MESSIAEN THE THEOLOGIAN

For Yvonne Loriod

Messiaen the Theologian

Edited by

ANDREW SHENTON
Boston University, USA

ASHGATE

Published by
Ashgate Publishing Limited
Wey Court East
Union Road
Farnham
Surrey, GU9 7PT
England
www.ashgate.com

Ashgate Publishing Company
Suite 420
101 Cherry Street
Burlington
VT 05401-4405
USA

British Library Cataloguing in Publication Data
Shenton, Andrew
  Messiaen the theologian.
  1. Messiaen, Olivier, 1908–1992–Criticism and interpretation. 2. Messiaen, Olivier, 1908–1992–Religion. 3. Spirituality in music.
  I. Title
  780.9'2-dc22

Library of Congress Cataloging-in-Publication Data
Messiaen the theologian / [edited by] Andrew Shenton.
    p. cm.
  Includes bibliographical references and index.
  ISBN 978-0-7546-6640-0 (hardcover: alk. paper) 1. Messiaen, Olivier, 1908–1992–Criticism and interpretation. 2. Music–20th century–History and criticism.
I. Shenton, Andrew
  ML410.M595M488 2009
  780.92–dc22

2009016970

ISBN 9780754666400 (hbk)

Bach musicological font developed by © Yo Tomita

Mixed Sources
Product group from well-managed forests and other controlled sources
www.fsc.org Cert no. SA-COC-1565
© 1996 Forest Stewardship Council
FSC

Printed and bound in Great Britain by
MPG Books Group, UK

Contents

List of Figures and Plates   *vii*

List of Tables   *ix*

List of Music Examples   *xi*

Notes on Contributors   *xiii*

Acknowledgements   *xix*

Editor's Note   *xxi*

Introducing Messiaen the Theologian   1
Andrew Shenton

PART I   MESSIAEN THE THEOLOGIAN

1   Religious Literature in Messiaen's Personal Library   15
    Yves Balmer

2   Messiaen as Preacher and Evangelist in the Context of European
        Modernism   29
    Peter Bannister

3   Messiaen's Saintly Naïveté   41
    Sander van Maas

PART II   MESSIAEN'S RELATIONSHIP WITH THEOLOGIANS

4   Olivier Messiaen and Cardinal Jean-Marie Lustiger: Two Views of
        the Liturgical Reform according to the Second Vatican Council   63
    Karin Heller

5   Messiaen's Relationship to Jacques Maritain's Musical Circle and
        Neo-Thomism   83
    Douglas Shadle

6   Messiaen and Aquinas   101
    Vincent P. Benitez

PART III   MESSIAEN, POETS AND THEOLOGICAL THEMES

7   Dante as Guide to Messiaen's Gothic Spirituality   127
       Robert Fallon

8   Five Quartets: The Search for the Still Point of the Turning World
          in the War Quartets of T. S. Eliot and Olivier Messiaen   145
       Andrew Shenton

9   The Charm of Impossibilities: Mystic Surrealism as Contemplative
          Voluptuousness   163
       Stephen Schloesser

PART IV   THEOLOGY IN MESSIAEN'S MUSIC

10   'Une œuvre simple, solennelle ...': Messiaen's Commission from
          André Malraux   185
       Nigel Simeone

11   Olivier Messiaen and the Avant-Garde Poetics of the *Messe de la
          Pentecôte*   199
       Robert Sholl

12   Messiaen as Explorer in *Livre du Saint Sacrement*   223
       Luke Berryman

13   Buddhist Temple, Shinto Shrine and the Invisible God of
          Sept Haïkaï   241
       Cheong Wai Ling

Glossary of People   *263*
Select Bibliography   *271*
Index   *287*

List of Figures and Plates

Figures

7.1   Symmetrical form and prime numbers in Dante and Messiaen   132

7.2   Outside-to-inside (closing fan) process of rearranging end-rhymes
in a sestina   133

7.3   Symmetrical permutation moving inside-to-outside
(or opening fan)   135

7.4   Symmetrical, crossed form of the *Turangalîla-symphonie*   135

7.5   Mount Purgatory, Dante's earthly paradise, is located on the
opposite side of the earth from Zion, not far from Messiaen's
earthly paradise of New Caledonia   137

7.6   Salvador Dalí's watercolour of Malecoda, a demon from
canto 23 of *Inferno*   142

11.1   Messiaen's table of rhythms for the 'Entrée', *Traité IV*, p. 88   208

13.1   Surface symmetry in the programmes of *Sept Haïkaï*   260

Plates

8.1   Poster for the premiere of the *Quatuor pour la fin du Temps*   151

10.1   Messiaen's handwritten plan of the orchestral layout for the
performance of *Et exspecto* in the choir of Chartres Cathedral   197

13.1   Buddhist temple gate guardians *Ni-o* [仁王] at Todaiji [東大寺],
Nara [奈良]   243

13.2   Different perspectives of the torii at Itsukushima Shrine [厳島神社],
Miyajima [宮島]   245

List of Tables

6.1   Formal outline of first half of *La Transfiguration*, 'Perfecte conscius
      illius perfectae generationis'   118

10.1 Guests at the performance of *Et exspecto resurrectionem*
      mortuorum in La Sainte-Chapelle, 7 May 1965   195

13.1 The superimposition of three tiers of chords in *Chronochromie* and
      Éclairs   247
13.2 An overview of *Sept Haïkaï* V   254
13.3 The shifting roles of the eight violins in *Sept Haïkaï* I, II, IV, V
      and VII   256

List of Music Examples

5.1   Arthur Lourié: *Procession*, bars 7–11   91
5.2   Arthur Lourié: *De ordinatione angelorum*, bars 1–7   91
5.3   Francis Poulenc: *Litanies à la vierge noire: Notre-Dame de Roc-
        Amadour*, bars 9–16   92
5.4   Olivier Messiaen: *Poèmes pour Mi*, 'Les deux guerriers', bars 1–6   95

6.1   Olivier Messiaen: *Trois petites Liturgies*, 'Psalmodie de l'Ubiquité
        par amour'   112
6.2   Olivier Messiaen: *La Transfiguration*, 'Perfecte conscius illius
        perfectae generationis'   114
6.3   Olivier Messiaen: *La Transfiguration*, 'Tota Trinitas apparuit' (basses)   116
6.4   Olivier Messiaen: *La Transfiguration*, 'Tota Trinitas apparuit'
        (sopranos)   116
6.5   Olivier Messiaen: *La Transfiguration*, 'Tota Trinitas apparuit'
        (chorus)   117
6.6   Olivier Messiaen: *Méditation III*, 'langage communicable'   120
6.7   Olivier Messiaen: *Saint François*, scene 5, 'L'Ange musicien'   122
6.8   Olivier Messiaen: *Saint François*, scene 8, 'La Mort et la
        nouvelle Vie'   123

11.1 Olivier Messiaen: 'Entrée (Les langues de feu)', opening   209
11.2 Olivier Messiaen: 'Sortie (le vent de l'esprit)', end   212
11.3 Olivier Messiaen: Transformation of three musical ideas in *Messe
        de la Pentecôte*   214
      (i)   'Entrée (Les langues de feu)' opening   214
      (ii) 'Offertoire (Les choses visibles et invisibles)' 4/4/1–2 and
              final bar   214
      (iii) 'Offertoire (Le don de Sagesse)' opening   214
      (iv) 'Consécration (Le don de Sagesse)' 16/2   214
      (v)   'Communion (Les oiseaux et les sources)' 18/1/1 and
              18/5/2/beats 3–4   215
      (vi) 'Sortie (le vent de l'esprit)' opening, 22/4/3 and 27/1/4   215

12.1 Olivier Messiaen: 'Sortie (le vent de l'esprit)', end   231
12.2 Olivier Messiaen: 'Offrande', 'La joie' in 'langage communicable'   233
12.3 Olivier Messiaen: 'Offrande', end   233

13.1   Olivier Messiaen: *Sept Haïkaï* I, bars 1–3 (reduction)   247
13.2   Olivier Messiaen: *Sept Haïkaï* IV, bars 1–4 (reduction)   249
13.3   Olivier Messiaen: *Sept Haïkaï* V, bars 1–8 (reduction)   252

Notes on Contributors

Yves Balmer is a graduate of the Conservatoire National Supérieur de Musique et de Danse in Paris. He recently completed his music doctorate on the reception history of Messiaen's music, under the direction of Joelle Caullier. A former researcher-associate at the Bibliothèque nationale de France (BnF) Department of Music, he was in charge of the classification and inventory of the Loriod–Messiaen archives. Balmer is currently a Maître de conférences (Associate Professor) at the Ecole Normale Supérieure in Lyons and, since 2008, a professor of musical analysis at the Paris Conservatoire.

Peter Bannister received a master's degree in musicology from King's College, Cambridge, UK before completing his training as a French Government scholar in Paris with Geneviève Ibanez, Michel Beroff (piano) and Naji Hakim (composition), where he subsequently carried out research into the history of organ improvisation for the Leverhulme Trust. His awards include prizes at international music competitions in Chartres, Nuremberg (organ improvisation) and San Sebastián (composition) as well as the *Prix André Caplet* of the Insitut de France for musical composition. His works have been performed at venues including the Théâtre des Champs-Elysées, Bourges, Chartres, Chichester and Villingen Cathedrals, Rencontres Musicales de La Prée, London South Bank Centre, St John's Smith Square, Festival Klangbogen Wien; he has made frequent recital appearances as an organist and pianist (BBC TV, Radio France, Notre-Dame de Paris, RAI, Vienna Cathedral), and has given masterclasses, lectures and papers in the UK, France, Croatia, Sweden (Gothenburg International Organ Academy) and the USA. Recent projects include the oratorio *Et iterum venturus est* in memory of Olivier Messiaen, premiered by the Ensemble Orchestral de Paris at La Trinité, Paris on December 9, 2008. He is a member of the board of directors of SOLI DEO GLORIA Inc. (Chicago), an organization dedicated to the promotion of new sacred music. He lives in Paris.

Vincent P. Benitez is Assistant Professor of Music at the Pennsylvania State University where he teaches graduate and undergraduate courses in music theory and applied organ. He holds two doctoral degrees in music: the PhD in music theory from Indiana University, and the DMA in organ performance from Arizona State University. Benitez is the author of *Olivier Messiaen: A Research and Information Guide* (Routledge, 2008). He has published articles on Messiaen in *Music Analysis, Dutch Journal of Music Theory*, *Journal of Musicological Research,* the *Poznan Studies on Opera*, *Music Theory Online*, and the *College Music Symposium.*

Benitez is currently writing a book on Messiaen's *Saint François d'Assise*, the subject of his dissertation at Indiana University.

Luke Berryman is a graduate musicology student at King's College, London. He was born in Oxford, England, and went on to study undergraduate music at the city's University at Magdalen College. There he was awarded both an academic Exhibition and an Instrumental Scholarship. He worked with Laurence Dreyfus and Julian Johnson, and gained a first-class honors degree. He also has an MM in musicology from Boston University. Luke also studied piano with Niel Immelman of the Royal College of Music, London, and has recently given recitals in Boston, Oxford and London.

Cheong Wai Ling is Professor at the Music Department, The Chinese University of Hong Kong. She received the PhD from Cambridge University, where she studied with Derrick Puffett. Her scholarly works on music composed in the twentieth century and, more specifically, the music and theoretical writings of Olivier Messiaen have been published by *Acta Musicologica*, *Journal of the Royal Musical Association*, *Music Analysis*, *Perspectives of New Music*, *Revue de Musicologie*, and *Tempo*.

Robert Fallon is Assistant Professor of Musicology at Carnegie Mellon University and specializes in the music of Olivier Messiaen. His chapter on Messiaen's bird style was published in *Olivier Messiaen: Music, Art, and Literature* (Ashgate, 2007) and his study of the opera *Saint François d'Assise* appears in *Messiaen Studies* (Cambridge University Press, 2007). His initial work on Messiaen's Gothic spirituality appears in *Musique, art, et religion* (Symétrie, 2009). He has published on Stravinsky, Messiaen, and Danielpour in journals such as *Journal of Musicology, Tempo, Notes*, and *Modern Fiction Studies* and in the book *Jacques Maritain and the Many Ways of Knowing* (Catholic University of America Press). He has written program notes and delivered lectures for the San Francisco Opera, Cincinnati Opera, New York City Opera, Cal Performances, and The University of Chicago Presents. He holds a PhD from the University of California at Berkeley.

Karin Heller, a native Austrian and a French citizen, is a Catholic theologian. She obtained her first doctoral degree in theology with specialization in studies on marriage and the family at the Lateran University, Rome. She also holds a doctoral degree in history of religions and religious anthropology from the Sorbonne University, Paris. In 2000, she obtained an *Habilitation* in dogmatic theology at the Ludwig-Maximilians-University of Munich, Germany. During her tenure as a visiting professor at the Institut Catholique de Paris and the University of Metz, she was also involved in the implementation of liturgical music at Sainte-Jeanne-de-Chantal, former parish of Cardinal Jean-Marie Lustiger. She served as an Associate Professor of Dogmatic Theology at the Theological Faculty of Lugano, Switzerland, for eight years, and she has also taught in Ireland, Italy, and

Spain. She is now an associate professor of theology at Whitworth University, Spokane, WA, USA. Her work relates to dogmatic and biblical theology, Christian spirituality and vocation, myths within contemporary literature, ecumenism, and the relationship between man and woman. She received both the Summer 2004 Research Fellowship granted by Whitworth's Weyerhaeuser Centre and the Whitworth Faculty Research and Development Summer Scholarship in 2006. She was named Whitworth University's 'Most Influential Professor 2007'.

Sander van Maas is an assistant professor of musicology at the University of Amsterdam and lecturer in music aesthetics at the Conservatory of Amsterdam. As a postdoctoral researcher he is presently involved in the project New Music and the Turn to Religion (funded by the NWO program The Future of the Religious Past). He is currently preparing a book entitled *The Sense of Soul*, which deals with a philosophical analysis of those musical experiences that—either within religious contexts or outside—are referred to as experiences of (the) 'soul'. His publications include an interdisciplinary study on Olivier Messiaen, *Doorbraak en Idolatrie: Olivier Messiaen en het geloof in music* (Eburon, 2003), which is published in an expanded and revised version in English as *The Reinvention of Religious Music: Olivier Messiaen's Breakthrough Toward the Beyond* (Fordham University Press, 2008). For more information see <home.medewerker.uva.nl/s.a.f.vanmaas/>.

Stephen Schloesser is an Associate Professor of History at Boston College. A member of the Society of Jesus, he was ordained a Catholic priest in 1992 after receiving his MDiv from the Weston Jesuit School of Theology in Cambridge, MA. He received his PhD in History and Humanities from Stanford University in 1999 and is the author of *Jazz Age Catholicism: Mystic Modernism in Postwar Paris, 1919–1933* (University of Toronto Press, 2005).

Douglas Shadle is a doctoral candidate in musicology at the University of North Carolina at Chapel Hill, where he is writing a dissertation on nationalism in nineteenth-century American symphonies. He has presented papers at the annual meetings of the American Musicological Society and the Society for American Music and has served as Student Forum co-chair for the latter. In June 2007, he received an Andrew Mellon Fellowship from the Historical Society of Pennsylvania and the Library Company of Philadelphia to conduct research on the early development of classical music in Philadelphia. He holds a BM in viola performance from the University of Houston and an MA in musicology from the University of North Carolina.

Andrew Shenton holds bachelor, masters and doctoral degrees from London University, Yale and Harvard respectively. His first professional music training was at The Royal College of Music in London, where he studied under a scholarship from The Royal College of Organists. In 1991, Dr. Shenton moved to the USA to study at the Institute for Sacred Music, Worship and the Arts at Yale and then for a PhD in musicology at Harvard University. Dr. Shenton holds the Fellowship diploma of the Royal College of Organists. He has given recitals in such venues as King's College, Cambridge, Westminster Abbey, St. Paul's Cathedral, London, St. Thomas Church Fifth Avenue (New York debut), and Washington National Cathedral. He has toured extensively in Europe and the USA as a conductor, recitalist and clinician, and his two solo organ recordings have received international acclaim. In addition to diplomas in both piano and organ Dr. Shenton holds the Choir Training diploma of the Royal College of Organists. He has been the recipient of numerous scholarships and awards including a Harvard Merit Fellowship and Harvard's Certificate of Distinction in Teaching. He has served on the faculties of Yale University and The Catholic University of America, has presented at several conferences and published numerous articles including essays on Messiaen in collections by Ashgate and Cambridge University Press. His monograph *Olivier Messiaen's System of Signs: Notes Towards Understanding His Music* (Ashgate, 2008) won the 2009 Miller Book Award. Dr. Shenton serves on the faculty of Boston University, where he directs the Master of Sacred Music program and the Boston University Messiaen Project [BUMP].

Robert Sholl is a Lecturer in Academic Studies at the Royal Academy of Music, London, and has taught at King's College, London and at The Royal College of Music. His doctorate, *Olivier Messiaen and the Culture of Modernity* is currently being revised for publication. Robert is a member of the Theology through the Arts research group, a founding co-editor of <oliviermessiaen.net>, and most recently, editor of *Messiaen Studies* (CUP, 2007). He has recently given papers on Messiaen at Washington DC (AMS), Princeton, Brown and Boston Universities, King's College London, the Royal Academy of Music and the Royal College of Music. In 2008 he organized a major conference at the Southbank Centre on Contemporary Music and Spirituality as the first event in Southbank's Messiaen Festival, and he will be the co-editor (with Sander van Maas) of a forthcoming set of related studies. Robert studied the organ with Olivier Latry (Titulaire Organiste de Notre-Dame de Paris), and currently tutors for the Royal College of Organists. He has recently given recitals in the *Festival de la Musique Sacrée* at the Cathedral of St-Malo, at La Madeleine (Paris), Westminster Abbey, and St Paul's Cathedral and at Notre-Dame de Paris. Future plans include recitals in Paris and Australia, and a disc of commissioned electroacoustic music.

Nigel Simeone is a musicologist and conductor who was appointed Professor of Historical Musicology in the Music Department at Sheffield University in October 2003. He was born in London in 1956 and is a graduate of Manchester University. After working in music publishing and as a music antiquarian, he taught in secondary schools for several years before becoming a university lecturer. He taught in the Music Department at the University of Nottingham from 1996 until taking up a post in 1998 at Bangor University, where he worked until moving to Sheffield. Nigel has collaborated with Peter Hill on three significant Messiaen books: A *Messiaen Reader* which will publish Messiaen's most important letters, articles, speeches and other writings, many of them for the first time, with annotations, commentaries and essays by the authors; a biography, simply entitled *Messiaen* published by Yale University Press in October 2005 to critical acclaim, and subsequently published in German (Schott, 2007) and French (Fayard, 2008, in a new, expanded edition); and a study of Messiaen's *Oiseaux exotiques* published by Ashgate in 2007. Nigel has been invited for the last six years to be a guest lecturer at the Messiaen Festival that takes place each summer in the French Alps (La Grave, Hautes Alpes), as well as being invited to lecture on Messiaen in Britain, France, Switzerland, Germany, Canada and the USA. He also writes on musical and cultural life in Paris since 1900, with specific current projects on the 1930s and on music under the German Occupation of the city (1940–44). He is interested in Broadway musicals and is currently working on the history and aesthetics of Broadway cast recordings, and on various other Broadway-related projects, and has recently published a monograph on Bernstein's *West Side Story* (Ashgate, 2009).

Acknowledgements

I am greatly indebted to the many friends and colleagues who have provided specific support to the Boston University Messiaen Project [BUMP], which was the driving force behind so many projects in the years up to Messiaen's centenary, including this one. I am especially thankful to my colleagues at the School of Music and the School of Theology at Boston University for their good-humoured encouragement of my work and the wise council of many, especially Jeremy Yudkin.

For this collection of essays I am profoundly grateful to the contributors for their willingness to turn spoken papers into readable ones and for their expertise in so many areas. My assistant Holly Reed gets bountiful laurels for her help with every aspect of both BUMP and this volume. I am also indebted to Christopher Murray who translated Yves Balmer's essay, Nigel Simeone for permission to use the cover photo (which is of Olivier Messiaen outside Sainte Trinité in Paris and which comes from Nigel's private collection), and Luke Berryman who proofread and checked facts.

I'm grateful to the music editor at Ashgate, Heidi Bishop, and her team, and especially to Sarah Price and Barbara Pretty.

Finally, the contributors and I acknowledge the enormous amount of work done by Yvonne Loriod-Messiaen in support of her husband's music over many decades and especially in the years since his death. Her dedication is an inspiration and a gift to those who love Messiaen's music and it is with much admiration that we dedicate this volume to her.

Editor's Note

In preparing this collection for publication I have been guided by the following principles:

> Language: where an English translation is available, references are to that version except where French is commonly used by English speakers (for example, for titles of Messiaen's compositions and for the *Traité*). Similarly, the original French for quotations has been omitted unless the source is unpublished or the meaning obscure and subject to more than the usual degree of interpretation (such as in some of the poetry quotations).

> *Traité de rythme, de couleur et d'ornithologie*: references to this are given as '*Traité*', followed by the volume number in Roman numerals, followed by the page reference, for example: *Traité V,* p. 119. The fifth volume is published in two parts which have been labelled *V/i* and *V/ii* respectively.

> Because the contributors are an international group of scholars their essays retain something of their individual voices; however, grammar, spelling and punctuation conform to Ashgate house style except where an original source differs, in which case it is given precedence. Issues of capitalization (notoriously inconsistent in French) conform to previous volumes in Ashgate's Messiaen series, and to the authoritative biography of Messiaen by Peter Hill and Nigel Simeone (Yale, 2005).

Introducing Messiaen the Theologian

Andrew Shenton

Olivier Messiaen (1908–92) was one of the most influential composers, teachers and performers of the twentieth century, yet he has not been afforded the same degree of attention as composers such as Schoenberg or Stravinsky. There are currently only a handful of books in English that deal with his style and only two that concentrate on his biography. Messiaen is also one of the most widely performed and recorded composers of the twentieth century, but although his popularity is increasing, the theological component of his music continues to provide a serious impediment for some of his audience. It is often reported that he considered it his good fortune to have been born a Catholic and he is often quoted as having said that 'the illumination of the theological truths of the Catholic faith is the first aspect of my work, the noblest and no doubt the most useful'.[1] For a composer whose music was a way of expressing his faith, this aspect of his life is clearly worth further investigation.

Under the aegis of the Boston University Messiaen Project [BUMP] a conference was held at Boston University in the autumn of 2007. A group of scholars, theologians and musicians gathered to discuss one aspect of Messiaen's life and work that had so far been largely neglected: Messiaen the Theologian. The conference participants endeavoured to move away from what Messiaen himself said about his life and work and instead offered a rich context for listening to his music with understanding.

This collection of essays, developed from papers read at the Boston conference, is divided into four parts, each of which deals with a specific aspect of Messiaen's theology. The essays cover a wide variety of topics such as Messiaen's personal spirituality, the context of Catholicism in France in the twentieth century, comparative study of Messiaen with writers such as Dante and Maritain, and analysis of his music in a theological context. In addition to contributing to the understanding of several major works, including *Quatuor pour la fin du Temps*, *Messe de la Pentecôte*, *Livre du Saint Sacrement*, *Sept Haïkaï* and *Saint François d'Assise*, the collection provides a basic framework for understanding the issues surrounding Messiaen's theology by contextualizing French Catholicism in the twentieth century, understanding the role of lay leadership in the French Catholic Church, highlighting the problems associated with making music 'speak' of

---

[1] Claude Samuel, *Olivier Messiaen: Music and Color. Conversations with Claude Samuel and Olivier Messiaen*, trans. E. Thomas Glasow (Portland, OR, 1994), p. 20.

Catholic truths, issues of interpretation, and by discussing the key figures in Messiaen's musical and theological world.

In order to provide a framework for Messiaen's life as a theologian it is important to understand something of the history of Catholicism in France in the late nineteenth and early twentieth centuries and some key concepts and terms used in these essays. For many readers, most of this will likely be new material and, because of its huge cast of characters, there is a glossary of people at the end of this volume that is designed to contextualize some unfamiliar names. Perhaps the most important historical factor to remember is that Messiaen lived in a time of both political and theological ferment that touched all aspects of social existence.

In the civil and political realm, Messiaen was born into a period of history in France known as the Third Republic, a republican parliamentary democracy that lasted from 1870 until the Vichy regime (1940–44). A provisional government ruled for a short time after the Second World War (1944–46) and was followed by the Fourth Republic (1946–58) and, currently, the Fifth Republic (1958–present). The Third Republic was established following the defeat of Napoleon III during the 1870 war against Prussia. In 1908, the year in which Messiaen was born, Paris, like other European capitals, was in its 'Belle Époque'. This retrospective appellation defined a 'beautiful era' for the upper classes that lasted from the late nineteenth century to the First World War. Though there was significant national and personal introspection during the period 'l'entre-deux-guerres' (the French expression for the period between the two wars that embodies the spirit of the time), during this period Europe was essentially at peace and it was a time of rapid growth, spurred by innovations in science and technology. The arts were radically transformed: Expressionism replaced Impressionism as the new avant-garde; Art Nouveau dominated design throughout much of Europe until the First World War; and many other movements such as Fauvism, Futurism and Surrealism flourished and were in turn superseded by new ideas. World fairs and new modes of transport meant easier access to the exotic and spurred a growth in orientalism and the fashion for Chinoiserie and Japanoiserie in costume and design. In music, cabaret theater became popular, as did operettas and music in salons and cafés. In literature, as with the other arts, Realism and Naturalism developed into Modernism, and writers such as Émile Zola and Marcel Proust stretched the boundaries of both technique and imagination.

During these same years of the twentieth century the Catholic Church was trying to redefine its position and influence amidst tumultuous cultural change.[2] There continued to be a struggle between those who wanted a strong Roman

---

[2]   For a more detailed introduction to the basic tenets of Catholicism, Catholicism in France in the twentieth century and Messiaen's theology see Andrew Shenton, *Olivier Messiaen's System of Signs: Notes Towards Understanding His Music* (Aldershot: Ashgate, 2008), pp. 17–34. See also: James C. Livingston, *Modern Christian Thought*, vol. 1 (Upper Saddle River, NJ: Prentice Hall, 1988); James C. Livingston, Francis Schüssler Fiorenza, Sarah Coakley and James H. Evans, Jr, eds *Modern Christian Thought*, vol. 2 (Upper Saddle

Catholic presence in society and government, and those who wanted a more restricted involvement. Rooted in conflicts dating to the medieval period of history, these forces are called 'ultramontanism' and 'gallicanism' respectively. Ultramontanism is the movement that supported the prerogatives and authority of the papacy, with the intention of freeing the Roman Catholic Church from the jurisdiction and control of civic powers. Gallicanism was the movement seeking to minimize the authority of the pope in civil affairs. Another important concept and movement of the time was that of 'laïcité' [laicity or laicism], which strictly means the separation of church and state, but which from the late nineteenth century came to mean the freedom of public institutions from the influence of the Catholic Church, and now means that the French government is legally prohibited from recognizing any religion. In France, separation of the church and state officially became law in 1905. In 1870, at the First Vatican Council, the contstitution *Pastor Aeternus* was accepted, which established both the primacy of the pope and his infallibility.

Less than ten years later, in 1879, Pope Leo XIII issued the encyclical *Aeterni Patris*, which established the teachings of Thomas Aquinas as the sole appropriate expression of theological endeavour. Thomism had always been an influential category of thought, but prior to *Aeterni Patris* it had taken two distinctive forms: Neo-Scholasticism represented the burgeoning interest in medieval scholastic theology and philosophy and its reclamation as a shield against growing dissention and change in theological circles; and Neo-Thomism, which was a much narrower category referring specifically to the study of the teachings of Thomas Aquinas. Following the issuance of *Aeterni Patris*, however, the emphasis on Aquinas's teachings alone made the appellation Neo-Thomism the more appropriate frame of reference.

Not all theologians found this turn to Neo-Thomism acceptable, and many began to move in new and creative directions that combined Thomism with new ways of thinking. Broadly speaking these theologians called for a 'return to the sources', or for 'resssourcement' as it came to be known, moving away from the limitations and rigours of scholasticism in its many forms. Labelled disparagingly by its detractors as 'la nouvelle théologie', advocates of this path sought to restore Catholic theology to its original purity of thought and expression by returning to the original sources, traditions and symbols of the Christian faith: scripture and the writings of the Church Fathers. Several prominent theologians who are associated with this new theology are referred to or quoted by Messiaen, including Henri de Lubac, Pierre Teilhard de Chardin, Hans Urs von Balthasar, Yves Congar, Marie-Dominique Chenu, Louis Bouyer and Etienne Gilson.

In returning to original sources, the work of Thomas Aquinas remained vital to the Catholic understanding of many important concepts central to the doctrine, including ontology, cosmology and the metaphysical proof of God's existence.

River, NJ: Prentice Hall, 2000); and Marcellino D'Ambrosio, '*Ressourcement* Theology, *Aggiornamento*, and the Hermeneutics of Tradition', *Communio* 18, no. 4 (1991): 530–555.

Indeed, the *Summa Theologiae* by Aquinas is arguably second only to the Bible in importance to the Roman Catholic Church. In the Motu Proprio *Doctoris Angelici* (29 June 1914), Pope Pius X summarized the importance of a Neo-Thomist understanding of the church, noting:

> [...] the capital theses in the philosophy of St. Thomas are not to be placed in the category of opinions capable of being debated one way or another, but are to be considered as the foundations upon which the whole science of natural and divine things is based; if such principles are once removed or in any way impaired, it must necessarily follow that students of the sacred sciences will ultimately fail to perceive so much as the meaning of the words in which the dogmas of divine revelation are proposed by the magistracy of the Church.[3]

As a formal response to decades of change, Pope John XXIII convened the Vatican's Second Ecumenical Council (commonly known as Vatican II), which he opened in 1962 and which was closed by Pope Paul VI in 1965. 'Aggiornamento', an Italian term literally meaning 'bringing up to date', was one of the key words used during the Second Vatican Council to mean a spirit of change, openness and modernity. Vatican II addressed many key issues in its four major sessions and produced a number of important documents such as *Lumen Gentium*, the Dogmatic Constitution on the Church, and *Sacrosanctum Concilium*, the Constitution on the Sacred Liturgy. *Lumen Gentium* discusses, for example, the hierarchical structure of the Church, the role of the laity and the role of the Blessed Virgin Mary. *Sacrosanctum Concilium* is concerned with general principles for the restoration and promotion of the Sacred Liturgy, especially in encouraging active participation of the faithful and in more clearly defining the role of music and the arts in liturgical practice.

This is the tumultuous theological and civil environment in which Messiaen was raised and lived out his religious convictions. He lived during an extraordinary time of *renouveau catholique* or Catholic Renewal (a renewal movement in the early twentieth century France that was both a literary and social movement seeking to return to the original values of Catholicism), and during an era of strong Neo-Thomism united with a revitalized and renewed theological endeavour aimed at reclaiming the origins of the faith ('ressourcement') that culminated in a period of ecclesiastical 'updating', or 'aggiornamento'. It is against this rich tapestry of social, economic, political, musical and religious change that Messiaen accepted the challenges of being a faithful member of the laity by sharing in the three offices of Christ – priestly, prophetic and royal – by 'engaging in temporal affairs and directing them according to God's will [...] and to illuminate and order all temporal things' (Catechism of the Catholic Church (1992) §§871–872, 882).

---

[3] http://maritain.nd.edu/jmc/etext/doctoris.htm, accessed September, 2008.

The contributors to this collection are internationally recognized scholars working in a number of disciplines. They utilize a broad range of methodologies including exegesis, theological studies and semiotics, with the specific aim of addressing directly the largest group of people who come across Messiaen's music: the audience.

The first part of the volume, simply entitled 'Messiaen the Theologian', enlarges what we know about Messiaen's own theology from an analysis of works in his library and then sets out to uncover his relationship to the musical avant-garde as a Christian composer. In the first essay, Yves Balmer sheds light on Messiaen's personal library and postulates how some of these books may have influenced his thinking. As a cataloguer of the Loriod-Messiaen collection at the Bibliothèque nationale de France, Balmer has had unique access to Messiaen's library and in his essay he lists the citations concerning Catholicism in Messiaen's monumental *Traité de rythme, couleur et d'ornithologie*, creating a typology of the works and authors cited according to their origin (scripture, writings by saints, Catholic artists, theologians, etc.). This typology permits the virtual recomposition of the Catholic volumes in Messiaen's private library, focusing upon works that we can assume held a particular significance for the composer because of their citation in the *Traité*. Balmer examines the relationship between various French Catholic movements and these writings, in an attempt to better define the portraits of Messiaen the Catholic and Messiaen the reader of Catholic literature.

Peter Bannister investigates Messiaen's unusual position within the musical avant-garde in Western Europe after 1945 as an expositor of unfashionable Catholic doctrine in a predominantly hostile intellectual environment. During a period when overtly Christian composition was generally viewed with deep suspicion by the artistic vanguard, Messiaen's artistic credibility remained essentially undented even with those unsympathetic to his beliefs (the critical controversy of the 1940s known as 'Le Cas Messiaen' notwithstanding). Indeed, he can be said to have evangelized the secular world of the concert hall with works such as *Couleurs de la cité céleste* and *La Transfiguration* and even the opera house with his monumental *Saint François d'Assise*, in a unique musical dialogue with the culture of modernity. This constitutes a continuation and development of Messiaen's pre-1945 trajectory both in words and music, stemming from a particular theological outlook concerning the relationship between the sacred and secular. A major factor in the success of Messiaen's project is his bold synthesis of ancient and modernist elements in a highly individual theological rainbow at a time when the avant-garde largely regarded any reference to tradition as regressive. On a technical level, this is exemplified by Messiaen's openness to the atonality of the Second Viennese School (attempting to bringing serial techniques into an explicitly Christian framework in pieces such as the *Livre d'orgue*). The rootedness of Messiaen's music in the physicality of sound discloses an affirmative theology of creation's goodness in stark contrast to the negative dialectics of much composition after the Second World War, while his ongoing engagement with Modernism derives from his eschatological hope. Bannister concludes that this musico-theological stance can provide material for reflection on the part of composers of younger generations.

Sander van Maas addresses the construction and meaning of the 'naïve' in Messiaen. Questions concerning this term in relation to the composer abound. Which elements of Messiaen's music, statements and attitudes are associated with this notion? In what sense is this notion applied, and how can this usage be understood in cultural-historical terms? What is the relation between Christian faith and the naïve? Why should Messiaen's alleged naïveté be 'impressive' and 'provocative,' as musicologist Richard Taruskin contends? How does the naïve come about and function in the context of self-conscious modernity? Addressing these and related questions van Maas suggests ways to make sense of an aspect of Messiaen that continues to inspire respect in both his fans and critics.

In the second part of the collection, three writers explore Messiaen's relationship with key theologians. Karin Heller highlights Messiaen's life and work as a church musician within the twentieth-century Church of France and in particular his relationship with Cardinal Jean-Marie Lustiger, Archbishop of Paris from 1981 to 2005. In a more or less ideologically pressured context, Messiaen remained faithful to the Gregorian renewal movement initiated by Solesmes, a Benedictine monastery famous as the source of the restoration of Benedictine monastic life in France under Dom Prosper Guéranger after the French Revolution, while other currents exalted liturgy as an appropriate tool for evangelization and committed themselves to composition of church music in vernacular language. Hostilities and misunderstandings between the ecclesiastical authorities and Messiaen's art led him to limit his production of church music and to transfer the idea of the Catholic liturgy into concert halls. Heller contends that this effort, together with his strong interest in nature, reflects a view proper to Romantic theology. Cardinal Lustiger's admiration for Messiaen is best expressed in his statement: 'I hear in Messiaen's music the inspiring power of the Word and the expression of a musician who has received the Word; I found [in this music], through the meditation expressed by the musician, aspects that helped me to understand in a new way the Word he commented on'. Lustiger's affinity with Messiaen's music is rooted in a deep conviction that liturgy is God's way *par excellence* of making himself visible through the Word. This explains why scripture became absolutely central during Lustiger's ministry as a pastor of the Parisian church of Sainte-Jeanne-de-Chantal. Called to implement liturgical reform in the wake of the Second Vatican Council, Lustiger wrote, together with the church organist and composer Henry Paget, a contemporary liturgical repertoire entirely at the service of the Word of God. What made these programmes unique was not only the exclusive use of vernacular scripture texts, but their structure. This mirrors Messiaen's genuine combination of scripture and music in his own work.

Douglas Shadle explores Messiaen's relationship to the Catholic philosopher Jacques Maritain's musical circle and to the movement known as 'Neo-Thomism', a modern revival of the theological and philosophical systems of St Thomas Aquinas led by Maritain. Shadle notes that Maritain's philosophical reach extended much farther into Parisian musical life than we currently recognize. Before the Second World War, Maritain and his wife Raïssa developed intimate relationships with several prominent musical luminaries. Olivier Messiaen, however, now considered the twentieth century's premier Catholic composer, appears strangely to have sidestepped Maritain's influence. Had he not, his fate might have been substantially different. In order to understand this unpredictable development, Shadle explores the theological and musical milieu in which Jacques Maritain played a central role. Drawing on Thomas Aquinas's medieval theology, Maritain's philosophy of art orients artistic production away from emotional expression and focuses instead on art's foundation in the intellect. His closest musical companions, Igor Stravinsky and Arthur Lourié, adopted many of his fundamental ideas in their own writings and attempted to create a 'Neo-Thomist' musical style. Maritain's ideas also entered into broader critical discourse in music periodicals, as a wide circle of important composers and critics responded positively to his views. Indeed, their continued adoption of a broadly defined neo-classical aesthetic was a direct response to his philosophy. Although they appeared at the height of Maritain's influence on Parisian musical life, Messiaen's earliest religious compositions bear no apparent stylistic resemblance to neo-classicism or Lourié's musical Neo-Thomism. His sacred works from the 1930s, for example, differ markedly in style from those of both Poulenc and Lourié, two of Maritain's closest allies. Viewed in the light of its theological context, however, the radical separation between Messiaen's music and that of Maritain's circle makes more immediate sense. Like several prominent Catholic theologians, Messiaen rejected Neo-Thomism's austerity in favour of a biblically oriented outlook. Consequently, his style and success paralleled the thought and widespread theological acceptance of two of his favourite contemporary theologians, Romano Guardini and Hans Urs von Balthasar.

Clearly, understanding the work of Thomas Aquinas is key to grasping the Catholic religious ethos of the time and essential to comprehension of both Messiaen's music and his theology. The essay by Vincent Benitez focuses on Thomist theology and its relationship to and influence on Messiaen's aesthetics and compositions. Benitez opens by introducing us to Aquinas and his theology, especially the *Summa Theologiae*, the essential practical manual of Christian Theology. He continues by considering Aquinas's theological ideas, particularly his synthesis of faith and reason and their place in the *renouveau catholique* in France. Using examples from several important works such as the *Trois petites Liturgies, La Transfiguration de Notre-Seigneur Jésus-Christ*, and *Saint François d'Assise*, Benitez discusses Aquinas's influence on Messiaen's music. He argues that Messiaen had a profound understanding of Thomistic thought and incorporated its precepts into his music so that every technique at his disposal was used to produce music that glorifies God.

The third part of this collection highlights Messiaen's relationship with certain poets, noting similarities in theological themes. Despite numerous efforts to define Messiaen's relationship to Roman Catholicism, scholars have reached no consensus about the foundation of his musical theology. Studies have discussed his connection to several medieval figures, including Sts Aquinas, Francis, Bernard and Bonaventure as well as to such modern figures as Chateaubriand, John XXIII, Maritain, Couturier, Chardin, Lubac and von Balthasar.[4]

Each of these sources adds to our understanding of Messiaen's theology. Nevertheless, a late medieval theology now called 'Gothic theology' synthesizes several important strands of this medieval tapestry. In his essay, Robert Fallon is the first to show the influence of Gothic spirituality on Messiaen, who Fallon argues was guided in this tradition by his reading of Dante. That Dante was not a theologian, but a poet, can only have appealed to Messiaen the musician. Fallon explores how Messiaen may have interpreted these comparisons and how he could have encountered Dante, and discusses formal similarities between Messiaen and Dante, including the use of symmetry, prime numbers and *retrogradatio cruciformis*. Finally, Fallon points out many parallelisms in their views of theology, particularly in reference to Tristan, Bernard, Francis, Aquinas and Bonaventure, the Neo-Platonic doctrines of illumination and emanation, bird metaphors, rainbows, the music of the spheres, the abyss of hell and the varieties of perfection found during the slow ascent to Paradise. Because these characters and theological principles appear in the works of both Messiaen and Dante, Fallon suggests that Dante was the artist whom Messiaen chose as his Bloomian precursor.

T. S. Eliot's *Four Quartets* were first published in 1943; Olivier Messiaen's *Quatuor pour la fin du Temps* was published in 1944. Both works were written during the Second World War although both contain earlier material. My own essay sketches the composition and publication of both works and analyses certain

---

[4]   For Aquinas see C. C. Hill, 'Saint Thomas Aquinas and the Theme of Truth in Messiaen's Saint François d'Assise', in *Messiaen's Language of Mystical Love*, ed. Siglind Bruhn (New York: Garland Publishing, 1998), pp. 143–167; for St. Francis see Larry W. Peterson, 'Messiaen and Surrealism: A Study of His Poetry', in *Messiaen's Language of Mystical Love*, ed. Siglind Bruhn (New York: Garland Publishing, 1998), pp. 215–224; for Saints Bernard and Bonaventure see Robert Fallon, 'Messiaen's Mimesis: The Language and Culture of the Bird Styles' (PhD diss., University of California at Berkeley, 2005) and 'The Record of Realism in Messiaen's Bird Style', in *Olivier Messiaen: Music, Art and Literature*, eds Christopher Dingle and Nigel Simeone (Aldershot: Ashgate, 2007), pp. 115–136; for Chateaubriand see Robin Freeman, 'Trompette d'un Ange secret: Olivier Messiaen and the Culture of Ecstasy', in *Contemporary Music Review* 14, no. 3–4 (1996): 81–125; for John XXIII see Christopher Dingle, '"La statue reste sur son piédestal": Messiaen's La Transfiguration and Vatican II', in *Tempo*, no. 212 (2000): 11; and for Maritain, Couturier, Chardin, Lubac, and von Balthasar see Fallon, 'The Record of Realism' and 'Two paths to paradise: Reform in Messiaen's Saint François d'Assise', in *Messiaen Studies*, ed. Robert Sholl (Cambridge: Cambridge University Press, 2007), pp. 206–231 and also 'Messiaen's Mimesis' and 'Knowledge and Subjectivity in Maritain, Stravinsky, and Messiaen', in *Jacques Maritain and the Many Ways of Knowing*, ed. Douglas Ollivant (Washington, DC: American Maritain Association, 2002), pp. 284–302.

primary themes in each that concern the nature of the human experience of music and music as a means of mediating or negotiating time. Messiaen's *Quatuor* is dedicated to the Angel of the Apocalypse, who raised a hand towards heaven saying: 'there shall be no more Time'. In this essay I am not concerned with the Apocalyptic programme or the circumstances surrounding the first performance. Instead, I investigate two things: first, some theological and philosophical issues regarding the end of time, and in particular how the cessation of time might be conceived in human terms and described, in Eliot's words, as the 'still point of the turning world'. Second, I discuss whether we might dare to abandon Messiaen's Christian programme altogether and, if we do, what meaning, if any, does the music have. There is no record of T. S. Eliot and Messiaen having met (though it is likely they were aware of each other's work), so this essay is speculative. But, at some point we have to put away the musicology and face the music. When we do, we have to listen carefully to what the music says to us on a deep and personal level, freed from his verbal accoutrements and from our conscious analysis.

This section ends with Stephen Schloesser's essay entitled 'The Charm of Impossibilities: Mystic Surrealism as Contemplative Voluptuousness'. In his *Technique of My Musical Language* (1944) Messiaen declared: 'One point will attract our attention at the outset: the *charm of impossibilities* … at once voluptuous and contemplative'. Calling for the hastening by prayer of the coming of the 'liberator' who would be 'both a great artisan and a great Christian', Messiaen invoked lines by two writers. First, Pierre Reverdy, a poet whose work and thought were essential to the invention of post-First World War surrealism. Second, Ernest Hello, a writer whose work and thought, central to nineteenth-century Catholic Revivalism [*renouveau catholique*], aimed at carrying out the mission of Dom Prosper Guéranger's monumental *l'Année liturgique* – namely, to penetrate beyond the *historique* and the *théologique* into the *mystique*. Was Messiaen's invocation of the nineteenth-century *mystique* and the twentieth-century *sur-réaliste* an arbitrary juxtaposition of two personal interests, or is there a serious internal connection between them? Schloesser argues for a connection by setting out the context of Jazz Age Catholicism and then reading within it the figures that Messiaen invoked as his primary influences in the 1944 text: his mother, Cécile Sauvage (poetess); William Shakespeare (dramatist of the magical); Paul Claudel (symbolist poet and icon of the *renouveau catholique*); Paul Reverdy and Paul Éluard (surrealist poets); Ernest Hello (nineteenth-century Catholic Revivalist; symbolist writer; author of *contes extraordinaires*, short stories of the macabre in the vein of Edgar Allan Poe); Benedictine monk Dom Columba Marmion (twentieth-century Catholic revivalist; heir to the *mystique* tradition of Dom Guéranger); and a figure that Messiaen does not mention but perhaps should have: Charles Tournemire, symbolist musician and composer of *l'Orgue mystique*, inspired by and modelled on Guéranger's *l'Année liturgique*.

In the final part of this collection, four writers discuss theological issues in specific works by Messiaen. Nigel Simeone documents the genesis of *Et exspecto resurrectionem mortuorum* from its commission by the French Ministry of Culture to its private premiere in La Sainte-Chapelle in Paris (6 May 1965), and its public premiere in Chartres Cathedral (20 June 1965). Although the work ended up being for an orchestra of woodwinds, brass and metallic percussion without text (although all five movements have epigraphs taken from the Bible and the title comes from the Nicene Creed: 'And I look for the resurrection of the dead'), Simeone presents evidence that Messiaen was considering writing a mass, a *De Profundis* or even a requiem to fulfill this commission. It is interesting to have insights into the mundane life of Messiaen as well as his spiritual life as he pondered how to write a piece that was to be in honour of the dead of the two world wars, just as it is also of interest to see something of the reception history of one of his pieces written for 'vast spaces: churches, cathedrals, even in the open air and on mountain tops'.

Robert Sholl discusses the influential organ work *Messe de la Pentecôte* in the context of the avant-garde. Messiaen's interest in the Surrealist movement in the 1940s was perhaps unsurprising. Surrealism represented a radical modernist aesthetic that attempted to re-integrate aesthetic experience into life through the politicization of art. At the vanguard of the revolutionary avant-garde aesthetic, Messiaen's students (including Berio, Boulez, Stockhausen and Xenakis), unwittingly inherited his spirit of confrontation and regeneration. Even as they searched for autonomy and authentic expression down supposedly secular paths, their work entailed a reaction to and a continuation of Messiaen's theological, aesthetic and compositional preoccupations. The search for a non-ideological and transcendental autonomy without God (for Boulez, Berio and Xenakis at least), would founder on its own epistemological rocks. For an ardent Catholic such as Messiaen, faith was his means of politicization and also a means to re-orientate such avant-garde politics. Yet, by attempting to redirect the search for the absolute in Western music towards God, Messiaen also revealed that theological concerns were inextricably connected to the bedrock of avant-garde thought. This study examines these concerns in relation to a small compositional period in Messiaen's output (1948–53). It investigates how Messiaen's music of this period engaged with and transformed the radical aesthetic of the avant-garde, and how it afforded him the impetus to renew and refresh his musical language.

Luke Berryman's essay acknowledges the need to reassess Messiaen's frequently misconstrued late works. Even today, innovative musical approaches to a familiar theological programme in his final organ work, *Livre du Saint Sacrement* (1986), remain largely unrecognized. New ideas are especially abundant in the last movement, 'Offrande et Alleluia final', as evidenced through critical comparison with finale toccatas serving similar programmatic purposes in the earlier organ cycles. These experiments make the *Livre* of special interest within his output, yet scholars frequently overlook it, perceiving it as either a series of disconnected written-out improvisations, or as an arbitrary summation to the organ oeuvre. A close examination of the music, and the circumstances in which it was being composed, reveals that the *Livre* is not, as writer Paul Griffiths has suggested, a 'garland of mementoes'. Neither is it a summation, as many scholars often suppose. In fact in *Livre du Saint Sacrement*, far from simply revisiting his familiar techniques (which had been exemplified on a grand scale in his monumental opera *Saint François*), Messiaen appears to discard many of them in favour of new ventures. By comparing Messiaen's approach to his programme in the final movement of the *Livre*, 'Offrande et Alleluia final', with toccata movements serving similar programmatic purposes and standing in similar positions in their respective organ cycles ('Dieu parmi nous', 1936; and 'Le vent de l'esprit', 1949), Berryman begins to elucidate the purposes and outcomes of these experiments. It becomes apparent that the *Livre* does not tally with musicologist Christopher Dingle's commonly accepted portrait of Messiaen in the 1980s as a contented old man who is 'at peace with the world'. Only once we have finally rejected this image will we be able to approach an understanding of Messiaen's untamable desire for musical experimentation. In his final works it seems that, far from being contented, Messiaen may even have been questioning the success of some of his older techniques and continuing to search for new methods of expressing his personal theology.

In the last essay, Cheong Wai Ling discusses the 'invisible temple' of *Sept Haïkaï*. If Messiaen's claim to have given 'Gagaku', the fourth movement and centerpiece of *Sept Haïkaï*, a 'Christian dimension' proves intriguing, 'Miyajima et le torii dans la mer', the following piece of the set, may strike us as even more perplexing in makeup. Apart from the use of an octachordal soundband to imitate the shō playing of gagaku music, 'Miyajima et le torii dans la mer' is deprived of all other Japanese musical elements. Instead, there is a rich display of French birdsong, Greek rhythm and, most unexpectedly, what Messiaen refers to as the 'theme of chorale'. Even though the torii (a traditional Japanese gate) of Miyajima – unlike any other torii in that it is set up in the sea rather than on land – is commonly construed as a gateway that leads to the Shinto shrine, Messiaen takes a different perspective and views through the torii not the Shinto shrine but rather the open sea. This explains his conception of the torii as leading to what he calls 'an invisible temple', which he remarks emphatically is 'the *true* temple'. The idea of an invisible temple and, by extension, an invisible God might have led Messiaen to arrive at the unexpected but nonetheless symbolic intrusion of a chorale. Cheong argues that Messiaen's use of such non-Japanese elements as French birdsong, Greek rhythm and, above all, the 'theme of chorale' tells of a hidden programme, a metaphor that is shrewdly withheld from his copious commentaries on the music.

Finally, one excellent essay from the Boston conference was not included in this collection since it was already committed for publication elsewhere: David Butler Cannata, 'Messiaen Reads the Infancy Gospels: The Vingt Regards sur l'Enfant-Jésus as Christology', in *Quomodo cantabimus canticum? Studies in Honor of Edward H. Roesner*, eds David Butler Cannata, Gabriela Ilnitchi Currie, Rena Charnin Mueller, and John Louis Nádas (American Institute of Musicology, 2008), pp. 235–77.

PART I
Messiaen the Theologian

Chapter 1

Religious Literature in Messiaen's Personal Library

Yves Balmer

> Personal libraries allow us to materialize in the most visible manner the interface
> between the act of creation and the social space in which that act is immersed.
>
> – Paulo D'Ioro and Daniel Ferrer[1]

The eclecticism and the sheer number of references cited in Messiaen's *Traité de rythme, de couleur et d'ornithologie*, combined with third-party reports of the composer's monumental literary knowledge, give clear proof that Messiaen possessed a vast and varied library.[2] Still, to date, there have been few studies of Messiaen's private library and preferred reading materials, despite existing research that has revealed the heuristic potential of such investigations.[3] The present study elaborates upon the concept of Messiaen as a reader. It does not seek to discover how specific texts may have influenced the composer personally or musically, but rather to sketch a portrait of the composer through the medium of the texts he read.

There is currently no formal catalogue of Messiaen's personal library.[4] This study draws from a body of some 600 references to works or authors contained

---

[1]   Paulo D'Ioro and Daniel Ferrer, *Bibliothèques d'écrivains* (Paris: CNRS Editions, 2001), p. 7.

[2]   For example, see Pierrette Mari: 'And then there is reading, that vice [which in Messiaen] is never quenched', in Pierrette Mari, *Olivier Messiaen* (Paris: Seghers, 1965), p. 10, as well as multiple reports from the students of Messiaen in the work of Boivin.

[3]   See Gareth Healey, 'Messiaen – Bibliophile', in *Messiaen: Music, Art and Literature*, eds Christopher Dingle and Nigel Simeone (Aldershot: Ashgate, 2007), pp. 159–172, and Andrew Shenton's article listing works read by Messiaen cited in the first chapter of his *Traité*, Andrew Shenton, 'Observations on time in Olivier Messiaen's *Traité*', in the same volume, pp. 173–190. For heuristic potential see Roger Chartier, *Ecouter les morts avec les yeux* (Paris: Collège de France/Fayard, 2008), and *Les Bibliothèques d'artistes* (Paris: INHA, 2008), proceedings of the conference 'Les bibliothèques d'artistes 20ᵉ – 21ᵉ siècles', held 9–12 March 2006 at the Institut National d'Histoire de l'Art (Paris) <http://inha.fr/IMG/pdf/partenaire-prog9mars.pdf> (accessed 25 July 2008).

[4]   A few books from his library have been donated to the Fonds Loriod-Messiaen of the Bibliothèque nationale de France. See Yves Balmer, *Catalogue des concerts du fonds Loriod-Messiaen de la Bibliothèque nationale de France* (Yves Balmer: 2008), p. 7–9. See: <http://catalogue.bnf.fr/ark:/12148/cb41224412f/PUBLIC>.

in the seven volumes of Messiaen's theoretical magnum opus, the *Traité*, with the intention of reconstructing not the *definitive* version of Messiaen's library, but rather, an impression of that collection's essence. While there are certainly lacunae in this portrait, it is nevertheless based upon a set of works read by the composer and judged by him to be of interest and worthy of citation in his own writings. Beyond the coherence lent to this corpus by the identity of its reader, it was an interest in possible links between these references that motivated this investigation, with the hope that it will broaden our knowledge of the composer through the medium of his readings, which he presented in his writings as some of the sources of his art. A personal library, and more particularly, a group of books known to have been read by their owner, reveals something about the owner's taste and choices. It contains traces of his personal intellect. These traces have implications on both the personal and social levels.

Messiaen came from a family of intellectuals and was therefore well read. It is no surprise therefore that he provided references for most of the citations in the *Traité*.[5] These references constitute a clear collection of primary source material while also hinting at the composer's sense of their usefulness. The first chapter of volume 1 of the *Traité*, entitled 'Le Temps', for example, is based primarily on the juxtaposition of citations pulled from a variety of texts, revealing Messiaen as a reader who compiles material from multiple sources. The sum of this heterogeneous set of citations creates a strange new whole, reminiscent of the eclectic construction of Messiaen's musical language.[6]

It is possible to define several coherent groups within the whole of Messiaen's citations; however, the majority of references are the names of composers (see appendix, p. 26). Messiaen also refers to a number of painters. It is harder to discern other groups because the texts come from a variety of disciplines including literature, poetry, musicology, ornithology and philosophy. This essay explores two key points gleaned from the *Traité*'s textual references. First, Messiaen's literary references contain a clear set of readings rooted in the Catholic Literary Renaissance. Second, Messiaen's frequent citation of the collective work *Les Rythmes et la vie* (discussed in detail below) provides an opportunity to understand his discovery of seemingly secular authors via the Catholic milieu.

---

[5]   Pierre Messiaen, a lycée teacher, also taught for many years at the Institut Catholique de Paris (ICP). For more biographical information see Yves Balmer, '*Je suis né croyant ... Aux sources du catholicisme de Messiaen*', in *Musique, art et religion dans l'entre deux-guerres*, eds Sylvain Caron and Michel Duchesnau (Lyon: Symétrie, 2009), pp. 365–389.

[6]   See for example Pierre Boulez, 'Vision et révolution', in *Regards sur autrui: Points de repère, tome II* (Paris: Bourgois, 2005), pp. 436–443.

Olivier Messiaen, a reader influenced by the Catholic Renaissance

In late nineteenth-century France, a movement developed that became known as the 'Christian Intellectual Renaissance'. According to historian Hervé Serry, this movement encompassed 'all of the debates, public entreaties, essays, novels and poetry up until the early 1930s written by authors identifying themselves as Catholic and intended as specifically literary and more generally intellectual'.[7] The Christian Intellectual Renaissance found a more explicitly literary expression with the advent of the Catholic Literary Renaissance, founded by a group of writers determined, according to Serry, to 'forge a Catholic aesthetic that, in their spirits, would serve as spearhead for the religious reconquest of the "eldest daughter of the Church" whose straying into "secularism" had culminated with the 1905 French law on the separation of Church and State'.[8] Most of the movement's writers were converts to Catholicism and included Paul Claudel, Charles Péguy, Georges Bernanos and François Mauriac.[9]

Messiaen shared with these writers a rejection of Enlightenment ideals, asserting his distaste for the work of French philosopher Jean-Jacques Rousseau, much like Ernest Hello, one of the movement's precursors.[10] The 'condemnation of the infernal foursome of Voltaire, Rousseau, Hegel, and Renan' was a major theme throughout Hello's work.[11]

Messiaen's literary references in the *Traité* include writers who were precursors to the Christian Intellectual Renaissance, writers solidly positioned within the movement itself, and philosophers who followed in its footsteps. Among the nineteenth-century authors who prefigured the Catholic Renaissance and embodied

---

[7]   Hervé Serry, 'Le double jugement de l'art est-il possible? Les impasses d'une critique catholique dans trois polémiques littéraires et religieuses de l'entre-deux-guerres', *La Société d'études soréliennes: Mil neuf cent*, 26/1 (2008): 73–90.

[8]   Hervé Serry, *Naissance de l'intellectuel catholique* (Paris: La découverte, 2004), p. 7.

[9]   See Adrien Dansette, *Histoire religieuse de la France contemporaine: l'Église catholique dans la mêlée politique et sociale* (Paris: Flammarion, 1965), pp. 698–704. See also Frédéric Guguelot, *La conversion des intellectuels au catholicisme en France 1885–1935* (Paris: CNRS Editions, 1998). For more on the writers see also the work of Hervé Serry, particularly 'Déclin social et revendication identitaire: la "renaissance littéraire catholique" de la première moitié du XXe siècle', *Sociétés Contemporaines* 44 (2002): 91–109, and Hervé Serry, *Naissance de l'intellectuel catholique*. See also Stephen Schloesser's, *Jazz Age Catholicism: Mystic Modernism in Postwar Paris, 1919–1933* (Toronto: University of Toronto Press, 2005).

[10]   Claude Samuel, *Entretiens avec Olivier Messiaen* (Paris: Belfond, 1967), p. 181. This opinion of Rousseau disappeared from the definitive version of the interviews published in 1999. In this sense, Messiaen holds similar views to his father who denounced on several occasions 'the values of 1789'. See, for example, Pierre Messiaen, 'Péguy poète national et chrétien', *La revue des Amis de Saint-François* 29 (1941): 19–24.

[11]   François Angelier, 'Hello, l'explosion de l'unité', in Ernest Hello, *Paroles de Dieu. Réflexions sur quelques textes sacrés* (Grenoble: Million, 1992), p. 18.

its spiritualist essence stands Ernest Hello, who is also known for his influence on Messiaen's *Visions de l'Amen*.[12] Hello (1828–85) represents a model Catholic writer, described by essayist François Angelier as a man whose 'influence on the mystical literature of the 19th and 20th centuries is as pregnant as it is discreet: [author] Georges Bernanos claims to owe "everything" to him, [poet and diplomat] Paul Claudel praises his "dazzling strokes of lightening," and [Nobel laureate] André Gide makes reference to him. Echoes of Hello's writing can also be heard in the work of [prominent contemporary writers] Julien Green and Dominique De Roux.'[13] Hello's position as a precursor to the Christian intellectual movements also stems from his determining influence on Léon Bloy while Hello was still alive.[14] Bloy would later become the Godfather of Jacques Maritain,[15] one of the key figures in the Christian Intellectual Renaissance.[16]

Another precursor to the Christian intellectual movement quoted by Messiaen is Maurice de Guérin, a poet of Christian and spiritualist sensibilities.[17] For example, Messiaen cites a long passage from Guérin's poem *Centaure* to clarify the effect of the 'gradual slowing of durations' in the Indian rhythm *Lakskmîça* (tâla number 88 in Messiaen's list in *Traité I*, p. 296):

> Slept on the threshold of my retirement, the sides hidden in the cave and the head under the sky, I followed the spectacle of the shades. Then the foreign life that had penetrated me during the day detached from me drop by drop, turning over to the peaceful centre of Cybele, as after the heavy shower the remains of the rain attached to the foliages make their fall and join water.[18]

---

[12]   Cited in Olivier Messiaen, *Traité III* and *Traité V*.

[13]   Angelier, 'Hello, l'explosion de l'unité', p. 18.

[14]   Also found in a biography of Hello: Patrick Kechichian, *Les usages de l'éternité: Essai sur Ernest Hello* (Paris: Seuil, 1993), p. 95, as well as a work by Bloy dedicated to Hello: Léon Bloy, *Ici on assassine les grands hommes: par Léon Bloy: avec un portrait et un autographe d'Ernest Hello* (Paris: Mercure de France, 1895). See also Claude Barthe's preface to Ernest Hello, *L'Homme: la vie, la science, l'art* (Paris: Editions de Paris, 2003), pp. 9–20.

[15]   Maritain was born in a liberal Protestant milieu. His wife, Raïssa, was a Russian Jewish émigré. Through the influence of Léon Bloy, in 1906 they converted to Catholicism. See a lecture by Maritain: 'En hommage à notre cher Parrain Léon Bloy' [In tribute to our beloved Godfather Léon Bloy] in Jacques Maritain, *Approches sans entraves* (Paris: Fayard, 1973), p. 41. See also Frédéric Guguelot, *La conversion des intellectuels au catholicisme en France.*

[16]   For the sake of preserving the traces of social networks we should also cite that Hello's posterity depends upon the publication of his *Textes choisis* in 1945 by Stanislas Fumet, publisher and friend of Pierre Messiaen: Ernest Hello, *Textes choisiset présentés*, ed. Stanislas Fumet (Paris, Fribourg: W. Egloff, 1944).

[17]   Cited in Olivier Messiaen, *Traité I*, p. 329.

[18]   Ibid., p. 329.

A Christian figure who considered that 'Man's heart is the place of union between the sky and the earth, the meeting point of God and the animal within humanity', Maurice de Guérin was a poet in close touch with nature with whom Messiaen identified.[19] François Mauriac, one of the major figures of the Catholic Literary Renaissance, later wrote a preface for an edition of Guérin whom he considered as a reference for the movement. Mauriac described Guérin's poems as 'the most beautiful of our literature'.[20]

Other authors cited by Messiaen in his *Traité*, including Paul Claudel, Emile Baumann and Pierre Reverdy, were directly involved in the Catholic Literary Renaissance. These three writers all published in Plon's collection *Roseau d'or* edited by Jacques Maritain and Stanislas Fumet.[21] Claudel characterized the Catholic Literary Renaissance as 'one of the most interesting literary revolutions to take place in our country'.[22] He noted: 'For centuries all of our poets' efforts have gone towards the creation of a fictitious land where the Gospel never sets foot, a place ignorant of Christ's Revolution and moral code and reigned over by the gods of paganism'.[23]

Messiaen also refers to Pierre Reverdy, one of his favourite poets, who also belonged to the Catholic Literary Renaissance.[24] In reality, Reverdy was thirstier for the absolute than a true Catholic or mystic, but he converted to the Catholic faith for a period of time, and lived near the Benedictine Abbey of Solesmes from 1926 onwards. In 1927, Reverdy published the poem 'Le Gant de crin'

---

[19]   Citation of Guérin by G. S. Trebutien, in Maurice de Guérin, *Maurice de Guérin: journal, lettre et poèmes* (Paris: Lecoffre, 1898), p. VI. Charles Du Bos writes: 'The sounds of nature, [Maurice de Guérin] tells us: "I will always listen to them. When one sees me dreaming, it's because I am thinking of their harmonies." Maurice "listens"; he "considers the horizon"; he stays "for hours on end" without moving, waiting, under the protection of "a certain place", of a certain "tree", from which, like cluster of wisteria flowers, his entire being is suspended. Entirely passive and entirely active: "the sounds of nature", slowly and gradually, transform themselves inside of him, transmitting the refrain of their cadences, weaving a supple and melodious garland: "oh ! how lovely they are, these natural sounds, the sounds that spread through the air, that rise with the sun and follow it, following the sun like a grand concert follows a king"'. Charles Du Bos, 'Le Génie de Maurice de Guérin', in Maurice de Guérin, *Le Centaure. La Bacchante: précédés de La génie de Maurice Guérin, par Charles du Bos* (Paris: Falaize, 1950), pp. 17–18.

[20]   François Mauriac, 'Préface' à Maurice de Guérin, *Le Centaure. La Bacchante*, p. 11.

[21]   For more on 'Le Roseau d'or', see Philippe Chenaux, *Entre Maurras et Maritain: une génération intellectuelle catholique (1920–1930)* (Paris: Cerf, 1999), pp. 68–78.

[22]   Claudel's *L'annonce faite à Marie* and *Le Repos du septième jour* are cited by Messiaen. See Messiaen, *Traité I*, p. 64; *Traité IV*, p. 118; *Traité V/i*, p. 256; *Traité V/ii*, p. 586.

[23]   Preface by Paul Claudel to Louis Chaigne, *Anthologie de la renaissance catholique* (Paris: Alsatia, 1938), n. p.

[24]   Cited in *Traité I, V, VI* and *VII*.

[The Horsehair Glove] in the *Roseau d'or* collection. Many of his other poems were also featured in the collection's collective volumes.

There is one more literary work that Messiaen cites (in the third volume of his *Traité*), which relates to the Catholic Renaissance: Baumann's *Nourritures célestes*. Emile Baumann (1868–1941) wrote the preface for the translation of *L'Imitation de Jésus-Christ*, published by the Catholic editor Desclée de Brouwer.[25] His work is penetrated with a mystical, sorrowful Catholicism in the tradition of Léon Bloy and Joris-Karl Huysmans. Some of Baumann's works were reprinted (a few appeared for the first time) in a collection called 'Catholic Renaissance Anthology at the beginning of the twentieth century',[26] in which the editor's biographical study of Baumann refers widely to the Catholic Renaissance.[27]

There remains a third category of references, those Catholic thinkers and philosophers who were part of the Catholic Literary Renaissance. First, there is Messiaen's reference to Dom Columba Marmion (1858–1923) and his well-known book *Le Christ dans ses mystères* (1919). In a work that traces the major themes of Marmion's thinking, cleric Canon Cardolle remarks:

> Certainly laymen [...] contributed considerably to the spiritual *élan* between the two World wars, including Bloy, Psichari, Péguy, Légaut, and Thibon. But at the present time, Marmion remains one of the most heeded of our spiritual guides. A survey was made among Belgian Catholics during the [First World] War which asked, "Do you read religious books? Which titles and authors?" The name most frequently mentioned was that of Marmion'.[28]

Marmion is a spiritual writer whose works are problematic, lying somewhere between spirituality and theology. They invoke a typically nineteenth-century spirituality marked by devotion to the Sacred Heart, the Eucharist and the Virgin

---

[25]   *L'imitation de Jésus-Christ: traduction nouvelle de Charles Grolleau: préface d'Emile Baumann* (Paris/Bruges: Desclée de Brouwer, 1933).

[26]   See the 45 texts by Baumann edited by Maugendre in Louis Alphonse Maugendre, *La Renaissance catholique au début du 20ᵉ siècle: Emile Baumann (1868–1941)* (Paris: Beauchesne, 1968), pp. 125–231. The other titles of this collection, all with the same author, are *La Renaissance catholique au début du 20ᵉ siècle: Georges Dumesnil: L'Amitié de France* (Paris: Beauschesne, 1963); *La Renaissance catholique au début du 20ᵉ siècle: Biographie de Joseph Lotte: Suivi de textes choisis de Joseph Lotte* (Paris: Beauchesne, 1964); *La Renaissance catholique au début du 20ᵉ siècle: L'abbé Lucien Chatelard (1883–1916)* (Paris: Beauchesne, 1966); *La Renaissance catholique au début du 20ᵉ siècle: Eusèbe de Bremond d'Ars (1888–1958)* (Paris: Beauchesne, 1968); *La Renaissance catholique au début du 20ᵉ siècle: Louis Bertrand (1866–1941)* (Paris: Beauchesne, 1971).

[27]   See the study by Louis Alphonse Maugendre, *La Renaissance catholique au début du 20ᵉ siècle: Emile Baumann (1868–1941)*, pp. 50–80.

[28]   J. Cardolle, *Aux Jeunes. Et toi, connais-tu le Christ vie de ton âme? D'après l'œuvre de Dom Marmion* (Paris/Bruges: Desclée De Brouwer, 1949).

Mary. They are anchored in the writings of Saint Thomas Aquinas, along with those of Saint Paul and Saint John and *The Rule* of Saint Benedict.[29]

Messiaen cited other contemporary Catholic philosophers such as Jean Guitton, (a disciple of Henri Bergson, who Messiaen also cited), as well as Gustave Thibon.[30] Both were Thomist philosophers like Marmion, emphasizing the fact that although Messiaen never refers to Jacques Maritain, the most celebrated of contemporary Thomist thinkers, he does cite Aquinas directly in volumes 1, 3, and 7 of his *Traité*.[31]

The reconstitution of Messiaen's virtual library using his litany of references to specific authors in his *Traité*, throws into relief – in the context of his literary references – a considerable number of texts from the French Catholic Literary circles of the early twentieth century. It is logical to assume that the formation of this collection dates to the composer's youth, but we must also take into account the fact that these references define an environment, a particular social sphere and manner of perceiving the world at a given historical moment. They are specifically Catholic and share their references to Saint Thomas Aquinas. These texts were organized around the (admittedly diffuse and polymorphous) dominant paradigm of Catholic Revival in late nineteenth- and early twentieth-century France. This was a movement in which Messiaen's intellectual father (Pierre) and his poet brother (Alain) were both involved. One of Pierre Messiaen's colleagues, Louis Chaigne, compiled the first anthology of the Catholic Literary Renaissance, and his editor at the publishing house Desclée De Brouwer was none other than Stanislas Fumet himself.[32]

---

[29]   Mark Tierney, *Dom Columba Marmion: Une biographie* (Paris: Buchet/Chastel, 2000), pp. 307–325.

[30]   Gustave Thibon was a Christian philosopher who contributed to the *Revue Thomiste* and *Études Carmélitaines*. See the contents of *Études Carmélitaines*: <http://perso.p-poirot.mageos.com/tabledesvolumes.htm> (accessed 7 October 2007).

[31]   For more on the influence of Thomist philosophy over Thibon see Hervé Pasqua, *Bas-fonds et profondeur: Critique de l'idôlatrie et métaphysique de l'espérance: Essai sur la philosophie de Gustave Thibon* (Paris: Klincksieck, 1985).

[32]   On the friendship between Chaigne and P. Messiaen see Louis Chaigne, *Itinéraire d'une espérance: Pages de journal* (Paris: Beauchesne, 1970), p. 181. Chaigne published an important *Anthologie de la renaissance catholique* in three volumes, which introduced the authors of the Catholic Literary Renaissance (see Louis Chaigne, *Anthologie de la renaissance catholique*). The first volume (1938) contains a preface by Claudel (see n. 23 above). Both men knew each other, as a signed copy in this author's personal collection from Fumet to P. Messiaen attests: 'To Pierre Messiaen, who brings Shakespeare to life. Best wishes.' Written in Stanislas Fumet, *L'Amour* (Paris: Desclée de Brouwer, 1939). Fumet was also Pierre Messiaen's editor at the publishing house Desclée, and commissioned Pierre's translation of Shakespeare (see Stanislas Fumet, *Histoire de Dieu dans ma vie* (Paris: Editions du Cerf, 2002), p. 396). Alain Messiaen kept company with Fumet, as Fumet's memoires attest, Stanislas Fumet, *Histoire de Dieu dans ma vie*, p. 691.

Discovery of a key work: *Les Rythmes et la vie*

In the first volume of his *Traité* Messiaen makes several references to the collective work *Les Rythmes et la vie* [Rhythms and life]. The fact that this work is not mentioned in the acknowledgements at the end of the volume makes it difficult to identify, particularly as two books bear the same title.[33] One was published in Lyon and, although undated, would seem to date from 1934;[34] the second was printed in Paris in 1947.[35] The two books are related to each other – the 1947 version, containing 14 articles, is a revised and expanded version of the original, which contains only nine. In the first volume of the *Traité* Messiaen refers explicitly to *Les Rythmes et la vie* three times. A comparison of the two versions confirms that all three references are only found in the 1947 edition.[36]

Messiaen's three explicit references to *Les Rythmes et la vie* cite the doctor René Biot, the economist Jean Chevalier and the philosopher Gustave Thibon.[37] Further comparison between the table of contents of *Les Rythmes et la vie* and the index of Messiaen's *Traité* reveals that three other authors cited by Messiaen in his *Traité* contributed to *Les Rythmes et la vie*: the philosopher Jean Guitton, the author François Guillot de Rode and the physicist Jean Thibaud. Though Messiaen fails to mention it, his citations of Guitton and Guillot de Rode both come from *Les Rythmes et la vie*.[38]

The physicist Jean Thibaud contributed a very long article to *Les Rythmes et la vie*, which Messiaen does not cite directly. Messiaen does, however, quote Thibaud's book *Vie et transfiguration des atomes* [Life and transfiguration of the atoms], which happens to be the only source for his aforementioned article. Messiaen probably discovered Thibaud's book via his article in *Les Rythmes et la vie*.

There are thus six references from *Les Rythmes et la vie* in Messiaen's *Traité*, enough to qualify the work as one of the cornerstones of Messiaen's theories on rhythm. The articles are:

> Jean Guitton: 'Introduction – The Significance of Rhythm'
> Jean Thibaud: 'Rhythm in Physical Reality: From Atom to Star'

---

[33]   Messiaen, *Traité I*, p. 369.

[34]   Groupe lyonnais d'études médicales, philosophiques et biologiques, *Les Rythmes et la vie* (Lyon: Lavendier, 1934).

[35]   Maxime Laignel-Lavastine, ed., *Les Rythmes et la vie* (Paris: Plon, 1947).

[36]   Thus correcting the identifcation of this work in the list of works consulted by Messiaen in writing the first chapter on time from the first volume of the *Traité* given by Andrew Shenton in, 'Observations on time in Olivier Messiaen's *Traité*', pp. 188 and 189.

[37]   All cited in the *Traité I*, p. 29.

[38]   Guitton is cited in Olivier Messiaen, *Traité I*, p. 41, in the context of a list of definitions of time: 'Rhythm is an alternation: the passage from the self to the other and from the other to the self' [without reference]. The citation comes from the introduction written by Jean Guitton of the 1934 edition: *Les Rythmes et la vie* (Lyon: Lavendier, 1934), p. 9.

René Biot: 'Sexual Activity'
Jean Chevalier: 'Rhythm in the World of Economics'
François Guillot de Rodes: 'Rhythm and Dance'
Gustave Thibon: 'The Rhythms of Spiritual Life'

Upon reading the *Traité*, one is struck by the variety of sources Messiaen calls upon in laying out his theories on time. Yet one also notes his dependence upon a single collective work containing articles on rhythm by experts in a number of different fields (philosophy is covered by Guitton, and Thibon; physics by Thibaud; medical science by Biot; economics by Chevalier; theatre, choreography and dance by Guillot de Rodes). The discovery of this collective work among Messiaen's readings reveals that seemingly varied references may come from common sources. More importantly, by studying how these articles came to be published in one collective volume (discussed further below), one discovers that *Les Rythmes et la vie* is hardly as secular as its title would suggest. Rather, it falls entirely within the vein of the Catholic Renaissance.

To the reader who takes into consideration the scientific and religious climate in the France of the 1930s, the 1934 version of *Les Rythmes et la vie* is clearly the product of a Catholic milieu and related to the Catholic Renaissance. The book was compiled under the direction of the doctor René Biot, a professor of medicine at the University of Lyons and published under the aegis of the *Groupe lyonnais d'études médicales philosophiques et biologiques*. This Lyons research group was formed to investigate possible links between biology and psychology, and tried to respond to social and moral issues through medical science. Though the group's name does not betray its Catholic inspiration, all of the issues examined through the lens of medical science contained in this collective volume are issues dear to Catholic morality. One example is the question posed by the secretary general of the association, René Biot, in his introduction to the volume. He tidily sums up the group's tone, asking: 'Can a doctor consider Man if he overlooks God'? This publication, with its focus on medical science, is typical of the tendency towards scientific mediation during the 1930s. The search for a 'new humanism' during these years gave rise to initiatives popularizing scientific advances.[39] *Les Rythmes* was a specialized publication written for a general audience, with a clearly stated religious background. This was the same strategy adopted by the Christian Intellectual Renaissance, which refused both the anti-rationalism of the ultramontanists and the anticlerical rationalism of certain scientists. In effect, the Christian Intellectual Renaissance sought to reconcile the Christian faith with the freedom of personal spirit.

The 1947 version of *Les Rythmes* reprints two-thirds of the articles from 1934 and adds eight new articles. Despite this considerable change, the tone of the second volume continues to position itself within the same Catholic mindset.

---

[39] See François Chaubet, *Histoire intellectuelle de l'entre deux guerres* (Paris: Nouveau Monde, 2006), p. 36.

The 1947 publication was edited by a professor of medicine, Laignel-Lavastine, who also contributed to the 1934 version and whose Catholic faith was attested to by both his contemporaries and his disciples. The second edition of *Les Rhythmes* was published as part of Plon's collection *Présences*, which also included many Catholic authors such as Gabriel Marcel, Jacques Maritain, and Jean Guitto. The collection was edited by Daniel-Rops who, at the time, was one of France's most prolific, widely read, and highly regarded Catholic writers. Daniel-Rops was also an esteemed Catholic critic alongside Jacques Maritain and Pierre Emmanuel.

Both versions of *Les Rythmes et la vie* were published during the height of the Catholic intellectual movement. They can perhaps even be thought of as committed to the Catholic cause. Though the general content of their articles does not deal explicitly with religion, (aside from some citations of Guitton and Thibon, who were both Catholic intellectuals), once the origin of these articles is recognized it is possible to conclude that Messiaen's seemingly secular references (such as those to Thibaud, Biot, Chevallier, and Guillot de Rodes) are in fact drawn from a Catholic publication. If these essays had not been published in a compilation such as *Les Rythmes et la vie*, it would have been difficult to find a link between them and Catholicism, a link that becomes clear within the context of their common citation by Messiaen. In other words, it is *through* his religious culture, clarified in the first part of this article, that Messiaen discovers his secular references.

The books read by Messiaen and cited in the *Traité* make it possible to begin to define our knowledge of Messiaen's intellectual universe. Most of his literary references are related to the Catholic Renaissance, while other works such as *Les Rythmes et la vie* are still bathed in a Catholic intellectual milieu, even when they do not explicitly deal with religion. This observation is also pertinent when one considers other works cited by Messiaen such as *A la gloire de la terre* [To the glory of the earth], written by the geologist Pierre Termier, whose biography reveals him to be fervent Catholic well versed in the works of Bloy et Maritain.[40] Messiaen's cultural references are clearly those of a man shaped by the spirit of French Catholic intellectual circles in the 1920s and 1930s. The citation of such works in a text written after the Second World War reveals this culture is firmly rooted in the composer's character. Certain of Messiaen's aesthetic concerns, particularly his interest in rhythm, should be re-evaluated in light of this new knowledge. In the preface to the second edition of *Les Rythmes et la vie* signed by the *Présences* group one reads: 'While one of the essential elements of Man, rhythm is also one of the most mysterious. [...] To all those who have followed our

---

[40]   Termier is cited in *Traité I, II* and *IV*. According to biographers Hudson and Mancini, 'From 1905 to Bloy's death in 1917 the Bloys and the Maritains saw each other very frequently, often along with other young men and women including Pierre and Christine van der Meer, Georges Auric the composer, Georges Rouault the painter, and Pierre Termier the geologist (who, with Bloy, believed that the Garden of Eden was the lost city of Atlantis)'. Deal Wyatt Hudson and Matthew J. Mancini, *Understanding Maritain: Philosopher and Friend* (Macon, GA: Mercer University Press, 1987), p. 81.

work over the last ten years, we hope to present one of its themes here. [Rhythm is one of the most] fertile subjects for the contemporary man to choose as the subject of his meditation or for a study in and of itself.'[41] It is remarkable to note that a Catholically oriented research group was interested in the notion of rhythm as an object of investigation and meditation.

We might reasonably draw the following conclusion: Messiaen's interest and concern about rhythm stand before a double background. There are on the one hand the musicians and their theoretical thoughts about this important musical factor, among which we have to mention Maurice Emmanuel and Marcel Dupré, whose heir and follower Messiaen is as a former student and professor at the Conservatoire de Paris; on the other hand, there are the less known reflections on this matter within Roman Catholic intellectual circles, whose influence on Messiaen has been ignored until now. Future studies will now be able to reference both aspects of Messiaen's interest, which, given the nature of his commitment to Catholicism, are inseparable.

---

[41]   Laignel-Lavastine, *Les Rythmes* (1947), p. II.

APPENDIX

Composers cited in the *Traité de rythme, de couleur et d'ornithologie*

Name of composer	Volume of *Traité*
Adam de la Halle	*V, VII*
Albeniz, Isaac	*I*
Auric, Georges	*VII*
Bach, Johann Sebastian	*I, III, IV, V, VII*
Balakirev, Mily	*VII*
Bartok, Béla	*I, II, IV, VI, VII*
Beethoven, Ludwig van	*I, II, IV, V, VII*
Berg, Alban	*I, II, III, VII*
Berlioz, Hector	*I, III, VII*
Bizet, Georges	*VII*
Borodin, Aleksander	*VII*
Boulez, Pierre	*I, II, III, IV, V, VII*
Bulow, Hans von	*I*
Cage, John	*I, VII*
Chopin, Frédéric	*I, II, III, IV, V, VI, VII*
Couperin, François	*VI*
Dallapiccola, Luigi	*VII*
Debussy, Claude	*I, II, III, IV, V, VI, VII*
Delvincourt, Claude	*I, III, VII*
Dukas, Paul	*III, VI*
Dupré, Marcel	*I, IV*
Eloy, Jean-Claude	*III*
Emmanuel, Maurice	*I, VII*
Falla, Manuel de	*I, II*
Folquet de Marseille	*I, VII*
Franck, César	*VI*
Frescobaldi, Girolamo	*IV*
Gesualdo, Carlo	*VII*
Gluck, Christoph Willibald	*IV*
Grieg, Edvard	*II, VI*
Grigny, Nicolas de	*IV*
Henry, Pierre	*VII*
Honegger, Arthur	*II, VII*
d'Indy, Vincent	*I, IV*
Janequin, Clément	*I*
Jolivet, André	*I, II, III, VII*
Kodály, Zoltan	*VII*

Name of composer	Volume of *Traité*
Le Jeune, Claude	*I, V*
Leibowitz, René	*I, III, VII*
Lesur, Daniel	*VII*
Ligeti, György	*IV, V*
Liszt, Franz	*VI*
Lully, Jean-Baptiste	*I*
Machaut, Guillaume de	*I, III, IV, V*
Maderna, Bruno	*IV*
Martenot, Maurice	*I, II*
Martinet, Jean-Louis	*VII*
Massenet, Jules	*III, VI*
Milhaud, Darius	*I, II, VI, VII*
Monteverdi, Claudio	*I, II, III, IV, V, VII*
Mussorgsky, Modest	*I, II, III, VI, VII*
Mozart, Wolfgang Amadeus	*I, III, IV, V, VII*
Nguyen-Thien Dao	*IV*
Nigg, Serge	*VII*
Penderecki, Krzysztof	*IV*
Poulenc, Francis	*VII*
Rameau, Jean-Philippe	*IV, VI*
Ravel, Maurice	*I, II, III, IV, VI, VII*
Rimsky-Korsakov, Nikolai	*II, VII*
Roussel, Albert	*I*
Rudel, Jaufré	*VII*
Sauguet, Henri	*VII*
Schaeffer, Pierre	*I, II, IV*
Schmitt, Florent	*VI*
Schoenberg, Arnold	*I, II, III*
Schumann, Robert	*IV, VI*
Stockhausen, Karlheinz	*I, II, V*
Strauss, Richard	*II*
Stravinsky, Igor	*I, II, III, V, VI, VII*
Tournemire, Charles	*IV*
Varèse, Edgar	*I, II*
Villa-Lobos, Heitor	*I, II*
Wagner, Richard	*I, II, III, IV, V, VI, VII*
Weber, Carl Maria von	*VI, VII*
Webern, Anton	*I, II, III, VII*
Wyschnegradsky, Ivan	*VII*
Xenakis, Iannis	*V*

Chapter 2

Messiaen as Preacher and Evangelist in the Context of European Modernism

Peter Bannister

Since the work of Bach scholars Philip Spitta and Albert Schweitzer in the late nineteenth century, it has become a truism in discussions of sacred music that there are five rather than four Christian evangelists, the fifth being the author of the *St Matthew* and *St John Passions*, the B Minor Mass and the mere matter of over a thousand other pieces. Curiously, when asked by Brigitte Massin whether he would appreciate the epithet 'the Bach of modern times', Olivier Messiaen replied somewhat ambiguously: 'I suppose I ought to take it as a very great compliment. It would be undeserved.' When then asked by Massin whether he could detect a resemblance between himself and the Leipzig Thomaskantor, his answer was a categorical 'No, not at all'.[1]

Without wishing to make of the composer of *La Transfiguration* the 'Sixth Evangelist', I would nonetheless contend that Messiaen has a unique place in late twentieth-century music by virtue of his unashamed proclamation of specifically Christian doctrine in an intellectual environment far more hostile than that of eighteenth-century Saxony. Refusing to limit religious music to the church, Messiaen evangelized the secular musical world from his first orchestral works of the 1930s to the towering later achievements of *La Transfiguration*, *Des Canyons aux étoiles…* or *Saint François d'Assise*. The consciously apologetic dimension of this enterprise, addressing the culture of modernity, is one of the most important and most controversial aspects of Messiaen's output. I will outline his trajectory as a preacher through music, word and personal example, suggesting reasons for the success, albeit not uncontested, of Messiaen's approach.

When considering this aspect of his career, a paradox is immediately apparent. Six decades of church service at La Trinité undoubtedly qualify Messiaen as one of his century's greatest liturgical musicians, hence the inevitable comparisons with Bach. However, unlike Bach, Messiaen's music is clearly not primarily intended for the liturgy.[2] Indeed, he emblematically re-contextualizes the word 'liturgy' in the title of the *Trois petites Liturgies de la Présence Divine*, a concert

---

[1]   Brigitte Massin, Olivier Messiaen: *une poétique du merveilleux* (Aix-en-Provence: Editions Alinéa, 1989), p. 59.

[2]   Highly idiosyncratic exceptions being the *Messe de la Pentecôte* and the unpublished Mass for eight sopranos and four violins of 1933.

work that falls within his own category of 'religious' as distinct from 'liturgical' composition: 'Liturgical music is exclusively dependent on the [church] service, whereas religious music spans all times and places, touching the material as much as the spiritual, and in the end finds God everywhere'.[3]

Although this well-known definition dates from Messiaen's later life, writing religious works for performance outside the confines of the church is a constant of his artistic strategy, as abundant examples from his early compositions demonstrate. In some cases the context is intimate, such as that of Messiaen's little-known cantata *La mort du nombre* of 1930 or the more familiar song-cycles *Poèmes pour Mi* (1936) and *Chants de terre et de ciel* (1938). The recourse to and writing of religious texts in an essentially private sphere of musical expression might in itself seem unremarkable. What is arguably more significant is that Messiaen brings explicitly Christian subject-matter into the inherently public domain of orchestral music. This is already evident in his very first composition in the genre to be performed, the *Banquet eucharistique* of 1928 (whose title surprised his teacher Paul Dukas), followed by a succession of pieces written in a short period: *Les Offrandes oubliées* (1930), *Chant simple d'une âme* (1930), *Le Tombeau resplendissant* (1931), *Hymne au Saint-Sacrement* (1932) and the orchestral version of *L'Ascension* (1933).[4]

It is worth underlining the singularity of this approach in 'an environment where faith plays little part', as Maurice Emmanuel remarked in his testimonial of 1931 endorsing Messiaen's application for the post at La Trinité.[5] With another supporter of his candidacy, Charles Tournemire, being his most obvious musical template, Messiaen's early sacred concert works, together with his authorship of numerous articles and aesthetic engagement as a member of *La Jeune France*, initiate a lifelong dialogue with secular culture. In doing so, Messiaen can be seen as remaining faithful to and indeed developing the aesthetic stance of the Catholic intellectual revival of the early twentieth century.[6]

---

[3]   *Conférence de Notre-Dame* (Paris: Editions Leduc, 1978), essentially re-iterated in the *Conférence de Kyoto: November 12, 1985* (Paris: Leduc, 1985), as well as in interviews with Claude Samuel and Brigitte Massin among others.

[4]   The *Banquet eucharistique* was actually programmed as *Le Banquet céleste* at its one and only performance at the Paris Conservatoire on 22 January 1930.

[5]   Quoted in *Messiaen* by Peter Hill and Nigel Simeone (New Haven, CT/London: Yale University Press, 2005), p. 35. The present essay constitutes, to a certain extent, an attempt to interpret the previously unavailable material that these two authors have recently brought to light.

[6]   French Catholicism's innovative inter-war aesthetic is discussed at length in Stephen Schloesser's insightful *Jazz Age Catholicism: Mystic Modernism in Postwar Paris 1919–1933* (Toronto: University of Toronto Press, 2005). Discussion of Tournemire's influence on Messiaen (also central to Robert Sholl's PhD thesis *Olivier Messiaen and the culture of modernity* (London: British thesis service, 2003)) should not be restricted to consideration of the latter's pre-war works – comments from the *Traité* equally point to Tournemire's

Le cas Messiaen

By the time of the Second World War, the apologetic dimension of Messiaen's music, and especially his written and spoken glosses, had become unmistakeable. The exceptional (and for many exceptionable) nature of the latter is obvious in the case of the *Quatuor pour la fin du Temps* (1941), not merely in Messiaen's idiosyncratic vocabulary, but also in the utter contrast with its immediate context.[7] Messiaen's provocative disregard for the supposed boundary between sacred and secular resurfaces in his spoken introductions to the *Vingt regards* given during their first performance at the Salle Gaveau and most famously in the music, original sung text and commentary to the *Trois petites Liturgies de la Présence Divine* of 1945. The violence of the critical reception to Messiaen's wartime works and the ensuing polemics known as *le cas Messiaen* [The Messiaen Controversy] can be seen as the logical consequence of both the content and above all the style of his highly personal form of apologetics.

Space does not permit full discussion of this furious and archetypically Parisian controversy, but a central element of the case against Messiaen was that, although his musicianship was almost universally admired, his commentaries (dismissed by Claude Rostand in a particularly virulent attack as 'the most appalling sacred jargon imaginable'), aroused widespread hostility for their literary style and apparent lack of audible connection with the music itself.[8] A prime example is Robert Delannoy's assault on the *Quatuor* published in *Les Nouveaux temps* on 13 July 1941, charging Messiaen with naïveté in positing a one-to-one correspondence between his intentions and their realization.[9] Objecting to the composer's admittedly exalted statement that 'such an act of faith should be expressed by resolutely revolutionary and superhuman sonic means', Delannoy denounces Messiaen's 'fanatical subjectivity, a Lucifer-like arrogance in wishing to describe light'. Furthermore, he asserts that Messiaen seeks to evoke 'the power of a personal miracle' in his music and then 'calmly announces that he has succeeded'. Essentially the same allegation is made by Bernard Gavoty, writing in *Le Figaro* under the pseudonym

---

improvisations as a blueprint for the *Messe de la Pentecôte*, the form of which obviously parallels that of the offices of Tournemire's *L'Orgue Mystique*.

[7] To sense the force of this juxtaposition see the remarkable prison camp bulletin entitled *Le Lumignon*, which Nigel Simeone has made available online at <www.oliviermessiaen.net>.

[8] In *Carrefour*, 21 April 1945, quoted and rebutted by Daniel-Lesur in 'Trois Petites Liturgies de la Présence Divine d'Olivier Messiaen', *Revue Musicale de France* (1 April 1946).

[9] Quoted *in extenso* in Rebecca Rischin, *For the End of Time: The Story of the Messiaen Quartet*, (Ithaca, NY: Cornell University Press, 2003); my translation from the French edition of Rischin's *For the End of Time, Et Messiaen composa: genèse du 'Quatuor pour la fin du Temps'* (Paris: Ramsay, 2006), pp. 160–162. All English translations in this essay are mine unless otherwise stated.

'Clarendon' following the première of the *Vingt regards* at the Salle Gaveau in March 1945: 'An ambitious plan: to express the inexpressible. Critical sense is abandoned. [...] There is a persistent contradiction here: like a lunatic creator of a vanished museum, the composer announces marvels when he speaks, but which the piano immediately refutes. [...] Is this heaven? No, it's purgatory.'[10]

Some evidence perhaps ought to be brought to bear in Messiaen's defence at this point. For example, in the case of the *Quatuor*, significant differences between the programme cited by Delannoy and the work's printed preface should be noted.[11] Not only does the latter omit the reference to 'resolutely revolutionary and superhuman sonic means', but Messiaen adds an important disclaimer, describing his evocation of God's eternity as 'a stammering attempt [*essai et balbutiement*], if one thinks of the overwhelming grandeur of the subject!' It would seem likely that Messiaen is here responding directly to Delannoy's critique: his acknowledgement of the impossibility of rendering the infinite by finite means indicates a degree of self-consciousness with which he perhaps should be credited more often.

Despite its frequently grandiloquent tone (reaching a paroxysm in the introduction to *Technique de mon langage musical* and an extraordinary article published in *Volontés de ceux de la résistance* [Willpower of the resistance], 16 May 1945 entitled 'Querelle de la musique et de l'amour' [Quarrel of music and love], it would be an over-simplification to see Messiaen's early literary work as entirely naïve and lacking in philosophical or theological sophistication. His introductory remarks to the *Offrandes oubliées* and the *Hymne au Saint-Sacrement* for the inaugural concert of *La Jeune France* (3 March 1936) are particularly insightful in their demonstration of self-critical awareness:

> 'The body lives through the spirit. Why deny the unknown power of the spiritual body to see the spirit itself through the body?' Thus wrote Saint Augustine. And it seems that true beauty is that which comes closest to this simple vision. Every artist thus needs to try, according to the words of Paul Valéry: 'to enlarge our conceptions to the extent where they become inconceivable'. This state of the spirit maintains a proper humility and contempt for the work itself: these are the necessary conditions in any quest for the new.[12]

I would nonetheless contend that, setting aside critical excesses and the sheer vitriol directed against the composer during the polemics of the *cas Messiaen*, a serious point arises from the controversy which scholarship should not dismiss. Following Messiaen's own self-analytical method, much musicology has concentrated on mapping his techniques with theological concepts. The question of what is lost – or maybe gained – 'in translation' into aural reality would perhaps benefit from the application of different methodology acknowledging that the intentions of

---

[10]   Quoted in Hill and Simeone, *Messiaen*, p. 142.

[11]   *Quatuor pour la fin du Temps* (Paris: Durand, 1942).

[12]   Quoted in Hill and Simeone, *Messiaen*, p. 62.

any composer are frequently undercut by the finished musical work considered as an independent entity with a life of its own. Careful reading of Messiaen's humorously self-deprecating comments in the *Traité* suggests that he was himself aware, at least retrospectively, of precisely this disjunction between his aims and their outworking.[13]

If posterity has vindicated Messiaen the musician, with the centrality of the wartime works reaffirmed by today's performers and audiences, the conclusion reached by *Le Littéraire* in 1946 at the end of an extensive enquiry indicates the general refusal of Messiaen's musical contemporaries to accept the indissolubility of the bond between the artist and the Christian apologist: 'Almost all [...] describe Messiaen as a very great musician of our time. The majority are also in agreement about rejecting all the literature and commentaries which the composer, or certain clumsy exegetes, place around his works, and concur that these do the music a disservice.'[14]

Messiaen and the post-war avant-garde: Crossing the desert?

The abrupt and startling stylistic change in Messiaen's music following this controversy and specifically the austerity and avant-garde experimentation of the works immediately subsequent to *Turangalîla* has occasioned much comment. One may or may not accept the link between the external circumstances of Messiaen's private life in the years preceding his marriage to Yvonne Loriod (particularly with respect to the harrowing mental disintegration of Claire Delbos), and the temporary submergence of Messiaen's characteristic melodic/harmonic idiom.[15] Similarly, the significance of the absence of religious works with orchestra in his catalogue between 1945 and 1963 (*Couleurs de la cité céleste*) is a matter of

---

[13]   Messiaen for example describes the second movement of the *Livre d'orgue* in these terms, discussing the music's relationship to I Corinthians 13, 12: 'The text juxtaposes the clarity of the beatific vision and the obscurity of faith. I only considered the latter, and particularly the incomprehensibility surrounding the Mystery of the Holy Trinity. But I was unable to realize my intention to express the darkness, and only managed to write a short and fairly nondescript dodecaphonic piece: no blackness, no confusion, no mystery' (*Traité III* (Paris: Leduc, 1996), p. 181.

[14]   *Le Littéraire*, 13/20 April 1946 (quoted in Hill and Simeone, *Messiaen*, pp. 166–167).

[15]   This interpretation is offered in 1960 (the year after the death of Claire Delbos) by Antoine Goléa, who already sees the Tristan Trilogy in terms of the sublimation of a relationship (compared to that of Wagner and Mathilde Wesendonck) whose consummation is clearly incompatible with Catholic doctrine (*Rencontres avec Olivier Messiaen*, Paris: Juillard, 1961, pp. 150–156). Although Hill and Simeone (*Messiaen*) conversely interpret *Harawi* as addressed to Claire Delbos, they too see a correspondence between Messiaen's musical evolution of 1949 and the dramatic, irreversible worsening of his first wife's condition due to post-surgical complications.

debate.[16] What is, however, certain is that the overtly public apologetics found in the wartime compositions (a direct and provocative challenge to secularism) disappear during the period in question. For all their adventurous musical language the *Messe de la Pentecôte* and the *Livre d'orgue* are more traditionally 'religious' works in the sense of being destined for church performance.[17] In the post-war years Messiaen's principal form of public aesthetic engagement arguably became his pedagogy at the Paris Conservatoire, Darmstadt and Tanglewood. Several factors can be identified that link this aspect of his activity with his espousal of the avant-garde and orientation away from religious themes: the confrontation with the predominantly secular agenda of international modernism, the radicality of Boulez and some of his other pupils' hostility to musical tradition, the need to compete with a forceful pedagogical rival in René Leibowitz, France's leading Schoenbergian, and in the case of the Conservatoire, the inappropriateness of religious argumentation in a state educational establishment.

Detractors of the avant-garde have sometimes viewed the 1950s as a crossing of the desert in which the broader crisis of musical language shackled Messiaen's creativity.[18] However, if the wilderness is seen as a place of purification rather than pure aridity, Messiaen's risky engagement with the artistic vanguard on its own terms rather than from the security of dogmatic statements and the somewhat self-legitimating system of the *Technique de mon langage musical* does not necessarily imply sterility. That he should have grappled with the issues, questioning his own position rather than dismissing the post-war debates as merely symptomatic of the decadence of modern society, testifies to a deepening of his attitude towards faith's relationship with culture. His impeccable avant-garde credentials, paradoxically gained through those experimental works such as the *Quatre études de rythmes* from which he later distanced himself, earned him the respect of those unable to share his Catholicism. Indeed, it was perhaps Messiaen's very refusal of easy answers, his solidarity with the struggles of the post-1945 generation and his refraining from manifesto-like proclamations that now constituted his form of witness.[19]

---

[16]   Arguing somewhat differently, Stephen Broad has speculated intriguingly that the lack of religious works from Messiaen's pen in the nine years following the *Livre d'orgue* could be correlated with the Vatican's denunication of the 'mania of novelty' and the 'so-called modern movement in art' in 1950–51 (Stephen Broad, *Messiaen and modern art sacré*, unpublished paper presented at the Fourth Biennial International Conference on Twentieth-Century Music, University of Sussex, UK, 2005).

[17]   Even if the première of the *Livre d'orgue* in the context of Pierre Boulez's concert series was an extremely public event with the church of La Trinité packed to overflowing.

[18]   This line is, for example, taken by Benoît Duteurtre in his stimulating if polemical *Requiem pour une avant-garde* (Paris: Robert Laffont, 1995), one of the most hotly debated texts on French artistic tendencies after 1945.

[19]   His pupil Alexander Goehr's quotation of Messiaen's admission to the class of 1955–56 that 'We are all in a profound night, and I don't know where I am going; I'm as lost

'Baptizing' the language of modernism

To speak of Messiaen as an evangelist during this period entails examining his 'evangelization' of technique itself. Characteristic of his approach is the experimentation with musical *objets trouvés* [found objects]. By this I mean those elements whose origin seems 'alien' to Messiaen's compositional system as defined by the *Technique de mon langage musical*, but that Messiaen subsequently integrates into his own personal Christian framework. One such example is the celebrated *Mode de valeurs et d'intensités*, the so-called *supersérie* that lit the touch-paper for the integral serialism of the 1950s. Although Messiaen only finally employed the technique in an overtly spiritual context much later, such an intention emerges in a fascinating diary entry from 1946 revealed by Peter Hill and Nigel Simeone, indicating that Messiaen's speculation is never entirely abstract:

> Large orchestra: write a ballet on Time. It is night on stage; a dancer – a man completely still – the creation of time – an angel with a rainbow halo enters, with a fearsome head, eyes rolled upwards to the beyond, no body, two Greek columns ablaze instead of legs. A hand which emerges from the clouds – the sun and a rainbow surrounding the head – a hallucinatory figure – when it appears, the man dances: it is Time; then the man *stops still*; the end of Time. He stands with his arms stretched out, not moving. Chords and resonances like those in my *Quatuor*, and a serial theme giving a series of twelve notes and series of timbres, one for each note, and one duration and nuance for each note. Develop timbres, durations and nuances according to the principles of serialism. […] Think of the star which opens the well to the abyss.[20]

The *Livre d'orgue* constitutes an extended attempt to place avant-garde technical devices in the service of a Christian theological purpose. In the *Livre* is arguably a subversive dimension in Messiaen's (mis-)appropriation of a musical language rooted in Viennese expressionism, alienated art belonging to the cultural world of Mahler, Freud or Egon Schiele with which Messiaen has little or no philosophical sympathy. In this respect, certain terms found in his discussion of the work in the *Traité III* are highly suggestive, such as Messiaen's description of the use of the series as a 'little sacrifice to the idols of the twentieth century', or his justification of the use of irrational rhythms as 'toying with the enemy'.[21]

The turn to birdsong in the 1950s equally responds to high modernism's preoccupation with the crisis of subjectivity. Here, the backdrop is not so much post-serialism as the other main current of the post-war avant-garde, *musique concrète*, with which Messiaen dabbled in 1952 (in the work *Timbres-Durées*) immediately

---

as you' is a moving testimony to his teacher's artistic integrity. (Alexander Goehr, *Finding the Key* (London: Faber & Faber, 1998), p. 56).

[20]   Hill and Simeone, *Messiaen*, p. 169.

[21]   Messiaen, *Traité III*, pp. 226–228.

prior to the composition of *Réveil des oiseaux*.[22] Birdsong is Messiaen's exit strategy from the aporia of the *après-guerre*; it offers him an objectivity with which to obviate the whole discussion of the caducity of subjective expression. The rationale remains eminently theological, as Messiaen regards birdsong as ontologically as well as temporally antecedent to human musical expression, proof of the rootedness of music in God's created order.[23] Birdsong allows Messiaen to affirm the Catholic theology of creation's goodness without requiring the restoration of tonality, while the risk of an anti-humanist stance (present in *musique concrète*) is avoided by the artistic shaping of the raw material necessitated by the composer's transcription of his ornithological sources for human instruments.

A final later example of the philosophical subversion of modernist techniques is the 'langage communicable' found in the *Méditations sur le mystère de la Sainte Trinité* and re-used in *Des Canyons aux étoiles…* .[24] Messiaen readily admitted to Claude Samuel the element of chance in 'transcribing' written texts into an idiosyncratic musical alphabet, parallels Mallarmé's 'throw of the dice' [*coup de dés*],[25] a phrase that Messiaen also uses in his stimulating discussion of John Cage's use of the *I-Ching*.[26] The contextualization of Messiaen's linguistic game in the avant-garde debates regarding subject and object is apparent, but he stresses his philosophical distance from Cage, whom he associates with unacceptable artistic nihilism.[27] Messiaen's qualification of Claude Samuel's juxtaposition of

---

[22]   *Timbre-Durées* for tape, written in collaboration with Pierre Henry.

[23]   Here I would argue against Antoine Goléa's negative interpretation of Messiaen's comment that 'It is in a spirit of self-mistrust, because I belong to this species, I mean the human race, that I took birdsong as my model' (Goléa, *Rencontres avec Olivier Messiaen*, p. 234). Goléa sees this as an inherent contradiction of his Catholicity, a passing phase of pessimism related to the tribulations of Messiaen's private life in the 1950s. On the contrary, the birdsong works can be viewed as having a liberating impact in the context of the composer's trajectory; regardless of his starting-point, Messiaen's compositional practice leads to an affirmative result (although there are moments of impressive bleakness such as the haunting 'Courlis cendré' that concludes the *Catalogue d'oiseaux*, it would seem difficult to interpret pieces such as 'Le Loriot' or *Oiseaux exotiques* as pessimistic).

[24]   In the piece 'Ce qui est écrit sur les étoiles' for the text 'Mené, Tequél, Parsin' as well as the Greek 'Agios o Theos, Agios ischyros, Agios alternatos' played on the tutti in movement V.

[25]   Claude Samuel, *Permanences d'Olivier Messiaen – Dialogues et commentaires*, (Arles: Actes Sud, 1999), p. 206.

[26]   Ibid., pp. 291–294.

[27]   Messiaen illustrates his stance with a thought-provoking parable: 'The life of Cage makes me think of the Chinese painter who, having been entrusted with decorating the walls of the emperor's palace, spent twenty years doing it. In the end, the emperor wanted to see the finished work, but the walls were still bare. Yet the painter had worked for twenty years – he had gradually wiped everything out.' (Samuel, *Permanences d'Olivier Messiaen*, p. 293).

However, Messiaen's attitude in 1952 seems to have been quite different: in a programme note for the radio broadcast of his *Timbres-Durées* composed in collaboration with Pierre

his optimism and Cagean pessimism neatly summarizes his position: 'My view of contemporary life isn't so optimistic.[28] I find it atrocious and full of crimes. But I hope in the future life which will be wonderful and will above all know no end.'[29]

Eschatological hope does not however mean abandoning the modern world to its fate: Messiaen the composer 'preaches' to his contemporaries by the very act of continuing to compose *works* rather than using experimentation with chance to deconstruct the notion of the art-work (the 'langage communicable' being already 'baptized' by virtue of its Scriptural and Thomist textual references).[30]

It is in the 1960s, beginning with *Couleurs de la cité céleste*, that Messiaen returns to explicitly public apologetics. His dialogue with secularism is exemplified by *Et exspecto resurrectionem mortuorum*, his response to André Malraux's commission commemorating France's war dead.[31] Sensing the metaphysical question (individual as well as societal) behind Malraux's request, Messiaen's decision to focus on the resurrection speaks for itself.[32] In this and subsequent works, his guiding vision of God's eternity remains essentially that of his early compositions, yet Messiaen has clearly travelled a long way artistically since the 1930s. Just as substantial theological reflection in his later works comes to complement (though not to supplant) devotional fervour, so Messiaen's musical vocabulary and expressive range attain a new fullness, the melodic-harmonic

---

Henry, he expressed his desire to pay homage to the 'prophets' who pointed to the way of renewal of musical language, 'the way that leads from Varèse to Boulez by way of Webern, Jolivet, John Cage and myself' (quoted in Hill and Simeone, *Messiaen*, p. 199).

[28] Significantly, Messiaen hints that his pedagogical responsibilities played a role in the maintaining of his own affirmative aesthetic stance: 'Nihilism is perhaps a very beneficial attitude for John Cage, but if I had adopted the theory at the Conservatoire, all my pupils would have committed suicide and my classroom would have been strewn with corpses!' (Samuel, *Permanences d'Olivier Messiaen*, p. 292).

[29] Ibid., p. 294.

[30] A preoccupation of the avant-garde since Adorno's extremely perceptive but highly pessimistic *Philosophy of New Music*, trans. Robert Hullot-Kentor (Minneapolis: University of Minnesota Press, 2006 [1941/1949]), in which he casts doubt on the possibility of aesthetic form as an image of reconciliation and totality in the face of barbaric, unreconciled reality.

[31] Stephen Schloesser has argued cogently for recognition of the importance of the context of the decade of bereavement after 1918 for the formulation of the inter-war progressive Catholic aesthetic, a programme for spiritual revival epitomized by Tournemire beginning the composition of his huge organ cycle *l'Orgue Mystique* with the celebration of the Resurrection, and with the office for Easter Sunday being completed on 11 November 1927, the anniversary of the armistice (see Schloesser, *Jazz Age Catholicism*, p. 309). The parallel with Messiaen's act of simultaneous memorialization and renewal in *Et exspecto* is a striking one.

[32] Messiaen cites Malraux as a prime example among self-declared agnostics who could better be described as 'believers in reverse [*croyants renversés*]', whose self-questioning in the face of death already constitutes an entry-point for the Gospel. (Samuel, *Permanences d'Olivier Messiaen*, p. 17).

richness of his pre-war idiom being integrated with the technical harvest of a modernist engagement that had at first seemed barren.[33] Moments of pure tonal affirmation are all the more powerful for no longer being self-legitimating. Here the seventh tableau of *Saint François*, the dramatic high-point of the opera where the saint receives the stigmata, perhaps provides the supreme musico-theological example. The tableau concludes ecstatically in a way not dissimilar to the ending of *L'Ascension*, yet this rapture is hard-won both dramatically and musically. 'Les Stigmates' commences with a sombre prelude whose anguished atmosphere is evoked by a 'mode de valeurs et d'intensités'. This is both a musical and spiritual journey from darkness to light: technique has been fully integrated with theology.

Messiaen's late synthesis of apparently contradictory elements should surely be seen as the result of a long process of artistic and spiritual maturation. It is worth emphasizing this development given that much writing on Messiaen, taking the composer's own statements at face value, has hitherto tended to stress the undoubtedly striking linear consistency of his aesthetic over the course of his career. Scholars have only recently started to probe the fissures in Messiaen's stage-managed public persona that are gradually emerging thanks to the unearthing of previously unpublished material from sources not submitted to the composer's self-censorship (such as his diary). As recent writers such as Rebecca Rischin and Siglind Bruhn have indicated, there is a considerable element of revisionism in Messiaen's statements dating from late in his career, obscuring the evolutionary aspect of his thought and smoothing over the inconsistencies and disruptions that are an inevitable part of an artistic journey spanning over 60 years.[34]

Conclusion

The question of Messiaen's effectiveness as an evangelist remains. Naturally, from a Christian standpoint, the impact of any preaching depends on the work of the Holy Spirit rather than human communication skills; however, Messiaen arguably presents a useful blueprint for Christianity's cultural engagement. Both negative and positive conclusions emerge from an evaluation of his 'homiletics'. Despite the intense spirituality, utter sincerity and enduring musical quality of his early work (itself constituting an important form of witness), I suggest that Messiaen's written apologetics were cruelly exposed by the critical furore of the 1940s.

---

[33]   The first signs of a loosening of modernist austerity can already be found as early as 1956 in the reappearance of tonal material in 'Le Loriot', movement 2 from the *Catalogue d'oiseaux*.

[34]   See Rischin, *For the End of Time*, and Siglind Bruhn, *Messiaens musikalische Sprache des Glaubens* (Waldkirch: Gorz, 2006). Examples are his frequently discussed refusal of the description of his music as mystical despite his pronouncement of 1944 that his works were 'mystically [...] religious' (*Technique de mon langage musical* (Paris: Leduc, 1944), p. 3), or his suspiciously contradictory assertions regarding 'sensuality'.

This cannot be entirely explained by the composer's own view of himself as a Catholic believer misunderstood by atheists.[35] Dominican organist R. P. Florand's description of 'a great musician who explains himself awkwardly as soon as he stops writing with notes' is not without foundation.[36] The 'commentaries where the limits of his culture appear all too obvious', although without question invaluable to scholarship, were generally perceived as extrinsic to his art.[37] In contrast, the force of Messiaen's later religious music – purified of fideism by the refining fire of interaction with the secular international avant-garde, which effectively barred the bringing in of the 'data of revelation'[38] to solve artistic problems – derives from far closer integration of theological and musical content, commanding respect if not necessarily doctrinal adherence.

Fundamental to the success of his endeavour is Messiaen's willingness to hold the complexity of modernity and the Church's ancient spiritual and musical heritage in creative tension via a *ressourcement* that is simultaneously backward- and forward-looking.[39] Here I believe that Messiaen's evangelizing embrace of modernism, both in terms of musical technique and intellectual engagement, can provide an example for contemporary religious composers seeking alternatives to the (dialectical) minimalism of Pärt, Gorecki or Tavener. Despite his expressed nostalgia for a medieval view of the artist as a craftsman glorifying God anonymously, Messiaen's praxis never abandons the present, framed as it is on one side by the ineradicable goodness of God's creation *ex nihilo* and on the other by an eschatological, Resurrection-based hope in the one who 'comes from the reverse side of time, goes from the future to the past and advances to judge the world'.[40]

---

[35]   As, for example, stated on p.1 of the *Conférence de Kyoto*: 'I am a believer, Christian and Catholic [...] speaking of God, the Divine Mysteries and the Mysteries of Christ, to people who do not believe them or who are not well-acquainted with religion and theology'.

[36]   'Y a-t-il un Cas Messiaen?', *Le Littéraire* (20 April, 1946).

[37]   Ibid.

[38]   The term is borrowed from Archbishop Rowan Williams's *Grace and Necessity* (London: Continuum, 2005), a significant retrieval of the aesthetics of Jacques Maritain as providing a potential theoretical basis for contemporary Christian art. A key element of Willliams's (and Maritain's) thought is the need for art whose beauty is generated by the work itself and not sought as a quality external to it. Their view of the artist as a craftsman working within parameters that are simultaneously autonomous *and* God-given, appealing to the Middle Ages against the cult of the individual in post-Enlightenment culture, closely parallels that of Messiaen. His negative response to Brigitte Massin's query as to a direct link between himself and Maritain other than their shared Thomism may seem surprising: the influence of the philosopher in the composer's milieu during the inter-war years should not be underestimated. (Massin, *Une poétique du merveilleux*, p. 178).

[39]   Messiaen's description of Tournemire's *Orgue Mystique* (in the journal *Syrinx*, May 1938) as a 'marvel of half-Gothic, half-ultramodern art' would seem equally applicable to his own dual approach.

[40]   Libretto to *Saint François d'Assise*, 7ème tableau.

Chapter 3
Messiaen's Saintly Naïveté

Sander van Maas

I consider myself naïve, and I hope to remain so for the rest of my life.
– Olivier Messiaen[1]

To brother Anthony, my bishop, brother Francis, I salute you. I am pleased that you teach sacred theology to the brothers providing that, as is contained in the Rule, you do not extinguish the spirit of prayer and devotion during study of this kind.
– Francis of Assisi[2]

If one were to have to compile a list of keywords regarding Olivier Messiaen, the list would probably begin with 'Catholic' followed closely by 'birdsong', 'colour' and perhaps 'Hindu rhythms'. In a top-ten list of adjectives used to qualify Messiaen, the word 'devout' would undoubtedly occur high on the list, probably followed closely by 'naïve'. The latter oft-quoted qualification is easily passed over. This is arguably so because it merely seems to refer to a benign quality in the person of Messiaen, or in the music that he is best known for, such as the *Quatuor pour la fin du Temps* and the *Turangalîla-symphonie*.

The more frequently words such as 'naïve' are used, however, the more the question arises concerning what exactly is said or meant by their use. Adjectives (or, for that matter, adverbs) are wonderful tools for analysis because they can act as levers to open up dimensions in 'Messiaen' experienced by many but mostly left unquestioned. The aim of this essay is to lift the word naïve and its correlates from their immediate contexts and to develop them into concepts for analysis. This work has already been started by various critics of Messiaen's music, two of whom I shall discuss more extensively, Paul Griffiths and Richard Taruskin.

Messiaen was not only a composer who entertained a seemingly vivid, albeit it soloistic, engagement with theology, he was also a religious practitioner. This is evident in his work as an organist at La Trinité, in his role as 'confesseur' for his students (as he formulated it) and as an inspiring visionary.[3] What seems most

---

[1]   Brigitte Massin, *Olivier Messiaen: une poétique du merveilleux* (Aix-en-Provence: Éditions Alinéa, 1989), p. 132.

[2]   Francis of Assisi, 'Letter to Brother Anthony (1223)', trans. Noel Muscat (amended), available online at <www.ofm.org.mt/noelmuscat/notes/Writings/DLP%20Cant% 20WSF % 2004.pdf > (accessed September 2008).

[3]   Claude Samuel, *Permanences d'Olivier Messiaen: Dialogues et commentaries* (Arles: Actes Sud, 1999), p. 301.

important in the dimension called 'the naïve' is that it does not primarily seek the religious in a theoretical position. This is not to say that Messiaen's alleged naïveté is an example of pure religious practice. As I will discuss, there are many elements in his work that display a highly informed and even cultured engagement with the naïve.

In order to be able to draw out the full implications of the naïve in Messiaen, I have chosen to make ample use of the stage performances of *Saint François d'Assise* that took place in June 2008 in Amsterdam, in the Netherlands. Messiaen's opera is a splendid case study for the meaning of the word 'naïve' because of its subject – the saint who loved to call himself 'ignorans et idiota' – and because the work is a summa of Messiaen's musical, aesthetic, dramatic and religious ideas. Most importantly, however, this production has unearthed aspects of the opera that have hitherto remained covered by those aspects of the saint that most resemble the composer: the predilection for colours, birds, music, poetry, mothers and love.[4] Beneath this layer of sensuous and affective saintliness, the production suggests, lies the question of evil in its various guises (sin, suffering, violence).

I shall start out, then, by drawing a picture of the Amsterdam production's visual details, which will support the ensuing discussion of the music in the second section. Throughout my analysis, the discussion of *Saint François* will focus on the second and eighth scene, which, incidentally, have many commonalities (Messiaen describes the latter scene as 'the same music, amplified and magnified'), and which present some of the most salient details of the whole opera. The third section of this essay presents an analysis of the use of the term 'naïve' with regard to personal character and religious faith in Messiaen. The application of the term to his music is studied in the fourth section, which presents, by way of a 'minor anthology', four different elements of the musically naïve that merit closer inspection. The fifth section returns to issues raised by the Amsterdam production by putting the naïve in the light of death and suffering, drawing together the theologies of Glory and of the Cross. In the final section, I shall argue for a reinterpretation of Messiaen's dealing with the (theological and practical) problem of evil.[5]

---

[4]   See for example Stephan Keym's impressive monograph on *Saint François* in which the subject of evil is routinely broached but not further elaborated. Keym, *Farbe und Zeit: Untersuchungen zur musiktheatralen Struktur und Semantik von Olivier Messiaens Saint François d'Assise* (Hildeshteim [etc.]: Georg Olms, 2002), pp. 46–60.

[5]   An important background for this essay is the longstanding debate in the psychology of religion concerning Paul Ricoeur's notion of 'second naïveté'. As is often forgotten, Ricoeur developed this thesis in the context of a book on the problem of evil: *The Symbolism of Evil* (New York and Evanston: Harper-Row, 1967). For a history of this debate see Patrick Vandermeersch, 'The Failure of Second Naiveté: Some Landmarks in the French Psychology of Religion', in *Aspects in Context: Studies in the History of Psychology of Religion*, ed. J.A. Belzen (Amsterdam – Atlanta: Rodopi, 2000). On second naïveté in Messiaen see also the final chapter of my *The Reinvention of Religious Music: Olivier Messiaen's Breakthrough Toward the Beyond* (New York: Fordham University Press, 2009).

Blackened crosses: *Saint François d'Assise* in Amsterdam

Up to 2008 there had been at least nine staged performances of *Saint François d'Assise*. After the premiere in 1983 at the Opéra Garnier in Paris, the work had been staged in London (1988), Salzburg (1992 and 1998), Leipzig (1998), Berlin (2002), San Francisco (2002), Bochum (Germany, 2003), and again in Paris (Opéra Bastille, 2004). The nine performances at the Muziektheater in Amsterdam in June 2008 were directed by Pierre Audi, for whom this production marked his 20th anniversary as artistic director of De Nederlandse Opera. The Residentie Orchestra and choir of De Nederlandse Opera were conducted by Ingo Metzmacher. The team further included two longstanding collaborators of Audi's, Jean Kalman for stage and light design, and Klaus Bertisch for dramaturgy. The main roles were sung by Rod Gilfry (Francis), Camilla Tilling (the Angel), Hubert Delamboye (the Leper), Henk Neven (Frère Léon) and Tom Randle (Frère Massée).

The stage of Amsterdam's huge Muziektheater was extended well into the audience area for the production: the first dozen rows were sacrificed to make a space large enough to accommodate the entire orchestra.[6] As a whole, the shape of the floor was quasi-circular to the eye of the spectator. Throughout the first act, in the centre of the front stage, on the black floor, a large pile of simple, black wooden crosses were arranged like an oval shaped bush. To the right of this bush stood a tall black cross, which had various extensions so as to make it resemble a tree. To the left there was a moveable bridge, light wood-coloured, with steps at both ends. The bridge held up a curtain adorned with faint stripes suggestive of the Umbrian hills. On the reverse the bridge, remaining invisible during the first scene, was a simple cross, similar to the ones used for the bush, but light in colour. The change from the first to the second scene consisted of a number of choristers turning the bridge around to display its cross, and turning the curtain into a backdrop. The bridge, the pile of crosses and the large cross-tree were the main stage props during the first act.

Throughout the production the use of colour was very restricted. Scene 1 started in matte black: the stage floor, the big tree-cross, the pile of smaller crosses, the darkness of the back stage hidden behind a traverse, bridge-like scaffolding, the hooded robes of the choristers. Scene 8 ended, in conformity with Messiaen's directions, with a blinding white light. This light was projected into the venue from the back wall of the stage, in a square array of light bulbs. Primary colours only made their first appearance with the Leper in the third scene: he was wrapped in plastic suit of black-and-yellow diagonal stripes ('I am like a leaf stricken with mildew: all yellow with black spots …').[7] The first moment of vivid colour was

---

[6]   For reasons of space I have limited this description of the opera scene to a functional minimum. The Amsterdam performances were released on DVD by Opus Arte in 2009 (Catalogue number OA1007D).

[7]   The translation of the libretto and of the stage directions used throughout this essay is by Felix Aprahamian, in the CD booklet to *Saint François d'Assise* (DG 445176–2), 1999.

the Angel's appearance, as the Angel-Musician, in scene 5. Here, dressed in a transparent plastic mantle adorned with geometric patches of colour, predominantly red, blue and green, the Angel played the 'Music of the Invisible' holding two fluorescent rods. Other manifestations of colour in the otherwise black-and-white palette, the dim colours of the friars' robes notwithstanding, were the school-children's robes used in 'The Sermon to the Birds' (scene 6), which were earth colours: yellow, green, blue and red. The school children were an innovation by Audi introduced as a class of aspiring little monks, who were taught about birds, and who also made the birds present by holding in their hands toy-like birds on sticks. Finally, in scene 7, red blood dripped from the stigmatized hands that were projected onto the scaffolding towers positioned on either side of the stage.

On the whole, the style and atmosphere of the stage resembled other productions by Audi's team, such as *Der Ring des Nibelungen* that gained fame in the 1990s;[8] but the Wagnerian chiaroscuro sits uneasily with Messiaen's world of light, as does Audi's preference for a minimalistic symbolism. These stylistic clashes, however, are only propaedeutical to the more tectonic frictions in these performances that I will try to describe and interpret below.

What the music says

For many spectators, including myself, the first impression of this staging of *Saint François d'Assise* was one of discomfort. The second act, in particular, makes an awkward impression, which is only partly due to its relatively weak function in the whole of the opera.[9] At the beginning of this act the choristers turn the bridge around, making the cross visible. Francis walks up its steps to the centre, placing his hands on the railing as if overlooking a landscape. Three friars position themselves below in front of the bridge, facing the audience. Along the round edge of the stage a line of choristers is positioned, hoods covering their heads and their faces directed at the pile of black crosses at centre stage.

The atmosphere is grim. The light is dim all around, spotlights to some extent highlighting Francis. The music of the second act features the special effects in the strings that signal, as the ensuing scenes of the opera will confirm, evil and fear. The first such elements are heard in scene 1, when Francis evokes the terror of the long walking journey he has undertaken and the refusal of entry by the monastery's doorkeeper (more about this below). From his slightly elevated position Francis

---

[8]   Audi's *Ring* was released on four DVDs by Opus Arte in 2006.

[9]   In the context of the first act its function is to lead up the scene with the Leper. Francis is shown to come to understand that God not only approves of things beautiful but also permits the existence of ugliness. Francis then decides he needs to practice his love for ugly beings, such as lepers. The scene, however, does not show how this understanding comes about, nor what the friars' role is in this process. This leaves the spectator searching for the meaning and unity of what is shown.

starts to sing the first of the four stanzas of the 'Canticle of the Sun', which forms a significant part of this scene. The 'Canticle' is known as one of the key symbols of St Francis's cosmic approach to things divine. It suggests a saint who is not merely absorbed by an inner drama that makes him an alien in the world of the senses, but who, in an unprecedented fashion, seems to express his mystical experience through an appreciation of the world as it appears to the senses.

The Francis heard singing his 'Canticle' in Amsterdam, however, did not appear in this guise at all. Instead, the intense lyricism of Messiaen's setting of the 'Canticle' text sounded like a helpless, impotent expression of mere longing for spiritual connection. Francis very much appeared as though he were unable to make his praise reach its destination. The friars, like Francis, did not manage to convey any sense of joy. Aligned in front of the bridge they turned their back to the cross. Their *recto tono* recitation, which is complemented by the hooded chorus, sounded heavy and mechanical and conveyed a sense of numbness.

Although it could easily be argued that the source of this grimness is to be found in the austerity, immobility, and blackness of the visual and choreographic elements, the source really seems to be the music. Herein lies the uniqueness of Pierre Audi's staging of *Saint Francis*: it brought out the dark qualities of the music and made these direct the visual aspects and the general atmosphere of the opera. What the second scene in particular reveals is how different the musical portrayal of the monks is from the libretto and the stage directions in the score. Whereas the latter seem to be in line with the popular image of the Franciscans as enlightened spiritual figures whose sensuous experience of religion contrasts with the bookishness of earlier (e.g., Benedictine) traditions, the music seems to place the friars in a much more sombre light.

The musical introduction to the scene introduces an alternation between ritualistic woodwind chords with a delicately Asian flavour, dry staccato notes on the flutes, and a set of strangely 'liquid' clocks ticking that exude an air of alienation. The element of alienation is then carried over to the main music of the scene. This music comes in three sections, the first two presenting a stanza of the 'Canticle' sung by Francis, followed by the brothers and the choir singing the lauds. The third section features Francis alone, descended from the wooden bridge and physically overwhelmed by the violence of the (French) word 'Saint!' sung by the choir from scaffolding towers on either side of the stage and from a traverse bridge. The sense of alienation returns each time the brothers sing the laudes music. It is mainly provoked by the extremely low, metallic rumbling of the ondes Martenot, which interrupts the singing – a timbre that travels from the ondes to the contrabassoon and the double bass – and the extraordinary 'howling' effect produced by a tuba with half-depressed valves. The mode of singing itself, the complete opposite of the *allégresse* [gaiety] Messiaen admired in the Solesmes tradition of Gregorian chant, does the rest.

Throughout the opera, Messiaen relies on semantic clichés in order connect both the music's effects and affects with the libretto and the stage actions. Low rumbles in the orchestra predictably signify terror, high bell sounds signify the

Angel coming, obvious glissandi signify the marvellous, and so on. Given these fairly unequivocal musical hints, it is surprising that Messiaen's score contains no stage directions that would support the content of the music in the second scene. If Francis and his friars really wander desperately in darkness as the music suggests, why did Messiaen not make this clear in his directions? The only darkness he refers to is that of the dim vaults of the monastery church:

> Interior of the little cloistered church, rather dark, with three successive vaults. In the rear and in the middle of the stage, a red lamp lit before a little altar indicates the presence of the Holy Sacrament. The curtain rises to reveal Saint Francis and the three Brothers (Sylvester, Rufus, Bernard) on their knees in prayer. Saint Francis to the right, the three Brothers to the left, facing him. To the right and left of the stage is the chorus (indistinct black shapes).

The Amsterdam performance of *Saint François* appears to have omitted the reference to the Holy Sacrament, which could have accounted for the friars being struck with awe, and would have justified terror in the music. However, as the 'terrible' music of the Holy ['Saint!'] presented shortly after is quite different from the eerie effects used earlier in the scene, that would not have completely removed the sense of alienation. Hence, the question remains: why are these effects here in the opera (and, for that matter, in similar passages in other scenes), and what does this reference to (the experience of) darkness really mean?

As I will discuss below, there is an immediate connection here with the notion of the naïve that concerns, although in a slightly different manner, both Francis and Messiaen.

The ideal of naïveté

In the critical reception of Messiaen it has become somewhat commonplace to test his work against the notion of a 'theology of Glory' (*theologia Gloriae*), that is, of a self-congratulatory faith that overlooks human fallibility and the Judgment to come. The concern here is whether the theological outlook of Messiaen's work is not too one-sidedly focused on the splendour of the divine, disregarding the drama of the Cross. The underlying accusation is that Messiaen oversteps ethics and human finitude in his ecstatic and triumphant fixation on divine glory.

The origin of this line of questioning may have been a question recorded by Almut Rößler in 1972 at a round table discussion with Messiaen. During that discussion a certain 'Mr Vos, a young theologian from Holland' asked the originally Lutheran question regarding the opposition between the theology of the Cross (*theologia Crucis*) and the theology of Glory.[10] The theme was taken

---

[10]   Martin Luther, *Heidelberg Disputation*, thesis 21. The Protestant concern with this opposition is again expressed by Karl Barth. Since Barth's work has had a considerable

up by Harry Halbreich in his biography of Messiaen, and has remained a point of reference.[11] In response to the question, Messiaen explains that the praise and joy that his music directs at the Creator is essentially praise for a God who, despite being infinite Other, has come to suffer with us in Christ. 'This is expressed', he says, 'by means of bird- and colour-themes' (Messiaen's example here being the second movement of his *Méditations sur le mystère de la Sainte Trinité*).[12] Messiaen further explains that his preference for the Apocalypse of John is a difficult one in that this biblical book is not just filled with marvellous events but with terror and catastrophe as well.

Because of this violence and destruction, Messiaen suggests that it is not easy to convert oneself time and again to the glory of God. Generalizing his point, he gives rare insight into his own struggle with faith:

> I'd like to give an example to illustrate my thoughts: When the Apostle Peter saw Christ walking on the water, he asked Him to give him his hand, so that he could walk on the water along with him. Christ gave him his hand, Peter looked at him and was able to walk on water in the same way. Suddenly he became aware of this, began to stumble and was in danger of drowning. He had doubted Christ who then said to Peter: 'Oh, man of little faith!' That's how it is for all of us every day. We must constantly strive afresh not to doubt and not to drown.[13]

Confessing at various occasions that he has 'no talent' for death and suffering and feels that 'sin isn't interesting', Messiaen supports and nourishes his public image of being naïve. 'I prefer flowers', is his simple response to what is probably the problem that haunts human existence most: evil.[14]

Yet, instead of provoking a scandal, this attitude is precisely what earns him and his work the most credit and admiration. Richard Taruskin, for instance, in a polemical review essay from 2003, praises *Saint François d'Assise* for remaining just on the right side of cliché, kitsch, bathos and, therefore, insignificance.

---

impact on the theological debate in the Netherlands, both Protestant and Catholic, the question may well have been inspired by his work. Cf. Karl Barth, 'Not und Verheissung der christlichen Verkündigung (1922)', in *Vorträge und kleinere Arbeiten 1922–1925* (Zürich: Theologischer Verlag, 1990), pp. 93–94.

[11] Harry Halbreich, *Olivier Messiaen* (Paris: Fayed/SACEM, 1980). See also the discussion by Andrew Shenton in his monograph *Olivier Messiaen's System of Signs: Notes Towards Understanding His Music* (Aldershot: Ashgate, 2008), p. 28.

[12] Almut Rößler, *Contributions to the Spiritual World of Olivier Messiaen: With Original Texts by the Composer*, trans. Barbara Dagg, Nancy Poland, and Timothy Tikker (Duisburg: Gilles und Francke, 1986), p. 52.

[13] Ibid., p. 53.

[14] Messiaen, *Olivier Messiaen: Music and Color: Conversations with Claude Samuel*, trans. E. Thomas Glasow (Portland, OR: Amadeus Press, 1994), p. 213; Rößler, *Contributions*, p. 52.

He contrasts the opera with other late twentieth-century spiritual works of music theatre (such as works by Osvaldo Golijov and the collaborative projects of John Adams and Peter Sellars) many of which, according to Taruskin, merely offer a 'panderfest' of 'consoling self-congratulation' presented as spirituality. In Messiaen, by contrast, Taruskin finds no such platitudes or banalities but something substantially different:

> The shallow obviousness of his libretto; the doggedly simple, maniacally static and didactic way he harps on a small fund of musically unprepossessing themes […]; his seeming ignorance – or perhaps his calculated neglect – of any semblance of ordinary stagecraft; the virtual banishment from the texture of counterpoint and thematic development (the usual guarantors of 'purely musical' interest), all bring to mind Pascal's dictum that the virtue of adherence to religious discipline is that it *vous fera croire et vous abêtira* ('it will make you believe, and make you stupid').[15]

Taruskin also notes that, 'Messiaen, supremely sophisticated in technique yet naively direct in expression as only a believer could be, works throughout the opera – indeed worked throughout his career – at the ticklish borderline of cliché'.[16] Instead of exploiting cliché, Messiaen allows his audience to experience the risk of platitudes and kitsch in order to bring them to the verge of religious ecstasy. Taruskin continues: 'The fact that, despite its many near approaches to it, Messiaen's opera manages after all to avoid kitsch while retaining its naiveté is perhaps its most impressive feat – and at the present cultural moment, dominated by a profusion of extremely artful spiritual kitsch, an enormously provocative one'.[17]

Taruskin attempts to make a case for the veracity of Messiaen's music when it takes risks (bordering on kitsch, bathos and insignificance) or when the sacred is evoked by means of 'uncanny otherness'. Naiveté, he suggests, supplies Messiaen's work with the seal of credibility, distinguishing it from the 'shabby topical hypocrisy' of the younger generation of spiritual composers. It is important to note here that, from the start, Taruskin's notion of naiveté is fraught with feelings of the sublime. I shall return to this below.

Although naiveté as a qualifier is primarily found in commentaries on his work, Messiaen himself did not shun it either. We do not have evidence that he used the word to qualify his works, as Taruskin and others do. He did, however, use it to describe his own person. In her book on the composer, Brigitte Massin quotes Iannis Xenakis, whose first encounter with his future teacher had been a memorable one. When Xenakis showed Messiaen his first works, he reports the latter to have responded by saying: 'You are a *naïf*'. As Xenakis appeared

---

[15]   Richard Taruskin, 'Sacred Entertainments', *Cambridge Opera Journal* 15, no. 2 (2003): 118.

[16]   Ibid., p. 118.

[17]   Ibid., p. 119.

somewhat shocked, Messiaen continued: 'No, it is not at all pejorative what I am saying to you, it is because I consider myself naïve, and I hope to remain so for the rest of my life'. The meaning of the qualifier 'naïve' used here by Messiaen is the issue under discussion. Xenakis understood it to refer to 'the intention to keep one's eyes open like a child, and to be marvelled by things, in both life and work'. 'And I really believe', Xenakis adds in conclusion, 'that he has remained exactly that: "marvelled" [*émerveillé*]'.[18]

If, generally speaking, presenting oneself as a *naïf* is paradoxical, this is certainly the case with Messiaen. Although he lived and worked in cities all of his life (from Avignon to Grenoble and Paris), and although his craft made him essentially dependent on cities as centres of culture, he liked to present himself as a countryman. More precisely he referred to himself as a *montagnard* [mountain dweller], a qualification he contrasted with the Cartesians who dominate the French capital. This tendency to locate himself outside of the official culture – withdrawing as he did to his country houses in the Dauphiné and the Cher – transpires also in the way he dressed and behaved. While he started out, in the first wave of public success, dressed in formal-looking suits and showy spectacles, this soon relaxed into the colourful shirts that became his trademark, always wearing the collar over his jacket and matching his blushing complexion. Evidently the outfit for going out into the woods hunting for birdsong – transforming nature into culture, the rural into the urban – was an even more pronounced mixture of the rustic and the artful. This public persona of Messiaen's seems in tune with his proclamation of disbelief in musical systems of human invention, stressing the foundational character of natural resonance, as well as with the provocative proposition of the bird music of the 1950s. Although this music arguably belongs to the most radical composed in the entire twentieth century, it was presented by him again with a mixture of rusticality and Latin learnedness.[19]

The tendency to create 'outposts' also transpires in the emphasis Messiaen put on the imaginary. His fondness for fairytales is well attested, as is his imponderable leap from these tales to the marvels of religion.[20] What creates the outpost is less the content of his tales or his faith than their mode of presentation. This mode includes many elements that defy the demands of the criticism and self-criticism that define post-Enlightenment modernity. For instance, it is a statement in itself to express oneself in the mode of fondness, riding unrestrictedly one's hobby-horses as Messiaen did so often and without request.[21] Massin quotes the *esprit*

---

[18]   Massin, *Une poétique du merveilleux*, p. 132.

[19]   This strategy refers not only to the urban naturalism of Rousseau but also to the religious tradition, originating with Saint Jerome, of the *sancta rusticitas*.

[20]   Characterizing this leap Paul Griffiths uses the term naïveté, adding that 'such *naïveté* can only be admired'. In Griffiths, *Olivier Messiaen and the Music of Time* (London/Boston: Faber and Faber, 1985), p. 22.

[21]   François-Bernard Mâche, a former student of Messiaen, related in Brussels in March 2008 (*Génération Messiaen* conference, organized by Brigitte Van Wymeersch),

de catalogue that characterizes many of Messiaen's explanatory texts, notably in those places where logical exposition seems more appropriate, according to the standards of rational exposition, than quoting a multiplicity of aspects as Messiaen does. Finally, there are the leaps of the imagination that defy the reality of the subject discussed, such as the claim that he wrote *Saint François* in four years and spent a neat four years more on its orchestration (the historical truth being less non-retrogradable).

The qualification 'a *naïf*' for a person can be, as Messiaen indicates in his conversation with Xenakis, something of an honorary nickname and may therefore be contested. Robert Craft, in his book detailing his friendship with Igor Stravinsky, mentions that he tried to convince the latter that Messiaen is 'a mystic and a Holy Roller rather than a *naïf*, which is I.S.'s epithet'.[22]

A minor anthology of the musically naïve

However much the naïve invites reduction to the person in question, reducing qualities of the work to the character of its author, it should always also be understood within the context of the work as such. Hence the question: What is the *musically* naïve? The answer is not easily given. There appears to be an endless richness within this single, and seemingly simple, concept. The naiveté of Gustav Mahler's *ländlers*, for instance, is quite different from the naiveté of Anton Bruckner. The radical simplicity of Erik Satie (or John Cage, for that matter) is not to be confused with the naïveté of Arvo Pärt's tintinnabuli music. The *faux-naïf* in Stravinsky differs from similar tendencies in Harrison Birtwistle. And so on.

Hence it seems justified to ask what, in Messiaen's compositions, gives us the musical experience of the naïve. Taruskin cites a number musical features in *Saint François* that help us isolate the phenomenon: shallow obviousness, dogged simplicity, (seeming) ignorance, and neglect of 'purely musical' substance. Working in a similar fashion, it is possible to isolate a few more such elements in the opera and in other works by Messiaen, and to develop them conceptually. I shall discuss three elements of Messiaen's musical naïveté: enthusiasm, the impossible and the cruel.

Enthusiasm

Enthusiasm is often regarded as a privilege of children and youth, but etymologically the term refers to a religious state, a 'being possessed by the gods' (also known

---

how Messiaen would take the score of *Catalogue d'oiseaux* and start telling his students, in his typically patient and lively manner, what was happening in the music – the sun coming up, birds awakening, etc. – as though he were reading a book to the youngest of children.

[22] Robert Craft, *Stravinsky: Chronicle of a Friendship* (Nashville/London: Vanderbilt University Press, 1994), p. 184.

as *mania*). Robert Craft's remark quoted above about Messiaen giving the impression of being a 'Holy Roller' refers to just this aspect of his music: the expressive features of an inward over-fullness that appear to press outward in uncontrolled vocal and bodily behaviour. However, even though his critics in late Second World War Paris may have detected something of this flavour – 'the ejaculatory manner of the spoken introductions' – in his enthusiastically pronounced programme notes at performances of the *Quatuor pour la fin du Temps*, Messiaen is no Pentecostalist.[23]

If enthusiasm can be the sign of genuine possession by the gods or the Holy Spirit, it must have something in common with the sublime. Enthusiasm, according to Immanuel Kant, is a state in which the mind attempts to overcome being overwhelmed by the invisible by means of an abstraction such as an Idea (in Messiaen this is often the Idea of eschatological redemption; in politics it can be the Idea of revolution).[24] The affect involved – passionate fervour – is an 'unpleasant pleasure' caused by the overstrained imagination that is then unbound. In Messiaen, enthusiasm does not seem sublime because of some form of possession (as in Pentecostalism), but because its concept is taken to its limits. The enthusiasm, for instance, of the fifth movement of *Turangalîla*, 'Joie du sang des étoiles', is too grand to be merely a form of subjective expression. It is raised to a slightly discomforting level, making one wonder if the subject of this movement is still to do with the human potential for praising the Creator. The ending of the fifth movement affirms this sense of discomfort: the sublime element – the *tremendum et fascinans* – is taken out of the eruptive music and turned into a sovereign expression of the Holy, leaving all reference to the praiser behind.

Furthermore, in *Saint François* the element of enthusiasm is mostly to be found in birdsong, which is responsible for the general sense of excitement whenever Good happens. Here the birds represent a perspective on the events from midway between earth and heaven. The birds act individually, but sometimes they resemble an ecstatic, collective *glossolalia* [speaking in tongues] such as in the *hors-tempo* passages of the 'The Sermon to the Birds'. Although they are the primary catalysts of affirmation, there is also a sense of constraint in their relentlessly exclaiming 'Yes'. The birdsong, especially in the style that is favoured by Loriod, is hard-edged, loud and brilliant. It is as though the over-fullness runs up against a limit that prevents relaxation of tension, like a bomb going off without the shell bursting. The birds express not just sublime enthusiasm, but also the pain of being cut off from the Glory they praise.[25]

---

[23] Peter Hill and Nigel Simeone, *Messiaen* (New Haven, CT/London: Yale University Press, 2005), p. 113.

[24] Immanuel Kant, *Kritik der Urteilskraft* (Hamburg: F. Meiner, 1963), p. 119 ff. (§ 29). Cf. Jean-François Lyotard's analysis of this passus in *L'enthousiasme: La critique kantienne de l'histoire* (1986).

[25] To this also belongs the occasionally *mechanical*, lifeless character of their interventions in the vocal parts and elsewhere in the opera. For more on this interaction

In sum, then, the enthusiasm in Messiaen, which on the surface appears as a figure of the naïve, hides the stakes of a destructive force that sooner or later overruns the initial references to childlike joy.

The impossible

The second element in the constitution of the naïve in Messiaen is the sense of unlimited possibility. This is what Paul Griffiths once referred to as Messiaen's 'saintly naïveté'.[26] The context was Griffiths's amazement that Messiaen would use, in *Quatuor*, certain musical materials which form what he describes as a 'a tune of banal perkiness'. For Griffiths, this music had a very strong reference and he felt that Messiaen had not paid any regard to this. 'It takes a sublime, even saintly *naïveté* to accept materials from Massenet and Glenn Miller, then use them to praise Christ as if they had never been employed for any baser purpose', Griffiths notes.[27] Messiaen's naïveté is here explained in terms that seem to highlight his square opposition to any historical determination. Whereas Theodor Adorno would claim that the historical development of the musical material would preclude the type of reinterpretation that Messiaen practices, Messiaen simply goes about it and manages to convince the listener with a unique result. What Messiaen attains, then, is so to speak the impossible. His music shows that it can go where, according to the law of historical determination, no music is allowed to go.

This specific feature can be considered either sublime or saintly. Messiaen's reinterpretation is, first, expressive of a sublime freedom. As Schiller has already noted about naïveté:

> every genius, in order to be one, must be naïve. [...] Unacquainted with the rules, the crutches of weakness and the taskmasters of affectation, guided only by nature or instinct, his guardian angel, he moves calmly and surely through all the snares of false taste in which he who is not a genius, if he is not clever enough to avoid them from afar, remains inevitably entangled.[28]

---

between life, affirmation and the mechanical see my *The Reinvention of Religious Music*, Chapter 5.

[26]   Griffiths, *Olivier Messiaen and the Music of Time*, p. 102. The notion of 'saintly naïveté' refers historically to the early Christian tradition of the *sancta simplicitas*, found in the work of Jerome (*Epist.* 57, 12, 4) around 395 AD. The notion appears also in Thomas à Kempis's *De imitatione Christi*, Book 4, Ch. 18 as *beata simplicitas*. Kempis's book, from the fourteenth century, was particularly appreciated by Messiaen, who used it as a source for the opera and often took it with him on his travels. Cf. Hill and Simeone, *Messiaen*, pp. 305, 374.

[27]   Griffiths, *Olivier Messiaen and the Music of Time*, p. 102.

[28]   Friedrich Schiller, *On the Naïve and Sentimental in Literature* (Manchester: Carcanet New Press, 1981), p. 28.

Second, what appears to be simple lack of taste or, more gravely, an error against the laws of the musical material, may ultimately be the expression of an unforeseen musical ethics. By reinterpreting musical materials that seemed lost because of their being over-determined by their historical use, Messiaen manages to give them a new life. 'The challenge of the religious artist', Griffiths writes, 'is to make all things sacred, and to deny the self that would discriminate'.[29]

The way in which Messiaen achieves this is not simply by playing the idiot (a word I shall return to below) and forgetting the meanings that history has sedimented in the material. As forgetting will not make this musical memory disappear, the challenge is rather to present the material, including its associations, in such a way that their law-like urgency disappears. This is achieved by creating a marvellous atmosphere that allows any transformation to take place, much as in fairy tales a figure can transform into any other object, and is perhaps even expected to do so.

The cruel

The final element in this minor anthology of the naïve in Messiaen, leads back to the key question of this essay. Messiaen's slogan about his lack of affinity with the themes of sin and suffering sits uneasily with the ideal of naïveté. In the naïve, the question of violence, and by implication the questions of sin and suffering, returns. An exquisite example of this is Harrison Birtwistle's opera *Punch and Judy*, which presents a ritualized version of the puppet play in stage format. In this opera, which was composed in the politically charged year of 1968, death, violence and cruelty are a matter of course. Although the piece is clearly composed for an adult audience, it remains particularly childlike to admire Punch for throwing his baby out of a fourth-story window because it cried too much. In *Punch and Judy*, extreme violence and death are portrayed, as one critic of this piece wrote, as 'pleasurable acts without lasting consequence' – a surprisingly religious formulation, and one that Messiaen would certainly have subscribed to.[30] However, the context in which this violence occurs remains alien to his world. In Messiaen's music, one does not encounter acts of violence between people. It was his expressed aim to write an opera in which traditional violent elements (murder, suicide and incest) would not play a role.

And yet Messiaen is reported to have had a fascination for particularly cruel characters such as Gilles de Rais, the occult companion of Joan of Arc who, according to folklore, was accused of horrendous crimes including the torture and murder of several dozens of children.[31] The remark about a lack of affinity with sin and suffering, then, is better understood as a preference for the 'winner's

---

[29]   Griffiths, *Olivier Messiaen and the Music of Time*, p. 102.

[30]   Donal Henahan, 'Atonal Punch and Judy is Slapstick for Adults', review in *New York Times*, 24 June 1988.

[31]   François-Bernard Mâche, on the above-mentioned occasion.

perspective' common to tales of cruelty, according to which the suffering and fate of the victims presents less of an issue. In *Saint François*, the majority of musical and musically coded violence is presented from such a perspective, the winner here being Jesus Christ, the sublime Pantocrator who presents himself in scene 7 as 'that after which was before' and 'that before which will be after'. This musical violence – a typical alternation of frightening *fortissimo* colour chords and bland *piano* chords – makes its first appearance in scene 2 when the choir sings, in French, 'Holy, Holy, Holy!'. As noted above, this passage stands for many others in Messiaen's oeuvre – often less explicit due to the lack of lyrics – where a similar *tremendum et fascinans* is evoked.[32]

The element of the cruel in the naïve leads back to the Amsterdam production of *Saint François* and the question of evil.

Defying the finite: Death, suffering and the naïve

Messiaen's representation of Francis in his comments depends to a large extent on the popular image of the saint as a man of the senses.[33] It is telling that Messiaen refers to Francis, who held the opinion that the beauties of the created world are the work of God, when he discusses the value of beauty for contemporary music. 'In that sense', he explains, 'I am very Franciscan'. He is referring specifically to the Francis of the 'Canticle of the Sun', the saint who 'was rich in sun, flowers, trees, birds, oceans, mountains [...] with everything that surrounded him'.[34]

There is, however, also another, more pessimistic side to St Francis. This darkness is folded into the sun-filled gaze that overlooks God's creation. It becomes manifest in the texts by St Francis himself, many of which focus on penitence, poverty, humility, obedience and austerity. Here, for example, is a typical passage from the First Rule of the Franciscan Order:

> And let us hate our body with its vices and sins, because by living carnally it wishes to deprive us of the love of our Lord Jesus Christ and eternal life, and to lose itself with all else in hell; for we by our own fault are corrupt, miserable, and averse to good, but prompt and willing to do evil; because, as the Lord says in the Gospel: from the heart of men proceed and come evil thoughts, adulteries, fornications, murders, thefts, covetousness, wickedness, deceit, lasciviousness,

---

[32]   The organ work *Apparition de l'église éternelle* is a point in case. Cf. the listeners' responses as staged and captured in Paul Festa's film *Apparition of the Eternal Church* (Independent, 2006). Many of these refer to the 'shock and awe' image of the divine that seems to be evoked by this work.

[33]   A typical example would be Massin, *Une poétique du merveilleux*, pp. 175–176.

[34]   Olivier Messiaen, *Music and Color*, p. 211.

an evil eye, false testimonies, blasphemy, foolishness. All these evils come from within, from the heart of man, and these are what defile a man.[35]

Francis, it appears, did not simply affirm creation as he had found it in his senses. He always aimed to get away from the sensible, exhorting his followers to do the same. According to his biographer Thomas of Celano, Francis later in his life even apologized for being in the vicinity of 'his brother the [physical] body'.[36] Since his death, the double vision regarding the world of the senses – simultaneously turning toward and away – has been articulated by Bonaventure in terms of *contuition*: 'God is contemplated *through* [the sensibles] as through vestiges, but also *in these*, inasmuch as He is in them through His *Essence, Power*, and *Presence*'.[37] Contuition is the ability to see the Cause of things in and through the things themselves.

Seen in this light, the general grimness of the Amsterdam performance of *Saint François* starts to fall into place. Audi and his collaborators chose to emphasize the mortification of the flesh and the moment of turning away from the sensible that is authentically Franciscan. Developing as it does from black to white, the performance represents 'the evolution of grace in the soul of Saint Francis' in terms of an *interruption* of the devious worldliness of the saint.[38] The spectator witnesses a negation of the sensible rather than a wholesome immersion in it.[39] As a result of this weakening of the sensible, the theological content provided by the libretto is highlighted. The visual asceticism 'theologizes' the opera, emphasizing as it does the bare bones of Francis's mysticism – the journey of the mind into God.

On the reverse side, this also lays bare the Achilles heel of the production. For the abstract and the schematic cannot be the final words in the representation of a saint who was so weary of the lure of abstraction. As an ideal of Franciscan practice, the naïve is an instrument for the spiritual 'containment' of this lure to turn away, but in the wrong – merely abstract – direction. As mentioned above, in

---

[35] *The Writings of St. Francis of Assisi*, trans. Paschal Robinson (1905), available online at <www.sacred-texts.com/chr/wosf/wosf06.htm#fr_264> (accessed September 2008).

[36] Quoted in Éphrem Longpré, 'Frères mineurs', in M. Viller et al., eds, *Dictionnaire de spiritualité: Ascétique et mystique, doctrine et histoire* (Paris: Beauchesne, 1964), tome V, p. 1292.

[37] Bonaventure, *The Journey of the Mind into God*, Chapter II.1. Translated from the Quaracchi Edition of the *Opera Omnia S. Bonaventurae*, Vol. V, 1891, pp. 295–316, available online at <www.franciscanarchive.org/bonaventura/opera/bon05295.html> (accessed September 2008).

[38] Massin, *Une poétique du merveilleux*, p. 190.

[39] The latter was more the case in Peter Sellars' version (1992/1998), balancing as it did on the borderline between the immanent and the transcendent. Concerning the Angel in scene 3, Sellars played explicitly on the 'perhaps': *perhaps* it was an angel (but maybe it was just a volunteer, a girl who helped out). Cf. Sellars' remarks in the documentary on this production made by Jean-Pierre Gorin, *Letter to Peter* (ORF/Loft/La Sept, 1992).

scene 1 we hear Francis explain to Brother Léon the nature of 'perfect joy' [*la joie parfaite*], a conversation based on the *Fioretti* and a short parable by the historical Francis himself.[40] In this parable, after a long and cold walk, Francis is refused access to his own hermitage and beaten away by the doorkeeper who shouts at him: 'Go away, you are a simpleton and an illiterate [*simplex et idiota*]'.

This insult is then used by Francis as an honorary nickname because it articulates two key values of his spiritual vision. First, the aspect of simplicity aims to contravene attempts by Satan to divide the soul into a *dipsychia* [double-mindedness] and to sow the seeds of dissension. Second, the figure of the *idiota* is meant as a warning against the pursuit of knowledge and abstraction as an end in itself. Audi's decision to splice the 'double vision' typical of contuition by emphasizing the 'black' moment of turning away from the world, risks the elimination of this essential aspect of Franciscanism.

Francis initially resisted theology, but later welcomed St Anthony of Padua as the first Franciscan theologian, recognizing the value of reflection. In the *Testament* written by St Francis, we read: 'And we ought to honor and venerate all theologians and those who minister to us the most holy Divine Words as those who minister to us spirit and life'.[41] The naïve, then, is a practical shield against the attempts by Satan to distract the friars from 'the spirit of prayer and devotion', that is, to counteract their continuous conversion to God. Through an emptying out of one's personal will (*kenosis*) it aims to achieve a state of wonder (cf. Messiaen's *émerveillement*) with regard to the world of the senses, and a preparedness to let the will of the Spirit take over.

The naïve is an implicit recognition of the existence and the power of evil in the world, and of the necessity to constantly counteract its workings. No mere turning away from the world (or flight into abstraction) will suffice in this respect. Evil needs to be confronted. The blackness of Audi's rendition, it could be argued in his defence, can also be understood to express this second darkness, which represents the darkness of the world rather than the darkness produced by negation. The experience of the former darkness is what seems to be suggested more particularly in the second scene. I shall return to this in the conclusion below.

In Messiaen's mind, too, the naïve and the experience of evil seem integrated, if only occasionally. Almut Rößler has suggested that Messiaen's views regarding sin and suffering had changed by the time he had finished *Saint François*.[42] Referring to his personal suffering while working on the physically large score of 'The Sermon to the Birds' with an increasingly bad back, she suggests that Messiaen had found his own experience, as a composer, of the Cross. Yvonne

---

[40]   François d'Assise, *Écrits*, Sources chrétiennes (Paris: Éditions du Cerf, 1981), No. 285, p. 119–121.

[41]   Francis of Assisi, *Testament*, in *The Writings of St. Francis of Assisi*. See also the chapter 'The Friars and the Universities' in John Moorman, *A History of the Franciscan Order: From its Origins to the Year 1517* (Oxford: Clarendon Press, 1968), pp. 123–139.

[42]   Rößler, *Contributions*, p. 52.

Loriod, too, emphasized on various occasions how Messiaen had suffered during his life (the cruel fate of his first wife being not the least of disasters to strike him). The underlying claim is that Messiaen, who responded to the question posed by 'Mr Vos' in hesitant terms, had finally found the connection between the theology of Glory – in particular the analogy of the Marvellous – and the theology of the Cross. Commenting on the stigmata scene, Messiaen said: 'From the dramatic standpoint, this is the most important scene in the whole work. I encountered the greatest difficulties in composing it, because I'm not a composer of pain, suffering, but a composer of joy. This is to say that this scene was totally contrary to my nature, but nevertheless I composed it with all my heart.'[43] The parallel with the Franciscan story could hardly be more explicit. In the period between *Turangalîla* and *Saint François* Messiaen's definition of joy really appears to have shifted. Wonderment has been (re-)connected with suffering. A few years later he would dedicate *Un sourire*, the work for small orchestra that he wrote for the Mozart bicentennial, to the newly found value of smiling through tears.[44]

The naïve's demon

The musical elements of the naïve discussed above have in common the tendency to defy the finite. Enthusiasm arises from a vision of something that cannot (yet) be seen: the ideal, which it presents to itself in abstract form. The 'saintly naïveté' of radical reinterpretation defies historical determinacy in favour of unlimited new readings. The cruel, finally, speculates on the infinite rebirth that undoes the finitude of its own object. Likewise, the main theme of *Saint François d'Assise* is death – human finitude – and how it shall be overcome in a movement of infinitization (perpetual dazzlement).

The first words of the opera are Frère Léon's mantra: 'I'm afraid, I'm afraid, I'm afraid, on the road, when the windows grow larger and more obscure, and when the leaves of the poinsettia no longer turn red'. Léon will remain the diagnostician of death throughout the opera. The second act presents death – for the first time recognized by Francis as the ugliness of some things in God's creation – as 'permitted' by Creator. 'Thou hast also allowed ugliness to exist, that the pustulating toad, the poisonous mushroom be found alongside the dragonfly and the bluebird.' The formula of 'permission' echoes the words of St Thomas Aquinas, for whom the problem of evil had remained an enigma. In his *Summa Theologiae*, Aquinas wrote: 'This is part of the infinite goodness of God, that he should allow evil to exist, and out of it produce good'.[45]

---

[43]   Messiaen, *Music and Color*, p. 241.

[44]   Other works from the same 'late' period, it should be added, suggest that the old sense of disconnected wonderment also continued to exist.

[45]   Thomas Aquinas, *Summa Theologiae*, (New York: Blackfriars – McGraw Hill, 1964–1980), Ia, q. 2, a. 3 ad 1.

Theologian Joseph Magee explains this phrase by suggesting that, 'knowing that God exists and is all-good and all powerful, the existence of evil is a mystery, but it does not undermine this knowledge. If God allows evil, then he must bring good out of it.'[46] At the end of Messiaen's opera, in scene 8 'Death and the New Life', evil is no longer 'permitted' but is lauded as an integral part of God's creation. 'Be praised, my Lord, for sister Death, for our sister bodily Death, Death! who no man can escape. Be praised, Lord!' Here, Death has become an event that wholly takes place within God, and merely repeats the death of *kenosis* that for some – such as for Francis – may take place during life. 'Blessed are those whom the first death will find submitting to Divine Will: the second death will do him no harm. Be praised, Lord!'[47]

Making death disappear: that is the ultimate stake of the naïve. The naïve is, as Nietzsche understood it, an extreme effort. 'Wherever we encounter the 'naïve' in art, we have to recognize the highest effect of Apollonian culture, which always first has to overthrow the kingdom of the Titans and to kill monsters, and through powerfully deluding images and joyful illusions must emerge victorious over the horrific depths of what we observe in the world and the most sensitive capacity for suffering.'[48] In the Amsterdam production, Francis does not die but walks slowly off stage leaving everyone else behind in wonderment. There is no body; his death does not produce a finite trace. Frère Léon fulfills his final duty and expresses what he experiences: 'He is departed ... like a silence, like a friendly silence which is touched by very gentle hands. He is gone ... like a tear, like a tear of clear water that drops slowly from a flower-petal. He has gone like a butterfly, a golden butterfly which flies from the Cross to go beyond the stars ... .' This deathless death is the most saintly thing in the whole opera and it crowns the enterprise of the naïve. Dramatically as well as musically this is the most dangerous moment because here the whole opera threatens to collapse into religious kitsch. And it almost does: the return of the Leper just before Francis disappears is kitsch as Hermann Broch understood it: the artistically endorsed demand that the stars and everything else that is eternal come down to earth for the sake of a human temporal gratification.[49]

Even more shocking than this kitsch – which is balanced out by the sublime violence of the final chorus – is the way Messiaen's Francis looked back on his life just a few moments earlier. What were the major events that need to be recollected at the hour of death? Was it the Leper (who, according to the Franciscan tradition,

---

[46]   Commentary by Joseph Magee available online at <www.aquinasonline.com/Topics/probevil.html> (accessed September 2008).

[47]   See the libretto, scene 8.

[48]   Friedrich Nietzsche, *The Birth of Tragedy out of the Spirit of Music* (1871), available online at <records.viu.ca/~Johnstoi/Nietzsche/tragedy_all.htm> (accessed September 2008).

[49]   Broch is here referring to the specific guise of the religion of art that he finds in Eichendorff. Hermann Broch, 'Notes on the problem of kitsch,' in *Kitsch: The World of Bad Taste*, ed. Gillo Dorfles (London: Studio Vista, 1968), 58–59.

may have been Christ in disguise) whose fate was intimately connected with Francis's own spiritual development? No. Was it the creation of the Order, whose friars were dependent on him as their 'mother'? Not really. He bids them goodbye in a rather routine fashion. Was it the stigmatization? No, this ultimate experience of Christ's suffering is not even mentioned. For Messiaen's Francis, it was the music and poetry that lead him towards God 'by image, by symbol, and in default of Truth'. At the close of the opera the naïve is again disconnected from the Cross in a slightly scandalous – for all too aesthetical – affirmation of the power of music and poetry, suggesting that scene 5, featuring the Angel-Musician, contains all that is really important in the work.

In conclusion: why then was scene 2 of the Amsterdam performance so unsettling? It is because it showed Francis and the friars in circumstances that scene 8 tells us do not exist. Here, the shield of the naïve seems temporarily lifted, and the confrontation with evil suddenly becomes lived experience. Scene 2 shows a darker sort of ignorance than found with Francis in scenes 1 or 3. The friars seem to be straying and the music tells us there is an immediate threat. One would expect the opera to stage a confrontation between this Dionysian evil and the powers of Light along the lines Messiaen presented in 'Combat de la Mort et de la Vie' from the organ cycle *Les Corps glorieux*. Or, perhaps even more fitting in this monastic setting, it could have included an engagement with the monastic demonologies. What the opera presents instead is a view of the Cross that is extremely Apollonian and therefore much closer in concept to that perceived by theologian Hans Urs von Balthasar. In Balthasar's theology, the Cross refers to Christ's triumph over the forces of darkness accomplished on Holy Saturday. According to Balthasar, on the Cross 'the contradiction that is sin, its mendacity and illogicality, is assumed within the logic of Trinitarian love'.[50] The confrontation between darkness and the Light has in a sense always already taken place, far above the heads of the friars. Here, as in *Saint François*, the traditional theological connection between the naïve and the experience of evil is ultimately broken, and an alternative reality is presented: one in which death and suffering have lost their prime religious importance.[51]

---

[50] Hans Urs von Balthasar, quoted in Aidan Nichols, *Say It Is Pentecost: A Guide Through Balthasar's Logic* (Edinburgh: T&T Clark Press, 2001), p. 120.

[51] Since death and suffering are rapidly loosing their privileged place in Western societies as well, this alternative reality may help us understand why Messiaen's music continues to have such enormous impact on contemporary audiences, and why this is because of, rather than in spite of, the religious outlook suggested by his work.

PART II
Messiaen's Relationship with Theologians

Chapter 4

Olivier Messiaen and Cardinal Jean-Marie Lustiger: Two Views of the Liturgical Reform according to the Second Vatican Council

Karin Heller

Jean-Marie Lustiger was born in 1926, 18 years after Olivier Messiaen. Both of them lived and worked in the context of the Church of France, challenged by major social changes and bitter political struggles common in the twentieth century. In the first part of this essay, my purpose is to highlight the period from the end of the nineteenth century to the opening of the Second Vatican Council in 1962. This period was marked by a Catholic revival movement that put great emphasis on liturgy and sacred music. An analysis of Messiaen's relationship to Catholic liturgy completes this part. In the second part, I deal with the introduction of liturgical reform in Paris and the way in which Jean-Marie Lustiger and Olivier Messiaen responded to this major challenge. An analysis of Lustiger's implementation of the liturgical reform during his tenure as pastor of Sainte-Jeanne-de-Chantal highlights the difference between his interpretation of the reform and that of Messiaen.

Olivier Messiaen and Jean-Marie Lustiger in the context of the twentieth-century Church of France

On liturgical movements and sacred music

During the period between the two world wars, France had largely become a 'mission field', in the sense that the gap between the Catholic Church and French civil society had massively increased. In spite of a still impressive number of priests, religious and ecclesiastical institutions, the Church of France underwent an important breakdown of the Christian faith affecting all categories of people, but in particular the working classes. Books such as Y. Daniel's and J. Godin's *France, pays de mission* (1943) and Henri de Lubac's *Le drame de l'humanisme athée* (1944) provided a warning, but they were ignored by the great majority of French Catholics.

The causes of this situation are manifold. Three years before Messiaen's birth, the Church of France had to deal with a dramatic change due to a vote of the French Parliament, which established the separation of church and state in 1905. In addition, French Catholicism had constantly been overshadowed by political tussles and tensions for centuries. At the beginning of the twentieth century, the Church of France struggled with Protestantism, the Enlightenment, human sciences, atheism, the French government and secularization. Catholics identified with political parties and failed to recognize one another as brothers and sisters in Christ. The Church of France was divided. One faction gathered around the idea of tradition, which it understood as a society faithful to the monarchy. The other around the vision of progress, a significant feature of the Third Republic, the name given to the political era in France from 1870 to 1940. After the Second World War, this evolution led to the formation of right- and left-wing Catholics.

The struggle sustained by the Church of France *ad intra* and *ad extra* was also made visible by the foundation of the Benedictine Abbey of Solesmes in 1832 under the leadership of Dom Prosper Guéranger. In fact, Pope Gregory XVI, who authorized the founding of the abbey, charged it with restoring the sound traditions of the pontifical jurisprudence and of the sacred liturgy. For much of French society, Gregorian chant and the associated Thomism were identified with ultramontanism, but also associated with the idea of a restoration of the monarchy.[1] This movement was seriously affected by the separation of church and state, which forced the Benedictine community of Solesmes into exile on the Anglo-Norman Isle of Wight between 1901 and 1922.

The exclusive use of Latin within liturgy delineated two categories of people: the clergy as the active carrier of the liturgy on the one hand, and the people as a more or less passive receiver on the other. Liturgy was a matter for specialists and among these specialists the Benedictines at Solesmes were the most prominent. Dom Guéranger, the founder of Solesmes, wrote a series of 15 volumes entitled *L'Année liturgique* [The Liturgical Year] in support of his movement. Later, Dom Columba Marmion, Abbot of the Belgian Benedictine Abbey of Maredsous, summarized this standard work in one volume entitled *Le Christ dans ses Mystères* [Christ in his Mysteries] and thus made it accessible for a large number of Catholics, including Olivier Messiaen.[2]

The form of piety proper to the nineteenth century centred on fostering emotion and fervour through visits to the Blessed Sacrament, as well as other spiritual exercises. Impressive musical performances supported these exercises. According to the custom of this time, Mass could not be interrupted by people receiving communion. Therefore, Catholics received communion either at the beginning of

---

[1]   Stephen Schloesser, *Jazz Age Catholicism: Mystic Modernism in Post-war Paris, 1919–1933* (Toronto: University of Toronto Press, 2005), p. 283.

[2]   With regard to the influence of Dom Marmion on Messiaen's *La Nativité du Seigneur* cycle, see the extensive analyses of Brigitte Massin, *Olivier Messiaen: une poétique du merveilleux* (Aix-en-Provence: Éditions Alinéa, 1989), pp. 68–73.

Mass or at its conclusion. This solution had the advantage of not disturbing the piety of the priest, who alone consumed the Eucharist during the celebration. It also did not disturb the piety of the people, who perceived Mass as a thanksgiving for communion received or as a preparation for receiving communion.[3]

Dom Lambert Beauduin (1873–1960), a Benedictine monk of the Mont-César Abbey close to Louvain, challenged this vision. Beauduin perceived the liturgy and the Eucharistic celebration as the origin of the Church. This led Beauduin to launch what became known as a popular Liturgical Movement at the Catholic Congress of Malines in 1909. The movement was a first attempt to make liturgy more democratic. Dom Beauduin's intuition fostered within the clergy and the people a desire for spiritual renewal, which aimed at a better 'understanding of the liturgy' and a 'partaking in the liturgy'. Confronted with strong opposition, the movement could fortunately refer to the *Motu proprio 'Inter sollecitudines'*, issued by Pope Pius X on November 22, 1903, which mentioned *expressis verbis* in its preamble 'the *active participation* in the most holy mysteries and in the public and solemn prayer of the Church' (emphasis mine).[4]

In 1944, the desire for renewal led the Church of France to establish the so-called Centre de Pastorale Liturgique (CPL).[5] Its main concern was to make liturgy accessible to the people. In order to reach this goal, two solutions were considered. The first supported the project of a liturgy adapted to the various categories of people; the second advocated for an adaptation of the people to the liturgy. What was at stake was nothing less than the fundamental question of the nature of liturgy. The first group perceived liturgy as a tool of evangelization and a means of communication with non-Christians. The second, represented in particular by the French theologian Louis Bouyer, conceived liturgy as the expression of the Church's life, having Mass at its centre.[6]

In 1954, ten years after the foundation of the CPL, its leadership had to recognize that liturgy could only be made accessible to people after a period of explanation and evangelization. The Liturgical Movement, nevertheless, accepted with difficulty the idea of a fundamental relationship between scripture and liturgy, the latter being inseparable from the hierarchical and apostolic nature of the Church.[7] In this regard, Louis Bouyer mentioned with consternation the hostile attitude

---

[3]   Louis Bouyer, *Dom Lambert Beauduin. Un homme d'Eglise* (Paris: Casterman, 1964), p. 55.

[4]   Ibid., pp. 33–53.

[5]   Pie Duployé, *Les Origines du Centre de Pastorale liturgique, 1943–1949* (Mulhouse, 1968). See also *Études de Pastorale Liturgique, Vanves 26–28 janvier 1944*, Coll. Lex Orandi 1 (Paris: Editions Savator, 1944).

[6]   Louis Bouyer, *Memories*, p. 96. Unpublished document in possession of the author.

[7]   Louis Bouyer, 'Ce qui change, ce qui demeure dans la liturgie', *La Maison-Dieu* 40 (1954): 104. Bouyer bears witness to these difficulties, which finally led him to break with the Centre de Pastorale liturgique. See *Le Métier de Théologien. Entretiens avec Georges Daix* (Paris: Editions France Empire, 1979), pp. 51–53, 65, 74–78.

of the Prior of Solesmes.[8] This rejection had ideological foundations, because Solesmes perceived the CPL as a challenger of its own liturgical conceptions and feared a loss of influence on French Catholic society. This reaction had to be understood within the context of a movement supported by Rome, which had aimed at a victory over Gallicanism in the wake of the Modernist crisis. In order for this to be successful, Cardinal Dubois, archbishop of Paris from 1920 to 1929, favoured Gregorian liturgy, which spread not only to all levels of the Catholic Church of France, but also internationally in association with French colonialism. Therefore, the community of Solesmes, after its return from exile on the Isle of Wight in 1922, had become a precious support to this project, which survived after Cardinal Dubois vacated the archbishopric.[9]

As a consequence, two musical schools developed in a more or less ideologically pressured context. One was the school of Solesmes, which gained national influence through the foundation of the Schola Cantorum in 1894 in Paris. This school was opposed to the republican Conservatoire National Supérieur de Paris, which was historically and ideologically rooted in the Enlightenment. Both schools engaged in ideological struggles, which periodically rekindled the tensions between the Church, church musicians, and French society.[10]

With time, however, the attempt by Solesmes to introduce exclusively Gregorian liturgy within French parishes failed because many of these communities were not able to match the exacting liturgical expectations of Solesmes. For this reason, the liturgical movement launched by Dom Lambert Beauduin at the Catholic Congress of Malines in 1909, met with real success. Beauduin's proposal included: (1) increasing the use of vernacular missals so that the congregation could follow what the priest said at the altar; (2) the introduction of 'dialogue' Masses, in which at a Low Mass the people said aloud with the server all the Latin responses and joined the priest in the *Kyrie*, *Gloria*, *Credo*, *Sanctus*, *Benedictus*, and *Agnus Dei*; and (3) teaching congregations to sing simple chants for the ordinary of the Mass.[11] In the wake of these proposals, the Church of France realized a great number of so-called paraliturgies. These paraliturgies, in the tradition of the German *Bet-Singmesse* [Pray-and-Sing-Mass], combined chants and prayers in the vernacular language while the priest pronounced all Latin prayers privately at the altar.

Under the influence of the movement supported by the CPL, French church musicians such as Joseph Samson (1888–1957), Choirmaster at the Cathedral of Dijon, and the priest-musicians Fr Joseph Gélineau SJ, and Fr Lucien Deiss CSS, composed many pieces in the vernacular language and polyphonic style, including the Psalter, translated from the Hebrew by the Bible of Jerusalem.

---

[8]   Louis Bouyer, *Memories*, p. 96.

[9]   Stephen Schloesser, *Jazz Age Catholicism*, pp. 300–301.

[10]   For more details regarding the 'war' between the two schools, see Stephen Schloesser, *Jazz Age Catholicism*, pp. 283–287.

[11]   Anthony Miller, 'Music in a Vernacular Catholic Liturgy', in *Proceedings of the Royal Musical Association, 91st Sess., 1964–1965* (Oxford, 1964–65), p. 27.

The paraliturgical movement undoubtedly rekindled community life. Some of these experiments, however, reflected extremely idiosyncratic liturgies, marked by partial or even total substitutions of biblical readings for secular literature, which was considered more accessible to people. This tendency strongly increased in the middle of the 1960s during which time French society underwent a significant change in worldview.[12]

The liturgical Constitution *Sacrosanctum Concilium*, issued by the Second Vatican Council in 1963, represented a consecration of Bouyer's views. His understanding of the relationship between scripture and liturgy made an important impact on Jean-Marie Lustiger. Lustiger was particularly fascinated by Bouyer's vision of the historical continuity between Judaism and Christianity, of the spiritual newness of the Gospel, and he clearly perceived the fundamental link between the Jewish Passover and the Lord's Supper.[13] Progressively, Lustiger came to the firm conviction that 'the norm of theology is not the human spirit', but that it is found 'in the Church's faith which recognizes God's revelation in scripture and in [the Church's] tradition'.[14] Consequently, Lustiger's view of liturgy developed along the line of Bouyer's central tenets on liturgy and theology.

Messiaen's relationship to the liturgy of the Church

Olivier Messiaen was appointed principal organist of the Parisian church of La Trinité in 1931. As with any organist's position, Messiaen was responsible directly to the church's pastor, who alone was in charge of the parish finances and employing staff. Curé Hemmer, to whom Messiaen had submitted his application, was not in a particular hurry to hire the young organist who was still only 22 years old. In a second letter to Hemmer, Messiaen anticipated the pastor's probable concern about an exhibition of 'tendencies which were too modern' for the congregation at La Trinité. Messiaen noted that 'it is important not to disturb the piety of the faithful by using chords which are too anarchic'.[15] In other words, the position of a church organist was conditioned on the capacity to renounce personal dispositions, to commit to compromises and to avoid disagreements. Later, Messiaen continued to bear witness to these cautions, especially in his first compositions for organ. This was due in no small part to the protests and critiques fostered in particular by 'old female parishioners, who heard the devil in the organ pipes'.[16]

---

[12]   Séraphin Berchten, 'Inquiétudes sur le sort de la Musique sacrée', *Musique sacrée. L'Organiste* 95 (1966): pp. 7–11.

[13]   Jean-Marie Lustiger, *Choosing God, Chosen by God: Conversations with Jean-Louis Missika and Dominique Wolton* (San Francisco: Ignatius Press, 1991), p. 276.

[14]   Ibid., p. 160.

[15]   Claude Samuel, *Permanences d'Olivier Messiaen: Dialogues et Commentaires* (Arles: Actes Sud, 1999), p. 91. See also: Peter Hill and Nigel Simeone, *Messiaen* (New Haven, CT/London: Yale University Press, 2005), p. 35.

[16]   Claude Samuel, *Permanences d'Olivier Messiaen*, p. 196.

Preconciliar conditions in parishes of Paris

Messiaen's tenure of more than 60 years at La Trinité coincided with a period of major change: the progressive fading away of parish life typical for the nineteenth century and the equally progressive emergence of a parish open to a dialogue with the world in the wake of the Second Vatican Council. According to Messiaen's own testimony, the six pastors in charge during his tenure 'avoided conflicts by a wise adaptation of the liturgical style proper to each public.'[17] During the weekend, La Trinité offered nine Masses. Messiaen usually played the organ at three Sunday Masses. The first was dedicated to Gregorian chant; the second to Classical and Romantic music; for the third, at noon, Messiaen was authorized to improvise more freely and to play his own compositions. This last one became also known as the 'Mass for fools', a name that designated all those enthusiasts who gathered to hear Messiaen improvise.[18]

The church of La Trinité stood in contrast to other churches in Paris, such as Saint-Séverin, Notre-Dame-des-Champs, Saint-Louis-d'Antin or Sainte-Odile, insofar as the pastors of La Trinité never engaged in preconciliar liturgical experiments. Since 1947, Saint-Séverin had paved the way for liturgical realizations in the vernacular language. In 1950, in this church, the Jesuit Joseph Gélineau experimented with use of his own compositions based on a French translation of the Hebrew Psalter, before they were published. One year later, in 1951, a remarkable collaboration with Michel Chapuis, principal organist of Saint-Germain l'Auxerrois and Notre-Dame-des-Champs, was at the origin of the restoration of the Saint-Séverin organ by the famous Alsatian organ builder Alfred Kern. The same year, Saint-Séverin formed a church choir. Thus, singing by the parish community, together with communion (which at Saint-Séverin was received by a large number of the congregation), became the most important pillars of growth in Christian life through liturgical renewal.[19]

In 1960, La Trinité, on the contrary, was only in a state of preparation for liturgical change and this preparation consisted of reading books chosen by the pastor.[20] Up to this date a musical programme on a Sunday at La Trinité is typified by this programme from 4 June 1950:

- High Mass: *Kyrie*, *Gloria* und *Agnus Dei* from Mozart's Mass in C Major; *Sanctus* and *Benedictus* by Planchet (a former choirmaster of La Trinité); *Graduale*: double choir by Leisring.

---

[17]   Ibid., p. 31.

[18]   Memoires of Olivier Glandaz, who took part in the restoration of the organ at La Trinité and was Messiaen's friend for many years. See '1908–2008 Messiaen's centenary' <www.glandaz.com/messiaen2008.htm> (accessed 23 April 2008).

[19]   Luc Perrin, *Paris à l'heure de Vatican II* (Paris: Editions de l'Atelier/Editions Ouvrières, 1997), pp. 171–175.

[20]   Ibid., p. 178.

- Vespers: *faux-bourdons* of the Renaissance time.
- Adoration of the Blessed Sacrament: *Quam dilecta* by Codès-Mongin (present choirmaster); *Sub tuum* for string quartet and harp by Planchet; *Tu es Petrus* by Fauré; *Tantum ergo* by Salomé (another former organist of La Trinité); *Cantate Domino* by Bonichère (predecessor of choirmaster Planchet).[21]

According to Fr. Jean-Pierre Schaller, vicar at La Trinité from 1956 to 2000, Messiaen's contribution was made up of improvisations based on the Psalms of the day.

Olivier Messiaen at the organ of La Trinité

With the exception of an unpublished mass for eight sopranos and four violins dating from 1933–34 and the motet *O Sacrum Convivium* (1937), Messiaen did not compose any music specifically for the liturgy. His organ output consists of more than 60 separate movements, many of which can be used liturgically but most of which he intended for concert use.[22] In the liturgical context, Messiaen's predilection was for organ pieces and not for vocal music. Messiaen adopted, for the most part, the technique of his teacher Charles Tournemire, principal organist of Sainte-Clothilde. Tournemire was influenced by 'the ideology of the Solesmes Schola', but he also distanced himself from Solesmes by using 'passionate' materials for expressing 'the idea of eternalist chants'.[23] This method was effectively a 'musical exegesis of texts', which 'suggests the invisible' and thus gives paramount importance to improvisation.[24] In other words, Tournemire's method consists of a musical comment on or a musical paraphrase of biblical and liturgical texts according to the norms established by the *Motu propio Inter solliditudines* (1903), which states that the principal office of sacred music:

> is *to clothe with suitable melody the liturgical text* proposed for the understanding of the faithful, its proper aim is *to add greater efficacy to the text*, in order that through it the faithful may be the more easily *moved to devotion* and better disposed for the reception of the fruits of grace belonging to the celebration of the most holy mysteries.[25]

Tournemire and Messiaen adopted this principle. Consequently, they can by identified as Symbolists and Surrealists insofar as both of them used allegories,

---

[21]   *Bulletin La Trinité*, 4 June 1950.

[22]   Jean-Rodolphe Kars, 'L'œuvre d'Olivier Messiaen et l'Année liturgique', *La Maison-Dieu* 3 (1996): 97–98.

[23]   Stephen Schloesser, *Jazz Age Catholicism*, p. 303.

[24]   Ibid., p. 289.

[25]   *Motu propio Inter solliditudines* (1903) [emphasis mine].

metaphors, homonyms, plays on words, symbols, and other imaginative associations, in order to provoke in their listeners both emotion and devotion.

The symbolist movement reacted to dry Catholic intellectualism proper to the eighteenth century. It is represented for example by the French poet Paul Claudel (1868–1955), whose works made an exceptional impact on Messiaen. The surrealists in turn reacted to a strong positivistic current. The positivists established a philosophical movement that excluded the possibility of a world beyond reality and, for this reason, its opponents such as Pierre Reverdy (1889–1960) and Paul Éluard (1885–1952) developed an impetuous desire to provide some sort of representation of the invisible world. Their enterprise inspired the Catholic renewal movement of the nineteenth and twentieth centuries, which aimed at the representation of the 'invisible mysteries' of Christ made visible in liturgy and the sacraments. Reverdy and Éluard, together with the writer and philosopher Ernest Hello (1828–1885), a contemporary of Dom Marmion, were also profoundly influential on Olivier Messiaen.[26]

According to Messiaen, his compositions were based on his individual choices and personal study of biblical texts, liturgical prayers and the works of certain theologians.[27] In other words, this choice reflects Messiaen's personal views of the Catholic faith. In the wake of Romanticism and Symbolism, what was at stake for Messiaen was not the intellect, but the heart. He himself explains that his purpose is to express 'the marvel of the Christian faith' and 'to respect the colour of the liturgical feast, the colour of the readings of the day and that of the texts of the plain-chant'.[28] Biographers Peter Hill and Nigel Simeone qualify his intent as: 'emotional sincerity, put at the service of the dogmas of the Catholic faith expressed through a new musical language – or at the very least an attempt to achieve this'.[29]

Messiaen assumes the limits of his musical interpretations at the service of the dogmas of Catholic theology when he writes in the preface to his organ cycle *Méditations sur le mystère de la Sainte Trinité*:

> Music in juxtaposition [to language based on conventions] does not express anything directly. It can suggest, express a sentiment, an estate of soul, touch the subconscious, and widen dream capacities, all of which represent tremendous powers: it absolutely cannot 'say' and give information in a precise way.[30]

[26]   See Stephen Schloesser, this volume, Chapter 9, pp. 163–82.

[27]   Claude Samuel, *Permanences d'Olivier Messiaen*, pp. 18, 123 and 209. See also 'Olivier Messiaen analyse ses œuvres', in *Olivier Messiaen Homme de Foi* (Paris: Trinité Media Communication, 1995): pp. 31–67.

[28]   Claude Samuel, *Permanences d'Olivier Messiaen*, pp. 18, 33. See also Joachim Havard de la Montagne, 'Olivier Messiaen (1908-1991)', *Musica et Memoria* 42 (1991): 25–26.

[29]   Hill and Simeone, *Messiaen*, pp. 59–62.

[30]   Samuel, 'Olivier Messiaen analyse ses œuvres', p. 49.

Therefore, consideration of Messiaen as a theologian has to be distinguished from those church theologians who elaborate models of theological thoughts that inform and explain the mysteries of the Catholic faith in a language based on theological realities forged by scripture and the various church traditions. Consequently, one may say that Messiaen's oeuvre reflects his personal research on music as well as his personal vision of the Christian revelation. This fact is well highlighted by Lustiger, who underlines the 'coincidence between [Messiaen's] integral artistic production and [his] spiritual itinerary'.[31]

Messiaen's approach to the Catholic truths is similar to that of Hans Urs von Balthasar whose theological reflection is comprised more of personal intuition and charisma than of a traditional use of scientific methods proper to the exploration of Catholic dogmatic theology. Most significantly, von Balthasar is for Messiaen 'the greatest of the contemporary theologians'.[32] Both of them are marked by the same constant use of the categories of mystery, poetry, symbols, figures, themes, transpositions, mixtures, colours and sounds. All of these realities are related or juxtaposed to one another, superimposed, given a hierarchical structure, associated with sacred numbers such as three or seven, combined with particular letters, space and rhythms.[33]

In the case of von Balthasar, this aptitude produced a discourse made of affirmations, interrogations, digressions, confirmations, abundant information related to scripture, philosophy, the Fathers, Catholic dogmas, human sciences and modern culture. As a result, von Balthasar's discourse is characterized by a certain *flou*, a word that may perhaps be translated as a 'blur' or a 'lack of clarity'. This *flou* is expressed by the author's difficulty in clearly determining and reaching his goals, a fact that may explain some of the more monumental aspect of his oeuvre. In the case of Messiaen, the same aptitude produced a musical language, which proceeds in the same way and also results in more and more monumental compositions. Two major reasons, highlighted by musicologist Hélène Cao, explain Messiaen's epistemology. The first is a combination of theological reflection and an attraction for the marvellous. The second is rooted in the fact that 'the elements of his language have their origin in a sensorial and intuitive approach, before being organized and rationalized'.[34]

The *flou* that affected Messiaen's methodology is also brought to the fore in his very personal concept of the hierarchy of function for music. He distinguished three kinds of music: liturgical, spiritual and coloured. Early in his career liturgical music ranked before the others; however, he later changed the primacy to spiritual music and finally he recognized the eternal aspect of coloured music,

---

[31]   Ibid., p. 8.

[32]   Samuel, *Permanences d'Olivier Messiaen*, p. 18.

[33]   Ibid. See also also Joachim Havard de la Montagne, 'Olivier Messiaen (1908-1991)', *Musica et Memoria* 46 (1992): 51.

[34]   Hélène Cao, 'Olivier Messiaen: de la poésie du réel aux mystères de la foi', *Saint François d'Assise Messiaen, L'Avant Scène Opéra* 223 (2004): 3–9.

while liturgical and spiritual music had to be related to temporality. On another level, only Gregorian chant was considered by Messiaen as truly liturgical music. Nevertheless, this kind of music could be related to birdsong, which expressed God's mystery and divine nature, which in turn could also be found in oriental expressions.[35] Consequently, one may perhaps agree with Catholic priest and musicologist Pascal Ide that Messiaen's entire music production 'is penetrated by his faith', but some doubts may remain when it comes to qualifying all of his music as 'sacred', 'theological' or 'mystical'.[36]

New light can be shed on this war of words if one considers the historical context in which Messiaen had lived and worked. The terms 'sacred', 'theological' and 'mystical' have to be related to currents of dialectic realism, which tried to establish relationships between theology, history, mysticism, and practical life in the nineteenth and twentieth centuries. Within these currents, Messiaen's approach is not only similar to those of the Symbolists and Surrealists, but also those of the Romantic theologians such as Friederich Schleiermacher and Novalis (the pseudonym of Friedrich von Hardenberg). These theologians took particular efforts to express their view of theological realities by means of the arts. Messiaen shared a common interest in the theology of the Middle Ages with these theologians and, in their wake, drew inspiration from Christian revelation, platonic love between man and woman, nature and creation, and from myths and poetry. The view of Messiaen, like those of many Romantic theologians, is characterized by an emphasis on God's infinite being, a 'universal poetry' and 'harmony of nature'.[37]

All of these views can be intimately linked not only to traditional church based liturgies, but to worship performed in a civil building or as an 'open air' event. Messiaen's efforts to move the liturgy into the concert hall and his keen interest in nature are similar to those of the Romantic theologians. François-René, Vicomte de Chateaubriand, one of the most famous French Catholic representatives of the Romantic movement, perceived in the instinct of the animals, and in particular in

---

[35]   See Olivier Messiaen, *Conférence de Notre-Dame: prononcée le 4 décembre 1977 à Notre-Dame-de-Paris* (Paris: Editions Alphonse Leduc, 1978).

[36]   Pascal Ide, 'Messiaen et la musique sacrée', in *La musica sacra nelle chiese cristiane. Actes du Congrès international d'études, Rome, 25–27 janvier 2001*, eds Académie Nationale Sainte Cécile, Conseil Pontifical de la Culture and Institut Pontifical de Musique Sacrée (Bologna: Alfa Studio, 2002): 187–196.

[37]   Friedrich Schleiermacher, 'On the Essence of Religion', in *On Religion: Speeches to its Cultured Despisers* (Cambridge: Cambridge University Press, 1996), pp. 18–54. Messiaen and Novalis drew their inspiration from an unconsummated love, in which both saw a model of 'divine love'. In the case of Messiaen this love is represented by Tristan and Yseult; in the case of Novalis by 'Sophie', a woman with whom Novalis was in love and who died at a young age. Messiaen bears witness to his convictions of a 'perfect harmony of nature' and its 'purity', which echo the views of an idealism proper to the romantics. See Samuel, *Permanences d'Olivier Messiaen*, pp. 24, 32, 42, and 44. For Pascal Ide, Messiaen is most significantly a musician amazed by God's infinity. See Ide, 'Olivier Messiaen, un musicien ébloui par l'infinité de Dieu', *Nouvelle Revue théologique* 4 (1999): 436–453.

birdsong, the organizing will of God. Chateaubriand's writings abound in lyric descriptions of the great variety of winged creatures whose songs are hymns to the eternal God and are an enchantment ordered by God's providence.[38] Again, Messiaen's predilection for birdsong suggest that if his music can be qualified as 'theological', and if the term 'theologian' can be applied to him, it should be intended in the sense in use by German and French Romanticism.

The Application of the Liturgical Reform According to the Second Vatican Council in Paris

Olivier Messiaen in the crossfire of the liturgical reform

Curé Jacques Hollande (1901–91) was at the head of La Trinité during the difficult years of the application of the liturgical reform (1957–72). Hollande was the first director of the so-called 'Mission de Paris', a movement of priests that aimed at an evangelization of the working classes through a total immersion in their life conditions. In 1954, the Vatican terminated this experiment and Jacques Hollande submitted to this decision. His appointment as *curé* of La Trinité was certainly associated with a painful change in his life, leading him from ministry with the working classes to the bourgeois 9th arrondissement of Paris.[39] The sanction of the priest-worker experiment pronounced by Rome meant that Hollande was not inclined himself to take the initiative for making major changes in parish life at La Trinité. In fact, G. Lahotte, the first vicar of La Trinité, hailed him as a man with 'a sense for measure' and 'a balanced judgement', an 'enemy of controversy, discussion, and newness'.[40] The introduction of the liturgical reform at La Trinité for Hollande was above all a matter of obedience to church hierarchy driven by an apostolic desire to convey the Gospel to all mankind. In this perspective, he was convinced that 'the advantages, which overcome whatever regrets, are at the origin of progress'. Thus, 'neither immobility, nor agitation were recommended at the hour of the Council'.[41]

A parish that had never opened up to liturgical experiments before the Second Vatican Council was quite unprepared for the reception of the various ordinances issued by the Parisian Cardinals Maurice Feltin (1949–66), Pierre Veuillot (1966–68) and François Marty (1968–81). The first ordinance, the subject of heavy criticism and loud protest by church musicians, dealt with the suppression of the various

---

[38]   Viscount de Chateaubriand, *The Genius of Christianity or the Spirit and Beauty of the Christian Religion*, Book V, *The Existence of God Demonstrated by the Wonders of Nature*, trans. Charles I. White (Baltimore: J. Murphy; Philadelphia: J. B. Lippincott, 1856).

[39]   *Bulletin La Trinité*, November 1972, 'Extrait de l'homélie de Monseigneur Pézeril à l'installation du Père Guinchat'.

[40]   *Bulletin La Trinité*, October 1972.

[41]   *Bulletin La Trinité*, February, March and May 1965.

classes of funerals and wedding ceremonies. Until the Second Vatican Council, the Church of France distinguished ten classes of funerals of which the last one was stipend free (people did not have to pay anything if they were poor, but the service was also the 'minimum'). The classes allowed people to affirm their social status or to make it clear that they had money. This was the problem. All of these offered a different kind of service, with different types of church decoration and different music. In 1962, a decree abolished all these classes, which were replaced by a unique 'parish ceremony'. The decree prescribed humble and simple materials for this ceremony as well as music 'proper to the dignity and the religious character of the event'. According to the decree, useless effects and ostentation had to be avoided.[42] This ordinance reduced the musical programmes at funerals and made it impossible to use the main organ during the ceremonies. Church musicians and organists began to fear for their employment. Therefore, some of them started a polemical campaign in the press.[43] La Trinité confronted these polemics by the appeal to abide by the statements published in *La Semaine religieuse de Paris*, the official organ of the archdiocese, and also the Catholic Newspaper *La Croix*. The advice was supported by a partial reproduction in the same bulletin of an interview given by Monsignor Veuillot published by *La Croix*.[44]

The changes introduced by the ordinances between 1964 and 1969 led rapidly to a dramatic transformation in the style of worship for High Mass and Vespers.[45] This in turn had important consequences for the musicians, because the abolition of High Mass and Vespers, which both had significant musical content, would lead to the progressive extinction of choirs, choirmasters, orchestras and cantors, as well as organists. 'For most of them, the reform of church music was quite exclusively presented under a painful aspect', wrote Catholic theologian Hugues Cousin in the wake of a survey amongst organists in a major French city (this is what the document says; the city is not named).[46] For the curé of La Trinité, Jacques Hollande, the application of the liturgical reform was a matter of inner conversion and spirit; however, the presentation of the reform took largely the aspect of a 'change of rubrics' and the ensuing debate focused more on the use or the suppression of Latin than on problems of spiritual life.[47] The announcements of new theological issues were usually explained to the congregation as either the

---

[42]   *La Semaine Religieuse de Paris*, 10 November 1962, pp. 1163–1165.

[43]   *France-Soir*, 13 December 1962; *Le Figaro*, 20 and 27 December 1962; *Le Figaro*, 5 January 1963; *La Croix*, 11 January 1963.

[44]   *Bulletin La Trinité*, January and February 1963.

[45]   An article published by *La Trinité* in July–August 1965, entitled 'Les Vêpres du 15 août' discusses this suppression of traditional Vespers.

[46]   H. Cousin, 'Les organistes et la réforme liturgique', *Notes de Pastorale liturgique* 69 (1967): 13.

[47]   *Bulletin La Trinité*, December 1962; March 1965; July–August 1965.

will of the church hierarchy, an attempt by the church Council to improve the life of worship of the community, or as apostolic necessities.[48]

Olivier Messiaen, like other organists and church musicians, was bound by the decisions made by ecclesiastical authorities. As a gifted musician and composer, Messiaen certainly underwent a great number of hardships through the administration of rules that reduced liturgical music to a kind of 'dusty backyard visited mostly by modestly talented choirmasters'.[49] Lustiger, in his homily on the occasion of Messiaen's funeral, referred to these sufferings, noting the 'sometimes mortal separations, divisions, hostilities and misunderstandings' that existed between the Church and Messiaen's art.[50] Messiaen's career as a church musician was marked by conflict because he was deeply committed to the Catholic faith and never considered a break with the Church, but he also never renounced his conviction that 'Gregorian chant was the only musical style that qualified as liturgical'.[51]

Messiaen was not actively involved on an institutional level in the application of the liturgical reform. He was not an official member of the diocesan commission for sacred music established by Cardinal Feltin in 1964, but he did participate in the first session of the commission presided over by Monsignor Delarue.[52] During this session, church musicians such as Gaston Litaize, Joachim Havard de la Montagne, Jean Langlais and Messiaen perceived the 'active participation' of the congregation in the liturgy as a threat to the well-established *scholae*. In addition, they identified the breakdown of Latin services with the progressive loss of the classical church repertoire, namely Renaissance polyphony and Gregorian chant. Consequently, many church musicians ran the risk of being made redundant because of the lack of music requiring professional performance. Therefore, these members of the committee put great emphasis on articles 36, 54 and 116 of the *Sacrosanctum Concilium*, which stipulated the use of Latin texts and of Gregorian chant, in particular for the parts of the Ordinary of the Mass sung by the congregation. Other committee members relied on the fact that authority was given to the bishops to decide to what extent the vernacular language was to be used. The polemic over these issues was often fierce. In the end, the above-named members left the commission because they believed that their views were not taken seriously by the episcopal authorities.[53]

---

[48]   *Bulletin La Trinité*, February 1961; February and March 1964; January 1965; June and October 1969.

[49]   Harry Halbreich, 'Une théologie sonore. Par la connaissance vers l'inconnaissable', in *Olivier Messiaen Homme de Foi*, p. 24.

[50]   Jean-Marie Lustiger, 'Musicien de l'Invisible', in *Olivier Messiaen Homme de Foi*, p. 8.

[51]   See *Lecture at Notre-Dame: An address presented at Notre-Dame Cathedral in Paris, December 4, 1977*, trans. Timothy J. Tikker (Paris: Alphonse Leduc, 2001 [1978]).

[52]   *La Semaine Religieuse de Paris* 2 (1964): 26–27. See also: Joachim Havard de la Montagne, *Mes longs Chemins de Musicien* (Paris: Editions L'Harmattan, 2001), pp. 72–76.

[53]   See Havard de la Montagne, *Mes longs Chemins de Musicien*, 74–76.

Olivier Messiaen was certainly frustrated with liturgical reform. The organ builder Olivier Glandaz recounted that Olivier Messiaen refused to accompany new vernacular hymns and antiphons with the organ.[54] When questioned about his views on liturgical reform, Messiaen was evasive and answered by glorifying the role of Gregorian chant and noting his admiration for composers who remained anonymous.[55] Thus, Messiaen avoided public polemic. Throughout the years, this polemic increased, particularly among church musicians who were concerned about the decline of Latin usage.[56] In this context, Messiaen was allied with his former teacher Maurice Duruflé, as a member of the honorific committee of Una Voce, an association founded on 19 November 1964 in Paris. Una Voce partially supported the *Sacrosanctum Concilium* and were in favour of Latin liturgy, Gregorian chant and the ecclesiastical arts of the Roman Catholic Church.[57] For this reason, Messiaen is sometimes associated with groups faithful to Archbishop Marcel Lefebvre, founder of the Society of St Pius X (SSPX) and one of the leading opponents of the liturgical reforms associated with the Second Vatican Council. Messiaen, however, never actually became a follower of the schismatic community gathered around Lefebvre and his Seminary at Ecône.

Jean-Marie Lustiger and liturgical reform

Jean-Marie Lustiger was 43 years old when he was appointed *curé* of the Parisian church of Sainte-Jeanne-de-Chantal by Cardinal Marty in 1969. The parish was located in the 16th arrondissement and had never taken part in preconciliar paraliturgical experiments. Lustiger began his ministry the same year as the promulgation of Pope Paul VI's missal. In the previous year, the ordinances on liturgical reform were followed by the strike and student protests that led to the eventual downfall of the De Gaulle government in a series of events now known as 'May 1968'. What Lustiger witnessed was the progressive transformation of the hope for renewal fostered by the Second Vatican Council into the opposite of the Council's aims. He wrote:

> Instead of renewing the Institution by an effort of interior conversion and rejuvenation, there was a reconditioning of people who felt their heritage to be an oppression and alienation. They 'alienated themselves' and were in a sense going to change dramatically. They 'decompensated', as psychologists say.[58]

---

[54]   In a personal conversation with this author.

[55]   *Musica et Memoria* 42 (1991), p. 26.

[56]   Aimé Martimort, 'La réforme liturgique incomprise', *La Maison-Dieu* 192 (1992): 86.

[57]   Joachim Havard de la Montagne, 'Olivier Messiaen (1908–1992)', Musica et Memoria, 46 (1992): 51.

[58]   Jean-Marie Lustiger, *Choosing God*, p. 273.

A couple of months before his relocation to Sainte-Jeanne-de-Chantal, Lustiger went on vacation to the United States where contacts within the American Roman Catholic Church put him in touch with priests and religious- and lay-persons devastated by activities similar to those of 'May 1968' carried out by a liberation movement in France. In the United States the liberation movement started at the University of Berkeley and was associated with anti-Vietnam war protests. Lustiger came to the conclusion that 'the only "pastoral ministry" capable of resisting ideological pressures was the one defined by the following structural elements: relationship to the community, service to the Word, worship, organization of charity, personal relationship to the faithful'.[59] In a Church context, where emphasis was not on liturgy and the sacraments, but on what was called 'the gospel within life', Lustiger made an audacious choice for the parish community he was put in charge of and made liturgy his priority.

Lustiger's decision was backed up by two important considerations. First, given the reduction of the number of priests, the only time when people would have a relationship with a priest was the Sunday liturgy. Second, Lustiger was convinced that 'the Christian liturgy is not primarily the fulfilment of rites; it is a historical act as a time and place of redemption, of salvation, and God's presence; it is an act in which Christ's disciples participate in his unique history'.[60] For Lustiger, priests and people were not the owners of the liturgy as actors and spectators are the creators of a spectacle. For him, 'all are both actors, collaborators with God, and spectators of the work of God in themselves'.[61] In addition, Lustiger distanced himself from a perception of the sacraments as visible signs of an invisible grace, an attitude typical of post-Tridentine theology, which emphasized making the invisible visible. Faithful to the Jewish representation of God's presence in the world, Lustiger envisioned liturgy as God's action to make Himself visible in His people to whom God convened His Word at Mount Sinai and throughout history by scripture. This comprehension of liturgy explained why scripture became absolutely central to all aspects of worship at Sainte-Jeanne-de-Chantal, including the musical programmes.[62] For Lustiger, what made music so special within liturgy was precisely its absolute relationship to the Word of God.[63] This feature was exactly what Lustiger admired in Messiaen's compositions. In an interview with Jean-Michel Dieuaide Lustiger said: 'I hear in Messiaen's music the inspiring power of the Word and the expression of a musician who has received the Word; I found [in this music], through the meditation expressed by the musician, aspects that helped me understand in a new way the Word he commented on.'[64]

---

[59]   Ibid., p. 275.

[60]   Ibid., p. 288.

[61]   Ibid., pp. 292–293.

[62]   Ibid., pp. 284–285.

[63]   Jean-Michel Dieuaide, 'La Musique, Parole de Dieu prononcée par des voix humaines', interview with Jean-Marie Lustiger, *Voix Nouvelles* 43 (2005): 10.

[64]   Ibid.

Lustiger's view of music as an integral part of the sacred liturgy

On his arrival at Sainte-Jeanne-de-Chantal in 1969, Lustiger chose to use exclusively French biblical texts for the music programmes. While Messiaen focused on improvisations and never composed pieces to be performed by a congregation, Lustiger wanted compositions based on large parts of the Sunday readings that could be performed by a cantor, a choir and the congregation. For this purpose Lustiger hired Henry Paget, a Church musician who had studied organ under Pierre Cochereau and Michel Chapuis at the National Conservatory of Strasbourg, where he obtained the distinction of 'First prize for organ'. Awarded prizes for harmony, for counterpoint and fugue as a student at the Conservatoire National Supérieur de Paris, Paget collaborated with Lustiger in the creation of hundreds of musical pieces written for each Sunday of the three liturgical cycles. Since 1993, Paget has held the position of Professor of Organ at the Institut Catholique de Paris. Like Messiaen, he is also Professor at the Schola Cantorum de Paris (2005) and has given many concerts in France, Germany, Italy, Switzerland, Belgium, Luxembourg and the United States. Paget and Lustiger shared with Messiaen a common interest in the mystery of Incarnation (for which Paget and Lustiger collaborated on a notable *Christmas Oratorio* in 1979), but they differed from Messiaen in their emphasis on compositions for Good Friday, a day of the liturgical year for which Messiaen never wrote a significant piece.[65] What really separated them from Messiaen was their collaboration in the field of vocal music in the vernacular language, which raised the congregation to the level of a truly active participant for the entire celebration.

The starting point for Paget and Lustiger was usually a refrain drawn from scripture, repeated by the congregation at various moments in the Mass. Then different pieces were progressively added, sung by the cantor or the choir. The two men described their settings as 'short cantatas'. Their music was analysed by Lucien Deiss on the release of their audio-recording *Veilleur, où en est la nuit?*[66] According to Deiss, what made these programmes unique was not only the exclusive use of scripture texts, but also their structure. 'In fact', Deiss wrote, 'we do not face stereotypes like the alternation of a refrain and strophes. The structure as well as the text stem from the Gospel.' He continues by noting that these compositions 'have the form of a dialogue and a drama, a form that highlights the logical structure of the [Gospel's] account and action into which the congregation, by the proclamation of a scripture text, interfaces as a protagonist'.[67] The alternation of the various liturgical actions affirmed the identity proper to each

---

[65]   Harry Halbreich, 'Une théologie sonore', p. 26. Henry Paget wrote a Passion according to St John for two voices, choir and organ (2005), as well as seven short motets a cappella on the last seven words of Christ on the Cross (2005).

[66]   Lucien Deiss, 'Cantate brève à la messe de onze heures', *Communio* 6 (1978): 87–91.

[67]   Ibid., p. 89.

actor of the liturgy. The priest celebrant, the deacon, the readers, the choir, the cantor and the congregation all respond to one another, and the result is a unified action.

The 'short cantata' composed for the last Sundays of the liturgical Year A illustrates this type of presentation. The gospel readings are drawn from the Gospel according to Matthew, chapters 24 and 25 (the English translation follows the arrangements of the biblical texts made by Lustiger who uses the French translation of the Bible of Jerusalem). During these Sundays the congregation repeatedly sings the refrain: 'The bridegroom was late, and they all grew drowsy and fell asleep. But at midnight there was a cry, "The bridegroom is here! Go out and meet him"'. (Matthew 25: 6). The choir or the cantor continues by proclaiming: 'if the householder had known at what time of the night the burglar would come, he would have stayed awake and would not have allowed anyone to break through the wall of his house. Therefore, you too must stand ready.' The congregation repeats: 'Therefore, you too must stand ready' and the choir or the cantor continue: 'because on a day you do not expect and at an hour you do not know, the Son of man is coming' (Matthew 24: 43, 44 and 50).

These 'short cantatas' are completely different from those spiritual songs akin to popular music in their level of technical difficulty and broad appeal. They also differ from those 'neutral' songs in the vernacular language used without distinction for all kinds of sacramental celebrations, including baptism, marriage or funeral.

The reception of the music programmes offered at Sainte-Jeanne-de-Chantal

Until the arrival of Jean-Marie Lustiger at Sainte-Jeanne-de-Chantal, many parishioners had never thought about music other than in terms of entertainment, relaxation, passive reception or as a bridge between two liturgical actions. Consequently they were surprised by this musical presentation of scripture. Two reactions could be observed. The first concerns a minority. These persons were irritated by the cantatas or rejected the melodies, which were perceived as 'incomprehensible', 'without harmony' or 'not appropriate for a worship service'. The cantatas were described as 'too intellectual' and unfavourably compared to opera. These reactions were a symptom of the difficulties people had in relinquishing preconciliar conceptions of the liturgy and being open to change in the wake of the Second Vatican Council. Many people reacted negatively to the increased use of scripture in liturgy combined with an individualistic perception of the sacraments and indeed of the entire work of salvation. Many people were looking within liturgy for what matched their personal taste and capacity. They did not understand that the problem was not the music, but their limited view of God's Word and of the sacred mysteries.

The majority of people had the second reaction. For them, what happened was an authentic revelation. With time, listening to and taking part in what at first seemed 'intolerable', people progressively perceived the Word of God as an overabundant font of spiritual life. In the words of Deiss, what made the 'short cantatas' so special was precisely the fact that they 'helped the congregation go beyond its capacities, and not remain a prisoner of the most narrow limits of its imagination, desires and habits'.[68] This result was due in no small part to the presence of Henry Paget at the organ at each of the six Sunday Masses. This fact highlights the key position of the organist and of sacred music in introducing liturgical reform and in developing the liturgy according to the new conciliar norms.

In order for this to be successful, a cordial dialogue and a mutual understanding between the pastor and the organist were fundamental. For the cantatas, Lustiger chose and arranged the biblical texts and his selection suggested a certain structure for the music pieces. The musical interpretation and composition, in turn, belonged entirely to Henry Paget. Their combined efforts were based on their submission to scripture. The partnership between Lustiger and Paget proved that there could be a liturgy entirely faithful to the norms issued by the Second Vatican Council and the musical church tradition of the past, because their collaboration included each musical style recognized by the Church.

In an address to the members of the French-speaking federation 'Amis de l'Orgue' [Friends of the Organ], Lustiger underlined the importance of liturgists challenging the organist by asking him or her for 'something else' and for 'much more' than was usually provided. Too often parish priests and liturgists undermine the organist's aesthetic and spiritual experience and ignore a tremendous resource for initiating the congregation into 'the Christian celebration of the "mysteries"'.[69] But, most importantly, Lustiger presented a series of pointed questions that are fundamental for a positive reception of the liturgical reform. He writes:

> Is there a leitmotiv? What is its function? What about the entrance piece and how much intensity should be given to it? What about the link between the moments of the proclamation of and the listening to God's Word? What should be repeated and remembered throughout the entire piece? What are the appropriate means for doing this, because some elements are perhaps superfluous? How should one consider the succession of particular moments, which may be marked by powerful and contrasting emotions? How should one consider the succession of words pronounced by a single person, be it the president, the celebrant, the priest, the bishop, and words uttered by the entire congregation? How should we think about desires and wishes expressed here and there, evaluate their balance or their relationship with regard to the other parts of the liturgy? Where can we find the most apt models for western and in particular French culture? Quite often, indeed, evangelical celebrations typical of the Southern part of the US, those of black communities, furnish an implicit model for celebrations: is this the only model possible? Is it convenient for our culture and our tradition? What should we think about the enthusiasm caused by Byzantine or Russian court music a couple of decades ago? What do they evoke in our memory of the past?

---

[68] Ibid., p. 90.

[69] Jean-Marie Lustiger, 'Adresse au Symposium des Amis de l'Orgue', *Communio* 4 (2000): 67.

How should we explain the absolute rejection of Gregorian chant as re-established over the nineteenth century and its passive resurgence in recorded music or in concert? How should we receive the classical tradition of the cantata? What should we think about the transition of opera to liturgy from the time of the sixteenth century and the great pieces for the liturgy created for orchestra and choir that resulted from this tradition?[70]

Conclusion

My purpose here has been to highlight Olivier Messiaen's profession as a church musician in the particular context of the twentieth-century Church of France and the liturgical reform applied in Paris. The most important difference between Olivier Messiaen's and Cardinal Jean-Marie Lustiger's views of the liturgical reform can be expressed as follows. As a professional church musician Olivier Messiaen was influenced by currents proper to the nineteenth and twentieth centuries, which rooted the Catholic renewal in Romanticism, Symbolism and Surrealism. In this perspective, liturgy was mostly perceived as a work of the Church, which made the invisible visible.

In the wake of the Second Vatican Council, liturgy came to be perceived as the *Mysterium paschalis*, that is to say as 'an action of Christ the priest and of His Body, which is the Church', in its connection with Trinitarian life (*Sacrosanctum Concilium*, 7–13). This view did not exclude preconciliar perception, but enlarged it. Moreover, the Council reached a deeper comprehension of the Word of God perceived as 'the support and energy of the Church […] the pure and everlasting source of spiritual life'. This fact called for 'easy access to Sacred Scripture […] provided for all the Christian faithful' (*Dei Verbum*, 21–22). These Christological, Trinitarian and ecclesiological aspects, based on scripture, should become normative for liturgy and sacred music. Consequently, Jean-Marie Lustiger developed an understanding of sacred music as a service to the Word of God, realized in particular through vocal music, which made scripture a source of inspiration for people's everyday existence.

The implementation of liturgical reform initially met with incomprehension due to lack of preparation and lack of an appropriate pedagogy. Some people were unprepared for such a change, which challenged habits and traditions conveyed over centuries. Others, on the contrary, hastened to suppress chants and customs in the name of 'the spirit of the Council'. New modes of worship were introduced without time for reflection and maturation. The exclusiveness of both sides often deepened the rifts within the Church of France, already marked by controversies over many centuries.

Interestingly, Lustiger himself was not immune from misunderstandings. The liturgical programmes of Sainte-Jeanne-de-Chantal remained unique and were

---

[70]   Ibid., pp. 69–70.

not adopted by other Parisian parishes or French-speaking communities. This phenomenon cannot be linked to technical problems. The real difficulty has to be identified with the two following human factors. First, in a Roman Catholic context, an organ, a professional organist, a cantor and a choir remain dependent on a cleric and a congregation willing to make the liturgy a real priority. Second, the implementation of the liturgical reform postulated a view of the liturgy that was not a mere copy of the past, but the expression of the Church yesterday, today and tomorrow. Messiaen's parish struggled with these issues along with the other Catholic parishes of France. His personal answer to these struggles was to keep clear of compositions that were imbued with the conciliar norms. This decision is perhaps regrettable, but does not diminish his dedication to authentic sacred music during his tenure as organist at La Trinité.

On 28 March 1989, Olivier Messiaen was given the prestigious Paul VI Award by the Paul VI Institute of Brescia, Italy, in recognition of his entire oeuvre. In the address delivered in the presence of the French composer at Notre-Dame de Paris, Lustiger underlines the challenges positively overcome by Messiaen in these particularly troubled times. First, Lustiger notes that Messiaen's music bears witness to a humanism open to God. Written to serve a people gathered together for worship, his oeuvre does not depend on a public chosen in advance. In fact, the challenge of every church musician is to overcome an always threatened solipsism and narcissism by leading people beyond themselves. Second, Lustiger hailed Messiaen as a composer entirely dedicated to 'the necessary, but also insufficient intimate connection between the quest for God and the expression of the Beautiful'. Indeed, this connection is very often broken. In their mediating function between God's Word and mankind, artists are torn between holiness and aesthetic pleasure. In order to overcome this challenge, the organist is called to apply to himself all of the spiritual disciplines. 'When this happens for a church musician', Lustiger remarks, 'the obstinate and patient quest of the true artist, his humble submission to the research on what cannot be grasped and cannot be divided, the continuous fading away of energy, and the uncertainty of the result, find an analogy in the ascension of the mystic who wants to be obedient to the obscure light given to him by the Lord and Redeemer of all'.[71]

---

[71]   Jean-Marie Lustiger, *Allocution à l'occasion de la Remise du Prix Paul VI à Olivier Messiaen, 28 mars 1989*. Unpublished document available at the Archbishopric of Paris, 22, rue Barbet-de-Joüy, F-75007, Paris.

Chapter 5

Messiaen's Relationship to Jacques Maritain's Musical Circle and Neo-Thomism

Douglas Shadle

Jacques Maritain, the eminent Roman Catholic philosopher, had such high hopes for his friend Arthur Lourié that in 1936 he boldly added him to the canon of great composers:

> Every great poet brings us the promise and the testimony that this insurmountable double conflict [between art and beauty, and beauty and the person] might be overcome. In the fire, he reconciles the person, art, and beauty. If we attach such a degree of importance to the musical output of Arthur Lourié, then today it brings us such a testimony, and with a force rarely equalled.[1]

This is certainly high praise, but why Lourié? For Maritain, Lourié was the sole musical manifestation of Neo-Thomism, a broad philosophical project that had occupied him for over two decades. As a system, Neo-Thomism attempted to solve modern philosophical and theological problems using St Thomas Aquinas's medieval theological methods.[2] In the hands of a Catholic layperson such as Maritain, it was a novel and precise way to confront contemporary philosophical approaches that did not coalesce with the received wisdom of Catholic tradition. Lourié, a disciple and close friend of Maritain, similarly challenged modern trends of musical composition with a style that presented the most sacred of Catholic music, plainchant, in a modern but approachable context that resonated with Maritain's ideas. In that same year, 1936, a much less well-known organist and composer, Olivier Messiaen, laboured at his equally profound spiritual project: the musical expression of Roman Catholic doctrine. Unlike Lourié, Messiaen embraced musical modernism in all of its eclectic variety. Plainchant did play a role in his compositional processes and output, but it is certainly not the only, or even the primary, component of his music. He absorbed and reformulated a

---

[1]   Jacques Maritain, 'Sur la musique d'Arthur Lourié', *La revue musicale* 17, no. 165 (April 1936): 266.

[2]   For an introduction to Maritain's Neo-Thomism in context, see Gerald A. McCool, *The Neo-Thomists* (Milwaukee, WI: Marquette University Press, 1994), pp. 77–96.

vast array of styles and musical sounds. Today, Messiaen has achieved iconic status as the twentieth century's most important Catholic composer, as well as one of the most innovative musicians of any creed, whereas the music of Arthur Lourié lives in almost total obscurity. A wave of intellectual change rocked Roman Catholic theology in the twentieth century that, surprisingly, relegated Lourié to the subordinate position he now occupies in musical scholarship.

Musicological evidence alone cannot explain fully such a sudden and permanent reversal of fortune. Viewed in the light of twentieth-century theological developments, however, this shift reflects two broader changes in Roman Catholic thought: *ressourcement*, or 'return to the sources', and *aggiornamento*, literally 'bringing up to date'. These two ideas mutually reinforce one another in what is popularly called '*aggiornamento* through *ressourcement*': by returning to theological sources before Aquinas, theology could once again penetrate the contemporary human experience. Maritain and the Neo-Thomists, who dominated official Catholic theology in the first half of the century, wished to confront idealism, positivism and modernism of all kinds solely with the rigour of Aquinas's rational, orderly proofs. Just as the Neo-Thomist influence was reaching its crest in European Catholic circles, though, other theologians such as Karl Rahner, Henri de Lubac, Hans Urs von Balthasar and Romano Guardini were instead turning away from their scholastic training and attempting to confront modernity by diversifying their theological influences. The combined work of these theologians, which came to fruition in the documents of the Second Vatican Council (Vatican II), now ranks among the highest intellectual achievements of the Roman Catholic Church in any era. Maritain's Neo-Thomism, on the other hand, quickly fell out of favour and currently carries little weight in Catholic philosophical and theological thought. Like Balthasar and Guardini, two of his favourite theologians, Messiaen also rejected Neo-Thomism in favour of a more eclectic style that could very well be called a musical '*aggiornamento* through *ressourcement*'. This rejection was instrumental in establishing and continuing his status as an acclaimed Catholic composer.

The rise of musical Neo-Thomism

Though profound, Maritain's philosophical influence on musical life in inter-war Paris remains largely uninvestigated.[3] Between the two world wars, several Parisian musical luminaries were closely associated with Maritain and his wife, Raïssa.

---

[3]   Scholars have briefly noted Maritain's connection to Igor Stravinsky only. See Louis Andriessen and Elmer Schönberger, *The Appollonian Clockwork: On Stravinsky*, trans. Jeff Hamburg (Oxford: Oxford University Press, 1989), pp. 81–96; Charles M. Joseph, *Stravinsky & Balanchine: A Journey of Invention* (New Haven, CT: Yale University Press, 2002), 76; Richard Taruskin, *Stravinsky and the Russian Traditions: A Biography of the Works through 'Mavra'* (Berkeley: University of California Press, 1996), p. 1587; Stephen Walsh, *Stravinsky: A Creative Spring, Russia and France, 1882–1934* (New York: Alfred

The couple first entered Parisian musical circles in 1905 when they began meeting frequently with pianist Ricardo Viñes in the home of Léon Bloy, a controversial Catholic mystic and novelist. From 1915 to 1925, the Maritains befriended, in turn, Georges Auric (through Viñes and Bloy), Jean Cocteau (through Auric), Arthur Lourié, Erik Satie (on his deathbed), Igor Stravinsky and Roland-Manuel, a composer-critic. Several other musicians and critics remained firmly within their social circle and often visited their home in Meudon, which became a popular hub of intellectual discussion on Sunday afternoons. The Maritains even convinced some of their musical friends to receive the sacraments again for the first time. Despite their social and spiritual successes, only Lourié and Roland-Manuel actually joined the Maritains in their study of Aquinas, which required a degree of mental rigour that others were apparently not willing to cultivate. Nevertheless, Neo-Thomist ideas percolated throughout Parisian musical culture.

Maritain published his first authentically Neo-Thomist book, *Art et scolastique*, in 1920.[4] The book's central premise is that art is an 'intellectual virtue' of the 'practical order' in the 'sphere of making': 'Art is the undeviating determination of works to be made.'[5] This rather abstruse formulation actually widens the scope of what one might consider 'art', because beauty is not an essential element in his definition. Taking the standard Thomist definition of Beauty, 'id quod visum placet [that which pleases when seen]', as a point of departure, Maritain goes on to explain how the fine arts are distinguished from all others: 'The work to which the fine arts tend is ordered to beauty; as beautiful, it is an end, an absolute, it suffices of itself.'[6] Works of fine art, then, serve no utilitarian function. Instead, they delight the intellect by radiating the invisible beauty imparted on them in the act of making. As these works participate in beauty, Maritain invests artistic creation with supernatural significance, believing that artistic creation is a continuation of God's creative acts. Such a view raises the importance of artists themselves, who have a 'peculiar dignity' in their co-creative acts.[7] Artists consequently have an isolated and lonely existence:

> [Art] delivers one from the human; it establishes the *artifex* – artist or artisan – in a world apart, closed, limited, absolute, in which he puts the energy and intelligence of his manhood at the service of a thing which he makes. This is true of all art; the ennui of living and willing ceases at the door of every workshop.[8]

A. Knopf, 1999), p. 432; and Walsh, *Stravinsky: The Second Exile, France and America, 1934–1971* (New York: Alfred A. Knopf, 2006), p. 96.

[4]   Maritain did publish a defense of Thomism in 1914, *La philosophie bergsonienne: études-critiques* (Paris: Rivière & cie, 1930), but *Art et scolastique* was the first of his books to treat an original topic using Thomist ideas.

[5]   Jacques Maritain, *Art and Scholasticism*, trans. Joseph W. Evans (Notre Dame, IN: University of Notre Dame Press, 1974 [1962]), p. 9.

[6]   Ibid., p. 33.

[7]   Ibid., p. 60.

[8]   Ibid., p. 9.

Nevertheless, according to Maritain, artists cannot remain secluded from the world if they do not wish to be accused of idolatry: 'It is absolutely necessary therefore that the artist, *qua* man, work for something other than his work, for something better loved. God is infinitely more lovable than art.'[9] The book's trajectory, then, moves from a broad but precise definition of art to the role of the individual fine artist in society. For Maritain, the Thomist foundation that set this trajectory corrects the prevailing trends in modern aesthetics, 'which, considering in art only the fine arts, and treating the beautiful only with regard to art, run the risk of vitiating both the notion of Art and the notion of the Beautiful.'[10]

Although *Art et scolastique* reads like a formal academic treatise, there is a clear political dimension to the text. Maritain finds more than one occasion to distinguish his Thomism from German idealism, the 'subjectivist "venom" which has infected metaphysics in the wake of the Kantian revolution'.[11] Perhaps more surprisingly, *Art et scolastique* also draws heavily on Jean Cocteau's 1918 essay, 'Le coq et l'arlequin', certainly an unconventional source. Like Cocteau, Maritain equates late nineteenth-century German music, especially Wagner, with artistic decadence.[12] By castigating Wagner specifically, Maritain gained allies among certain French musical nationalists and inserted himself into the decades-old debate about Wagner's place in French concert halls.[13] More broadly, though, the book was not a simple denunciation of German art and aesthetics; it served as a springboard for launching France's triumphant re-entry into modern artistic culture. The style of the treatise itself embraces Cocteau's notion that 'tradition appears at every epoch under a different disguise'.[14] The academic tone of the book belies its radical acceptance and support of modern French composers such as Erik Satie, whom, according to Maritain, even Aristotle, the source of Thomist metaphysics, 'no doubt would have liked'.[15] Rhetorically aligned with Cocteau, Maritain's ideas garnered easy acceptance among Cocteau's followers. They also appealed to Stravinsky, who had already begun to mix musical 'tradition' with the 'modern' in his earliest neo-classical works.

Composers and critics alike began adopting Maritain's rhetoric and ideas not long after *Art et scolastique* first appeared. Cocteau, for example, took Maritain's statement about the artist's workshop and applied it to Stravinsky, commenting:

---

[9]   Ibid., p. 70.

[10]   Ibid., p. 4.

[11]   Ibid., p. 167.

[12]   Ibid., p. 57. See also Stephen Schloesser, *Jazz Age Catholicism: Mystic Modernism in Postwar Paris, 1919–1933* (Toronto: University of Toronto Press, 2005), pp. 190–194.

[13]   See Jane Fulcher, *The Composer as Intellectual: Music and Ideology in France, 1914–1940* (New York: Oxford University Press, 2005), pp. 28–31.

[14]   Jean Cocteau, *Le Rappel à l'ordre*, in *Œuvres Complètes de Jean Cocteau*, vol. 9 (Paris: Marguerat, 1946), p. 32. Schloesser, *Jazz Age Catholicism*, pp. 151–152.

[15]   Maritain, *Art and Scholasticism*, p. 17. Maritain later claims: 'I know nothing in contemporary production more sincerely *classical* than the music of Satie'. Ibid., p. 53.

'This composer, embroiled in his work, clothed in it, harnessed to his work like the old one-man-band, stripping off and piling up around himself pieces of musical bark, is all of a piece with his room.'[16] Stravinsky himself used scholastic metaphysical language in a 1924 essay written for a New York-based magazine, *The Arts*: 'My Octuor [*Octet*] is a musical object. This object has a form and that form is influenced by the musical matter with which it is composed. The differences of matter determine the differences of form. One does not do the same with marble that one does with stone.'[17] Reviewing Stravinsky's piano sonata in 1925, Arthur Lourié also invoked scholastic metaphysics, in this instance by noting the interplay between inner and outer forms: 'The original classical forms catalyze new ideas in him, totally enfolded in new forms – but the deceptive appearance is that of outdated ideas and forms – and the realized work constitutes an organism in itself.'[18] The conductor Ernest Ansermet, a champion of Stravinsky's music, drew on Maritain's idea of the work of art's objective givenness suggesting: 'Every musical work is for the listener a succession of musical facts that are organized in the memory and understanding. […] the work is of a purely musical nature and objective character.'[19] Finally, adopting Maritain's concept of the 'artifex', Roland-Manuel described Stravinsky's 1925 piano concerto as having 'the marvellous naïveté of the genial artisan'.[20]

The source of these critical views did not go unnoticed. In an article sardonically titled 'Thomas et les imposteurs', critic Henri Monnet assessed current debates about artistic 'objectivity' and pointed an accusatory finger at Maritain: 'I know who is responsible for these verbal onslaughts: it is St Thomas, St Thomas, or at least Mr Ansermet and his good guide, Mr Jacques Maritain.'[21] Monnet questioned the value of applying Thomist principles to music criticism and called Ansermet, Lourié, and author Boris de Schloezer (by no means a professed Neo-Thomist) 'disciples of Maritain' who 'speak Thomist language'. Monnet also expressed apprehension about 'the danger of the excess of intellect in the search for objectivity' and wondered if the emotions, not the intellect, might 'constitute the form of a perfectly ordered work of art'.[22] Both de Schloezer and Roland-

---

[16]   This passage comes from the 1924 appendix to 'Le coq et l'arlequin', 'Strawinsky Dernière Heure'. Cocteau, *Le Rappel à l'ordre*, p. 57.

[17]   Igor Stravinsky, 'Some Ideas about my Octuor', *The Arts* (January 1924): 4.

[18]   Arthur Lourié, 'La Sonate pour piano de Strawinsky', *La revue musicale* 6, no. 10 (1925): 100.

[19]   Ernest Ansermet, 'Introduction à l'œuvre d'Igor Stravinsky', *Revue Pleyel* 2, no. 18 (1925): 15–16.

[20]   Roland-Manuel, 'Concerto pour le Piano, de Stravinsky', *Revue Pleyel* 1, no. 10 (July 1924): 27–28.

[21]   Henri Monnet, 'Thomas et les Imposteurs', *Revue Pleyel* 3, no. 29 (1926): 13. The title is an allusion to a novel by Jean Cocteau, *Thomas l'Imposteur* (Paris: Gallimard, 1923).

[22]   Monnet, 'Thomas et les Imposteurs', p. 14.

Manuel wrote defensive responses to the article, but the controversy quickly waned as Neo-Thomist rhetoric became more mainstream.[23] Although they treated the subject negatively, Monnet and other sceptics were uncovering the notion of 'purity' as the primary intellectual focus of Maritain and his circle. Raïssa Maritain, Jacques's wife, later reminisced: 'The artistic conscience was truly purifying itself, tending toward that "discovery of the spiritual in the sensible" which not only defines poetry but defines the soul of every art, painting as well as music and the theater.'[24] In her mind, Satie and those in his orbit were stripping away the artifice, decadence and excess of Wagnerism, which was antithetical to Thomist and modern sensibilities alike.

The controversies over musical objectivity and purity dissipated in the mid-1920s, but Maritain's Neo-Thomism remained current in music criticism well into the next decade. Arthur Lourié was, unsurprisingly, the central propagator of Maritain's ideas, and he often put them at the service of Stravinsky's music. In a review of Stravinsky's *Œdipus Rex* (1927), for example, Lourié found the practical application of Thomist metaphysics in a compositional principle he called the 'dialectical' procedure:

> Contemporary musicians strive to construct their works dialectically; it is not a matter of seizing one of the dialectical procedures of the past, but rather to affirm dialectics as a method of musical construction. [...] The dialectical method is the only one that responds to the modern sensibility, for dialectical energy uniquely depends on the equilibrium between the 'what' and the 'how', which appears as the present ideal.[25]

Concern for music's 'what' – the essential form – and its 'how' – the style, or material – generates a dialectical energy, which is music's animating power, or 'entelechy', to use the term from classical and scholastic metaphysics. Lourié continued Thomist lines of thinking in his published commentary on Stravinsky's *Apollon musagète* (1928):

> Surmounting the individual element – the *animal* principle – Stravinsky's music tends, more and more, toward the *spiritual*. By this same token, it aims at the unity of the moral and aesthetic principle, a unity long since lost. In his previous works the choice between 'how' and 'what' was made thus: with an ever increasing tendency of the centre of gravity to shift toward the latter. [...] On the basis of this principle, Stravinsky created several works in which vulgar materials were elevated toward

---

[23]   Boris de Schloezer, 'A Mes Critiques', *Revue Pleyel* 3, no. 30 (1926): 13–15; Roland-Manuel, 'Reflexions sur la pureté', *Revue Pleyel* 3, no. 31 (1926): 15–17.

[24]   Raïssa Maritain, 'A Handful of Musicians', *The Commonweal* (29 October 1943): 33.

[25]   Arthur Lourié, 'Œdipus-Rex', *La revue musicale* 8, no. 8 (1927): 244.

pure forms. Then came a period in which equilibrium was established between 'how' and 'what'. Today, it is the latter that tends to prevail.[26]

Lourié suggests that Stravinsky's increasing attention to form – not necessarily its structure, but its essence – spiritualizes the music and unites morality with aesthetics. This unity is precisely what Maritain hoped an artist would achieve when he claimed that God, toward whom beauty in the fine arts leads the audience, is infinitely more lovable than art, the act of making a beautiful object.

Shortly after his reviews of *Œdipus Rex* and *Apollon musagète*, however, Lourié began to distance himself from the rhetoric of objectivity so prominent in his writing and that of others, notably Ernest Ansermet, in the early 1920s. By 1930, he deplored the inhumanity of what was being called objective, or 'pure', music, which often emphasized rhythm at the expense of other musical features. He argued instead that melody is music's most spiritual and transcendent element:

> Musicians and poets of the vanguard have, until very recently, been ashamed of melody and lyric moods […] I believe that this sense of shame may be explained by the fact that melody (any melody) is apt to reveal some intimate truth, the genuine psychological and spiritual substance of its maker. *Melody discloses the nature of the subject, not the object.*[27]

This turn to melody came in the wake of Maritain's 1927 republication of *Art et scolastique*. In the new edition, Maritain included an essay called 'The Frontiers of Poetry' in which he shielded his ideas from the 'inhuman' abuse of Thomist principles that occurred after the treatise's original publication. The union of morality and beauty that Lourié found in Stravinsky's works apparently did not trickle into the broader artistic climate. Lourié felt that artists had taken 'purity' too far:

> Where would the notion of "pure art" lead if pushed to its furthest logical extremes? To an art completely isolated from all that is not its own rules of operation and the object to be created as such, in other words, an art apart, freed, completely uninterested in man and things. Angelist suicide – through the forgetting of matter.[28]

Both Lourié and Maritain were responding to attitudes, like Monnet's, that Thomism removes the human from art, but they did not agree with this opinion. For them, Thomism penetrated to the very essence of what it means to be human.

---

26   Arthur Lourié, 'A propos de l'Apollon d'Igor Stravinsky', *Musique: Revue Mensuelle* 1, no. 3 (1927): 118.

27   Arthur Lourié, 'An Inquiry Into Melody', *Modern Music* 7, no. 1 (1929–30): 3–4.

28   Maritain, *Art and Scholasticism*, p. 123. By 'angelism', he meant an intellectual retreat from physical reality.

The problem for Lourié, then, became how to create a musical style that more accurately reflected what they considered an authentically Thomist vision.

Two competing visions of Catholic music: Lourié and Messiaen

Despite their best efforts, the Neo-Thomism of Maritain and Lourié was not the only conception of Roman Catholicism taking hold in inter-war France. The younger generation of Catholics to which Messiaen belonged began to interrogate the meaning of the word 'Catholic'. They rediscovered a personal dimension of Catholic faith that seemed lost on certain Church authorities. Through this reformulation of faith and Catholicism, they drifted away from established modes of thought. It is commonly held, for example, that Messiaen and his friends in the group La Jeune France came together in opposition to neo-classicism; however, this claim does not fully explain why Messiaen did not follow the Neo-Thomist path.[29] It is likely that he did not fully embrace Neo-Thomism because he did not wish to sacrifice the originality and individuality of his personal musical style. It is clear from his writings that Messiaen believed his unique emotional style perfectly suited his desire for religious musical expression. Moreover, it is very easy to misinterpret the Neo-Thomists' ideas as cold and impersonal. Messiaen probably wanted to avoid the confusion, and he even admitted that philosophical jargon terrified him.[30] He sought a more personal expression of faith that Lourié appears never to have found.

If we take Lourié at his word and broadly align Stravinsky's neo-classicism from the 1920s with Maritain's Neo-Thomism, we can understand Lourié's output from the late 1920s through the early 1940s as a newly reformulated Neo-Thomist style. In a radical stylistic departure from Stravinsky, and in an attempt to place melody at the centre of this new style, Lourié turned to Gregorian and Byzantine chant as stylistic foundations. Like Maritain, Lourié idealized the melodic freedom of liturgical chant, and he employed melodic styles akin to chant in two of his largest works from the period – the *Sonata Liturgica* (1928) and the *Concerto Spirituale* (1929–30). Two short motets from 1936 and 1943 – *Procession* and *De ordinatione angelorum*, respectively – also exemplify his style (see Examples 5.1 and 5.2).[31]

Both works open with clear allusions to plainchant, but each vocal utterance is nested within a thoroughly modern idiom. In *Procession*, the rhythmic drive of the piano contrasts with the nearly arrhythmic vocal entry; the brass timbres

---

[29]   See, for example, Robert Sherlaw Johnson, *Messiaen* (London: J.M. Dent & Sons, Ltd., 1975), p. 10.

[30]   Brigitte Massin, *Olivier Messiaen: une poétique du merveilleux* (Aix-en-Provence: Alinea, 1989), p. 178.

[31]   Raïssa Maritain supplied the texts for both works. She wrote the poem, 'Procession', and for the later work selected a passage from St Thomas Aquinas's *Summa Theologiae* (New York: Blackfriars – McGraw Hill, 1964–), I, Q. 108.

Example 5.1   Arthur Lourié: *Procession*, bars 7–11

Example 5.2   Arthur Lourié: *De ordinatione angelorum*, bars 1–7

and dissonant counterpoint function similarly in *De ordinatione angelorum*. In addition to their use of unabashedly chant-like melodies, both works have forms that faithfully present and clearly accentuate the overarching syntax of each text. As in the openings, each line or phrase floats timelessly above the preceding and succeeding instrumental interjections. Lourié accomplished three Neo-Thomist goals with this style: he retained the clarity and simplicity of 1920s neo-classicism; he incorporated his newly developed ideas about the primacy of melody; and he packaged Gregorian chant in a thoroughly modern harmonic idiom.[32]

Lourié was not alone in translating Neo-Thomist ideas into a musical style in the 1930s. Francis Poulenc, for example, who had recently experienced a reawakening of his own Catholicism, at times composed in a similar style.[33] His 1936 motet, *Litanies à la vierge noire*, bears an uncanny resemblance to *Procession* and *De ordinatione angelorum*, particularly in its melodic construction. After a mixed modal introduction on the organ, the sopranos enter, marked *humblement*, with a chant-like prayer of supplication, 'Lord, have pity on us' (see Example 5.3).

Example 5.3 Francis Poulenc: *Litanies à la vierge noire: Notre-Dame de Roc-Amadour*, bars 9–16

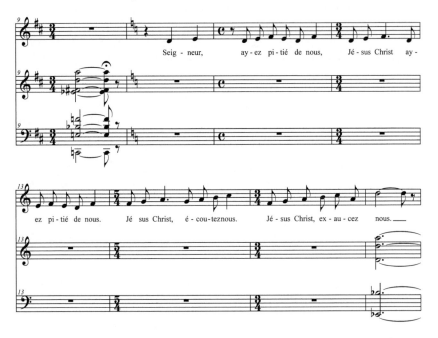

<hr />

32   Lourié was certainly not the only composer writing so-called 'modern' works with foundations in Gregorian chant. Charles Tournemire's *L'Orgue Mystique* also falls into this mould, but this work has a purely liturgical function that Lourié's paraliturgical works do not share.

33   Although it is unclear whether he was a personal acquaintance of the Maritains, he openly admired Jacques's writing. Poulenc's 'ideal library' included at least one book by Jacques Maritain that he presumably did not already own. Francis Poulenc, "'My Ideal Library'", in *Francis Poulenc: Music, Art, and Literature*, eds Sidney Buckland and Myriam Chimènes (Aldershot: Ashgate, 1999), pp. 140–144.

Although the organ plays more of a dialogic role in the work, giving the text's form a less clearly punctuated expression than the instruments in Lourié's two motets, *Litanies* certainly shares their character.

In addition to Poulenc, other composers close to Maritain socially or intellectually also wrote in melody-driven styles that, like Lourié's, combine modern elements with older styles, especially from sacred music traditions.[34] *Benedictiones* (1938), a motet by Roland-Manuel, for example, is a dissonant experiment in 'Neo-Renaissance' sacred polyphony. Although they did not employ the exact methods of Lourié and Poulenc, these composers strenuously avoided Schoenberg's 12-tone method, which they perceived as the lingering representative of Wagner's decadence. Lourié criticized dodecaphony with the term 'neogothic', which meant the style derived too exclusively from the emotions, an approach that Maritain and his friends would have repudiated.[35] From a compositional standpoint, then, musical Neo-Thomism was thriving, but alternative styles were emerging simultaneously.

The young organist and composer Olivier Messiaen did not accept Maritain's Neo-Thomism; in fact he rejected the 'mechanical' and 'impersonal' trends of 1920s neo-classicism – the same trends that Lourié likewise rejected – but his reasons for doing so differed significantly from Lourié's.[36] Unlike Lourié, Messiaen believed emotion and sincerity should be the source of religious and musical expression and 'at the service of the dogmas of Catholic theologies' and that the theological subject matter is 'The best, for it comprises all subjects. And the abundance of technical means allows the heart to pour out freely.'[37] This was the opposite view from many contemporary composers. For example, in a review of *La Nativité du Seigneur* (1935), Georges Auric, a Neo-Thomist sympathizer, claimed that with regard to Messiaen: 'On many issues we would be poles apart.'[38] Although Messiaen and the Neo-Thomists would have agreed on the intimate relationship of music and the supernatural, they held distinct views on the source of this relationship. By stating the importance of the artist's emotional expression, Messiaen rejected Maritain's notion that art is a virtue of the intellect; he continued

---

[34]   Composers such as Georges Auric, Arthur Honegger, Roland-Manuel, Maurice Jaubert and Nicolas Nabokov.

[35]   Arthur Lourié, 'Neogothic and Neoclassic', *Modern Music* 5, no. 3 (1928): 3–8.

[36]   The members of La Jeune France bemoaned the 'hard, mechanical, and impersonal' conditions of modern life, but their implication is that modern trends in music reflected these conditions. See Peter Hill and Nigel Simeone, *Messiaen* (New Haven, CT/London: Yale University Press, 2005), p. 63.

[37]   Olivier Messiaen, Program Notes for the Première of *La Nativité du Seigneur*, 27 February 1936, quoted in Robert Fallon, 'Knowledge and Subjectivity in Maritain, Stravinsky, and Messiaen', in *Jacques Maritain and the Many Ways of Knowing*, ed. Douglas Olivant (Washington, DC: American Maritain Association, 2002), p. 296.

[38]   Quoted in Hill and Simeone, *Messiaen*, p. 60.

his open avoidance of Thomist rhetoric in other contexts.[39] Although Messiaen was not proposing the same 'egocentric' (Lourié's term) principles as Schoenberg, he was treading dangerously close to the 'neogothic' realm.

Messiaen consequently approached style quite differently from Lourié, although like Lourié, he openly acknowledged the primacy of melody in all musical composition: 'The melody is the point of departure. May it remain sovereign!'[40] Messiaen also occasionally employed formulas from plainchant but did not present them with the same clarity and simplicity as either Lourié or Poulenc; he was much more interested in transplanting the melodic contours or forms of specific chants into a stylistically diversified context.[41] In *Poèmes pour Mi* (1936), a work whose overall conception as a setting of vernacular sacred poetry resembles that of Lourié's *Procession*, Messiaen chose not to write in the relaxed and ethereal idiom of plainchant. Instead, the work often borders on the operatic, as seen in the opening of the seventh song, 'Les deux guerriers' [The two warriors] (see Example 5.4). The vocal line is essentially a recitative, and his eventual orchestration of the work gives it Straussian proportions.

Without relying on Lourié's almost dogmatic resurrection of plainchant, Messiaen was quite open to non-traditional musical sources. The bulk of his 1944 treatise on his musical style comprises discussions of non-retrogradable rhythms, modes of limited transposition, birdsong, the music of India and a series of 'special chords', all stylistic elements that today's listeners associate almost exclusively with Messiaen. Although Messiaen and the Neo-Thomists apparently agreed on certain ideas, such as the primacy of melody, Messiaen had an arguably more universal – or, 'catholic' – soundscape from which to draw musical materials. This difference was profound. In retrospect, both approaches to musical composition might be dubbed 'authentically Catholic', but Lourié's music is rarely identified as such today.

Ressourcement and the fate of Pre-Vatican II Catholic music

The lasting impact of Messiaen's rejection of Neo-Thomism requires a closer look at theological changes taking place in European Catholicism – especially in France – in the 1930s and 1940s. Since 1879, the year of Pope Leo XIII's important encyclical *Aeterni Patris*, Neo-Thomism had been the dominant strand of Catholic

---

[39]   For example, at the first concert of La Jeune France (3 June 1936), he said, 'Emotional sincerity, put at the service of the dogmas of the Catholic faith expressed through a new musical language – or at the very least an attempt to achieve this. Such is the programme of Olivier Messiaen which he puts into practice in the *Hymne au Saint-Sacrement*, in *Les Offrandes oubliées*'. Quoted in Hill and Simeone, *Messiaen*, p. 62.

[40]   Olivier Messiaen, *The Technique of My Musical Language*, trans. John Satterfield (Paris: Leduc, 1956 [1944]), vol. 1, p. 13.

[41]   See his analysis of 'La Vierge et l'Enfant' from *La Nativité du Seigneur* (1935) in Messiaen, *The Technique of My Musical Language*, vol. 2, p. 16.

Example 5.4   Olivier Messiaen: *Poèmes pour Mi*, 'Les deux guerriers', bars 1–6

theology and the only official method taught in seminaries; non-practitioners faced official censure.[42] Gradually, though, Neo-Thomism was increasingly under attack along two specific fronts.[43] First, critics of Neo-Thomism argued against the historical validity of the approach, questioning whether contemporary Neo-Thomism authentically reflected what Thomas actually wrote, and second, they tried to determine if Aquinas's metaphysical system and method of argumentation were capable of accurately accounting for lived experience. Despite these attacks, Maritain and the powerful Roman Dominican, Fr. Réginald Garrigou-Lagrange, insisted on the universal applicability of Aquinas's thought. Maritain's famous expression, 'Vae mihi si non Thomistizavero' [Woe to me if I do not Thomistize], neatly sums up this attitude.[44] Other theologians such as Henri de Lubac and Hans Urs von Balthasar argued for a return to the Bible and the Church Fathers as sources for theology, and in order to apply these sources to the present day [*aggiornamento*], they also engaged with a wide variety of modern philosophical

---

[42]   José Pereira, 'Thomism and the Magisterium: From *Aeterni Patris* to *Veritatis splendor*', *Logos: A Journal of Catholic Thought and Culture* 5, no. 3 (2002): 149–155.

[43]   For a good introduction to these debates, see Marcellino D'Ambrosio, '*Ressourcement* Theology, *Aggiornamento*, and the Hermeneutics of Tradition', *Communio* 18, no. 4 (1991): 530–555.

[44]   Jacques Maritain, *Le Docteur Angelique*, in Jacques et Raïssa Maritai, *Œuvres complètes*, vol. 4, *Œuvres de Jacques Maritain, 1929–1932* (Fribourg: Editions Universitaires; Paris: Editions Saint-Paul, 1983 [1930]), p. 21.

approaches, especially German idealism, phenomenology and existentialism. Garrigou-Lagrange snidely called this approach, 'La nouvelle théologie', but it is more positively known as *ressourcement*.[45]

The historical critique of the official Neo-Thomism expounded by Garrigou-Lagrange took two basic forms: a burgeoning interest in textual criticism and a renaissance of patristics, the study of the Church Fathers. Though not a theologian, the philosopher and mediaevalist Etienne Gilson is most closely identified with the former approach, which influenced a generation of thinkers.[46] Unlike Gilson, theologians tended much more heavily towards the latter approach. For example, two French Jesuits, Jean Daniélou and Henri de Lubac, oversaw the publication of a series of patristic writings, which they called *Sources Chrétiennes*, whose goal was 'to provide a number of readers a direct access to these "sources," always overflowing with spiritual life and theological doctrine, which are the Fathers of the Church'.[47] Blending the two approaches, the French Dominican Marie-Dominique Chenu argued that in order to understand Aquinas, one must first explore his intellectual sources, primarily the Church Fathers.[48] The Neo-Thomist responses to *Sources Chrétiennes* and Chenu were equally damning. Dominican Marie-Michel Labourdette thought the *Sources* series had a 'hidden agenda' of permanently directing theological inquiry away from Aquinas.[49] Chenu fared worse: even before the publication of his treatise, the head of the Dominican Order removed Chenu from his post as Regent of Le Saulchoir, the French Dominican college where he had been teaching for nearly a decade.[50]

The return to historical sources brought on by *ressourcement* theologians involved much more than simple excavation; in fact, further study of the Bible and the Church Fathers spurred a radical re-orientation of theological methods toward

---

[45]   Garrigou-Lagrange did not coin the term, but he made it famous. See D'Ambrosio, '*Ressourcement* Theology', p. 531.

[46]   For an approachable example, see Etienne Gilson, 'Doctrinal History and Its Interpretation', *Speculum: A Journal of Mediaeval Studies* 24, no. 4 (1949): 483–492. On his influence, see Gerald McCool, *The Neo-Thomists*, 146–148.

[47]   Preface to Gregory of Nyssa, *Contemplation sur la vie de Moïse*, trans. Jean Daniélou (Paris: Cerf, 1942), p. 8, quoted in D'Ambrosio, '*Ressourcement* Theology', 541.

[48]   Marie-Dominique Chenu, *Introduction á l'étude de S. Thomas d'Aquin* (Paris: Vrin, 1950). See Fergus Kerr, *Twentieth-Century Catholic Theologians: From Neoscholasticism to Nuptial Mysticism* (Malden, MA: Blackwell Publishing, 2007), pp. 26–29.

[49]   Marie-Michel Labourdette, 'La théologie et ses sources', *Revue Thomiste* 46, no. 2 (1946): 353–371. See Brian Daley, 'The *Nouvelle Théologie* and the Patristic Revival: Sources, Symbols, and the Science of Theology', *International Journal of Systematic Theology* 7, no. 4 (2005): 367; and Aidan Nichols, 'Thomism and the Nouvelle Théologie', *The Thomist* 64, no. 1 (2000): 3–4.

[50]   Kerr, *Twentieth-Century Theologians*, 18–20.

experience and the subject.[51] Two German theologians, Romano Guardini and Hans Urs von Balthasar, led the way. In his *Welt und Person* (1939), for example, Guardini developed a novel theory of the person that he claims originated in the Bible and early Christian writings but that also drew inspiration from the writings of his contemporaries Martin Buber, Rudolf Otto, and the older Wilhelm Dilthey.[52] Balthasar rejected systematics altogether and believed theologians should start afresh from the original source of Christian revelation: Jesus Christ.[53] In several of his major works, he developed a Christo-centric theology that parried possible objections from a wide array of philosophical traditions, including German idealism and existentialism, which he held in high esteem even though they failed to answer fundamental questions about human reality. His approach, like Guardini's, contrasts sharply with the Neo-Thomist theologians, who wanted to continue using the scholastic method of repetitious definitions and proofs. In their formulation, divine revelation, handed down through tradition, is objective; the theologian's job is to clarify it systematically. Balthasar, Guardini, de Lubac and others focused instead on the dialectical relationship between the objective universality of divine revelation and one's personal response to it – a decidedly 'subjective' approach. The practitioners of *la nouvelle théologie* diversified and assimilated disparate conceptual sources into what was often a piecemeal exposition of fundamental doctrines.

The parallels between Messiaen's aesthetic attitude of the 1930s, which he maintained with modification throughout his career, and the theological attitudes of the *ressourcement* theologians are clear. Just as de Lubac, Balthasar and their circles drifted away from scholasticism in favour of a more direct approach to questions about the fundamental reality of Christian revelation, Messiaen used his highly unconventional emotionalism to illustrate the fundamental doctrines of the Church such as Christ's birth (*La Nativité du Seigneur*), sin and penitence (*Les Offrandes oubliées*), Christ's ascension into Heaven (*L'Ascension*), and the Sacrament of Marriage (*Poèmes pour Mi*, *Chants de terre et de ciel*). Also, like the *ressourcement* theologians, Messiaen created an eclectic style based on a wide array of sources. He absorbed all of these musical elements into a personal style that he appropriately called '*my* musical language'. Even Messiaen's continued

---

[51]   For a brief overview of the role of experience in official Church teaching, see Alessandro Maggiolini, 'Magisterial Teaching on Experience in the Twentieth Century: From the Modernist Crisis to the Second Vatican Council', *Communio* 23, no. 2 (1996): 225–243.

[52]   Robert A. Krieg, *Romano Guardini: A Precursor of Vatican II* (Notre Dame, IN: University of Notre Dame Press, 1997), pp. 34–35.

[53]   'To honor the tradition does not excuse one from the obligation of beginning everything from the beginning each time, not with Augustine or Thomas or Newman, but with Christ'. Hans Urs von Balthasar, *Razing the Bastions: On the Church in This Age*, trans. Brian McNeil (San Francisco: Ignatius Press, 1993 [1952]), p. 34.

interest in Eastern musical tradition, though it began much earlier, mirrored de Lubac's deep foray into certain aspects of Buddhism taken during the 1950s.[54]

Messiaen also faced criticism similar to that experienced by the *ressourcement* theologians. At times he defended his unique eclecticism and ultramodernism against certain detractors who probably struggled to categorize his novel style. He complained, 'Every subject can be a religious one on condition that it is viewed through the eye of one who believes. [...] As for those who moan about my so-called dissonances, I say to them quite simply that I am not dissonant: they should wash their ears out!'[55] Henri de Lubac in particular endured similar opposition from the established Neo-Thomists, who thought he was essentially dispensing with tradition in favour of modern understandings of Church doctrine. According to Garrigou-Langrange and his allies, without recourse to the supposedly objective methods of Thomism, theology would become 'relative', a harsh term of disparagement.[56] The *ressourcement* theologians however, were not relativists; each used new languages to serve tradition, which encompassed more than the systematic theology of the scholastics. By rejecting the impersonal and objective tendencies of Neo-Thomism and embracing a personal response to revelation, they were practising '*aggiornamento* through *ressourcement*'. Messiaen achieved the same result: his music embodied modern sensibilities, as other essays in this volume attest, while drawing on as wide an array of sounds as anyone of his generation.

At the Second Vatican Council, the *ressourcement* theologians and a related group, the transcendental Thomists led by Karl Rahner, won the theological battle against Neo-Thomism. The conciliar documents' emphasis on a personal response to divine grace reflects this victory.[57] The Council thus assured a secure position in Catholic thought for the theological trajectory begun by de Lubac, Balthasar, Rahner, and others. No one embodied the shift in theological method more than Karol Wojtyła, the Polish philosopher and theologian who became Pope John Paul II in 1978. Although he acknowledged the value and importance of Thomism, he did not believe in its primacy; his own approach to theology and philosophy blended classical metaphysics with the phenomenology of Max Scheler in an attempt to integrate the subjective and objective dimensions of the human person. On two separate occasions later in his papacy, he officially removed Thomism as

---

[54]   Although this connection is tenuous, it demonstrates how widely the pair searched for inspiration. Hans Urs von Balthasar, *The Theology of Henri de Lubac: An Overview*, trans. by Joseph Fessio and Michael M. Waldstein (San Francisco: Ignatius Press, 1991 [1976]), pp. 54–59.

[55]   Olivier Messiaen, 'Autour d'une parution', *Le Monde musical* (30 April 1939): 126, quoted in Hill and Simeone, *Messiaen*, p. 82.

[56]   Nichols, 'Thomism and the Nouvelle Théologie', pp. 3–4.

[57]   The evidence is overwhelming. For a group of concise interpretations, see David Schultenover, ed., *Vatican II: Did Anything Happen?* (New York: Continuum, 2007).

the sole theological and philosophical approach available to Catholic teachers.[58] Neo-Thomism's official reign, which began with *Aeterni Patris* in 1879, had effectively come to a close, at least for the present.

The defeat of the Neo-Thomists not only effectively silenced them, but also altered the historical reception of the original inter-war Neo-Thomists, in theology as well as in music. Throughout the period, Maritain, Lourié and their friends were a dominant force within the Parisian musical world, and they did not hide the central source of their inspiration, Catholic culture. Their ideas formed the basis of important critical discussions and shaped the directions that neo-classicism would take. In effect, to be Catholic meant sharing this group's beliefs about art. As a philosopher and layman, Maritain served as a bridge between the musicians' modern sensibilities and official Church theology. Fr. Réginald Garrigou-Lagrange, Maritain's mentor before the Second World War, was one of the fiercest opponents of *ressourcement* theology. Today, after the diminution of Neo-Thomist thought in Catholic circles, its practitioners such as Maritain and Garrigou-Lagrange are often seen as inhibitors of the new, fresh and young *ressourcement* theologians.[59] Lourié, who appears never to have embraced the changes taking place in Catholicism, unfortunately became a victim of circumstance, and he is now largely forgotten as a composer, much less a specifically Catholic composer. Messiaen, who sidestepped Maritain's brand of Catholic thinking, became all the more successful because he did so. His interest in developing a personal musical style as a direct response to God continues and will continue to resonate with contemporary Catholic thought as the theology underlying the Second Vatican Council steadily flourishes.

---

[58]   John Paul II, *Veritatis Splendor* (6 August 1993), §29; and John Paul II, *Fides et Ratio* (15 September 1998), §49. For a fuller discussion of these passages, see Pereira, 'Thomism and the Magisterium', 176–178; and Kerr, *Twentieth-Century Catholic Theologians*, pp. 169–170.

[59]   This is especially unfortunate in Maritain's case, because he did so much to reconcile authentic Catholic teachings with contemporary life.

Chapter 6
Messiaen and Aquinas

Vincent P. Benitez

I read many theologians; I always return to Saint Thomas Aquinas, the most modern and richest of them all.

– Olivier Messiaen[1]

From an early age, Olivier Messiaen was attracted to the writings of Saint Thomas Aquinas (*c.* 1225–74). Interested in theology as a teenager, Messiaen studied Aquinas's *Summa Theologiae* (1266–73), a practical manual of Christian theology summarizing doctrinal matters in a systematic and comprehensive manner. Throughout his life, Messiaen meditated upon the topics of the *Summa*. In an interview with Brigitte Massin, he expressed his admiration for the *Summa*'s unchanging organization of a thesis, followed by a series of arguments on each side of the issue, followed by a consideration of the thesis's content.[2]

In his monumental *Summa*, which was left unfinished at the time of his death, Aquinas focused on God and His essence, moral theology, and Christ and the benefits He conferred upon humankind.[3] These topics are divided into subtopics that Aquinas referred to as 'questions', which in turn are divided into questions that he referred to as 'articles'. Composing the foundation of the *Summa*, these nearly 3000 articles are the invariable elements mentioned in Messiaen's interviews with Massin. They typify the teaching activity of the *disputatio* [disputation] in which a theology master, while recognizing several plausible answers to a question, defended one against credible alternatives in the classroom. Thus, the *Summa* is organized in the following manner: (1) Aquinas would pose a question; (2) offer a series of arguments that seemingly provided correct answers to the question in a section entitled *Videtur* [It seems that]; (3) present a series of counter-arguments to the question in a section entitled *Sed contra* [On the other hand]; (4) provide what he considered to be the correct answers to the question in a section entitled

---

[1]   Jean-Christophe Marti, 'Entretiens avec Olivier Messiaen', in *Saint François d'Assise, L'Avant-Scène Opéra, Saint François d'Assise: Messiaen, Special Bilingual Program Book of the Salzburg Festival* (Paris: L'Avant-Scène Opéra, Opéra d'aujourd'hui, no. 4, 1992), 8–18. All translations are mine unless noted otherwise.

[2]   Brigitte Massin, *Olivier Messiaen: une poétique du merveilleux* (Aix-en-Provence: Éditions Alinéa, 1989), pp. 32, 178.

[3]   Throughout this essay, I employ masculine pronouns for God, in keeping with Aquinas's Christian theology.

Responsio [Reply]; and (5) close each question by disproving the arguments of the *Videtur* section.

Messiaen developed a compositional aesthetic steeped in Thomistic thought, as evinced by his remarks in interviews with Bernard Gavoty and Claude Samuel:

> God for me is manifest, and my conception of sacred music derives from this conviction. God being present in all things, music dealing with theological subjects can and must be extremely varied. The Catholic religion is a real fairy-story – with this difference, it is all true. I have therefore, in the words of Ernest Hello, tried to produce 'a music that touches all things without ceasing to touch God'. (Interview with Gavoty)[4]

> The first idea I wanted to express [as a musician], the most important, is the existence of the truths of the Catholic faith. [...] The illumination of the theological truths of the Catholic faith is the first aspect of my work, the noblest, and no doubt the most useful and most valuable – perhaps the only one I won't regret at the hour of my death. (Interview with Samuel)[5]

Messiaen's statement that God is present in all things, and his desire to touch all things without ceasing to touch God through his music, is derived from Aquinas's beliefs on how God is revealed through natural reason.[6] As stated in the *Summa*, observing creation enables one to deduce the existence of God and some of His divine qualities. Since God is the creator of the universe, the first cause of all things, He is present in His creation, indeed, in a rather intimate way. Human beings can therefore acquire knowledge of God through the observation of the created order. Aquinas also argued that knowledge of God resulting from natural reason is a preamble to faith, but not faith itself. Thus, Messiaen's conception of music in which he attempted to depict God as manifest in the natural world through a highly varied, theologically oriented music, illuminating the truths of his Catholic faith in the process, is aligned with Aquinas's teachings.

This essay will examine the various ways in which Aquinas's *Summa Theologiae* influenced the compositional aesthetics of Messiaen. First, it will consider Aquinas's theological ideas, particularly his synthesis of faith and reason, and their place in the Roman Catholic Church. The essay will then turn to the cultural milieu in which Messiaen grew up, which found the Catholic Church in France turning to Thomistic thought in order to oppose Modernism. Finally, it will

---

[4]   Bernard Gavoty, 'Who Are You Olivier Messiaen?', *Tempo* 58 (Summer 1961): 34.

[5]   Olivier Messiaen, *Olivier Messiaen: Music and Color: Conversations with Claude Samuel*, trans. E. Thomas Glasow (Portland, OR: Amadeus Press, 1994), pp. 20–21.

[6]   Saint Thomas Aquinas, *Summa Theologiae*, Part I, q. 2 ('Whether there is God'), art. 2 ('Can it be made evident?'); *Summa Theologiae*, Latin text, English translation, introduction, notes, appendices, and glossaries, 60 vols. (New York: Blackfriars–McGraw Hill, 1964), vol. 2, pp. 8–11.

explore how Aquinas inspired Messiaen's work as a composer by looking at pieces such as 'Psalmodie de l'Ubiquité par amour' from the *Trois petites Liturgies de la Présence Divine* (1943–44), selected movements from *La Transfiguration de Notre-Seigneur Jésus-Christ* (1965–69), *Méditations sur le mystère de la Sainte Trinité* (1969), and scenes 5 and 8 of *Saint François d'Assise* (1975–83).

Aquinas and his theology

The *Summa Theologiae* of Aquinas has been recognized as the most authoritative theological work for several centuries in the Catholic Church. In his effort to reconcile faith with reason, Aquinas synthesized the works of Aristotle and other classic authors – Christian, Greek, Islamic, and Jewish – in the *Summa*, bringing them all into line with Catholic doctrine. The accomplishment was immense, to say the least.[7]

Despite being accused of corrupting Christian theology with pagan thought by some thirteenth-century contemporaries, Aquinas, and his *Summa*, grew in favour with the Catholic Church. At the Council of Trent (1545–63), the *Summa* was to be found upon the altar alongside the Bible and the Decretals (a collection of papal rulings).[8] Saint Ignatius of Loyola (*c*. 1491–1556), the founder of the Society of Jesus, made the study of Aquinas mandatory for members of the Jesuit order.[9] In 1567, Pope Pius V declared Aquinas an Angelic Doctor of the Catholic Church.[10]

After suffering a decline in study during the seventeenth and eighteenth centuries, Thomistic thought experienced renewed interest beginning in the second half of the nineteenth century. Taking up the perennial theme of the relation between faith and reason in his 1879 encyclical *Aeterni Patris*, Pope Leo XIII recalled the Church to Aquinas by calling for a revival of the study of his works.[11] Viewing Thomistic thought as the epitome of Christian philosophy in which both

---

[7]   According to Will Durant, 'Improving upon the custom of his time, [Aquinas] made explicit acknowledgements of his intellectual borrowings [in his writings]. He quotes Avicenna, al-Ghazali, Averroës, Isaac Israeli, Ibn Gabirol, and Maimonides; obviously no student can understand the Scholastic philosophy of the thirteenth century without considering its [Muslim] and Jewish antecedents.' See Will Durant, *The Age of Faith: A History of Medieval Civilization – Christian, Islamic, and Judaic – from Constantine to Dante: A.D. 325–1300*, vol. 4, *The Story of Civilization* (New York: MJF Books, 1950), pp. 963–964.

[8]   Ibid., pp. 977–978.

[9]   Brian Davies, *The Thought of Thomas Aquinas* (Oxford: Clarendon Press, 1993), p. 16.

[10]   *Catholic Encyclopedia: St. Thomas Aquinas*, available online at <www.newadvent. org/cathen/14663b.htm> (accessed 7 March 2007).

[11]   Pope Leo XIII, 'Aeterni Patris', in *The Papal Encyclicals*, comp. Claudia Carlen Ihm, vol. 2, *The Papal Encyclicals: 1878–1903* (Raleigh, NC: The Pierian Press, 1990), pp. 17–27.

revelation and reality were in accord, Pope Leo recommended that it form the foundation of instruction in Catholic schools in order to combat the vagaries of modern philosophy since Descartes. This revival of Thomism, which as a by-product spurred interest in the Middle Ages on the part of Catholics, continued into the twentieth century. According to theologian and author Ralph McInerny, 'Chairs of Thomistic studies were founded, [...] societies were formed, journals [begun], [... and the] critical edition of the works of Thomas[,] which is called the Leonine after its patron Leo XIII[,] was inaugurated [...]'.[12] Finally, despite losing ground to other philosophies in Catholic intellectual circles of the 1960s, such as phenomenology, the enduring originality of Thomistic thought was reaffirmed by Pope John Paul II in his 1998 encyclical *Fides et Ratio*.[13]

Aquinas was the first Christian theologian to effect a synthesis of faith and reason when grappling with the reality of God. In order to better understand his harmonization of Greek and Christian thought, let us examine the impact Aristotle had, along with his Muslim and Jewish commentators, on Latin Christendom during Aquinas's lifetime. We shall then consider Aquinas's theological viewpoints vis-à-vis his quarrel with the Latin Averroists, Christian followers of the Islamic Aristotelian, Averroës.[14]

The availability of Aristotle's works in Latin translation, such as the *Physics* and *Metaphysics*, presented a major challenge to Christianity in the thirteenth century. Like their Muslim counterparts in the ninth century, and their Jewish counterparts in Spain in the twelfth century, Christian theologians felt impelled to reconcile Greek philosophy with their sacred doctrines. Besides being exposed to Aristotle and the works of other Greek authors, Latin Christianity likewise became acquainted with Muslim and Jewish philosophers, such as al-Kindi, al-Farabi, al-Ghazali, Avicenna, Ibn Gabirol, Averroës and Maimonides. As Will Durant writes: 'the rage for the new philosophy was an intellectual fever that could hardly be controlled. The Church [...] deployed her forces to surround and absorb the invaders. Her loyal monks studied this amazing Greek [Aristotle] who had upset three religions'[15]

The partitioning of Christian intellectual life in the thirteenth century into what was 'known' and what was 'believed' had become rather pronounced. Some Christians compartmentalized their thought, following Aristotle while

---

[12]   Ralph McInerny, ed. and trans., with an introduction and notes, *Thomas Aquinas: Selected Writings* (London: Penguin Books, 1998), p. xxvii.

[13]   Pope John Paul II, *Fides et Ratio*, available online at <www.vatican.va/holy_father/john_paul_ii/encyclicals/documents/hf_jp-ii_enc_15101998_fides-et-ratio_en.html> (accessed 20 May 2008).

[14]   Known as the Commentator, Averroës (*c*. 1126 – *c*. 1198), or Ibn-Rushd, was a significant figure in Islamic philosophy. He was a doctor, philosopher and scientist who, while writing on varied topics, was best known in Christian Europe for his commentaries on Aristotle.

[15]   Durant, *The Age of Faith*, pp. 954–955.

doing philosophy on the one hand, and espousing the Nicene Creed while engaged in theology on the other, suggesting that they accepted contradictories as simultaneously true.[16] This dichotomy of thought contributed to a noticeable turn from orthodoxy, with some Christians questioning certain dogmas of their faith. Aquinas attempted to fuse the 'known' and 'believed', determining that the only way to reconcile the two was to find truth in both.

Aquinas was motivated to reconcile faith and reason because of his dispute with the Latin Averroists. They adopted certain doctrines of Averroës derived from his commentaries on Aristotle, such as the world being co-eternal with God; or that natural law, not God, controlled the world; or that all humans have but one soul. Coalescing around the Belgian Siger de Brabant, a professor of philosophy at the University of Paris, the Latin Averroists also claimed that knowledge derived from the senses was independent of faith.[17] In the words of the Aquinas biographer G. K. Chesterton, they were advocating that:

> [the] Church must be right theologically, but [...] wrong scientifically. There are two truths; the truth of the supernatural world, and the truth of the natural world, which contradicts the supernatural world. While we are being naturalists, we can suppose that Christianity is all nonsense; but then, when we remember that we are Christians, we must admit that Christianity is true even if it is nonsense. In other words, [the Latin Averroists] split the human head in two [...] and declared that a man has two minds, with one of which he must entirely believe and with the other may utterly disbelieve. To many this would at least seem like a parody of Thomism. As a fact, it was the assassination of Thomism. It was not two ways of finding the same truth; it was an untruthful way of pretending that there are two truths. And it is extraordinarily interesting to note that this is the one occasion when the Dumb Ox [Aquinas] really came out like a wild bull.[18]

And like a wild bull, he did.[19] Aquinas argued against this position, maintaining that there was only one truth rooted in God. This truth was to be approached by

---

[16]   McInerny, *Thomas Aquinas: Selected Writings*, p. xxii.

[17]   A recognized leader of the Latin Averroists, Siger de Brabant (*c.* 1240–*c.* 1281–84) was a leading proponent of radical Aristotelianism. He taught a strict version of Aristotelian philosophy with no attempt to reconcile it with Christian theology, making him susceptible to the accusation that he was teaching contradictory truths. Ironically, Siger de Brabant, later in life, aligned himself increasingly with Thomistic precepts.

[18]   G. K. Chesterton, *Saint Thomas Aquinas: 'The Dumb Ox'* (New York: Image Books/Doubleday, 1956), p. 69. I use Chesterton's references to Siger de Brabant in this paragraph as representing Latin Averroists in general.

[19]   In a short polemical essay written in 1270 entitled *De unitate intellectus contra Averroistas*, Aquinas, believing in the complementarity of Aristotle with the Christian faith, argued specifically against what he believed to be Averroës' incorrect interpretations of Aristotle. See Ralph McInerny, *Aquinas Against the Averroists: On There Being Only One*

both faith and reason. Nothing discovered in nature could contradict faith, and nothing deduced from faith could contradict nature. Some truths, such as the Holy Trinity or the Incarnation, could only be known through faith, for they are beyond the scope of human understanding. For Aquinas, these are the *mysteries of faith*, emerging from divine revelation. Other truths, such as the composition of material things, could only be known through reason, for all knowledge emerges from the senses, which is made intelligible by the power of reasoning, while still other truths, such as the existence of God, are made known through both faith and reason. For Aquinas, these are the *preambles of faith*, or what faith presupposes, because they are true apart from revelation.

In his dispute with the Latin Averroists, Aquinas showed himself to be 'every bit as much the defender of Aristotle against misreading as he [was] a defender of the Christian faith'.[20] He incorporated Aristotelian thought in his philosophy and theology to a substantial degree, harmonizing the Greek philosopher's ideas with Christianity.[21] The Aristotelian assumption of intellectual knowledge arising from the senses, for example, dominated Aquinas's work. God makes Himself known to humankind through His creation. It is then through the inspiration of the Bible, followed by Christ Himself, that knowledge of God moves to the less obvious in the sensible world to what lies beyond this life. But in the final analysis, the trajectory of one's knowledge of God begins with sense perception.

In claiming knowledge of God's existence in the *Summa Theologiae*, Aquinas argued that one should move from the visible world of humanity to the invisible world of God, taking as his cue Romans 1:20: 'Ever since God created the world his everlasting power and deity – however invisible – have been there for the mind to see in the things he has made.'[22] As philosopher Brian Davies characterizes Aquinas's perspective: 'We do not start with a knowledge of God. We begin as knowing the world in which we live. So we will have to be content with reasoning to God's existence from that.'[23]

Intellect, Purdue University Series in the History of Philosophy, ed. Arion Kelkel et al. (West Lafayette, IN: Purdue University Press, 1993).

[20]   McInerny, *Thomas Aquinas: Selected Writings*, p. xxi.

[21]   As author and philosopher Brian Davies (*The Thought of Thomas Aquinas*, p. 16) observes, 'it would be wrong to say [...] that Aquinas is just an Aristotelian. Even when he supports Aristotle, the emphasis is not: "Aristotle said it, so it must be true." His usual line is: "It is true and Aristotle made the point well." [...] [A]s well as being influenced by Aristotle, [Aquinas] was also indebted to elements in the thought of Plato and to later writers of a Platonic caste of mind (Neoplatonists).'

[22]   *The Jerusalem Bible: Reader's Edition with Abridged Introductions and Notes* (New York: Doubleday, 2000).

[23]   Davies, *The Thought of Thomas Aquinas*, p. 25.

Thus in the *Summa*, Aquinas provided five rational proofs for the existence of God, his so-called 'Five Ways' [*Quinque viae*].[24] These proofs comprise arguments derived from: (1) change or motion – there must be a first cause behind the change or motion, without the first cause itself being changed or moved; (2) causation – there must be a first cause behind all other causes; (3) possibility and actuality – the possible, which may but need not be, derives its existence from the actual, which not only must be but also implies a being that is pure actuality; (4) the gradation of observable virtue – there must be something perfectly moral that is the source of the imperfect virtues found in the world; and (5) the goal-directed quality of nature – everything in nature is orderly, suggesting that it is governed by an intelligent being.

Aquinas believed that although we can ascertain God's existence, we cannot know what God is (i.e. His nature). Since He is not an object of sense perception, God defies comprehension; He is beyond definition or location in a genus, species, or class. Yet Aquinas posits that we can still get an idea of God's nature by considering the ways in which He does not exist. Thus, Aquinas proposes five qualities associated with God: (1) God is simple, without compositeness, such as matter and form; (2) God is perfect; (3) God is infinite, without limit; (4) God is immutable; and (5) God is one, without diversification within Himself.

For Aquinas, because God is existence itself, God must be in all things, and in the most intimate manner. Therefore, every existing thing brings us face to face with God. Human beings live in a world pervaded by God, hence the world is not only good but also holy. God leads humankind to Him by means of sense perception. Through things they can touch and ideas they can comprehend, human beings develop the spiritual awareness that can draw them closer to God.

Aquinas believed that humanity's ultimate goal was union with God, the source of eternal happiness and salvation.[25] This belief has certain ramifications for Aquinas, as noted by scholars Robert Pasnau and Christopher Shields:

> [S]ince God is the highest and first cause, the highest and best form of contemplation is our blessedness: it consists in grasping, insofar as we are able, God's essence, and it is a final culmination of our striving, something denied to us in this life but in some cases given after death. This is how and why Aquinas

---

[24]   Aquinas, *Summa Theologiae*, Part I, q. 2 ('Whether there is a God'), art. 3 ('Is there a God?'); (Blackfriars–McGraw Hill), vol. 2, pp. 12–19. Aquinas's arguments are indebted to Aristotle, Maimonides, Avicenna and Averroës. See Davies, *The Thought of Thomas Aquinas*, p. 26.

[25]   'There can be no complete and final happiness for us save in the vision of God.' See Aquinas, *Summa Theologiae*, Part I–II, q. 3 ('What happiness is'), art. 8 ('Is man's happiness the vision of God's very essence?'); (Blackfriars–McGraw Hill), vol. 16, pp. 84–85.

> can find himself in full agreement with the sentiment of I Corinthians 13:12:
> *Now we see through a glass, darkly, but then face to face.*[26]

While commenting upon ceremonial precepts associated with the Mosaic Law in the *Summa*, Aquinas suggested how human beings could get closer to God, move from the visible to the invisible, *see* through the dim mirror, but then face to face: through the light of faith and grace, conveyed through the language of poetry: 'Just as human reason fails to grasp the import of poetical utterance on account of its deficiency in truth, neither can it grasp divine things perfectly on account of their superabundance of truth; and therefore in both cases there is need of representation by sensible figures'.[27]

'Seeing' God does not mean that one 'comprehends' God. To comprehend something implies that one knows it perfectly, and as we have already discussed, this is not possible with God in this life, for the truth of God lies beyond human reason. Human beings grasp the divine essence in proportion to the light of faith and grace they receive. When expressed through poetical utterance, and despite any deficiencies in its transmission, this vision of God transcends human reason. In the final analysis, whether seeing or comprehending, the material, sensible and visible serve as signs for the spiritual, intellectual and invisible.

To summarize: Aquinas argues that the search for God is a fulfilment of the revelation that God has given to humankind, which is concerned with, among other things, an invisible world accessible only through faith.

The *renouveau catholique* in France

Messiaen grew up during the post-war *renouveau catholique* in France, the Catholic revival associated with the Church's crusade against modernism. In *Jazz Age Catholicism*, Stephen Schloesser defines the *renouveau* as a reconceptualization of Catholicism by 'certain cultural and intellectual elites not only as being thoroughly compatible with "modernity," but even more emphatically, as constituting the truest expression of "modernity." [The Church's] eternal truths were capable of infinite adaptation to ever-changing circumstances.'[28] In order to make this reconceptualization possible, Catholic elites appropriated three traditional Catholic ideas: (1) hylomorphism – a philosophical doctrine that describes reality in terms

---

[26]   Robert Pasnau and Christopher Shields, *The Philosophy of Aquinas*, The Westview Histories of Philosophy Series, ed. Alan D. Code et al. (Boulder, CO: Westview Press, 2004), pp. 214–215.

[27]   Aquinas, *Summa Theologiae*, Part I–II, q. 101 (The ceremonial precepts in themselves), art. 2 (Are the ceremonial precepts figurative?); (Blackfriars–McGraw Hill), vol. 29, pp. 118–121.

[28]   Stephen Schloesser, *Jazz Age Catholicism: Mystic Modernism in Postwar Paris, 1919–1933* (Toronto: University of Toronto Press, 2005), p. 5.

of inchoate matter and the causal force that defines it; (2) sacramentalism – a theological doctrine that considers created things as outward signs of invisible realities; and (3) transubstantiation – a theological doctrine that argues for the divine presence of Christ in the eucharistic bread and wine offered at Mass.[29]

This recasting of Catholicism is rooted in Aquinas's harmonization of faith and reason as articulated in the *Summa*. This is evident in Schloesser's characterization of hylomorphism, sacramentalism and transubstantiation as advancing

> a vision of the world as a dialectical composite of two interpenetrating planes of reality: seen and unseen, created and uncreated, natural and supernatural. As such, they offer an alternative way of imagining relationships. Two entities – God and world, divinity and humanity, even […] Catholicism and culture – need not be seen as two extended bodies in competition with one another […].[30]

During the *renouveau catholique*, the Catholic avant-garde challenged the prevailing positivism/historicism of the Sorbonne, considered the cultural-intellectual opposite of Catholicism, by seeking to depict essential truths that lie beyond sense perception. In the late nineteenth century, the word 'modern' connoted a secular world that excluded belief in the supernatural, whereas the word 'Catholic' connoted a besieged religion that was competing with modern culture and thought. That changed in post-war France. The Catholic elite became dissatisfied with realist modes of representation, which left the world devoid of meaning and mystery. They recognized modernity's meaningless, tragic side as evinced by the unprecedented trauma of the First World War. Consequently, the Catholic elite re-imagined the relationship between religion and culture so that faith and fact, grace and the grotesque, or religion and realism (derived from nineteenth-century positivism) could stand side-by-side, without a hint of irreconcilability. In a word, they embraced modernity in order to supply meaning to the nihilistic world in which they lived.

As Robert Fallon observes: 'During the Renouveau [c]atholique, Thomism was important not only to theologians, but to all ranks of French Catholics'.[31] It is hence not surprising that a devout young Messiaen, growing up during the *renouveau catholique*, would read Aquinas's *Summa Theologiae* in 1923 or 1924, and probably *Art et scholastique* by Maritain in 1927.[32] The interest in Aquinas, along with the Middle Ages in general, on the part of French Catholics prompted their artists and intellectuals to create new works of art from old materials, such as Scholastic philosophy, Gothic stained-glass windows, or plainchant. This principle

---

[29]   Ibid., pp. 6–7.

[30]   Ibid., p. 6.

[31]   Robert Fallon, 'Messiaen's Mimesis: The Language and Culture of the Bird Styles' (PhD diss., University of California at Berkeley, 2005), p. 283.

[32]   Massin, *Olivier Messiaen*, pp. 31, 178; see also Fallon, 'Messiaen's Mimesis', p. 287.

of rebirth, or *palingenesis*, encouraged Catholic artists to experiment with novel techniques when composing, creating, or presenting their work.[33]

Deeply influenced by the theology of Aquinas, and perhaps motivated by the aesthetic of palingenesis, Messiaen strove to align his compositional aesthetics with Thomistic doctrines by attempting to 'touch all things without ceasing to touch God', and through his belief that 'a theologically oriented music should be extremely varied' Like Aquinas, Messiaen believed that God is simple and joyous, and that Christian truth could be found in unlikely sources. Thus, Messiaen would not hesitate to juxtapose birdsongs, Far-Eastern elements, Greek metric patterns, Indian *deçi-tâlas*, modes, serial techniques and tonal elements in his theology of sound, paralleling Aquinas's philosophical synthesis of Christian, Greek, Islamic and Jewish works and teachings.

Aquinas's influence on Messiaen's music

Trois petites Liturgies de la Présence Divine

The direct influence of Aquinas on Messiaen appears for the first time in the 'Psalmodie de l'Ubiquité par amour (Dieu présent en toutes choses ...)', the third movement of the *Trois petites Liturgies de la Présence Divine*.[34] Written by Messiaen, the movement's text is Thomistic in tone, dedicated to the God who is present in all things. The first stanza describes God as being wholly in all places and in every place, giving existence to all things, and, through the phrase the 'successive you is simultaneous', eternal because He lacks succession, being simultaneously whole.

In his conversations with Antoine Goléa, Messiaen characterized these references to divine ubiquity, particularly the 'successive you is simultaneous', which describes the difference between time and eternity, as based on Thomistic thought.[35] They stem

---

[33]   Schloesser, *Jazz Age Catholicism*, pp. 7, 135–136, 306, and 317.

[34]   Robert Fallon has noted Aquinas's indirect influence on Messiaen's *Les Corps glorieux* (1939). He argues that Messiaen drew from the *Summa*'s passages on the corporeal qualities of resurrected saints (*Summa Theologiae*, Part III, 'Treatise on the Resurrection', qq. 82–85, 93 (New York: Benziger Bros, 1947–48)) when writing pieces such as 'Subtilité des corps glorieux', 'Force et agilité des corps glorieux', and 'Joie et clarté des corps glorieux'. See 'Messiaen's Mimesis', pp. 255–256. Another instance of Aquinas's indirect influence on Messiaen can be seen in the composer's offertory motet, *O sacrum convivium*, for unaccompanied choir, composed in 1937. Scholars have attributed the piece's Latin text to Aquinas.

[35]   Antoine Goléa, *Rencontres avec Olivier Messiaen* (Paris–Genève: Slatkine, 1984), pp. 48–49.

from Aquinas's discussion of time and eternity in the *Summa Theologiae*.[36] For Aquinas, time is the measure of movement: it is continuous and implies successive change, that is, a 'before' and 'after' in a mutable thing as exemplified by a finite linear sequence of natural numbers. Eternity, on the other hand, is the measure of the permanence of God: it is immutable, indivisible and simultaneous. Indeed, for Aquinas, to recognize both the immutability and indivisibility of eternity is to affirm the existence of God.

To convey the liturgy's sense of divine ubiquity, Messiaen employs a colourful array of harmonic, rhythmic and timbral elements, suggesting the multicoloured effects of stained-glass windows. As shown in Example 6.1, the piano sounds the total chromatic in each measure through melodic sequences of a tritone followed by a perfect fourth.[37] The celesta descends chromatically in parallel perfect fourths before reversing direction in bar 5 (not shown). The chords in the strings provide the musical texture with a forceful rhythmic impetus. The movement's colourful instrumentation consists of a piano, celesta, vibraphone, maracas, Chinese cymbal, tam-tam, female choir, ondes Martenot and strings, with the piano, celesta and vibraphone suggesting the sounds, according to Messiaen, of a Balinese gamelan orchestra.[38]

Stained-glass imagery is an important aspect of Messiaen's compositional aesthetics, serving as a metaphor for his music's luminous and didactic qualities. But more important, because Messiaen believed that the light of stained-glass windows is beyond time and space, its musical suggestion in 'Psalmodie de l'Ubiquité par amour' is an appropriate depiction of God, who is beyond time and space, or, in a word, simultaneous.

La Transfiguration de Notre-Seigneur Jésus-Christ

Messiaen continues to display his high regard for Aquinas by setting several passages dealing with Christ's Transfiguration from the *Summa* (Part III, q. 45) in the second half of *La Transfiguration de Notre-Seigneur Jésus-Christ*.[39] To suggest

---

[36] Aquinas, *Summa Theologiae*, Part I, q. 10 ('The eternity of God'), art. 1 ('What is eternity?'), art. 2 ('Is God eternal?'); (Blackfriars–McGraw Hill), vol. 2, pp. 134–141.

[37] Because of practical considerations, Messiaen reverses the direction of the sequence so that the perfect fourth becomes a perfect fifth.

[38] Robert Sherlaw Johnson, *Messiaen* (Berkeley and Los Angeles: University of California Press, 1989), p. 66.

[39] Although the utilization of Aquinas's texts in *La Transfiguration* is clearly the next major instance of the theologian's influence on Messiaen after *Trois petites Liturgies*, we should mention his inclusion of a Thomistic text in the preface to *Et exspecto resurrectionem mortuorum* composed in 1964 (Paris: Leduc, 1966). Messiaen cites a passage ('Homme-Dieu ressuscité, il est à la fois cause prochaine et cause instrumentale de notre resurrection' [As God and Man rising again, He is all together the proximate and instrumental cause of our resurrection]), presumably from the *Summa Theologiae* (Part III, q. 56

Example 6.1 Olivier Messiaen: *Trois petites Liturgies*, 'Psalmodie de l'Ubiquité par amour'

the mystery of the Transfiguration in this oratorio, Messiaen employs a variety of Latin texts. Besides the *Summa*, he sets passages from the Bible (Genesis, Psalms, Wisdom of Solomon (considered deuterocanonical by Roman Catholics and apocryphal by Protestants), the Gospels According to Saints Matthew and Luke, the Epistle of Saint Paul to the Philippians, and the Epistle to the Hebrews); the Office for the Feast of the Transfiguration; and the Roman Catholic Missal. Throughout *La Transfiguration*, theological considerations govern musical ones.

La Transfiguration is a liturgical act of praise for the concert hall.[40] It comprises two *Septenaries*, or groups of seven pieces. The second *Septenary* is approximately twice as long as the first, suggesting that it is more substantial from both theological and musical perspectives than its counterpart. Both *Septenaries* exhibit the same formal structure. The first and fourth pieces are gospel narratives describing the Transfiguration. Each narrative is followed by two movements that comment upon the events and ideas outlined in each gospel story. A chorale closes each *Septenary*.

As observed by Christopher Dingle, the theological concepts of 'light' and 'affiliation' underscore the biblical narratives associated with the Transfiguration.[41] According to gospel accounts of the event, the face of Jesus shone like the sun, and His clothes were imbued with a brilliant white light.[42] Emanating from a bright cloud (representing the Holy Spirit) that overshadowed Jesus and His disciples, the voice of God declared Jesus to be His Son, urging Peter, James and John to listen to Him. The idea of light is obviously linked with the radiant glory of Jesus' transfigured body, which all believers will mirror at their resurrection. Flowing from God's declaration about Jesus is the idea of affiliation, which denotes not only an extension of Jesus' relationship with God to all believers, but also their divine potentiality. For Dingle, affiliation transcends light, because it reveals the 'divine potentiality in human existence' manifested by the light of the Transfiguration. For this writer, light and affiliation have somewhat different meanings, based on his reading of Aquinas.

Through the divine light of His Transfiguration, Christ revealed His essential deity to His disciples by giving them a preview of His glorified, resurrected body. Through His divine power, Christ transfigures the bodies of all believers at their

---

('The resurrection of Christ as cause'), art. 1 ('Whether Christ's resurrection is the cause of our own resurrection'); (Blackfriars–McGraw Hill), vol. 55, pp. 70–71), in order to reinforce the second movement's theme of Christ's resurrection taken from Romans 6:9 ('Le Christ, ressuscité des morts, ne meurts plus; la mort n'a plus sur lui d'empire' [Christ, being raised from the dead, dies no more; death has no longer dominion over Him]).

40   Other pieces by Messiaen that fit into this category include *Trois petites Liturgies*, *Des Canyons aux étoiles ...* (1971–74) (Paris: Leduc, 1978), and *Saint François d'Assise*.

41   See Christopher Philip Dingle, 'Olivier Messiaen: La Transfiguration de Notre-Seigneur Jésus-Christ: A Provisional Study', 2 vols. (MPhil thesis, University of Sheffield, 1994), pp. 16–17.

42   See Matthew 17:1–13, Mark 9:2–8, and Luke 9:28–36.

resurrection into copies of His own. For their part, believers affiliate themselves with Christ by first conforming themselves to His Passion and Death, and then by participating in the likeness of His Resurrection, in order for them to have eternal life. Accordingly, affiliation has more to do with the idea of restoration than divine potentiality in human existence. In other words, through the Incarnation and work of Christ, God has restored humanity unto Himself.

Messiaen uses Aquinas's *Summa Theologiae* in the second *Septenary* to probe the theological significance of 'light' and 'affiliation'. For example, in 'Perfecte conscius illius perfectae generationis', the ninth movement of *La Transfiguration*, Messiaen employs a passage from the *Summa* (Part III, q. 45, art. 4, reply) in order to describe how affiliation – that is, how human beings are restored to God – is achieved: by conforming to the image of Christ, which takes place imperfectly in the believer through the grace received from baptism, and perfectly through His divine glory, which is foreshadowed in the Transfiguration. Example 6.2 shows how Messiaen expresses part of Aquinas's text in 'Perfecte': through a solo baritone chanting the words on a single note.[43]

Example 6.2   Olivier Messiaen: *La Transfiguration*, 'Perfecte conscius illius perfectae generationis'

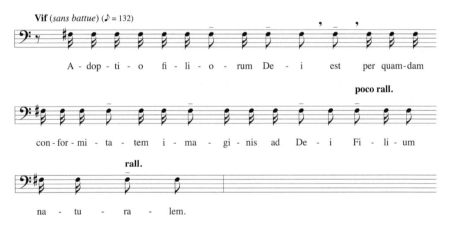

As Dingle points out, here and in *Terriblis est locus iste*, the work's 12th movement in which a text from the *Summa* is also used, are the 'only times in the entire oratorio that a solo voice is heard', pointing to the importance of Thomistic thought in Messiaen's theological outlook. In other words, for Dingle, Aquinas serves as preacher for Messiaen's concert hall liturgy.[44]

---

[43]   Later in the piece (beginning at Rehearsal 39), the solo baritone returns to recite more of Aquinas's text; this time, on a series of single notes (g–f–e♭).

[44]   Christopher Philip Dingle, '"La statue reste sur son piédestal": Messiaen's *La Transfiguration* and Vatican II', *Tempo* (April 2000): 11.

In 'Tota Trinitas apparuit', the 13th and penultimate movement of *La Transfiguration*, Messiaen uses Aquinas's *Summa Theologiae* one last time to conclude the work's final thoughts on the Transfiguration. The passage in question (Part III, q. 45, part. 4, reply, point 2) describes how the Holy Trinity is present in the bright cloud. Basses chant the beginning of the text on a melodic formula centred on g♯ (see Example 6.3). Sopranos then take over, singing a melisma on 'Tota Trinitas apparuit', emphasizing the words 'the whole Trinity appears', the main point of Aquinas's passage (see Example 6.4). Finally, a chorale ensues, with the chorus singing the last part of the text ('Pater in voce' [the Father through the voice], 'Filius in homine' [the Son through Man], 'Spiritus Sanctus in nube clara' [the Holy Spirit through the bright cloud]), interrupted twice by the song of the Bobolink (see Example 6.5).

Aquinas's imprint on Messiaen shows itself in yet another way in *La Transfiguration* by means of the wide array of compositional techniques employed. Messiaen's musical synthesis of varied elements in his works can be considered an analogue to Aquinas's philosophical synthesis of Christian and non-Christian writers. In essence, Messiaen is composing theologically oriented, highly varied music. Commentators have often criticized Messiaen for the so-called pagan and sensuous elements of his music, which, according to his critics, have no place in works that are supposed to convey the truths of Catholicism. But like Aquinas, Messiaen believed that God could be found in non-Christian cultures, especially in their musical aesthetics and techniques, and that the so-called sensuous elements found in his music, which often occur within static frameworks suggesting the suspension of time, were only reflective of the ecstatic love of an eternal God.

Let us return to 'Perfecte conscius illius perfectae generationis'. Table 6.1 is a formal outline of the first half of the piece. As reflected by this chart, the music contains a diversity of musical elements – North Indian music, Indian *deçi-tâlas*, colour chords enhanced by resonance elements, Tibetan music, birdsongs framed in Greek metric patterns, non-retrogradable rhythms, modes of limited transposition, and pitch and rhythmic ostinatos suggesting fourteenth-century isorhythm. No matter how eclectic the music may be, it 'works', pointing to Messiaen's creative compositional synthesis.

Méditations sur le mystère de la Sainte Trinité

In the *Méditations sur le mystère de la Sainte Trinité*, an organ work that followed *La Transfiguration*, Messiaen invented a new compositional technique known as the 'langage communicable' in order to spell out passages from Aquinas's *Summa theologiae* dealing with the Holy Trinity.[45] Using the German musical alphabet as a basis, Messiaen assigned a sound, pitch, and duration to each letter of the

---

[45]   The following explanation of the *langage communicable* is based on Messiaen's preface (*Le langage communicable*) to his *Méditations sur le mystère de la Sainte Trinité* (Paris: Leduc, 1973). For a detailed examination of the 'langage communicable', see

Example 6.3 Olivier Messiaen: *La Transfiguration*, 'Tota Trinitas apparuit' (basses)

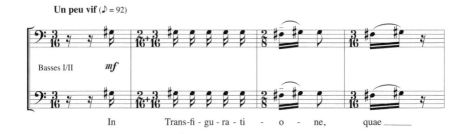

Example 6.4 Olivier Messiaen: *La Transfiguration*, 'Tota Trinitas apparuit'
              (sopranos)

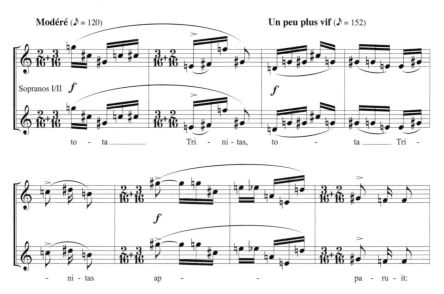

Example 6.5   Olivier Messiaen: *La Transfiguration*, 'Tota Trinitas apparuit' (chorus)

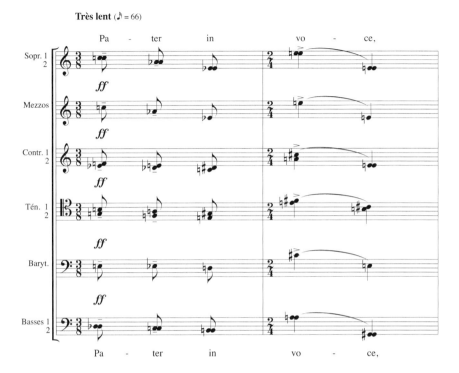

Roman alphabet, with pitch classes unifying different phonetic groups. In order to avoid wordiness, he omitted articles, pronouns, adverbs and prepositions, and spelled out nouns, adjectives, and verbs.[46] Messiaen employed a system of cases, as in the Latin declensions, via three musical formulas, representing, respectively, the genitive, ablative or locative; accusative or dative; and privative cases. The piece makes use of three leitmotifs, two of which depict the auxiliary verbs 'to be' and 'to have', while the other represents God through both forward and retrograde versions. Messiaen used the 'langage communicable' in the first, third

---

Andrew Shenton, *Olivier Messiaen's System of Signs: Notes Towards Understanding His Music* (Aldershot: Ashgate, 2008), pp. 69–158.

[46]   With respect to Messiaen's intention to avoid an 'accumulation of words' in the 'langage communicable', Andrew Shenton has pointed out that Messiaen's language actually includes 'some of the articles, pronouns, adverbs[,] and prepositions he claims to have omitted, and [that] he has not reduced the number of words significantly (the French translation of Aquinas in the *Méditations* uses 71 words, of which Messiaen sets 62)'. See Shenton, *Olivier Messiaen's System of Signs*, p. 94.

Table 6.1   Formal outline of first half of *La Transfiguration*, 'Perfecte conscius
illius perfectae generationis'

Segment	Musical materials	Rehearsal number
A	Sikkim music (*râgavardhana*/use of colour chords enhanced by resonance elements)	R1:1–2
D	Tibetan music (low B♭/C)	R1:3–5
C	Birdsong	R2:1–R4:8
A¹	Sikkim music (*laksmiça*/use of colour chords enhanced by resonance elements)	R5:1-3
B	Tibetan music (low B♭/C)	R5:4–6
C¹	Birdsong	R6:1–6
D	Descending gongs	R7:1–3
E	Unison passage sung by basses (two non-retrogradable rhythms; C/B♭–G♭)	R8:1–4
F	Multi-layered birdsongs/irrational rhythms	R9:1–5
G	Baritone solo (F♯–First lines of text by Saint Thomas Aquinas)	R10:1
C²	Extended birdsong	R10:2-R13:9
H	Unison choral passage (with modal harmonic support)	R14:1-R17:7
C³	Birdsongs	R18:1-R22:4
E¹	Harmonic/rhythmic cycles (suggestive of 14th-century isorhythm and the 'Liturgie de cristal' from the *Quatuor pour la fin du Temps*)	R23:1-R24:6
E²	Tutti unison (C/B♭)	R25:1-9

and seventh movements of the *Méditations*.[47] In this essay, we shall focus on the
third movement.

Messiaen utilized the 'langage communicable' in the third movement to express
the idea of God's essence, as stated in a sentence adapted from Aquinas's *Summa
Theologiae*: 'The true relationship with God is really identical to the essence'.[48]
For Messiaen, this means that:

[47]   The texts in question are: (1) Movement I: *Summa Theologiae*, Part I, 'Father, Son,
and Holy Ghost', q. 33 ('The Father'), art. 4 ('Whether to be unbegotten is proper to the
Father'); (2) Movement III: Part I, 'The Trinity', q. 28 (Relations in God), art. 2 (Is relation
in God the same thing as [H]is nature?), reply; and (3) Movement VII: Part I, 'Father, Son,
and Holy Ghost', q. 37 (The name 'Love'), art. 2 (Whether Father and Son love each other
in the Holy Spirit).
[48]   'La relation réelle en Dieu est réellement identique à l'essence.'

there is only one single, unique nature in God, the divine nature, and that the three persons constituting the Trinity are not three separate gods, but the same God; only their relationships allow them to be distinguished: the Father engenders the Son; the Son is engendered by the Father; both of them spiritually generate the Holy Spirit, and the Holy Spirit proceeds from the Father and the Son. The four relationships – paternity, filiation, spiration, and procession – exist for eternity in the one and only God and are identical to [His] essence.[49]

During a platform discussion on 11 June 1972 on the occasion of the European premiere of the *Méditations* at the Second Düsseldorf Messiaen Festival, Messiaen declared that the third movement 'contains [the] central thought [of the *Méditations*], namely: "In God, there is no distinction between Relation and Essence."'[50]

Within a trio texture, the right hand states the Thomistic sentence in the 'langage communicable' from the outset of the piece. As reflected by Example 6.6, articles and adverbs are omitted, words that use the alphabet are in plain type, cases are in parentheses, and the names of leitmotifs are either circled ('Dieu') or enclosed in parentheses ('est–verbe être'). Absent are the musical interpolations, such as birdsong, characteristic not only of the other movements but also of Messiaen's later music in general. The sentence is sounded in its entirety, straight through.

The dyads in the left hand and single notes in the pedal supply the right-hand line with a rhythmic counterpoint comprised of Indian *deçi-tâlas*. In the first ten measures of the piece (see Example 6.6), *pratâpaçekhara* is stated twice in the left hand, followed by *râgavardhana* and *varnamanthikâ*, respectively.[51] After that, the rhythmic patterns are repeated. *Rangapradîpaka* is stated several times in the pedal.

The *deçi-tâlas* enhance the movement's theme of divine essence by their extra-musical associations. In the preface to this movement, Messiaen describes *pratâpaçekhara* as evoking 'the strength that emanates from the countenance', *râgavardhana* as 'the rhythm that gives life to the melody', *varnamanthikâ* as 'the analysis of colour', and *rangapradîpaka* as 'luminous colour'. *Pratâpaçekhara* is the most consequential of the *deçi-tâlas* from a symbolic standpoint, as it is most closely related to the movement's theme. Although the other *deçi-tâlas* are more peripheral symbolically, being more descriptive than symbolic, they accentuate aesthetic themes important to Messiaen, especially that of colour.

The third movement of the *Méditations* is austere and stark in expressive quality. Its trinitarian symbolism is not as obvious as 'Le mystère de la Saint

---

[49]   Samuel, *Music and Color*, p. 126.

[50]   Almut Rößler, *Beiträge zur geistigen Welt Olivier Messiaens* (Duisburg: Gilles und Francke, 1984); trans. Barbara Dagg, Nancy Poland, and Timothy Tikker as *Contributions to the Spiritual World of Olivier Messiaen: With Original Texts by the Composer* (Duisburg: Gilles und Francke, 1986), p. 51.

[51]   *Pratâpaçekhara* consists of a ♩.♪♪; *râgavardhana*, a ♪♪ ♩.; *varnamanthikâ* (reduced by one ♪), a ♪♪♪♪ ♪♪; and *rangapradîpaka* (reduced by one ♪ for all but the last note, which is reduced by a ♪), a ♪♪♪♪♩ + ♪).

Example 6.6 Olivier Messiaen: *Méditation III*, 'langage communicable'

Trinité' from *Les Corps glorieux* (1939), the only other piece Messiaen wrote that directly addressed the subject of the Holy Trinity.[52] Thus, what is the point of this piece, or, for that matter, the use of the 'langage communicable' in the *Méditations*

52 For a discussion of the trinitarian symbolism of 'Le mystère de la Saint Trinité' in relation to the *Méditations*, see Shenton, *Olivier Messiaen's System of Signs*, pp. 32–34.

in general? The answers to these questions, as noted by Andrew Shenton, may lie with Aquinas's ideas about how Angels communicate.[53]

With the 'langage communicable', Messiaen may have been mimicking the speech of Angels in order to effect a greater closeness to God through his music. He can be seen as attempting to make the invisible real through a superhuman language of praise that transcends the poetry characterized by Aquinas as beyond human reason. In the preface to the *Méditations* (*Le langage communicable*), Messiaen described how Angels talk to one another, based on Aquinas's *Summa Theologiae* (Part I, Divine Government, q. 107 ('The speech of the [A]ngels')): 'If the angel, by its will, directs its mental concept with the view of manifesting it to another, immediately the latter perceives it: in this way the angel speaks to another angel.'[54] Furthermore, quoting Aquinas again, Messiaen noted how the intellectual operations of Angels transcend time and space. Although the abstract 'langage communicable' may not transcend time and space, it is certainly a part of a musical composition that conveys a substantive theology about the Holy Trinity.

Saint François d'Assise

For both Messiaen and Aquinas, God is the ultimate reality, possessing a dazzling superabundance of truth that lies beyond the comprehension of human beings. As a part of his compositional aesthetics, Messiaen strove to illuminate the theological truths of his Catholic faith through his music. Given the paramount importance of Aquinas's theology in the Catholic Church, it is not surprising that Messiaen would make Aquinas's idea on accessing the invisible world of God through faith the theological focus of his magnum opus, *Saint François d'Assise*.

Example 6.7 shows a passage from 'L'Ange musicien', scene 5 of *Saint François d'Assise*, in which the character of the Angel paraphrases the passage from Aquinas's *Summa Theologiae* dealing with God's superabundance of truth to the character of Saint Francis: 'God dazzles us by an excess of Truth. Music carries us to God by an absence of Truth.'[55] Messiaen explains this enigmatic phrase to Claude Samuel:

> The arts, especially music but also literature and painting, allow us to penetrate domains that are not unreal, but beyond reality. For the surrealists, it was a hallucinatory domain; for Christians, it is the domain of faith. "Blessed are those

---

[53]   See Shenton, *Olivier Messiaen's System of Signs*, pp. 147–148. Although this writer is indebted to Shenton's observations regarding the place of the Rosetta Stone and Aquinas in an interpretation of the 'langage communicable' and the *Méditations* as a whole, he offers a different interpretation of Messiaen's compositional intentions.

[54]   'Si l'ange, par sa volonté, ordonne son concept mental en vue de la manifester à un autre, aussitôt ce dernier en prend connaissance: de cette manière l'ange parle à un autre ange.'

[55]   'Dieu nous éblouit par excès de Vérité. La musique nous porte à Dieu par défaut de Vérité.'

who have not seen and who have believed." They haven't seen, but they have a secret intuition about what they don't see. Now, I think music, even more than literature and painting, is capable of expressing this dreamlike, fairy-tale aspect of the beyond, this 'surreal' aspect of the truths of faith. It's in that sense that music expresses the beyond with its absence of truth, because it isn't inside the actual framework of reality. God alone is the single true reality, a reality so true that it surpasses all truth.[56]

Example 6.7   Olivier Messiaen: *Saint François*, scene 5, 'L'Ange musicien'

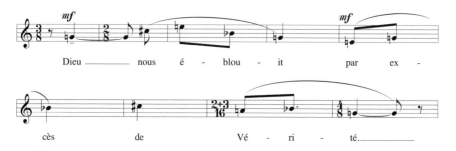

Messiaen's idea of divine dazzlement comports with Aquinas's belief that human beings cannot grasp the Truth and Light of God because they lie beyond their ability to perceive. Humanity needs signs and symbols, especially poetical ones, to better grasp the spiritual.

As shown in Example 6.8, Saint Francis recalls and modifies the paraphrased passage just before he dies in 'La Mort et la nouvelle Vie', scene 8 of *Saint François*, highlighting its importance in Messiaen's thinking: 'Lord! Music and poetry have led me to You: by image, by symbol, and by absence of Truth. [...] Deliver me, enrapture me, dazzle me forever with your excess of Truth.'[57]

Accordingly, at his death, Saint Francis finally understands the Truth and Light of God. He began his spiritual journey by lacking truth; at the end of his trek, he

[56]   Samuel, *Music and Color*, p. 233.

[57]   'Seigneur! Musique et Poésie m'ont conduit vers Toi: par image, par symbole, et par défaut de Verité. [...] Délivre-moi, enivre-moi, éblouis-moi pour toujours de ton excès de Vérité.' At a lecture given in Kyoto on 12 November 1985, Messiaen declared that this text summarized the theological message of *Saint François d'Assise*. See Olivier Messiaen, *Conférence de Kyoto: November 12, 1985*, trans. into Japanese by Naoko Tamamura (Paris: Leduc, 1988), p. 18. For a study of the Thomistic Theme of Truth in *Saint François*, see Camille Crunelle Hill, 'Saint Thomas Aquinas and the Theme of Truth in Messiaen's *Saint François d'Assise*', in *Messiaen's Language of Mystical Love*, ed. Siglind Bruhn, Studies in Contemporary Music and Culture, ed. Joseph Auner, vol. 1 (New York: Garland Publishing, 1998), pp. 143–167.

Example 6.8   Olivier Messiaen: *Saint François*, scene 8, 'La Mort et la nouvelle Vie'

reaches spiritual fulfilment by absorbing the truths of the faith through musical and poetical images, not abstract concepts.

Conclusion

The *Summa Theologiae* of Aquinas influenced Messiaen's compositional thinking throughout his life. Messiaen had a profound understanding of Thomistic thought and incorporated its precepts into 'a music that touched all things without ceasing to touch God'.[58] In a conversation this writer had on 22 May 2006 in Paray-le-Monial, France with Père Jean-Rodolphe Kars, former concert pianist and close friend of Messiaen, on the role of religion in Messiaen's music, Père Kars best summarized the relationship between Messiaen and Aquinas. He characterized Messiaen as a modern-day, musical counterpart of Aquinas. He referred to Messiaen's music as a holy music, with every compositional technique contributing to the goal of revealing the splendour of God.

---

[58]   Père Pascal Ide, a Thomistic scholar and priest at La Trinité, has remarked about the depth of Messiaen's grasp of Aquinas in 'Olivier Messiaen théologien?' (see *Portrait(s) d'Olivier Messiaen*, ed. Catherine Massip, with a preface by Jean Favier (Paris: Bibliothèque nationale de France, 1996), p. 40).

PART III
Messiaen, Poets and Theological Themes

Chapter 7
Dante as Guide to Messiaen's Gothic Spirituality

Robert Fallon

In a recent film, three people express horror and fascination while listening to Messiaen's imposing *Apparition de l'église éternelle* (1936):

> Ricky Ian Gordon (composer): It's like Dante's *Inferno*!
> Elizabeth Povinelli (anthropologist): […] kind of Dante in descent […]
> Harold Bloom (literary critic): [long pause] You know, if I were put down in the Inferno, and was told that for all eternity I was going to be listening to this, I would repent me of all my sins.[1]

Uttered at different times and in different places, these independent comparisons of Messiaen to Dante suggest that both artists conjure a sense of overwhelming, judgmental and supernatural solemnity. Yet even though most of Messiaen's music is light, melodious, ebullient – completely different from the dark *Apparition* – the comparison with Dante still holds. The strongest tie between these most Catholic of artists lies not in their ability to evoke hell, but in their mutual focus on heaven. Dante's *Paradiso* resonates not only in Messiaen's *Éclairs sur l'au-delà...*, but also in his numerous other compositions that evoke celestial serenity.

Surprisingly, Messiaen never acknowledged Dante's influence. For a composer who published books on Mozart, Debussy and Ravel and freely claimed inspiration from hundreds of painters, poets, philosophers, theologians and musicians, Messiaen's silence on Dante is puzzling. For a Roman Catholic composer who championed the Middle Ages, his overt silence raises questions. Messiaen referred to Dante in print only twice. He first mentioned Dante in an article on Paul Dukas's opera *Ariane et Barbe-bleu*, where he admires Dante's summative learning: 'In the manner of a Dante, or a da Vinci, he [Dukas] embodied the intellectual achievements of his own time'.[2] Messiaen's other reference to Dante appears in his *Traité*, where he describes how Blue Rock Thrushes congregate in the Baux

---

[1]   Paul Festa, dir., *Apparition of the Eternal Church*, DVD (2006).

[2]   Olivier Messiaen, 'Ariane et Barbe-Bleue', translator unknown, liner note in Paul Dukas, *Ariane et Barbe-Bleue*, dir. Armin Jordan (Erato LP 750693, 1984), p. 11; originally printed as '*Ariane et Barbe-Bleue* de Paul Dukas', *Revue musicale* 166 (May–June 1936): 79–86.

valley in the south of France. Citing Frédéric Mistral, the nineteenth-century poet and revivalist of Occitan and troubadour poetry, Messiaen explains that this valley may have inspired Dante's vision of hell.[3] By suggesting that Dante interested him only because he visited a place where birds live, Messiaen could hardly have downplayed his influence any more.

In the musicological literature, too, Messiaen has been linked with Dante only in passing. Audrey Eckdahl Davidson's book on the Tristan Trilogy (*Harawi*, *Turangalîla-symphonie* and *Cinq Rechants*) notes that Dante placed Tristan in the second circle of hell, which punishes lust. She also notes how *Harawi* shares the conceit of eyes so important to the *Vita nuova*'s rendering of love.[4] Similarly, Malcolm Hayes calls the slow movements of *Les Offrandes oubliées*, *L'Ascension* and *Quatuor pour la fin du Temps* 'a musical counterpart of the Empyrean in Dante's *Paradiso*'.[5]

I find it likely, however, that Dante relates to Messiaen more profoundly than such casual comparisons suggest. As Virgil guided Dante, so Dante guided Messiaen's artistic and spiritual cosmology. For example, most of the medieval *dramatis personae* in Messiaen's world of influences appear in the *Commedia*. Both artists have connections to Giotto and Richard of St Victor, both discuss the troubadour Folquet de Marseilles, the musician-lover Tristan, and Saints Bernard of Clairvaux, Francis of Assisi, Bonaventure and Thomas Aquinas.[6] That he was a poet-theologian can only have appealed to Messiaen.

In the following sections, I explore four points of contact between Messiaen and Dante: biography, technique, theology and imagery. By recognizing Dante as a seminal figure among Messiaen's influences, we stand to gain a greater appreciation of the history, artistry and theology of Messiaen's 'Gothic spirituality'.[7]

---

[3]   Messiaen, *Traité de rythme, de couleurs, et d'ornithologie*, Vol. 2 (Paris: Alphonse Leduc, 1999), p. 599.

[4]   Audrey Eckdahl Davidson, *Messiaen and the Tristan Myth* (Westport, CT: Praeger, 2001), pp. 4, 52.

[5]   Malcolm Hayes, 'Instrumental, Orchestral and Choral Works to 1948', in *The Messiaen Companion*, ed. Peter Hill (Portland, OR: Amadeus Press, 1999), p. 167.

[6]   For Dante's reference to Folquet de Marseilles, see *Paradiso* IX; for Tristan, see *Inferno* V; for Bernard of Clairvaux, see *Paradiso* XXXIII and XXXI; for Francis of Assisi, see *Paradiso* XI, XXXII; for Bonaventure, see *Paradiso* XI and XII; for Thomas Aquinas, see *Paradiso* X–XIV and XX; for Richard of St Victor, see *Paradiso* X and, for Richard's connection to Messiaen, see Anne Keeley, 'In the Beginning Was the Word? An Exploration of the Origins of Olivier Messiaen's *Méditations sur le mystère de la Sainte Trinité*', unpublished paper delivered at Messiaen*2008* International Centenary Conference, Birmingham, UK, 23 June 2008.

[7]   I called an aesthetic based on Gothic spirituality 'double realism' in 'The Record of Realism in Messiaen's Bird Style', in *Olivier Messiaen: Music, Art and Literature*, eds Christopher Dingle and Nigel Simeone (Aldershot: Ashgate, 2007), pp. 115–136, and developed this idea in 'La spiritualité gothique de Messiaen et le *renouveau catholique*',

A term borrowed from art history, Gothic spirituality refers to the twelfth- and thirteenth-century Parisian belief, influenced by Neo-Platonism, that the material world could lead to the spiritual world.[8] It explains how looking at an ornate Gothic reliquary or the brilliant colours of a stained glass window can exalt the soul. Art historian Marchita Mauck characterizes Gothic spirituality as 'the translucency of glass and jewels, the weightlessness, harmony, and unity of Gothic architecture symbolically express[ing] the ineffable presence of God, the immaterial True Light to which the believer aspired to ascend'.[9] This ascent from materiality to spirituality derives from Christian Neo-Platonism, which holds that creation emanates from the superabundant being of the Trinity and exemplifies traces of that being in a hierarchy that illuminates the soul more brightly the closer it rises towards God.[10]

Dante undergoes the transformative process of Gothic spirituality by traversing this world and entering the next. In *La vita nuova*, he relates how, as a boy, he felt a deeply spiritual love for Beatrice, a beautiful young woman who died at age 25. In the three canticles of the *Commedia* – *Inferno*, *Purgatorio*, and *Paradiso* – he relates how, 'midway in our life's journey', he became lost in a dark wood. He finds his spiritual and artistic way with the guidance of the ancient poet Virgil, who leads him down through the nine circles of hell and up through the nine terraces of Mount Purgatory. At the top of the mountain, Virgil puts Dante into the care of the beatific Beatrice, who guides him through the light upon light of the nine spheres of paradise until he reaches the Empyrean, where Christ, Mary and the greatest of the apostles and saints dwell in eternity. The *Commedia* tells

---

translated into French by Martine Rhéaume, in *Musique, arts et religion dans l'entre-deux-guerres*, eds Sylvain Caron and Michel Duchesneau (Lyon: Symétrie, 2009), pp. 347–64.

[8] For use of the term 'Gothic spirituality' in the art historical literature, see for example, Horst Woldemar Jansen and Anthony F. Janson, *History of Art: The Western Tradition*, 6th edn (Upper Saddle River, NJ: Prentice Hall, 2004), text on light in Chartres Cathedral near Figure 11–18; F. R. Ankersmit, *Sublime Historical Experience* (Palo Alto, CA: Stanford University Press, 2005), p. 91; William D. Wixam, 'Medieval Sculpture at the Cloisters', *The Metropolitan Museum of Art Bulletin* 46, no. 3 (Winter 1988–89): 29; Wendell D. Garrett, 'The First Score for American Paintings and Sculpture, 1870–1890', *Metropolitan Museum Journal* 3 (1970): pp. 307–335; and Herbert Schade, 'Images', in *Encyclopedia of Theology: A Concise Sacramentum Mundi*, ed. Karl Rahner (New York: Continuum International Publishing, 1975), p. 684.

[9] Marchita Mauck, 'Gothic spirituality', in *The HarperCollins Encyclopedia of Catholicism*, ed. Richard P. McBrien (New York: HarperCollins, 1995), pp. 575–576.

[10] For a good overview of late medieval Christian Neo-Platonism, see Justo L. González, 'The Augustinian Tradition in the Thirteenth Century', in *A History of Christian Thought*, Vol. 2 (Nashville, TN: Abingdon Press, 1971), pp. 241–254; Frederick Copleston, SJ, 'The Pseudo-Dionysius', in *A History of Philosophy*, Vol. 2 (New York: Doubleday, 1993), pp. 91–100; and Ewart Cousins, 'Introduction', in Bonaventure, *Bonaventure: The Soul's Journey into God; The Tree of Life; The Life of St. Francis*, trans. Ewert Cousins (New York: Paulist Press, 1978), pp. 1–48.

the progress of Dante's soul at the same time it teaches the theology of the Roman Catholic Church.

Biographical connections

The date and manner of Messiaen's first encounter with Dante are unknown. The first substantial evidence of Dante's influence, however, appears at the end of the Second World War. In 1944, Messiaen was 35 years old, the proverbial midway through his life's journey of 70 expected years and the age that Dante says he traveled through hell, purgatory and paradise. The following year, Messiaen recorded in his journal that he wished to compose a 'Paradis' for orchestra that includes 'chasms above and below'. And while at work on the epic *Turangalîla-symphonie* in 1946, he planned a 'Symphonie théologique' for orchestra – a project that sounds like it might have been a musical counterpart to Dante's epic theological poem.[11]

Throughout these years, Messiaen's wife Claire Delbos exhibited signs of prolonged mental illness that Messiaen experienced as a deathlike loss, as depicted in the valedictory imagery of *Harawi: Songs of Love and Death*. If Dante was on his mind, Claire's metaphorical death may have reminded him of Beatrice's early death. Their names, after all, convey related meanings – Beatrice means 'blessed' while 'Claire' connotes 'bright and shining' – the same light-filled quality that Dante used to describe the blessed in *Paradiso*. As Dante ascribed the number nine to Beatrice in *La vita nuova*, so Messiaen honoured Claire in the nine movements of *Poèmes pour Mi*.

Both Messiaen and Dante refashioned their lives in their art. For example, Dante is the lead character in his own poetry, and his beloved Beatrice is probably not only a literary invention, but also a real woman who moved him profoundly. Messiaen's art is similarly autobiographical. From *Le Tombeau resplendissant*, which laments the death of his mother, to the song cycles of the mid-1930s that exalt his wife and son, from the *Quatuor pour la fin du Temps*, which reflects his wartime internment, to the Tristan Trilogy, which shows his entrapment in forbidden love, Messiaen composed much of his own life into his music.

---

[11]   Peter Hill and Nigel Simeone, *Messiaen* (New Haven, CT/London: Yale University Press, 2007), pp. 159, 169. For a discussion that tangentially links Messiaen to Arthur Lourié, whose works *Sonata liturgica* (1928) and *Concerto spirituale* (1930) evoke the piety of a 'Symphonie théologique', see Fallon, 'Composing Subjectivity: Maritain's Poetic Knowledge in Stravinsky and Maritain', in *Jacques Maritain and the Many Ways of Knowing*, ed. Thomas Ollivant (Washington, DC: Catholic University of America Press, 2002), pp. 284–302.

Formal connections

Biographical parallels aside, several of Messiaen's formal techniques closely follow Dante's prosodic and symbolic structures. Dante famously invented *terza rima* in the *Commedia* and composed the Trinitarian 3 times 33 cantos, plus one more to total 100, the square of the perfect number 10. Such numerological and constructivist designs are also found outside the *Commedia*, where I see two techniques that Messiaen appears to have borrowed.

The first technique groups subsections of pieces in symmetrical designs that involve prime numbers. Dante arranged the poems in *La vita nuova* into a symmetrical series that alternates groups of short poems with single long canzonas in the pattern [10–1–4–1–4–1–10], totaling 31 poems (a prime number). He followed a similar numerological construction at the centre of the *Commedia*. As Charles S. Singleton noticed in 1965, the number of lines in the seven central cantos of *Purgatorio* (and thus of the whole *Commedia*) form a symmetrical series: [151–145–145–139–145–145–151]. The first, central, and last numbers of this series are prime numbers and also reduce to prime numbers by numerological addition (1+5+1 = 7; 1+3+9 = 13).[12] He further notes that these cantos can be grouped [3–1–3], totaling 7 cantos, a prime. Similarly, Messiaen grouped the seven movements of *Les Corps glorieux* into three books [3–1–3], where the single movement was the longest of the seven (another prime number), and structured the *Catalogue* into symmetrically alternating groups of shorter movements with longer single movements: [3–1–2–1–2–1–3], totalling 13 movements (a prime number).[13] *Sept Haïkaï*, *Des Canyons aux étoiles…*, and *Éclairs sur l'au-delà…* follow similar plans (see Figure 7.1).[14]

---

[12] Charles S. Singleton, 'The Poet's Number at the Center', *Modern Language Notes* 80, no. 1 (1965): 1–10; see also Robert M. Durling, 'Number, Light, Motion, and Degree at the Center of the *Comedy*', in Dante, *Purgatorio* (New York: Oxford University Press, 2004), pp. 610–612. Singleton does not discuss the role of prime numbers in his article, but he does find other symmetries around the centre of the poem. Significantly, he notes that the theme of *Purgatorio* XVII, where this symmetry occurs, focuses on 'love, which is shown to be the all-embracing and all-motivating force of creatures and creator' (p. 1), a theme that was dear to Messiaen.

[13] Messiaen's fascination with prime numbers may have its origin in the troubadours' use of prime numbers. A common stanza length in troubadour poetry has five lines. Arnaut Daniel's song 'L'aur' amara' has six stanzas of 17 lines (a prime number) and a seven-line envoy (a prime), totaling 109 lines (another prime); similarly, Andreas Capellanus's twelfth-century *The Art of Courtly Love* lists 31 rules of love. See Arnaut Daniel, 'L'aura amara', in *Lyrics of the Troubadours and Trouveres: An Anthology and a History*, trans. Frederick Goldin (Garden City, NY: Anchor Books, 1973), pp. 210–216.

[14] For more on Dante's arrangement, see Barbara Reynolds, 'Note on the Structure of the *Vita nuova*', in Dante, *La vita nuova*, trans. Barbara Reynolds (London: Penguin Books, 1969), p. 101.

Dante

La Vita nuova	10–1–4–1–4–1–10	31 poems (prime)
Commedia	3–1–3	7 central cantos (prime)

Messiaen

Les Corps glorieux	3–1–3	7 movements (prime)
Catalogue d'oiseaux	3–1–2–1–2–1–3	13 movements (prime)
Sept Haïkaï	3–1–3	7 movements (prime)
Des Canyons aux étoiles…	5–2–5	movements (primes)
Éclairs sur l'au-delà…	5–1–5	11 movements (prime)

Figure 7.1   Symmetrical form and prime numbers in Dante and Messiaen

For Messiaen, prime numbers signify the unity, indivisibility and simplicity of God. He measured many of his phrase lengths, particularly in his bird style, to prime numbers of semiquavers in order to relate creation to divinity.[15] While Thomas Aquinas hardly mentions primes, Dante refers to them at least three times. In *De vulgare eloquentia*, for example, he writes about different poetic lines, all of which use prime numbers:

> Although Italian poets have made use of the three- and the eleven-syllable line, and of all kinds in between, those of five, seven, and eleven are the most frequently used, and after them that of three more than any other.[16]

Because prime numbers are often called the elements of all numbers, as all other numbers may be factored into primes, Dante writes in *Paradiso*:

> [Heaven's] own motion unfactored, all things derive
> their motions from this heaven as precisely
> as ten is factored into two and five.[17]

Similarly, in the first canto of *Paradiso*, Beatrice herself says that 'The elements / of all things […] whatever their mode, observe an inner order. It is this form / that makes the universe resemble God'.[18] Dante's numerological use of prime numbers could be the source of Messiaen's belief that prime numbers, 'by the simple fact

---

[15]   For more on Messiaen's use of prime numbers, see Fallon, 'The Record of Realism'.

[16]   Dante, *Literature in the Vernacular* [*De vulgari eloquentia*], trans. Sally Purcell (Manchester: Carcanet New Press, 1981), par. 44.

[17]   Dante, *The Divine Comedy: Paradiso* XXVII, trans. John Ciardi (New York: Penguin Books, 2003), 115–117.

[18]   Dante, *Paradiso* I, 101–105.

of not being divisible into equal fractions, represent an occult force (for you know that divinity is indivisible)'.[19]

The second formal structure I find common to Dante and Messiaen is what scholars call *retrogradatio cruciformis* or *retrogradatio cruciata*, but what Messiaen called interversion or 'symmetrical permutation'.[20] Most people today recognize it as the operation that determines the ordered rearrangement of end-words in a sestina (see Figure 7.2). Copying the troubadour Arnaut Daniel, who invented the sestina, Dante's sestinas follow a criss-crossing pattern of rearranging words that moves from the extremes towards the middle. Although Messiaen first explored this operation in his *Technique de mon langage musical* and appears

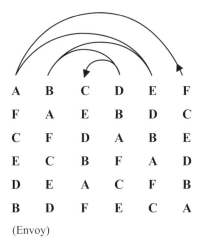

A	B	C	D	E	F
F	A	E	B	D	C
C	F	D	A	B	E
E	C	B	F	A	D
D	E	A	C	F	B
B	D	F	E	C	A

(Envoy)

Note: Each letter represents an end-word and each row of letters represents a stanza. This operation is also known as *retrogradatio cruciformis* or *retrogradatio cruciata*.

Figure 7.2   Outside-to-inside (closing fan) process of rearranging end-rhymes in a sestina

[19]   Olivier Messiaen, *Music and Color: Conversations with Claude Samuel*, trans. Thomas Glasow (Portland, OR: Amadeus Press, 1994), p. 79.

[20]   Robert M. Durling, 'Introduction', in *Petrarch's Lyric Poems: The Rime Sparse and Other Lyrics*, trans. and ed. Robert M. Durling (Cambridge, MA: Harvard University Press, 1976), p. 16. A possible source for Messiaen's initial use of the word *interversion* is Alfred Jeannroy, *La Poésie lyrique des Troubadours* (Toulouse: Éduard Privat, 1934), which describes the hermetic poetic style of *trobar clus* with the term *entrebescar los motz*, a phrase he notes that others relate to the word *intervertir*, the noun form of which would be *interversion*. See Jeannroy, *La Poésie lyrique*, p. 34, n. 5.

to have first used it in *Île de feu 2*, his most elaborate example of it appears in *Chronochromie*.[21]

Like Messiaen's symmetrical permutation, the sestina mediates between stasis and change, mutability and immutability. Dante scholar Robert Durling notes that the sestina limns human temporality. The cyclicity of *retrogradatio cruciformis*, he says, captures the simultaneously changing and recurring nature of the world and 'the embeddedness of human experience in time'.[22] Michael and Marianne Shapiro, authors of *Figuration in Verbal Art*, agree, writing: 'The revolutions of the rhyme words in the sestina within a necessarily linear progression (dictated by the temporality of language) make the poem a place of intersection between cyclical and linear conceptions of time.'[23] Similarly, Messiaen described 'symmetrical permutation' as a necessary result of the interaction between human and inhuman quantities. The number of permutations in any given set is determined mathematically by calculating the factorial of the number of objects. Five objects, for example, yields $5 \times 4 \times 3 \times 2 = 120$ permutations. Because this number grows extremely rapidly (seven objects yields 5040 permutations), Messiaen said: 'their number is so high that it would require half a lifetime to write them and several years to play. It's therefore necessary to choose.'[24] His choice was to impose the operation of symmetrical permutations that first appeared in sestinas by Arnaut Daniel and Dante Alighieri. By following the process the same number of times as there are items to reorder, one arrives at the original sequence (see Figure 7.3).

Messiaen adapted *retrogradatio cruciformis* into a chiasmus in his Tristan Trilogy symphony, which portrays a human love that mirrors divine love (see Figure 7.4). To my knowledge, this symmetry in *Turangalîla*'s structure has not been identified in previous scholarship. The Introduction is linked to the Final, and the 'Chant d'amour' movements are symmetrically imbricated with the 'Turangalîla' movements. Though their music contrasts greatly in mood, the movements 'Joie du sang des étoiles' and 'Jardin du sommeil d'amour' share the consonantal sequence 'J – du s – d[e]' followed by a noun beginning with a vowel. The justification for regarding the symphony in two parts of five movements each rests on how movement V, halfway through the long work, functions as a major internal conclusion. The appearance of an intricate structure

---

[21]   He first called 'symmetrical permutation' by the name 'interversion', a term that is best understood in Messiaen as any reordering of events, whether systematic or not. He also described it as 'opening scissors' or 'opening fan' when the values spread apart or progress from the inside out (e.g. [1 2 3 4] becomes [3 2 4 1]) or 'closing scissors' or 'closing fan' when the values converge or progress from the outside in (e.g. [1 2 3 4] becomes [4 1 3 2]). See Messiaen, *Traité III*, pp. 7–15; 319–26; for his inchoate use of it in the *Technique de mon langage musical*, Vol. 2 (Paris: Leduc, 1944), see Ex. 126.

[22]   Durling, 'Introduction', p. 17.

[23]   Michael and Marianne Shapiro, *Figuration in Verbal Art* (Princeton: Princeton University Press, 1988), p. 99.

[24]   Messiaen, *Traité III*, p. 79.

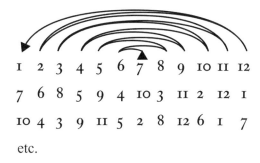

Note: The numbers typically represent the number of semiquaver notes in a note's duration.

Figure 7.3   Symmetrical permutation moving inside-to-outside (or opening fan)

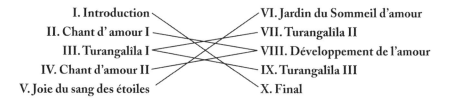

Figure 7.4   Symmetrical, crossed form of the *Turangalîla-symphonie*

characteristic of troubadour poetry in a work related to Tristan, who is often characterized as a troubadour, reveals Messiaen's melding of form and content in *Turangalîla*.

Symmetry necessarily focuses attention on the line of axis. Studies of comparative religion have found that such axes represent, as T. S. Eliot put it, 'the still point of the turning world'.[25] Religion scholar Mircea Eliade explains that this *axis mundi* 'at once connects and supports heaven and earth'.[26] Unlike his 'non-retrogradable rhythms', which represent the absence of time that theologians say characterizes eternity, Messiaen's symmetrical permutations and structural

---

[25]   T. S. Eliot, 'Burnt Norton', from *Four Quartets* (London: Faber & Faber, 1944), 'Burnt Norton' II, 62.

[26]   Mircea Eliade, *The Sacred and the Profane: The Nature of Religion*, 1965, trans. Willard R. Trask (Orlando: Harcourt, 1987), p. 36. I owe the connection between the sestina and Eliade to Marilyn Krysl, 'Sacred and Profane: the Sestina as Rite', *American Poetry Review* 33, no. 2: 7–12. For an excellent discussion of the expressive content of the sestina, see Margaret Spanos, 'The Sestina: An Exploration of the Dynamics of Poetic Structure', *Speculum* 53, no. 3 (July 1978): 545–557.

symmetries work on a large scale. By allowing ample time for each wing of the symmetry, these procedures seem to represent a dialogue between heaven and earth, the connection that defines the heart of Gothic spirituality.

Theological connections

The theological tradition that informs Messiaen's Gothic spirituality, a movement of the spirit that ascends from the visible to the invisible worlds, drew heavily from Christian Neo-Platonism. Exemplified by the writings of the Pseudo-Dionysius, Christian Neo-Platonism gave late medieval Christendom the hierarchical cosmology of nine spheres of heaven (accounting for the seven planets, nine choirs of angels, and so on) reflected in the *Commedia*. At the beginning of most cantos in the *Commedia*, Dante describes his location by naming the position of the planets and constellations of the zodiac. In *Paradiso*, he ascends through the nine heavens before he arrives at the Empyrean, the outermost sphere that contains all of creation. Messiaen recreates a similar cosmology. In *Des Canyons aux étoiles...*, his titular ellipsis suggests that there is a spiritual place beyond Aldebaran (mentioned in the score) and all the stars; in *Éclairs sur l'au-delà...*, he again portrays the stars (and his own astrological sign, Sagittarius) as mere stops on the way to the beyond.

If this cosmology was commonplace in the medieval world, the location of earthly paradise more closely connects Messiaen to Dante. In the *Purgatorio*, the penitents atone for their sins by climbing Mount Purgatory, whose pinnacle is a sort of earthly paradise. Located on the opposite side of the earth from Zion, where Christ died, the peak of Mount Purgatory leads to the entrance to the heavens.[27] Modern maps tell us that the point on the globe opposite Jerusalem (32°N, 35°E) is close to two French colonies in the South Pacific. Gauguin's earthly paradise of Tahiti (18°N, 150°W) is not far away. But closer still to the mythical Mount Purgatory lies New Caledonia (22°S, 166°W), the island paradise Messiaen invented for St Francis's dreams (see Figure 7.5). Stefan Keym's monograph on *Saint François d'Assise* likewise observes this similarity between Messiaen and Dante.[28]

Rising above the earth, Dante enters the increasingly luminous and glorious heavens. The closer his body and soul approach the Empyrean, the brighter and purer the surrounding light becomes. Christian Moevs, author of *The Metaphysics of Dante's Comedy*, explains this phenomenon as follows:

> The Neoplatonic tradition [...] spoke of an 'emanation' in degrees or stages, an outpouring of light from Light [...] in which each level of reality causes (gives

---

[27] For an illustration of Mount Purgatory lying opposite Zion, see Dante, *The Divine Comedy*, trans. John Ciardi, p. 318.

[28] Stefan Keym, *Farbe und Zeit: Untersuchen zur musiktheatralen Struktur und Semantik von Olivier Messiaens* Saint François d'Assise (Hildesheim: Georg Olms, 2002), p. 40.

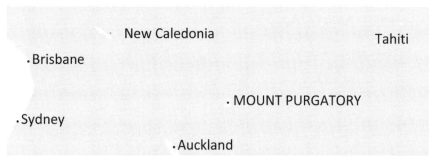

Figure 7.5   Mount Purgatory, Dante's earthly paradise, is located on the opposite side of the earth from Zion, not far from Messiaen's earthly paradise of New Caledonia

being to) the next, creating a chain of mediate links between attributeless self-subsistence and contingent finite being. Neoplatonic emanation [...] permeates Christian thought on creation.[29]

The *Commedia* is constructed around the theology of emanation and light imagery, usually associated with another Neo-Platonic concept, that of 'illumination', the process that guides the soul towards perfection. In *Paradiso*, Dante describes how creation emanates being in a hierarchical fashion:

> Within the heaven of peace beyond the sky
> there whirls a body from whose power arises
> the being of all things that within it lie.
> The next sphere, that which is so richly lit,
> distributes this power to many essences
> distinct from itself, yet all contained within it.
> The other spheres, in various degrees,
> dispose the special powers they have within
> to their own causes and effects ... .[30]

Dante also adopts light imagery at the very opening of *Paradiso*: 'The glory of Him who moves all things rays forth / through all the universe, and is reflected / from each thing in proportion to its worth.' In the speech he gives to Bonaventure, Dante combines these conceits of hierarchies of being and light:

> All things that die and all that cannot die
> are the reflected splendor of the Form

---

[29]   Christian Moevs, *The Metaphysics of Dante's* Comedy (New York: Oxford University Press, 2005), p. 109.

[30]   Dante, *Paradiso* II, 118–120.

our Father's love brings forth beyond the sky.
For the Living Light that streams forth from the Source
in such a way that it is never parted
from Him, nor from the Love whose mystic force
joins them in Trinity, lets its grace ray down,
as if reflected, through nine subsistant natures
that sempiternally remain as one.[31]

Messiaen shared Dante's Neo-Platonic preoccupation with being and light. Light imagery bathes his music, from his 'colour chords' to *Chronochromie*, and from *Couleurs de la cité céleste* to the weightless, light-filled final movements of *La Transfiguration*, *Saint François d'Assise* and *Éclairs sur l'au-delà*....[32] And his theology overtly addressed hierarchies of being. He told Claude Samuel, for example, that 'Every superior being assimilates the inferior being',[33] and wrote that religious art 'expresses ideas about a single being, who is God, but a being who is ever-present and who can be found in everything, above everything, and below everything'.[34] Such flirtation with pantheism, apparent also in his bird style and nature works, has long characterized Christian Neo-Platonism.[35]

Both Dante and Messiaen show this hierarchy of being in their portrayals of paradise. The successive spheres in Dante's ascent become ever more glorious, ineffable and dissociated from time and space. Even while each sphere is perfect because it is heavenly, each also has its own proper character since it functions in a hierarchy. Messiaen likewise composes a variety of states of perfection in such weightless adagios as the finales of *L'Ascension* and the *Quatuor*, the viol scene of *Saint François*, and the fifth and final movements of *Éclairs*. When such movements lift away from their initial tessitura and gradually approach stratospheric heights, Messiaen seems to map the ascent to heaven.

Finally, Dante and Messiaen share a theology of language and the first word. In his book on writing in the vernacular, *De vulgari eloquentia*, Dante follows Thomas Aquinas in asserting that angels have no need for language because they possess 'a most swift and indescribable sufficiency of understanding, whereby one becomes fully known to the other'.[36] Similarly, he says that animals do not need speech

---

[31]   Dante, *Paradiso* XIII, 52–60.

[32]   A further theological similarity may involve Dante's five references to rainbows, whose seven colours he associated with the seven gifts of the Holy Spirit. It is intriguing to speculate that Dante could be the source of the 'theological rainbow' Messiaen writes about in his *Technique de mon langage musical*.

[33]   Messiaen, *Music and Color*, p. 31.

[34]   Hill and Simeone, *Messiaen*, p. 80.

[35]   John Scotus Eriugena, for example, was condemned for the pantheism the Church found in his Neo-Platonic *On the Division of Nature*. Johannes Scotus Erigena, *Periphyseon* [On the Division of Nature] (Indianapolis: Bobbs-Merrill, 1976).

[36]   Dante, *De vulgari eloquentia*, p. 16.

because instinct enables members of like species to understand one another.[37] Messiaen echoed these theories in his essay on the 'langage communicable' that prefaces the score to the *Méditations sur le mystère de la Sainte Trinité*, but credits Thomas for the notion that angels do not need language.

Dante then wonders what the first word was. Answering that it must have been the word 'God', he says 'it seems absurd and abhorrent to reason that any thinking should have been named by man before God, by whom and for whom he had been created'.[38] Messiaen again follows Dante in the preface to the *Méditations*, where the first full word he writes in his 'langage communicable' is a special, musical 'word' for God that can sound either forward or backward: 'I thought it necessary to signal the attention of the listener the only important word in all of language, the word that is not the name of a king [as on a cartouche], but of the King of kings, the *Divine Name!*'[39] Messiaen alludes here to Christian Neo-Platonism, one of whose most influential texts was the Pseudo-Dionysius's *Treatise on the Divine Names*. This theory of the first word is not discussed by Thomas.

Imaginal connections

When reading the *Purgatorio* and *Paradiso*, it is impossible to ignore the ubiquitous imagery of music and birds.[40] In *Purgatorio*, 23 of 33 cantos resonate with music, while 28 of 33 cantos in *Paradiso* feature music; many of these cantos refer to songs, hymns, wings, flight and birds many times over. At each stage on the ascent of Mount Purgatory, the penitent chant a different prayer and at each level of heaven, a new music resounds from the choirs of angels. Dante names such chants as the *Miserere*, *Salve Regina*, *Te lucis ante terminum*, *Te deum laudamus*, *Vinum non habent*, and so on. At various times, as in *Purgatorio* 20 and 29, he also refers to the music of the spheres. Dante's constant references to heavenly chant and the

---

[37]   Ibid.

[38]   Ibid., p. 18.

[39]   Messiaen, *Méditations sur le mystère de la Sainte Trinité* (Paris: Leduc, 1973), p. v.

[40]   For more on music in Dante, see William Peter Mahrt, 'Dante's Musical Progress Through the *Commedia*', in *The Echo of Music: Essays in Honor of Marie Louise Göllner*, ed. Blair Sullivan (Warren, MI: Harmonie Park Press, 2004), pp. 63–73; Judith A. Peraino, 'Re-Placing Medieval Music', *Journal of the American Musicological Society* 54, no. 2 (Summer 2001): 209–264; John Stevens, 'Dante and Music', *Italian Studies* 23 (1968): 1–18; Nino Pirrotta, 'Dante *Musicus:* Gothicism, Scholasticism, and Music', *Speculum* 43 (1968): 245–257; Ambrogio Orlando, *La Commedia di Dante distributa per materia* (Florence: Sansoni, 1965), pp. 365–372; Reinhold Hammerstein, 'Die Musik in Dantes *Divina Commedia*', *Deutsches Dante-Jahrbuch* 41/42 (1964): 59–125 and *Die Musik der Engel: Untersuchungen zur Musikanschauung des Mittelalters* (Munich: Franke, 1962).

music of the spheres must have appealed to Messiaen, because his works are full of neo-Gregorian chant and the idea that earthly music mirrors heavenly concord.[41]

The same is true of Dante's birds, which populate these poems nearly as densely as does music. In *Purgatorio*, 19 of 33 cantos use bird imagery, while 20 of 33 cantos in *Paradiso* refer to birds. Much of the time, birds provide the vehicle for Dante's metaphors, as when he writes in *Purgatorio* 25:

> And as a little stork, eager to fly
> but afraid to leave the nest, will raise a wing
> then let it fall again – just such was I,
> the will within me now strong and now weak,
> eager to ask, but going only so far
> as to make me clear my throat, and then not speak.[42]

Another form of the *Commedia*'s bird imagery draws on the myth of the eagle, which alone among living creatures is able to stare into the sun. This ability makes the eagle a symbol of desire for God. Eagles appear in *De vulgare eloquentia*, when Dante refers to 'the eagle that seeks the stars', and in *Paradiso*, when Beatrice's eyes are raised to heaven and so surpass, he says, even the eagle.[43] Most famously, sparks in heaven form a cosmic eagle that appears in several cantos of *Paradiso*.

Because eagles in Dante symbolize striving for God, it is not surprising that Messiaen uses them in a similar way. Messiaen composed music for only five species of eagles among his approximately 350 bird species. Two of the five, the Bonelli's Eagle and Short-toed Eagle, along with a related bird, the Peregrine Falcon, cry out in the 12th movement of *La Transfiguration* because this movement portrays longing for closeness to God. As Messiaen writes in his note: 'The scene is set by the cries of mountain birds: Peregrine falcon and Bonelli's eagle. The light from "on high" becomes visible.' In his own 'succinct analysis' in the score, Messiaen writes that the movement came about when he looked into the snow on Mont Blanc, compared it with the sun, and suddenly understood that Christ's glory surpasses that of the saints as the brightness of the sun surpasses the brightness of snow. In looking at the snow and the sun, perhaps Messiaen portrays himself like the eagle, striving to close his distance from God.

Finally, as mentioned above, Messiaen drew from the same group of medieval standard-bearers as Dante. Richard of St Victor, Tristan, the troubadour Folquet

---

[41]   To my knowledge, the coinage 'neo-Gregorian' was first applied to Messiaen's melodies in Siglind Bruhn, *Messiaen's Contemplations of Covenant and Incarnation: Musical Symbols of Faith in the Two Great Piano Cycles of the 1940s* (Hillsdale, NY: Pendragon Press, 2007), p. 63, though it has been applied to modernist renditions of chant for many decades. This useful term must, of course, be kept distinct from its application to the international repertory of chant composed between the ninth and thirteenth centuries.

[42]   Dante, *Purgatorio* XXV, 10–15.

[43]   Dante, *De vulgari eloquentia*, p. 43; *Paradiso* I, 47–49.

de Marseilles, and Saints Bernard, Francis, Bonaventure and Aquinas all appear in the works of both artists. As Dante greets Arnaut Daniel in Purgatory, so does Messiaen employ the *retrogradatio cruciformis* of Daniel's sestina. And when Messiaen mentions Giotto's frescoes of Saint Francis, it calls to my mind Giotto's famous portrait of Dante. As Dante is the pre-eminent poet of Catholicism, so must Messiaen be regarded as the pre-eminent composer of Catholicism – at least since the Renaissance.

Conclusion

Having established numerous similarities between the two Catholic artists, I conclude by reflecting on how Dante came to figure so prominently in Messiaen's consciousness. Messiaen probably made his first connection to Dante through his mother, the poet Cécile Sauvage. Enumerating her taste for grandeur, a biography of Sauvage names Dante among her favourite artists: 'In painting, Poussin, Vélasquez. In music, Mozart, and above all Bach. In poetry, Dante and Shakespeare. And Racine.'[44] Sauvage's poetic roots emerged from French Romanticism, which revered Dante and often paired him with Shakespeare. Writer Henri-Marie Beyle, better known as Stendhal, wrote that 'The romantic poet par excellence is Dante', while the apex of French Dantisme probably occurred when Victor Hugo joined the swollen ranks of translators and called Dante the spiritual brother of Shakespeare.[45] Like T. S. Eliot after him, Hugo compares the spirituality of Shakespeare's this-worldliness to the spirituality of Dante's other-worldliness, a comment to which we can easily imagine the Shakespeare-loving Messiaen nodding with interest, if also uncertain assent.[46]

Despite the notable highpoint of Étienne Gilson's *Dante et la philosophie* (1939), French studies and translations of Dante waned in the years surrounding the Second World War. But in 1958, Alexandre Masseron published his version of the *Comédie*, which resonates with Messiaen's use of Masseron's book on St Francis that provided source material for his opera.[47] Furthermore, in 1960, Salvador Dalí contributed to the growing field of translations with his illustrated version of the *Comédie*. Because he once admitted to liking Dalí's depictions of monsters, could

---

[44]   Henri Pourrat, *La Veillée de novembre* (Uzès: Éditions de la Cigale, 1937), p. 130. I am grateful to Yves Balmer for providing me with this quotation.

[45]   Michael Pitwood, *Dante and the French Romantics* (Geneva: Droz, 1985), p. 13, quoting Stendhal's *Racine et Shakespeare*, ed. Pierre Martino (Paris: Cercle du Bibliophile, 1968–74), p. 45.

[46]   Pitwood, *Dante and the French Romantics*, p. 194.

[47]   In 1922, André Pératé published a version of *La Divine comédie* which may have come to Messiaen's attention because Pératé's version of Saint Francis's *Fioretti* contains the woodcut by Maurice Denis that Messiaen said influenced the scene of the Angel-Musician in his opera.

Messiaen have known of Dalí's watercolour of Malecoda, a demon from canto 23 of *Inferno*? (see Figure 7.6).[48]

Figure 7.6   Salvador Dalí's watercolour of Malecoda, a demon from canto 23 of
                Inferno
                © 2008 Salvador Dalí, Gala-Salvador Dalí Foundation / Artists
                Rights Society (ARS), New York

Another likely source in which Messiaen could have discovered Dante is the work of art historian Émile Mâle, whose book *L'Art religieux de la fin du Moyen Age en France: Étude sur l'iconographie du Moyen Age et sur ses sources d'inspiration* (1898) compares Gothic cathedrals and even the *Commedia* to symphonies. 'The *Paradiso* is all music and light', he writes, 'the souls themselves are singing lights, and all form vanishes in a splendour a thousand times brighter

---

48   Messiaen, *Traité I*, p. 68.

than that of the sun'.[49] Dante reappears at least four more times in *L'Art religieux de la fin du Moyen Age en France*, which paints him as a touchstone of Gothic sensibility and spirituality.

In sum, no other single source than Dante explains so thoroughly the fascination with the medieval techniques, imagery and theology that comprises Messiaen's Gothic spirituality. If Messiaen was inspired by Dante, the question arises why he kept his admiration hidden, since he acknowledged hundreds of other sources in his writings and interviews. One reason for Messiaen's silence could involve his history of dissembling. He fabricated the 5000 prisoners and broken cello string at the premiere of the *Quatuor pour la fin du Temps*; he falsely claimed he transcribed the birds in *Oiseaux exotiques* on his travels, even though they come from a set of commercial recordings; and he evaded questions about the similarities between Stravinsky's *Les Noces* and his *Trois petites Liturgies*.[50]

Repressing the influence of Stravinsky leads to a second explanation for Messiaen's silence about Dante, namely that artists often repress their strongest influences. Anne Sexton, for example, has said: 'Poets will not only hide influences. They will bury them.'[51] But Harold Bloom, who has shown he fears Messiaen as much as he respects Dante, lists repression of the 'precursor' as one of his modes of poetic influence. 'Every forgotten precursor', he says, 'becomes a giant of the imagination.'[52] It is not surprising, then, that in wishing to fashion an entirely original artistic persona, Messiaen would imagine and re-imagine Dante's technique, theology and imagery. By recognizing Dante's influence on Messiaen, we discover Messiaen's efforts to craft his artistic identity by updating pre-modern Gothic spirituality for the modern world.[53] In the end, Dante's powerful grip on Messiaen's imagination suggests that Messiaen's identity and inspiration emerged first from his faith, and only then from his art.

---

[49]   Emile Mâle, *The Gothic Image: Religious Art in France of the Thirteenth Century*, trans. Dora Nussey (New York: Harper & Row, 1972), p. 385.

[50]   For more on these moments of misguidance, see Hannelore Lauerwald, 'Er musizierte mit Olivier Messiaen als Kriegsgefangener', *Das Orchester* 47, no. 1 (1999): 21–23, and Rebecca Rischin, *For the End of Time: The Story of the Messiaen Quartet* (Ithaca: Cornell University Press, 2003), pp. 65–66; Robert Fallon, 'The Record of Realism in Messiaen's Bird Style'; and on *Trois petites Liturgies* see Jean Boivin, *La Classe de Messiaen* (Paris: Christian Bourgeois, 1995), pp. 324–325, and Matthew Schellhorn, '*Les Noces* and *Trois petites Liturgies:* An Assessment of Stravinsky's Influence on Messiaen' in *Olivier Messiaen: Music, Art and Literature*, pp. 39–61, 40–41.

[51]   Anne Sexton, 'The Barfly Ought to Sing', in *Ariel Ascending: Writings about Sylvia Plath*, ed. Paul Alexander (New York: Harper & Row Publishers, 1985), p. 182.

[52]   Harold Bloom, *The Anxiety of Influence: A Theory of Poetry*, 2nd edn (New York: Oxford University Press, 1997), p. 107.

[53]   For more on Messiaen's 'updating', see Fallon, 'Two Paths to Paradise: Reform in Messiaen's *Saint François d'Assise*, ed. Robert Sholl (New York: Cambridge University Press, 2007), pp. 206–231.

Chapter 8

Five Quartets: The Search for the Still Point of the Turning World in the War Quartets of T. S. Eliot and Olivier Messiaen

Andrew Shenton

> After the kingfisher's wing
> Has answered light to light, and is silent, the light is still
> At the still point of the turning world.
>
> – T. S. Eliot[1]

The *Quatuor pour la fin du Temps* [Quartet for the end of Time] by Olivier Messiaen and *Four Quartets* by T. S. Eliot are two significant works of art that were both published in their final form during the Second World War. The authors worked without any identifiable personal knowledge of the other although it is likely that later in their lives they were familiar with each other's work. It is all the more extraordinary then that a French Catholic musician and an Anglican American/ English poet would deal with some strikingly similar subject matter, especially since neither were writing typical war works.[2]

This essay sketches the composition and publication of both works and analyses certain primary themes that concern the nature of the human experience of music as a means of expression and as a means of negotiating time. After a brief introduction, I will comment on three common themes: time and technique, the 'unattended moment' and the 'still point of the turning world'.

Messiaen scholarship is, in many ways, still in its infancy, so there are still only a few books and articles about Messiaen's *Quatuor*. Anthony Pople wrote

---

[1]   T. S. Eliot, *Four Quartets* (London: Faber and Faber, 1944). 'Burnt Norton', IV, line 134. Quotations from *Four Quartets* are reproduced by kind permission of Faber and Faber Ltd (UK). Excerpts from 'Burnt Norton' in *Four Quartets* by T.S. Eliot, © 1936 by Houghton Mifflin Harcourt Publishing Company, renewed 1964 by T.S. Eliot; from 'East Coker' in *Four Quartets*, © 1940 by T.S. Eliot, renewed 1968 by Valerie Eliot; from 'The Dry Salvages' in *Four Quartets*, © 1941 by T.S. Eliot, renewed 1969 by Valerie Eliot; from 'Little Gidding' in *Four Quartets*, © 1942 by T.S. Eliot, renewed 1970 by Valerie Eliot; all reprinted by kind permission of Houghton Mifflin Harcourt Publishing Company (USA).

[2]   This term, most often applied to poetry, describes those works written in direct response to war. It came into effect largely after the First World War, which was catalogued to great effect by writers such as Rupert Brooke and Siegfried Sassoon.

an insightful handbook that covers technical and analytical aspects of the music and delves into the theology through a reading of Messiaen's own prefatory commentaries.[3] Rebecca Rischin has put the *Quatuor* in historical context and there are essays by, among others, Iain Matheson and Robert Sherlaw Johnson, that take up some of the extra-musical themes in the work.[4] Biographical information on Messiaen was scarce until the excellent work done by Peter Hill and Nigel Simeone. In their biography of Messiaen they situate the *Quatuor* in his chronology and provide archival information that elucidates the composition and reception history of the piece.[5]

For Eliot on the other hand, the literature is vast. Several major biographies detail aspects of his life. The two most authoritative of these, by Peter Ackroyd and Lyndall Gordon, are sympathetic to the problems of relating a poet's life to his work.[6] There are several collections of essays or monographs devoted exclusively to *Four Quartets* that document the compositional process and examine the poems' themes.[7] Inevitably this means pursuing the musical correspondences set up by Eliot's title. David Moody is sensitive to the problems of pressing the analogy of the quartet too far, but he does try to ascertain what exactly the four instruments (voices) are in the *Quartets*.[8] For Keith Alldritt, the *Quartets* comprise 'four dramatic monologues which interweave and combine but which always remain recognisable'.[9] Alldritt labels these voices the lecturer, the prophet, the conversationalist and the conjuror and offers an illuminating reading of the four poems from this perspective.

Many writers have connected Eliot and his work to specific composers, including Beethoven (notably the late quartets), Bartok (quartets 2–6), Tippett, Ives, Britten

---

[3]   Anthony Pople, *Quatuor pour la fin du Temps* (Cambridge: Cambridge University Press, 1998).

[4]   Rebecca Rischin, *For the End of Time: The Story of the Messiaen Quartet* (Ithaca, NY: Cornell University Press, 2003); Iain Matheson, 'The End of Time: A Biblical Theme in Messiaen's *Quatuor*', in *The Messiaen Companion*, ed. Peter Hill (London: Faber & Faber, 1995), pp. 234–248; Robert Sherlaw Johnson, 'Rhythmic Technique and Symbolism in the Music of Olivier Messiaen', in *Messiaen's Language of Mystical Love*, ed. Siglind Bruhn (New York: Garland, 1998), pp. 121–139.

[5]   Peter Hill and Nigel Simeone, *Messiaen* (New Haven, CT/London: Yale University Press, 2005). See especially pp. 94–104.

[6]   Peter Ackroyd, *T. S. Eliot* (London: Hamish Hamilton, 1984); Lyndall Gordon, *T. S. Eliot: An Imperfect Life* (London: Vintage, 1998).

[7]   See especially Helen Gardiner, *The Composition of 'Four Quartets'* (London: Faber & Faber, 1978); and Bernard Bergonzi, ed., *T. S. Eliot Four Quartets: A Selection of Critical Essays* (London: Macmillan, 1969).

[8]   A. David Moody, 'Four Quartets: Music, word, meaning and value', in *The Cambridge Companion to T. S. Eliot*, ed. A. David Moody (Cambridge: Cambridge University Press, 1994), pp. 142–157.

[9]   Keith Alldritt, *Eliot's Four Quartets: Poetry as Chamber Music* (London: The Woburn Press, 1978), p. 39.

and Stravinsky.[10] To my knowledge nobody has yet made a connection between Messiaen and Eliot partly because there is no documentary evidence of personal connection. So, like the connection of *Four Quartets* to Bartok and his quartets, this essay is speculative, but it provides another way of thinking about each work and it puts music to Eliot's words and vice-versa. Eliot has an epigraph to his *Quartets* by the late sixth century BCE Greek philosopher Heraclitus that reads: 'Although the word is common to most, men live as if each had a private wisdom of his own'. What he means by this is that although all (English) speakers share the same language, our interpretation of that language, of each of those words, is to a large degree private and personal. What this means for a comparative study of Messiaen and Eliot is that I have personally found connections between these works beyond any superficial theological or even biographical information about each man. I offer these up as a new way of approaching both works, acknowledging that I have my private wisdom about them as you do yours.

When listening to Messiaen I am increasingly convinced that at some point we have to put away the musicology and face the music. When we do, we have to listen carefully to what the music says to us on a deep and personal level, freed from Messiaen's verbal accoutrements and from conscious analysis. But, we also often have to try and express to others what the music means to us. Since we have no way to talk about music except in words, Eliot gives us a poetic way to engage with some philosophical and theological concepts in Messiaen's music. It is difficult trying to explain the meaning of a word in one language with that of another because subtlety and nuance are lost in translation. This is actually one of the themes of *Four Quartets*: the struggle of the poet trying to use words that:

> [...] strain,
> Crack and sometimes break, under the burden,
> Under the tension, slip, slide, perish,
> Decay with imprecision, will not stay in place,
> Will not stay still. (BN, V, 149)[11]

But, I am getting ahead of myself. Let me briefly contextualize the quartets for you.

---

[10] For reference to the Beethoven quartets see for example, Grover Smith, *T. S. Eliot's Poetry and Plays* (Chicago: Chicago University Press, 1956), p. 253 and David Barndollar 'Movements in Time: *Four Quartets* and the Late String Quartets of Beethoven', in *T. S. Eliot's Orchestra: Critical Essays on Poetry and Music*, ed. John Xiros Cooper (New York: Garland, 2000), pp. 179–194. For Bartok, see Hugh Kenner, *The Invisible Poet* (London: W. H. Allen, 1974), p. 261; and for Tippett, Ives, Britten and Stravinsky see the essays by Suzanne Robinson, J. Robert Browning, C. F. Pond, and Jayme Stayer respectively in *T. S. Eliot's Orchestra*.

[11] Quotations from *Four Quartets* are identified thus: (Quartet (by initials), movement, line).

Four Quartets

Although T. S. Eliot was born in the United States and studied at Harvard, he immigrated to England in 1914, became a citizen in 1927 (the year he converted to Anglicanism) and remained there for the rest of his life. Eliot was a renowned poet, dramatist and literary critic. He received the Nobel Prize in Literature in 1948 and is the author of such notable works as *The Waste Land*, *Murder in the Cathedral* and *Old Possum's Book of Practical Cats*.

   Four Quartets consists of four separate but connected poems published between 1935 and 1942. They were released under the collective title *Four Quartets* in 1943 in the United States and in 1944 in the UK. The four poems are:

> Burnt Norton (1935) (BN)
> East Coker (1940) (EC)
> The Dry Salvages (1941) (DS)
> Little Gidding (1942) (LG)

For Messiaen, calling his piece a quartet is one of simplicity and convention – any piece for four instruments can be called a quartet and, by the start of the twentieth century, the form of the piece can be anything from one to many movements. With regards to Eliot the answer is not so clear, though many have put forward valuable suggestions. Eliot told his friend John Hayward that he thought the title 'quartet' sets people on the 'right track', and explained that the title suggested to him 'the notion of making a poem by weaving together three or four superficially unrelated themes: the 'poem' being the degree of success in making a new whole out of them'.[12] Each poem is related to a season and an element: 'Burnt Norton' (air/spring); 'East Coker' (earth/summer); 'Dry Salvages' (water/autumn); 'Little Gidding' (fire/winter). Each consists of five sections or 'movements'. British poet Stephen Spender described the content of each movement thus: 'the first consisting of introduction and statement; the second, the transcendence of the theme of the first, in a lyric-like minuet, followed by a sustained meditative passage further developing the thought; the third, illustrative, through the metaphor of journey or pilgrimage of the theme of exploration; the fourth, a lyric; the fifth, a summary of the whole, and a return to the theme of the opening movement'.[13] The pattern for Messiaen's *Quatuor* can be described in similar terms: the first movement is his introduction; the second, his programmatic statement; the third, an illustration of an aspect of the theme; the fourth, an interlude; the fifth and eighth, are lyrics; and the sixth and seventh are a further development of the theme. What both works demonstrate is an organic and holistic conception of form that demonstrates

---

[12]   Letter dated 3 September 1942, quoted in Helen Gardiner, *The Composition of 'Four Quartets'*, p. 26.

[13]   Stephen Spender, *Eliot* (Glasgow: Collins, 1975), p. 155.

sustained development of themes from one part to another while at the same time introducing new ideas throughout.

In an unpublished essay dating from 1933, Eliot declared that the aim for his writing was to achieve '[…] poetry so transparent that in reading it we are intent on what the poetry *points at*, and not the poetry, this seems to me the thing to try for. To get *beyond poetry*, as Beethoven, in his last works, strove to get *beyond music*.'[14] Messiaen's aim for his music is similar: a struggle to get at what the music (and his own commentaries) *point at* and not the music itself. In fact, this desire to get 'beyond poetry' is a development from the Symboliste desire expressed by writer Paul Valéry as 'the common intention of several groups of poets to reclaim their own from music'.[15] Indeed Valéry himself writes about the musical effect of poetry and notes that:

> the meaning produced within you, far from destroying the musical form communicated to you, recalls it. The living pendulum that has swung from sound to sense swings back to its felt point of departure, as though the very sense which is present to your mind can find no other outlet or expression, no other answer, than the very music which gave it birth.[16]

Valéry was also aware, like Eliot, of the limitations of poetry, noting that the true communication between the poet and reader allows a freedom 'analogous to that which music allows to the hearer, although less extensive'.[17]

Music was important to Eliot. Scholar John Cooper describes it as Eliot's 'central symbol of the aesthetic state', and notes that it is, 'as such, the closest an earthbound intelligence, bent on practicing gestures of renunciation, can get to the divine'.[18] Eliot himself noted that poetry was an effective means of communication, but not at the same level as music. In his essay *Poetry and Drama*, written in 1957, Eliot declared: 'This peculiar range of sensibility can be expressed by dramatic poetry, at its moments of greatest dramatic intensity. At such moments, we touch the border of those feelings which only music can express. We can never emulate

---

[14]   In an unpublished essay 'English poets as Letter Writers', in the Hayward Collection, King's College, Cambridge. Quoted in Paul Murray, *T. S. Eliot and Mysticism: The Secret History of 'Four Quartets'* (London: Macmillan, 1991), p. 17.

[15]   Paul Valéry, *The Art of Poetry*, trans. Denise Folliot, with an Introduction by T. S. Eliot (New York: Pantheon Books, 1958), p. 42.

[16]   Ibid., p. 72.

[17]   Ibid., p. 157. In his essay 'Pure Poetry', Valéry goes even further, and compares the resources of the musician with that of the poet concluding that the musician 'only has to assemble well-defined and well-prepared elements', whereas the poet's language constitutes '*an effort by one man* to create an artificial order by means of a material of vulgar origin' (Ibid., p. 190).

[18]   Cooper, John Xiros, *T. S. Eliot and the Ideology of 'Four Quartets'* (Cambridge: Cambridge University Press, 1995), p. 162.

music, because to arrive at the condition of music would be the annihilation of poetry, and especially of dramatic poetry.'[19]

It is interesting to note that Messiaen was an avid commentator on his own music in a way that continues to paralyse other writers, who simply repeat what he said, respecting or perhaps guaranteeing the composer's invincible imprimatur; or, they echo his comments in a manner that more or less imitates his own style. Eliot on the other hand did not attempt to provide analysis or interpretation of his writing. There is a famous account of Eliot's refusal to elucidate his work: when a student asked Eliot what he meant by the line from *Ash Wednesday* (1930) 'Lady, three white leopards sat under a juniper tree' (II, 43), Eliot replied that he meant: 'Lady, three white leopards sat under a juniper tree'.[20]

Quatuor pour la fin du Temps

The circumstances surrounding the composition of the *Quatuor pour la fin du Temps* are unusual. Messiaen was just 32 years old when he was captured and taken to Stalag VIIIA, a prison camp about 70 miles east of Dresden. Three of his fellow prisoners were also musicians: the cellist, Étienne Pasquier; the clarinetist, Henri Akoka; and the violinist, Jean le Boulaire. Fortunately the violinist and clarinetist had managed to keep their instruments in captivity and a cello was found for Pasquier. In the camp Messiaen wrote what he described as 'an unpretentious little trio', for the three men, which they played in the camp washrooms.[21] This piece became the 'Interlude', the fourth movement of the eight in the *Quatuor*, and a germinal one for musical and rhythmic material. For some of the other movements Messiaen reused material from earlier works, probably due to lack of time for wholly new composition and perhaps partly to bring attention to his own work as he was at that time relatively unknown as a composer.[22]

The *Quatuor* was premiered in Stalag VIIIA on 15 January 1941, with Messiaen himself playing the piano (see Plate 8.1). The size of the audience varies

---

[19]   T. S. Eliot, 'Poetry and Drama', in *T. S. Eliot On Poetry and Poets* (London: Faber and Faber, 1957), p. 87.

[20]   Spender, *Eliot*, p. 129.

[21]   Antoine Goléa, *Rencontres avec Olivier Messiaen* (Paris: Juilliard, 1961), p. 62.

[22]   The fifth movement, 'Praise to the eternity of Jesus', for cello and piano, first appeared as part of the 'Festivals of Beautiful Water' for a sextet of ondes Martenot, written for the Paris Exposition of 1937; and the eighth, 'Praise to the immortality of Jesus', for violin and piano, is his arrangement of the second part of his *Diptyque* for organ, composed in 1930. According to Hill and Simeone, a note in Messiaen's archives shows that two of the movements originally had different titles: 'the sixth movement is given as "Fanfare" (changed to "Dance of fury, for the seven trumpets"), while the eighth movement appears as "Second praise ('louange') to the eternity of Jesus" (changed to "Praise to the immortality of Jesus")'. See Hill and Simeone, *Messiaen*, p. 101.

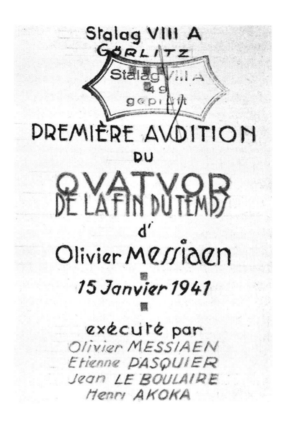

Plate 8.1   Poster for the premiere of the *Quatuor pour la fin du Temps*

in different accounts, but the effect of the music was universally felt.[23] At the time of the premiere a French language newspaper called *Lumignon* was produced in the camp. In the first issue, dated 1 April 1941, there was a review of the *Quatuor* which noted that: 'this music honours everyone. This is its true grandeur, which draws us to it.'[24]

The theme for the *Quatuor* is taken from the *Book of Revelation*, the last canonical book in the Bible. In *Revelation*, St John recounts that an angel visited him and called him to be a witness to what he sees in a series of visions. He then writes seven letters to the seven major churches in Asia warning them that Christ will be returning to earth. These letters describe the final judgment of God on the

---

[23]   Messiaen claimed there were 5000 at the premiere, Pasquier said around 400 and Charles Jourdanet (an audience member on the occasion) recalls '150 or so'. See ibid., pp. 100–102.

[24]   Quoted in ibid., p. 101. The review is signed with the initials V. M.

world using symbols and metaphors that require exegesis and are therefore open to a number of interpretations.

The *Book of Revelation* is powerfully evocative, but Messiaen warned against a superficial reading of it. He said: 'To regard the *Revelation* merely as an accumulation of cataclysms and catastrophes is to understand it poorly; the *Revelation* also contains great and marvellous periods of illumination, followed by solemn silences'.[25] Clearly, his music aims to express some of the less violent aspects of the story and, as the *Quatuor* lasts less than an hour, Messiaen obviously had to restrict the programmatic content to certain elements.

Messiaen wrote substantial notes in the preface to the score that tell us the general programme of the *Quatuor*, and of the form and content of individual movements. He also wrote in the score itself, annotating features such as birdsong and identifying important musical elements such as the rhythmic patterns in the cello and piano in the first movement, 'Crystal Liturgy'. The epigraph in the score declares that the work is 'in homage to the Angel of the Apocalypse, who raised a hand towards heaven saying "there shall be no more Time"'. In the first section of the preface, dedicated to a discussion of the subject of the *Quatuor* and to a commentary on each movement, he added the following passage:

> I saw a mighty angel coming down from heaven, wrapped in cloud, with a rainbow round his head. His face was like the sun, his feet like pillars of fire. He planted his right foot on the sea, his left foot on the land and, standing by the sea and the earth, he raised his hand to heaven and swore by him who lives for ever and ever, saying: There shall be no more time; but on the day the seventh angel sounds the trumpet, the hidden purpose of God will have been fulfilled. (*Revelation*, 10:1–7)

Since Messiaen himself stated 'I did not want in any way to make a commentary on the *Book of Revelation*, but only to justify my desire for the cessation of time', and because, in truth, the majority of the movements have only tangential connection to the apocalyptic theme, this essay does not discuss those sections or movements of the *Quatuor* explicitly related to the *Book of Revelation*, nor does it pursue any connections between notions of the end of time and the circumstances under which the piece was written and premiered.[26] Instead it delves deeper into some of the theological and philosophical issues regarding the end of time, and in particular how the cessation of time might be conceived in human terms and described as the still point of the turning world.

The titles of the eight movements of the *Quatuor* are as follows:

1. Crystal liturgy ['Liturgie de cristal']
2. Vocalise for the angel who announces the end of Time ['Vocalise pour l'ange qui annonce la fin du Temps']

---

[25]   Goléa, *Rencontres*, p. 70.
[26]   Ibid., p. 64.

3. The abyss of the birds ['Abîme des oiseaux']
4. Interlude ['Intermède']
5. Praise to the eternity of Jesus ['Louange à l'éternité de Jésus']
6. Dance of fury, for the seven trumpets ['Danse de la fureur, pour les sept trompettes']
7. Cluster of rainbows, for the angel who announces the end of Time ['Fouillis d'arcs-en-ciel, pour l'ange qui annonce la fin du Temps']
8. Praise to the immortality of Jesus ['Louange à l'immortalité de Jésus']

Thanks to these titles and his commentaries in the preface to the score, we know that Messiaen is specifically portraying the Angel of the Apocalypse in the first and third parts of the second movement, in the sixth movement, and also in part of the seventh movement. The fourth movement, the 'Interlude', has no thematic programme and is also not discussed in this essay, although Messiaen does note that it is related to the other movements 'by various melodic references'.[27] Movements 1, 3, 5 and 8 bear no direct relationship to events described in the *Book of Revelation* (although it is possible that the third movement, 'Abyss of the birds' refers to the bottomless pit described earlier in *Revelation* by the fifth angel).[28] These four movements, along with sections from the second and seventh movements, may, however, be related to the part of the epigraph ('there shall be no more Time') inscribed in the score, and I shall suggest some ways we might engage musically and theologically with them.

The end of Time

Immediately prior to the first performance of the *Quatuor* Messiaen gave a lecture in which he later recalled, 'I told them first of all that this quartet was written for the end of time, not as a play on words about the time of captivity, but for the ending of concepts of past and future: that is, for the beginning of eternity, and in this I relied on the magnificent text of the *Revelation*'.[29] Nearly two decades later he said, 'my initial thought was of the abolition of time itself, something infinitely mysterious and incomprehensible to most of the philosophers of time, from Plato to Bergson'.[30]

Messiaen and Eliot are both concerned with physical, philosophical and theological aspects of time. Both have a sense that the cessation of time may be a type of heaven or a unity with a god who is without beginning or end. Eliot writes of the passage of human time as 'a time for living and for generation' (EC, I, 10),

---

[27] Messiaen, *Quatuor pour la fin du Temps* (Paris: Durand, 1942), Prèface, p. ii.
[28] For references to the abyss (or bottomless pit) see *Revelation*, 9:1–5, 11:7 and 20:1–3.
[29] Goléa, *Rencontres*, p. 67.
[30] Ibid., p. 70.

echoing the famous passage in *Ecclesiastes*, and also of 'The time of the seasons and the constellations' (EC, I, 42), but he is more interested in philosophical aspects of time and these are best summarized by the opening passage of the first *Quartet*, 'Burnt Norton'. Eliot notes that:

> Time present and time past
> Are both perhaps present in time future
> And time future contained in time past. (BN, I, 1)

He ascertains the primacy of the present noting that:

> Time past and time future
> What might have been and what has been
> Point to one end, which is always present. (BN, I, 44)

Time as part of the human condition is not always pleasant or easy according to Eliot, who believes that 'Time past and time future / Allow but a little consciousness' (BN, II, 83), and suggests that 'Only through time time is conquered' (BN, II, 90).

In addition to the commentaries he wrote about his own music, Messiaen discussed in some detail different aspects of time in the first movement of his *Traité de rythme, de couleur et d'ornithologie*, written between 1949 and 1992 and compiled posthumously by his wife, Yvonne Loriod, according to a plan put forward by Messiaen himself.[31] According to Messiaen, 'The perception of time is the source of all music and all rhythm', which is why the first chapter of his treatise starts with a theological and philosophical discussion of time that is broad-ranging in its scope but often quite specific about how time relates to perception of music.

In the opening section of the first chapter, entitled 'Time and eternity', Messiaen defines both time and eternity by quoting St Thomas Aquinas, whose discussion in the *Summa Theologiae* makes the distinction that 'Eternity is an all-encompassing simultaneity, and in time there is a before and an after'.[32] Messiaen also describes angelic time in the *aevum*, that is 'the intermediary between time and eternity', and human time, which he explains as being characterized by 'periodic changes, through the alternation of two events, the first never being identical but similar'.[33] Like Eliot, Messiaen uses the familiar passage from *Ecclesiastes* (3:1ff) to illustrate human time: 'For everything there is a season, and a time for everything under

---

[31]   Olivier Messiaen, *Traité*. For a detailed analytical summary of the first chapter of the *Traité* see: Andrew Shenton, 'Observations on Time in Olivier Messiaen's *Traité*', in *Olivier Messiaen: Music, Art, Literature*, eds Christopher Dingle and Nigel Simeone (Aldershot: Ashgate, 2007), pp. 173–189.

[32]   Messiaen, *Traité I*, p. 7.

[33]   Ibid., pp. 7 and 8.

heaven: a time to be born, and a time to die.'[34] He then moves his discussion to the end of human time and quotes again in his *Traité* the passage from *Revelation* that is the key quote for his *Quatuor*: 'I saw a mighty angel coming down from heaven … '.[35] Although Messiaen's chapter in the *Traité* includes reference to more than 30 writers (including Einstein, Euclid and Newton) and includes discussion of such diverse topics as stellar time and geological time, he is clearly most interested in eternity and the notion that the Christian God is eternal.

Although the *Quatuor* is a comparatively early work, Messiaen is already deeply concerned with manipulating time, especially through rhythmic innovations. In the preface to the *Quatuor*, in addition to an explanation of the subject of the piece and a commentary on each movement, Messiaen included some performance practice advice, and a short summary of his novel and inventive rhythmic language. This explanation deals specifically with four techniques: first, added values (the addition of a note, rest or dot to a rhythm); second, augmentation and diminution of rhythms; third, non-retrogradable rhythms, that is to say rhythms that are palindromic; and lastly, rhythmic pedals (rhythms that provide a fundamental basis for the music). These four, plus Greek and Hindu rhythms and the use of polyrhythms (more than one rhythm played at the same time), give Messiaen a boundless range of rhythmic possibilities that can be astonishingly complex.[36]

In fact, Messiaen sought to manipulate time through many specific musical techniques including repetitive forms, structural units in mosaic patterns, isorhythmic motets, palindromes and symmetrical patterns, monothematicism, monotonality, unity of atmosphere, avoidance of conflict, neutralized dissonance, extremely slow tempos, static formal plans, fixed orchestration and relatively stable levels of tension.[37] There is clear evidence that later in life he was aware of the power a composer has over his material and of the effect that this has on the listener. In the first chapter of the *Traité*, Messiaen acknowledged that because the composer:

> knows in advance all the pasts and the futures [of the work] […] he can transform the present so that it touches the past or the future […] he can push his research in all possible forms offered by inversions or permutations of duration: forward

---

[34]   *Ecclesiastes*, 3:1 ff.

[35]   *Revelation*, 10:1 ff.

[36]   Lavignac's *Encyclopédie de la Musique* (the 120 deçî-tâlas listed by Sharngadeva in his treatise *Samgîta-ratnâkara*). A. Lavignac and L. de la Laurencie (eds), *Encyclopedié de la musique et dictionnaire du conservatoire* (Paris: Delagrave, 1913–31).

[37]   See for example, Paul Griffiths, *Olivier Messiaen and the Music of Time* (London/ Boston: Faber & Faber, 1985), and Diane Luchese, *Olivier Messiaen's Slow Music: Glimpses of Eternity in Time* (PhD dissertation, Northwestern University, 1998), especially chapter 2, pp. 10–65.

motion, retrograde motion, movement from the centre to the extremes, movement from the extremes to the centre, and a multitude of other movements.[38]

This manipulation of musical material affects the listeners regardless of their knowledge of any extra-musical programme so, to a certain extent, Messiaen's programme *is* going to be evident in the music even if the listener is not aware of the programme prior to hearing the music. The music does 'map' to the programme to a large extent and because the human response to music is broadly the same (for example, slow and quiet = calm), there is an extent to which Messiaen's broad intentions may be perceived without prior knowledge of the programme (or ignoring it). We can then perhaps understand Eliot when he says: 'We had the experience but missed the meaning' (DS, II, 93) and we can perhaps recover some of the meaning through listening, even if the listening is according to our own wisdom.

It is worth looking in some detail at a specific movement of the *Quatuor* to see how Messiaen pushed the boundaries of technique to a programmatic end. I have previously undertaken a brief hermeneutical analysis of 'Crystal liturgy' in which I discussed the curious and ambiguous title and attempted to relate it to the apocalyptic programme and to analyse the extra-musical elements including the epigraph and annotations in the score.[39] Messiaen's commentary for this first movement states: 'Between three and four o'clock in the morning, the dawn chorus: a blackbird or a nightingale soloist improvises, surrounded by a shimmer of sound, a halo of trills lost very high in the trees. Transpose this to the religious plane: you will have the harmonious silence of heaven.'[40] The most significant part of this description is the final sentence in which Messiaen asks us to make a huge leap of imagination (and faith) and transpose a mundane scene to a heavenly one. If we are willing and able to do this we might be able to hear the 'harmonious silence of heaven', an image Eliot suggests is perhaps a type of music 'heard so deeply / That it is not heard at all' (DS, V, 210).

There are two notable techniques in the 'Crystal liturgy' that contribute to the attempt at the negation of time and the illustration of heaven. The first is the use of 'isorhythm'. This technique combines a pattern of melodic or harmonic material (called the 'color') over a different pattern of rhythmic material of a different length (called the 'talea'). In 'Crystal liturgy', the piano has a sequence of 29 chords, which is played to a rhythmic sequence of 17 values. Once the rhythmic pattern has been completed it begins again on the 18th chord and then when the chord sequence has finished it begins again, this time on the 13th rhythm of the second time through the rhythmic sequence. Obviously it would take a long time to play out all the 493 possibilities of this isorhythm until the two sequences realign

---

[38] Messiaen, *Traité I*, p. 28.

[39] See: Andrew Shenton, *Olivier Messiaen's System of Signs: Notes Towards Understanding His Music* (Aldershot: Ashgate, 2008), pp. 65–67.

[40] Messiaen, *Quatuor*, Prèface, p. i.

at their respective beginnings, so what we hear is a fragment, one that is isolated and taken out of time.

The cello part in this movement is also organized using isorhythmic technique, but there is a further innovation in this part. The melodic material of the cello part, (the 'color'), is a five-note melodic shape. The innovation is to be found in the rhythmic ostinato, which is a 15-note figure made up of two cells, one of three notes and one of 12. Both of these are non-retrogradable, that is to say they are palindromic about their midpoint. We may not be aware of these subtleties when we are listening, but it is certain that Messiaen was aware of the effect they would have at some level on the audience as he manages his material towards both an explicit and implicit goal.

In Messiaen's commentary for this movement he describes the dawn chorus in a forest scene but suggests that it has a heavenly counterpart. Could it be that the clarinet and violin represent the mundane, planted on earth and fixed with birdsong, and at the same time a parallel universe unfolds in the piano and cello that allows us a distorted glimpse of heaven, where (to use St Paul's analogy) we see through the glass a little less darkly?

The unattended moment

One of the central themes in *Four Quartets* is a moment 'in and out of time', a moment of 'sudden illumination' where we perceive what Eliot described in his earlier poem *The Waste Land* as 'the heart of light, the silence'.[41] The timeless moment is a moment of spiritual fulfilment beyond description by mere words which 'strain, / Crack and sometimes break, under the burden' (BN, V, 149). It comes without warning, and, as I quoted above, Eliot suggests that although 'We had the experience but missed the meaning', the meaning can be recovered at least in part because 'approach to the meaning restores the experience / In a different form, beyond any meaning / We can assign to happiness' (DS, II, 94). In the fifth section of 'The Dry Salvages' Eliot summarizes the experience of the moment and outlines the action it behooves us as humans 'Caught in the form of limitation / Between un-being and being' (BN, V, 167), to take in order to restore the meaning:

> But to apprehend
> The point of intersection of the timeless
> With time, is an occupation for the saint–
> No occupation either, but something given
> And taken, in a lifetime's death in love,
> Ardour and selflessness and self-surrender. (DS, V, 200)

---

[41]   *The Waste Land* (London: Faber & Faber, 1922), I, 'The Burial of the Dead', line 41.

The timeless moment, the 'unattended moment', can happen anywhere. At these places we may be joined with time past and time future, but for Eliot the moment of sudden illumination can only be recalled as a moment in time because:

> [...] only in time can the moment in the rose-garden,
> The moment in the arbour where the rain beat,
> The moment in the draughty church at smokefall
> Be remembered; involved with past and future. (BN, II, 86)

The isolated moments are only 'hints and guesses, / Hints followed by guesses' (DS, V, 212), however, we are able to partly restore the meaning through a combination of 'prayer, observance, discipline, thought and action' (DS, V, 214).

This 'unattended moment' occurs many times in Messiaen's music. For example, in the *Méditations sur le mystère de la Sainte Trinité* Messiaen tries to describe God's tremendous presence, suggesting in 'Méditation IV' that 'the strangeness of the timbres and the bird song chosen should evoke an unknown dimension', and that 'all we can know of God is summed up by these words that are so complex and yet so simple: *He is*. Words that we can only comprehend in flashes, in rare and brief moments of illumination'.[42]

In the *Quatuor*, Messiaen is at one point explicit about this other-worldly moment. In the programme note for the seventh movement, he describes a state whereby in his dreams he remarks that: 'I hear and see ordered melodies and chords and familiar hues and forms; then following this transitory stage I pass into the unreal and submit ecstatically to a vortex, a dizzying interpretation of superhuman sounds and colours'.[43] His description is of mystical encounter and his language is revealing: unreal [*irréel*], ecstatic [*extase*] and superhuman [*surhumain*]. Musically the surreal dream is reinvisioned through trills, glissandi, tempo changes, coloured chords and arpeggiated figures, especially at figure K in the score, where the composer submits completely to the ecstatic experience. By putting this experience into music he is able to partly restore it and to share it with his listeners. As Eliot noted, 'approach to the meaning restores the experience / In a different form', so we are not able to duplicate Messiaen's dream exactly but, since he is a composer of remarkable genius, these musical 'hints and guesses' are often enough to allow any listener some sort of mystical encounter of their own.

Messiaen also tries to depict heaven itself. In the first movement, 'Crystal liturgy', this is an attempt to evoke the 'harmonious silence of heaven'. In the second movement, 'Vocalise, for the angel who announces the end of Time', the music is divided into three sections: the first and third parts are short and, in Messiaen's own words, 'evoke the power of the mighty angel, his hair a rainbow, and his clothing mist'. The second, more extended section portrays

---

[42]   Messiaen, *Méditations sur le mystère de la Sainte Trinité* (Paris: Leduc, 1973), preface to 'Méditation IV', p. 29.

[43]   Messiaen, *Quatuor*, Prèface, p. ii.

what Messiaen described as 'the ineffable harmonies of heaven'. The musical means of achieving this effect are, in Messiaen's words, 'soft cascades of blue-orange chords, encircling with their distant carillon the plainchant-like recitative of the violin and cello'.[44] Like the cluster of rainbows that surround the Angel of the Apocalypse, this heaven is vague and immaterial, serene and tranquil, echoing the paradoxical 'harmonious silence' Messiaen describes in the first movement. Messiaen's language signifies a religious heaven with its 'carillon' and 'plainchant'. This heaven is, of course, personal and unique, but it is interesting to note that is not predicated on any description of the New Jerusalem as describe in *Revelation* and, consciously or unconsciously, Messiaen never overburdens it with any dogmatic language that would preclude a non-Catholic from appreciating or even participating in this vision. In fact, as I have noted before, 'it is difficult for us to define an eschatology for Messiaen, because his oeuvre is not a catechism and does not address any defined Catholic notions of death, human destiny, the Second Coming or the Last Judgment'.[45]

The still point of the turning world

Recalling the unattended moment, or trying to regain it, requires for Eliot moving towards the 'still point of the turning world'. This concept is born of the philosophical model of serenity and stillness that imagines a single point at the centre of a circle or globe, which is a point of complete stillness. This state of grace, 'a condition of simplicity / (costing not less than everything)' (LG, V, 253), Eliot believes should be the pursuit of every Christian. The choice is to go by way of possession (the way up), or the way of dispossession (the way down), both of which the poems' epigraph from Heraclitus informs us will bring us to the same place, to 'the still point of the turning world' (BN, II, 62). Eliot has called for this serenity several times in the earlier quartets such as in *East Coker*, where he writes, 'I said to my soul, be still, and let the dark come upon you / Which shall be the darkness of God' (EC, III, 112), and he urges us that 'We must be still and still moving / Into another intensity / For a further union, a deeper communion' (EC, V, 204). This same attitude of prayer as the inspiration for our daily lives is also expressed in *Ash Wednesday* where Eliot writes: 'Teach us to care and not to care / Teach us to sit still' (VI, 211). Prayer is however, 'more / Than an order of words, the conscious occupation / Of the praying mind, or the sound of the voice praying', (LG, I, 46) it is 'a lifetime burning in every moment' (EC, V, 194).

The two 'Louange' movements of Messiaen's *Quatuor* are for me superb examples of how Messiaen has composed music that moves us to the 'still point'. Although perhaps heretical to those people who believe that Messiaen's word is the final one regarding comprehension of his music, we have to acknowledge that

---

[44]   Ibid., p. i.

[45]   Shenton, *Olivier Messiaen's System of Signs*, p. 27.

for many people Messiaen's text is an impediment to listening and although they may be drawn to the music they are not drawn to the programme. In truth, when I hear these movements I do not hear them as paeans to Jesus, though I may be partly conscious of Messiaen's commentaries. For me, the long and ecstatic phrases in the string parts and the regular pulsing of the piano are part of a formal design that transcends the mundane and is in many ways a transformative experience.

The form of these movements is important to the effect Messiaen is trying to create. Eliot, perpetually concerned with technique, suggests that:

> Only by the form, the pattern,
> Can words or music reach
> The stillness, as a Chinese jar still
> Moves perpetually in its stillness. (BN, V, 140)

Eliot's image of a Chinese vase that although stationary has perpetual circular movement by virtue of its shape and perhaps its painted design, is a strong parallel to Messiaen's music in these movements which itself moves perpetually in its stillness.

Messiaen may himself have had this experience of the unattended moment, of contact with the divine, many times, but, for most of us, as Eliot points out:

> [...] there is only the unattended
> Moment, the moment in and out of time,
> The distraction fit, lost in a shaft of sunlight,
> The wild thyme unseen, or the winter lightning
> Or the waterfall, or music heard so deeply
> That it is not heard at all [.] (DS, V, 206)

By giving his music an explicit programme Messiaen has asked for it to be more than 'absolute' music (music for its own sake), and he thereby assigns it a function beyond that required of a piece of music without a programme. Its success should therefore be judged, at least in part, on the fulfilment of extra-musical function. Messiaen's *Quatuor* has served us well if it has caused us to reflect even for a moment on war or enticed us to (re)read the *Book of Revelation* or to think about time and the way it affects our lives.

But, if it has helped us to mediate our relationship with our own God (bearing in mind the cautionary epigraph Eliot uses for his *Quartets* that 'although the word is common to most, we live as if we each had a private wisdom of our own'), then it has achieved both its implicit and explicit goals. The same is true for Eliot in his *Quartets*, although because his medium is language, his ideas and the ones they spark in us are perhaps easier for us to verbalize and therefore comprehend.[46]

---

[46]   For more discussion on the question of understanding, see Shenton, *Olivier Messiaen's System of Signs*, especially pp. 3–11, and 159–171.

In conclusion I would like to leave you with two thoughts that perhaps provide a way to understand Messiaen's theological music for both the Christian and the non-Christian alike. The first is simply stated in an essay by the English poet W. H. Auden:

> You cannot tell people what to do, you can only tell them parables; and that is what art really is, particular stories of particular people and experiences, from which each according to his immediate and peculiar needs may draw his own conclusions.[47]

Messiaen gives us much extra-musical information, but he is not proselytizing; rather he invites us to partake of the music and theology only to the extent we are willing and able.

Eliot himself summarizes our engagement with any music, and especially with the transformative aspect of music whether that is the transcendence of time, the moment of revelation or the move towards 'serenity, stillness and reconciliation'. In the fifth section of 'The Dry Salvages' (line 211), Eliot reminds us of the most crucial and overwhelming feature of music and its manifold capabilities:

> you are the music / While the music lasts.

---

[47]   W. H. Auden, 'Psychology and Art To-day', in *The Arts To-day*, ed. Geoffrey Gregson (London: John Lane, 1935), p. 18.

Chapter 9

The Charm of Impossibilities: Mystic Surrealism as Contemplative Voluptuousness

Stephen Schloesser

Is it nonsense? I wish it were. It sometimes sounds terribly sensible to me.
But, my dear Sebastian, you can't seriously *believe* it all.
Can't I?
I mean about Christmas and the star and the three kings and the ox and the ass.
Oh yes, I believe that. It's a lovely idea.
But you can't *believe* things because they're a lovely idea.
But I *do*. That's how I believe.

Evelyn Waugh[1]

1944: A refusal to mourn?

In 1944, Olivier Messiaen completed the *Trois petites Liturgies de la Présence Divine* [Three Small Liturgies of the Divine Presence]. His text is nearly pantheistic in its claims for divine immanence in the historical world of space and time.[2] Even in the best of times, such claims might have been expected to have had a difficult reception. These were not the best of times.

The premiere of the *Trois petites Liturgies* on 21 April 1945 contributed to the uproar now known as the 'Messiaen Controversy' [*Le Cas Messiaen*].[3] A half-century later, Claude Samuel looked back at the scandal: 'today's listeners must feel only astonishment and be at a loss to explain the violent and often offensive remarks provoked by the first performance of the *Trois petites Liturgies*'.[4]

---

[1]   Evelyn Waugh, *Brideshead Revisited: The Sacred and Profane Memories of Captain Charles Ryder* (Boston: Little, Brown, 1945), p. 86.

[2]   Olivier Messiaen, *Trois petites Liturgies de la Présence Divine* (Paris: Éditions Durand, 1952).

[3]   For an exhaustive study see Lilise Boswell-Kurc, 'Olivier Messiaen's Religious War-time Works and their Controversial Reception in France (1941–46)', (PhD diss., New York University, 2001). See also Peter Hill and Nigel Simeone, *Messiaen* (New Haven, CT/London: Yale University Press, 2005), pp. 142–167.

[4]   Claude Samuel, tr. Stewart Spencer; in liner notes for Messiaen, *Réveil des oiseaux. Trois petites Liturgies de la Présence Divine*, with Kent Nagano, Yvonne Loriod, et al.,

Perhaps – but then again, it is worth revisiting what it might have been like to listen to such immanentist effusions about divine presence in a blood-soaked city.

Messiaen began this composition in 1943, in occupied Paris, as the war's tide turned in favour of the Allies (following the Soviet repulsion of Hitler's forces at Stalingrad in January–February of that year). When Messiaen finished them in March 1944, Paris would still be awaiting its liberation in August. By the time they were first performed in April 1945, Paris had been liberated for eight months, but Hitler would not finally capitulate for another two weeks.

As many memorial plaques scattered throughout the city centre attest today, the Liberation of Paris in August 1944 was achieved only after a brutal urban battle – one final convulsion of violence piled up on four years of occupation, torture and executions. German snipers fired shots from the roof of the nave of Notre-Dame cathedral as the congregation assembled for the Te Deum thanksgiving service on 26 August. Although congregants took cover under their seats, Charles de Gaulle 'calmly stood through the service, joining fervently in the "Magnificat"'.[5] De Gaulle forbade Cardinal Emmanuel Suhard, the archbishop of Paris, from attending the service in his own cathedral. As chronicler Emmanuel Godin notes, 'because he had welcomed Marshal Pétain to Notre-Dame in April 1944 and in June 1944 had celebrated the funeral of Philippe Henriot, the collaborationist information minister assassinated by Resistance fighters, [Suhard] was considered as a traitor by the liberators of France. For some Christian-democrats, he also betrayed true Catholic values.'[6] This extraordinary assertion of a layman's military authority over the cardinal archbishop not only demonstrates how conflicted French Catholicism was in the summer of 1944; it also points to the bloody retribution against collaborators – the *épuration* [cleansing] – that would immediately follow the Liberation, tearing France apart.[7] The French needed decades to sort out the traumatic 'Dark Years' of German occupation and the collaborationist Vichy government.[8]

© 1996, 1992 by Erato Disques S.A., Erato 0630-12702-2, Compact disc.

[5]   Charles Williams, *The Last Great Frenchman: A Life of General de Gaulle* (New York: John Wiley & Sons, 1993), p. 275.

[6]   Emmanuel Godin, 'French Catholic Intellectuals and the Nation in Post-war France', *South Central Review* 17, no. 4 (Winter 2000): 45–60, at p. 47.

[7]   Larry Collins and Dominique Lapierre, *Is Paris Burning?* (New York: Simon and Schuster, 1965); Antony Beevor and Artemis Cooper, *Paris After the Liberation, 1944–1949*, rev. edn (New York: Penguin Books, 2004).

[8]   Julian Jackson, *France: The Dark Years, 1940–1944* (New York: Oxford University Press, 2001). The reception history of director Marcel Ophuls's documentary film *Le Chagrin et la pitié* [*The Sorrow and the Pity*] illustrates the long duration of the trauma. Released and shown on German and Swiss television in 1971, the work was not broadcast in France due to what Ophuls called 'censorship by inertia'. Another decade passed before it was shown in France (following the accession to power of François Mitterrand's socialist government). See Guy Austin, *Contemporary French Cinema: An Introduction* (New York: Manchester University Press; New York: St. Martin's Press, 1996), p. 22. For the long

While politics, war and personal experience led his contemporaries to capture modernity's existential angst with music that was darkly expressionistic, excruciatingly dissonant or whimsically aleatoric, Messiaen frequently declared: 'I have no wish to waste my time on harrowing subjects. I am a musician of joy.' When asked in 1963 to write a work commemorating the 25th anniversary of the outbreak of the war, Messiaen responded: 'Death? That exists, but I myself emphasize the Resurrection.' He refused to write a Requiem Mass and chose instead to compose *Et exspecto resurrectionem mortuorum*, based on words from the Nicene Creed: 'I look forward to the resurrection of the dead.'[9] Although Messiaen knew what it was like to be reproached for pursuing 'a kind of *theologia gloriae* which scarcely has anything to do with the actual situation of today's human being and his need for redemption',[10] one critic has concisely summed up his counter-cultural stance: 'Messiaen's music is different from its age not so much for the techniques it discovers but for its refusal to mourn. Not since Haydn perhaps, has a composer had the effrontery to be so happy, so serene: to suffuse his music with such confidence and composure.'[11]

Creation and Apocalypse.
Incarnation and Eschatology.
Immanence and Emanence.[12]
On the one hand, finding God everywhere in the here and now.
On the other hand, despairing of the here and now,
and hoping to find God in the there and then.
Seeming contradiction.
Apparent incompatibilities?
Or the charm of impossibilities?

---

duration of France's trauma see Henry Rousso, *The Vichy Syndrome: History and Memory in France since 1944* (Cambridge, MA: Harvard University Press, 1991).

[9] Yvonne Loriod in an interview with Peter Hill, in *The Messiaen Companion*, ed. Peter Hill (London: Faber & Faber, 1995), pp. 294–295.

[10] See remarks by Dutch theologian Johan Vos in a roundtable discussion (11 June 1972) transcribed in Almut Rößler, *Contributions to the Spiritual World of Olivier Messiaen*, trans. Barbara Dagg and Nancy Poland (Duisberg: Gilles & Francke, 1986), pp. 48–56, at p. 51.

[11] Bernard Holland, 'Remembering Messiaen with Works of His Own', *The New York Times* (10 November 1992).

[12] 'For to immanence, to the heart, Christ is redundant and all things are one. To emanence, to the mind, Christ touches only the top, skims off only the top, as it were, the souls of men, the wheat grains whole, and lets the chaff fall where? To the world fat and patently unredeemed; to the entire rest of the universe, which is irrelevant and nonparticipant; to time and matter unreal, and so unknowable, an illusory, absurd, accidental, and overelaborate stage.' Annie Dillard, *Holy the Firm* (New York: HarperCollins Perennial, 2003 [1977]), pp. 69–70.

Although Christian doctrine insists that these extremes be grasped simultaneously in tension, in practice this is a difficult thing to do – as several centuries of the Catholic/Protestant divide suggest.[13] Messiaen struggled to hold on to both. Where others saw only irreconcilable differences, Messiaen envisaged the 'charm of impossibilities'.[14] In a largely post-Christian milieu, he not only held on to religious faith; he pushed belief in divine immanence to its extreme precisely through his representations of transcendence.[15]

The brutal year of 1944 produced not only the *Trois petites Liturgies*, it also witnessed Messiaen's manifesto written at age 36: *Technique de mon langage musical* [The Technique of my Musical Language]. In the introductory notes to this work, Messiaen cited (in this order) the major influences on his thought: his mother, Cécile Sauvage (1883–1927); his wife, Claire Delbos (1906–59); William Shakespeare (*c.* 1564–1616); Paul Claudel (1868–1955); Pierre Reverdy (1889–1960) and Paul Éluard (1895–1952) (the two are linked); and Ernest Hello (1828–1885) and Dom Columba Marmion (1858–1923) (these two are also linked).[16] I will consider these influences under five rubrics: 'The Mystical'; 'The Symbolist'; 'The Fantastical'; 'The Surrealist'; and 'The Catholic'.

The mystical

Before discussing the writers on Messiaen's list, it is important to document the influence of a person he does not mention: Charles Tournemire (1870–1939), organist at Sainte-Clotilde in Paris. Although Messiaen does not acknowledge it, he owed a profound debt to Tournemire for his self-conception as a contemplative 'commenting on' sacred texts.[17]

---

[13]   Stephen Schloesser, 'The Unbearable Lightness of Being: Re-Sourcing Catholic Intellectual Traditions', *CrossCurrents* 58, no. 1 (Spring 2008): 65–94.

[14]   Olivier Messiaen, *Technique de mon langage musical. Texte avec exemples musicaux*, Vol. 1 (Paris: Alphonse Leduc, 1944), p. 6.

[15]   Here Messiaen is thoroughly consonant with Catholic tradition. Compare Gerard Manley Hopkins: '[A] being so intimately present as God is to other things would be identified with them were it not for God's infinity or were it not for God's infinity he would not be so intimately present to things'. Gerard Manley Hopkins, 'Comments on the Spiritual Exercises of St. Ignatius Loyola', in *The Note-books and Papers of Gerard Manley Hopkins*, ed. Humphrey House (New York: Oxford University Press, 1937), p. 316. See also Karl Rahner, *Foundations of the Christian Faith* (New York: Crossroad, 1978), p. 137.

[16]   Messiaen, *Technique*, p. 5.

[17]   Messiaen's lack of acknowledgment can be explained: he was a student in Marcel Dupré's organ class at the Conservatoire. Tournemire never forgave either Dupré (for taking the Conservatoire position he thought belonged to him) or Dupré's mentor, Charles-Marie Widor (who, Tournemire believed, had betrayed him). See Stephen Schloesser, *Jazz*

After his family moved to Paris in 1919 (following the First World War), the 11-year-old Messiaen entered the Conservatoire National Supérieur de Musique where he met Daniel-Lesur, also born in 1908. Daniel-Lesur's mother Alice, herself an accomplished composer, had been one of Tournemire's favorite pupils; she in turn engaged Tournemire as young Daniel's teacher. Daniel-Lesur served as Tournemire's deputy at Sainte-Clotilde from 1927 to 1937.[18] Messiaen too occasionally assisted as organist for Tournemire sometime after his introduction to the organ in Dupré's class in autumn that same year.[19] In August 1930, Messiaen wrote Tournemire that he had been 'trying to play' two of the 51 offices from Tournemire's monumental *L'Orgue Mystique* (1928–32). Exactly one year later (August 1931), a letter thanked Tournemire for his vigorous support of Messiaen's being hired as titular organist at La Trinité.[20] On 25 April 1932, both Messiaen and Daniel-Lesur (along with several other young star organists) played pieces from *L'Orgue Mystique* at a grand concert at Sainte-Clotilde, an evening event aimed at making the massive work familiar to a wider audience.[21]

Thus, when Messiaen came to write and publish his first work for organ, *Le Banquet céleste* [The Celestial Banquet] in the summer of 1928, he was most certainly familiar with Tournemire's *L'Orgue Mystique*.[22] The first part of Tournemire's cycle had been composed between late October 1927 through March 1928, and its first volumes went to press that same summer.[23] Messiaen's familiarity with Tournemire's method of improvising 'paraphrases' or 'commentaries' on liturgical texts would account at least in part for his insertion of the scriptural quotation on his own work's front cover.[24]

Age Catholicism: Mystic Modernism in Postwar Paris, 1919–1933 (Toronto: University of Toronto Press, 2005), pp. 297–299 (hereafter: Schloesser, JAC).

[18]   See Nigel Simeone's obituary for Daniel-Lesur in *The Musical Times* (2002), available online at <www.musicaltimes.co.uk/archive/0204/daniel_lesur.html> (accessed 13 May 2008).

[19]   Hill and Simeone, *Messiaen*, p. 22. Given the close relationship between Messiaen and Daniel-Lesur, one might speculate on the veracity of Dupré's later reminiscence that Messiaen had never seen an organ console before Dupré introduced him to it. Again, the Tournemire–Dupré antagonism would explain this possible inaccuracy.

[20]   See letters of Olivier Messiaen to Charles Tournemire dated 4 August 1931; 10 August 1931; and 17 September 1931; in Brigitte de Leersnyder, ed., *Charles Tournemire (1870–1939), Cahiers et Mémoires de l'Orgue 41* (Paris: Les Amis de l'Orgue, 1989), pp. 80–85. See also Schloesser, JAC, p. 308.

[21]   Tournemire's handwritten program for 25 April 1932 is reproduced in Leersnyder, *Charles Tournemire*, pp. 28–29. See also Schloesser, JAC, p. 320.

[22]   Hill and Simeone, *Messiaen*, p. 25.

[23]   Schloesser, JAC, pp. 309–312.

[24]   I am grateful to Nigel Simeone for furnishing a copy of the first edition of *Le Banquet céleste*. The quotation reads: 'He who eats my flesh and drinks my blood abides in me and I in him. Gospel according to Saint John'. For Tournemire's method, see Schloesser, JAC, pp. 302, 304, 308.

LE BANQUET CÉLESTE

'Celui qui mange ma chair et boit mon sang demeure en moi et moi en lui'

ÉVANGILE SELON SAINT JEAN

So, by 1928, at age 19, Messiaen perceived himself as working in the line of Tournemire as one who contemplates and 'comments on' liturgical texts. Messiaen would later use this very word: 'Insofar as I was an organist, I had the duty of commenting on the texts proper to the office of the day'.[25]

To understand Tournemire's project of *l'Orgue Mystique* – and, indeed, to understand the meaning of that problematic word *mystique* – we need to go back to the early part of the previous century.[26] Tournemire's *l'Orgue Mystique* was self-consciously intended as a musical application of the massive 15–volume work produced by Dom Prosper Guéranger (1805–75) at Solesmes Abbey beginning in 1841: *L'Année liturgique* [The Liturgical Year].[27]

Guéranger conceived of his work as a means of revivifying a religion that had not only narrowly escaped extinction after the French Revolution, but that he felt had become frigid even before that historical watershed. In addition to the coldness of Jansenist religiosity, the Romantic Guéranger felt that the acrimonious theological contests between Jansenists and Jesuits had made Catholicism an affair largely of the mind, not the heart.[28] Guéranger wrote in his preface: 'Let the Catholic who reads *The Liturgical Year* be on his guard against that coldness of faith, and that want of love, which have well-nigh turned into an object of indifference that admirable [liturgical] cycle of the Church'.[29] He wanted to change all that by means of a liturgical revival that would recover religion as a burning passion animating the individual believer's heart.

Guéranger's three-fold paradigm can be found in the chapter headings set out at the beginnings of each of the major liturgical seasons of his work. He made his method abundantly clear: first came the 'historical' ('l'Historique'), then the

---

[25]   Messiaen in Antoine Goléa, *Rencontres avec Olivier Messiaen* (Paris: Editions Slatkine, 1984), p. 38. Messiaen said that his epigraphs (taken from biblical or theological texts) were 'of the greatest significance' for the artist to study, inseparable from the origins of his music. See Rößler, *Contributions*, pp. 27–37, at 28.

[26]   At a loss for a category into which Messiaen might be placed, scholars and critics frequently refer to him as a 'mystical' composer. Messiaen disavowed the term and preferred 'theological' instead, saying that 'mystical' led people to think of 'a neurotic who has vague sentiments and ecstasies' whereas he thought of himself as 'a devout man who loved the sound, solid gifts of faith.' Messiaen in Rößler, *Contributions*, pp. 67–115, at p. 89.

[27]   The final volumes were not published until after Guéranger's death.

[28]   Guy-Marie Oury, *Dom Guéranger: Moine au coeur de l'église, 1805–1875* (Solesmes: Éditions de Solesmes, 2001), p. 332.

[29]   Dom Prosper Guéranger, OSB, *The Liturgical Year*, trans. Dom Laurence Shepherd, OSB, 15 vols. (Westminster, MD: Newman, 1952 [1948–1950]), Vol.1, p. 11.

'mystical' ('la Mystique'), and thirdly, the 'practical' ('la Pratique').[30] Investigating the 'historical' first exemplified the hottest trends of his day: the nineteenth century was marked by the elevation of historical research above all else. Indeed, Solesmes itself was best known for its paleographical studies that aimed at recovering the most accurate texts for its definitive editions of ancient liturgical chant.[31]

The reader of *The Liturgical Year* would initially be introduced to a major season (e.g. Christmastide) by surveying the history of its practice throughout the ages. But this was only a first step in a three-fold process. Guéranger was not primarily interested in leaving the reader with this kind of knowledge, the chilling historicist approach that he felt was killing religion.[32] Guéranger wrote: 'As the chief object of this work [*The Liturgical Year*] is to assist the devotion of the Faithful, we purposely avoid everything which would savour of critical discussion'.[33]

The 'historical' thus led immediately from a study of the past to the second stage – the 'mystical' – an individual's present appropriation of that past here and now. Guéranger's *mystique* of Advent demonstrates the method. He begins by quoting ancient sources distinguishing between three comings of Christ: the first was historical and the third will be eschatological (i.e. the final judgment). The second, however, is in the soul, here and now, mediating past and future. The historical coming was 'humble and hidden'; the eschatological coming will be 'majestic and terrible'; but here in the present, Christ's coming into the soul is 'mysterious and full of love.' Guéranger reiterates his point: 'These longings for a Messiah […] are *not a mere commemoration* of the ancient Jewish people; they have *a reality and efficacy* of their own'. Indeed, Guéranger makes a claim that is probably heterodox but nonetheless thoroughly resonant with the spirit of the Romantic era: 'In vain would the Son of God have come, nineteen hundred years ago, to visit and save mankind, *unless He came again for each one of us and at every moment of our lives*'.[34] This is the highly specific meaning of the 'mystical' in nineteenth-century Catholic Revivalism [*renouveau catholique*[35]]. As distinct

---

[30]	Dom Prosper Guéranger, OSB, *Historique, mystique et pratique des temps de l'année liturgique* (Grez-en-Bouère, France: Dominique Martin Morin, 1979).

[31]	Schloesser, JAC, pp. 31–33, 283–287.

[32]	David Strauss's *Life of Jesus Critically Examined* (1835), a meteoric event in positivist-historicist readings of religion, had first appeared just six years earlier. Strauss's work appeared in French translation soon after: David Friedrich Strauss, *Vie de Jésus ou examen critique de son histoire par le docteur David Frédéric Strauss*, trans. Émile Littré (Paris: Ladrange, 1839). Littré, the famous lexicographer who produced the *Dictionnaire de la langue française*, was a friend of Auguste Comte and a positivist philosopher in his own right. See, for example, Littré's *Conservation, revolution et positivisme* (1852), *Paroles de la philosophie positive* (1859), and *Auguste Comte et la philosophie positive* (1863).

[33]	Guéranger, *Liturgical Year*, Vol. 3, p. 109.

[34]	Guéranger, *Liturgical Year*, Vol. 1, pp. 29–30. Emphasis added.

[35]	For the *renouveau catholique* see Schloesser, JAC, p. 343, n. 93.

from the merely 'historical', which leaves the great religious moments in the settled past, the 'mystical' contemplates and comments on liturgical and scriptural texts, thereby facilitating new religious moments here and now – the coming of Christ into the soul, 'mysterious and full of love'.

A century later, increased inner fervour was also Tournemire's aim in the devastating wake of the First World War. In 1927, responding to calls by his student Joseph Bonnet (who gave him a complete set of Guéranger's multi-volume *Liturgical Year*), Tournemire decided to compose a mammoth musical cycle for the entire liturgical year. Having prepared himself by means of a sojourn at Solesmes, Tournemire took texts from the various liturgical offices of each Sunday and wrote musical 'paraphrases' of them. (Tournemire used both *paraphraser* and *commenter* [to comment on] to describe his work.) These compositions are not intended as theological 'expositions' or *explications du texte*; rather, they are meant to be devotional meditations, imaginative ruminations that seep deeply into the listener and inflame the heart. Tournemire laid out his self-understanding in his unfinished manuscript on the 'Exalted Mission of the Organist in the Church' by quoting Ernest Hello (who, as will be seen below, was a seminal influence in Messiaen's intellectual development): 'Higher than reason, *orthodox mysticism* sees, hears, touches, and feels that which reason is incapable of seeing, hearing, touching and feeling'.[36]

In sum: Messiaen's method, derived from Guéranger via Tournemire, is at one with the Catholic Revivalist project of *la Mystique* – The Mystical.[37] It aims at immanence – which is to say *presence*; not so much an increase in knowledge as an increase in feeling, most especially of love.

The Symbolist

The Symbolist movement was distinct from Catholic Revivalism as well as intimately related to it. Symbolism was a direct response to (and intended to be a repudiation of) positivism.

---

[36] In Schloesser, JAC, pp. 299–303, 304, 308, 310.

[37] Julian Tölle suggested in 1999 that Messiaen's work should be situated within the broader cultural context of the *renouveau catholique*. More recently, Siglind Bruhn has also connected Messiaen to this movement by pointing to his father's associations. The doctoral research of Yves Balmer offers the most substantial evidence of Messiaen's father's acquaintance with this milieu. See Julian Christoph Tölle, *Olivier Messiaen, Éclairs sur l'au-delà...: die christlich-eschatologische Dimension des Opus ultimum* (New York: Peter Lang, 1999), pp. 223–224; Siglind Bruhn, *Messiaen's Contemplations of Covenant and Incarnation: Musical Symbols of Faith in the Two Great Piano Cycles of the 1940s* (Hillsdale, NY: Pendragon Press, 2007), pp. 19–30; Yves Balmer, '"Je suis né croyant...", Aux sources du catholicisme d'Olivier Messiaen', in *Musique, art et religion dans l'entre-deux-guerres*, eds Sylvain Caron and Michel Duchesneau (Lyon: Symétrie, 2009), pp. 417–441; and Balmer's essay in the present volume.

Positivism held, in the words of Auguste Comte, that by the nineteenth century, the human race had passed through the same three phases of human knowledge that individual human beings do: in childhood one is a theologian; in adolescence one is a metaphysician; but in adulthood, one abandons the search for unseen causes, and accepts the condition of 'positive knowledge' – we know only what we can positively observe. Gustave Courbet's formulation is more picturesque:

> Above all, the art of painting can only consist of the representation of objects which are visible and tangible for the artist [...] I maintain, in addition, that painting is an essentially *concrete* art and can only consist of the representation of *real and existing* things. It is a completely physical language, the words of which consist of all visible objects; an object which is *abstract*, not visible, non-existent, is not within the realm of painting.[38]

Note Courbet's equivalences: what is real and existing is what is physical and visible. Conversely, what is abstract and not visible is, by extension, non-existent.

Positivism was the animating ideology that undergirded the Third Republic, the French state created during the 1870s (in the wake of the devastating catastrophe of the Franco-Prussian War and the Paris Commune [1870–71]). As French statesman Léon Gambetta said even before its founding: 'What we propose to do is to apply positivism in the political order'. The Republic's assault on Catholicism reached its zenith beginning in 1901. In 1903, religious orders were expelled and properties confiscated. In 1905, the Act of Separation of Church and State removed in a single sweep all the church's property, culminating five years of anti-clerical legislation.[39]

Not surprisingly, Catholicism reacted violently to such provocations. After the Act of Separation of Church and State was passed in December 1905, Pope Pius X (who had only recently assumed the papacy in 1903) issued two encyclicals denouncing the separation. Then, as if to underscore the roots of political republicanism in positivist historicism, Pius issued two more condemnations of what has come to be known as 'Roman Catholic Modernism'.[40] This complex crisis centred on the fundamental problem of the relationship between emanence

---

[38]   Schloesser, JAC, pp. 19–20.

[39]   Schloesser, JAC, pp. 26, 53–54.

[40]   The two encyclicals denouncing the French separation of church and state were *Vehementer nos* (2 November 1906) and *Une fois encore* (6 January 1907). The two documents condemning the 'Modernists' were the syllabus of errors *Lamentabili sane exitu* (3 July 1907) and the encyclical *Pascendi dominici gregis* (8 September 1907). For Roman Catholic Modernism and integralism, see Schloesser, JAC, pp. 54–56; and Schloesser, '*Vivo ergo cogito*: Modernism as Temporalization and its Discontents: A Propaedeutic to This Collection', in *The Reception of Pragmatism in France and the Rise of Catholic Modernism, 1890–1914*, ed. David G. Schultenover (Washington, DC: Catholic University of America Press, 2009), pp. 21–58.

and immanence – or rather, *Transcendence and Immanence*.[41] If the seventeenth century had been about the 'domestication' of the transcendent, the nineteenth century was about its eradication.[42] In December 1908, Messiaen was born into a family that mirrored this politico-religious maelstrom: to a fervently Catholic father and a mother who practised no organized religion.

In contrast to this multivalent positivism arose Symbolism. For the Symbolists, true reality cannot be seen but merely 'suggested' or pointed to. The external world as we see it is a 'forest of symbols', a world of 'correspondences' in the words of Charles Baudelaire. There are visible realities that correspond to (and hence are capable of suggesting to us) invisible realities.[43] Stéphane Mallarmé puts the method with precision. Since reality can never be 'copied' but only pointed to, 'The ideal is to *suggest* [*suggerer*] the object. It is the perfect use of this mystery which constitutes the symbol. An object must be gradually evoked in order to show a state of soul.'[44]

Although the concept is ethereal the method was actually quite concrete. Invisible realities could be 'suggested' by taking texts about non-realistic or anti-realistic subjects – from the Bible, from classical antiquity, ancient mythologies, the 'Orient,' or the esoteric – and 'commenting on' or 'paraphrasing' them in some way. Richard Wagner's operas would be the most well-known example of the movement. Tournemire was clearly a thoroughgoing Symbolist.

Claude Debussy's opera *Pelléas et Melisande* (premiered in 1902), a setting of Maurice Maeterlinck's Symbolist text, made an enormous impact on Messiaen as a boy. As an adult, he was self-consciously explicit about the relationship between Maeterlinck's libretto and Debussy's composition, noting: 'Where the text suggests, the music explains; where the text hides and symbolizes to excess, the music reveals; the music "tears the veil" and speaks the truth'.[45] The Tristan and Isolde legend would preoccupy Messiaen from 1945 to 1948 (perhaps as a Symbolist retreat from the religious furore over 'the Messiaen Controversy').

One can think of nineteenth-century Symbolism as a kind of secularized sacramentalism. During the epoch of many conversions to Catholicism by

---

[41]   Gabriel Daly, *Transcendence and Immanence: A Study in Catholic Modernism and Integralism* (New York: Oxford University Press, 1980).

[42]   William C. Placher, *The Domestication of Transcendence. How Modern Thinking about God Went Wrong* (Louisville: Westminster John Knox Press, 1996).

[43]   See Stephen Schloesser, 'From Spiritual Naturalism to Psychical Naturalism: Catholic Decadence, Lutheran Munch, and *Madone Mystérique*', in *Edvard Munch: Psyche, Symbol, Expression*, ed. Jeffery Howe (Chestnut Hill: McMullen Museum of Art, Boston College, 2001), pp. 75–110, see especially pp. 81–82.

[44]   See Schloesser, JAC, p. 215.

[45]   Olivier Messiaen, *Traité VI*, p. 53; Gareth Healey, 'Messiaen – Bibliophile', in *Olivier Messiaen. Music, Art and Literature*, eds Christopher Dingle and Nigel Simeone (Aldershot: Ashgate Publishing, 2007), pp. 159–171, at p. 163. The 'veil' very likely refers to Henri Bergson's aesthetic theory. See Schloesser, JAC, p. 63.

intellectuals – a trend that skyrocketed in direct proportion to the state's measures taken against the Catholic Church – Symbolism became a 'half-way house' en route to religious conversion.[46] The iconic figure linking the *renouveau catholique* to Symbolism was the poet and ultra-Catholic convert, Paul Claudel – a figure Messiaen mentions in his 1944 list of influences.

Commenting on Claudel's *Art poétique* [Poetic Art] (1907), published the year before Messiaen's birth,[47] the scholar Wallace Fowlie writes:

> The poet sees every created thing in perpetual movement. We move by coming into contact with all the other things in the world. By this constant movement we waste ourselves and finally perish. 'Tout périt. L'Univers n'est qu'une manière totale de ne pas être ce qui est.' [Everything perishes. The universe is nothing but a total way of not being what is.] Existing within this movement, we unconsciously tend to deny that which is constant. This is our separation from God. […]
>
> The human spirit alone is able to comprehend something of the bond which exists between the instability of the world and the stability of God. By naming an object, as the poet does, man rescues it from its fate of dissolution. In *Traité de la Connaissance* Claudel reaches a definition of man and of the poet as the one whose function is to *represent* (or reproduce) the creation of the Creator. 'Tout passe, et, rien n'étant présent, tout doit être *représenté*.' [Everything passes and, since nothing is present, everything must be *represented*.] All the parts of the world find in man, in the incorruptible part of man, an intelligence which understands them and which is able to offer them to the One who created them in the beginning.[48]

Claudel's vision can be seen echoed throughout Messiaen's works: a world in constant Heraclitean motion and perishing, which is saved – i.e. given some measure of Parmenidean stability – by the 'poet' who can re-present that which is never actually present. Claudel's attention to the eternal, the only stable force in a world always passing out of existence, is shot through with a certain melancholy. This melancholic sense of the tragic seems manifest in Messiaen's representations of immanence such as 'Dieu parmi nous' ['God among us'] from *La Nativité du Seigneur* (1936) and the *Trois petites Liturgies* (1944); even as life pushed him towards representing emanence and transcendence in pieces such as *Apparition de l'église éternelle* [Apparition of the Eternal Church] (1931), *Couleurs de la cité céleste* [Colors of the Celestial City] (1963) and *Éclairs sur l'au-delà...* [Illuminations on the Beyond] (1987–91).

---

[46]   Schloesser, JAC, p. 36.

[47]   Paul Claudel, *Art poétique: connaissance du temps, traité de la co-naissance au monde et de soi-même: développement de l'église* (Paris: Mercure de France, 1907).

[48]   Wallace Fowlie, *Paul Claudel* (London: Bowes & Bowes, 1957), pp. 31–2. Emphasis original. Translations mine. See also: Stephen Schloesser, '"Not behind but within": *Sacramentum et Res*', *Renascence* 58/1 (Fall 2005): 17–39.

To some extent Messiaen inherited this (repressed) melancholy from his mother, Cécile Sauvage, yet another influence in his 1944 list.[49] Messiaen is frequently quoted reflecting on the poetry Sauvage wrote while she was pregnant with him. He had a keen appreciation for coincidence and he loved that she had written about a boy who would become a musician.[50] It is striking, however, that he doesn't comment on how melancholic its conclusion is. Sauvage anticipates the grief she will have after Olivier has left her womb

> And now he's born! I'm all alone, I feel
> Within me the hollow of my blood take fright;
> With inner smell I search the shadow of him, with
> Secret female sense. [...]
> Ah! How small I am, my soul cast down,
> As, when the seed has taken flight, its husk
> Falls back to earth with all the dried-out matter.
> O heart abandoned in the wind! Poor nest![51]

Sauvage's lines exemplify Claudel's anxieties: we live in a world of perpetual becoming and perishing. But although Sauvage shared Claudel's melancholy, she does not seem to have shared his correlative attraction to the eternal – one shared by her son as well as her husband.

In addition to Claudel, Messiaen names another Symbolist: Ernest Hello. Sometime around 1933 (i.e. about five years after the death of his mother and two years after receiving the post at La Trinité), Messiaen's brother Alain introduced him to Hello's book entitled *Paroles de Dieu* [Words of God].[52] First published in 1877, its method (both mystical and Symbolist) is made clear in the subtitle 'Reflections on Several Sacred Texts'.[53] The method is all the more evident

---

[49]   On the occasion of the premiere of *Saint-François d'Assise*, Messiaen 'observed that not only had he always felt constitutionally unable to compose a Passion, but he had found even writing the saint's death scene extremely difficult'. Bruhn, *Messiaen's Contemplations*, p. 39.

[50]   Claude Samuel, *Olivier Messiaen: Music and Color: Conversations with Claude Samuel*, trans. E. Thomas Glasow (Portland, OR: Amadeus Press, 1994), p. 15.

[51]   Cécile Sauvage, '*L'Ame en bourgeon*' [The Budding Soul], trans. Philip Weller; in Dingle and Simeone, *Music, Art and Literature*, pp. 191–251, at p. 234.

[52]   Olivier Messiaen in an interview with Brigitte Massin; in Massin, *Messiaen: une poétique du merveilleux* (Aix-en-Provence: Éditions Alinéa, 1989), p. 155.

[53]   A renewal of interest in Hello began around 1910 and increased after the First World War: *Paroles de Dieu: Réflexions sur quelques textes sacrés* (Paris: Perrin et cie) was republished in 1923 thanks largely to Stanislas Fumet. Perhaps not coincidentally, Fumet's key work on Hello was reissued at the war's end and just two years after Messiaen's *Visions*: Stanislas Fumet, *Ernest Hello, ou le Drame de la Lumière*, rev. edn (Fribourg and Paris: Egloff and the Librairie de L'Université de Fribourg, 1945 [1928]); see also Hello, *Textes*

when one looks at any chapter, each of which begins with a line or two from scripture (quoted in both the Latin Vulgate and French translation) followed by Hello's contemplative reflections. *Paroles de Dieu* would become one of the most influential books in Messiaen's early intellectual development. Its final chapter, entitled simply 'Amen', became the basis for the wartime composition *Visions de l'Amen* (1943).[54]

One of the most curious aspects of this book is its fourth section devoted to 'Tears in the Scriptures'. (Note again the theme of perishing and loss.) Among the tears considered by Hello are tears in the desert; tears of the children of Israel; tears of Anna and Samuel; of Ezekial, Esdras, Jeremiah and Daniel; of the widows without tears; the tears of God the Father; and also the tears of Jesus at the tomb of Lazarus: 'And Jesus wept'. This attention to material bodily functions like tears, sweat, and blood is yet another mark of Catholic Revivalists, whether highly sophisticated (like Hello) or more popular (like Anne-Catherine Emmerich on whose *Dolorous Passion of our Lord Jesus Christ* [1833] Mel Gibson based the script for his movie *The Passion of the Christ* [2004]).

Messiaen's work shares this same genealogy. For example, in his analysis of the 'Amen of the Agony of Jesus' (from *Visions*), Messiaen quotes Hello: 'Perhaps the crucifixion was felt in a more terrible manner in the Mount of Olives than on the cross. For on the cross it was felt in reality. In the Mount of Olives it was felt in the mind. The sweat of blood is the word of this terror.' He then explains that the low Cs at the end of the piece are meant to 'fall like drops of blood'.[55] In the world of Hello and Claudel, Symbolist transcendence and mystical immanence intermingle. They are 'contemplative', yes … but theirs is a *voluptuous* contemplation, dripping in bodily manifestations.

> The blood which is the Eternal Word,
> God who is in the mouth of his creature, in this
> heart in which he basks,
> This gulp of real wine![56]

---

choisis et présentés, ed. Stanislas Fumet (Fribourg: Egloff, Librairie de l'Université, 1945). For Fumet see Schloesser, JAC, pp. 176, 181, 188, 294.

[54]   See Goléa, *Rencontres*, pp. 95–102; Messiaen, *Traité III*, pp. 229–275.

[55]   Messiaen, *Traité III*, pp. 244, 248; quoting Ernest Hello, *Paroles de Dieu*, p. 245. As Jeffery Howe shows, this linkage between Symbolism and bodily suffering is already present in Gustave Moreau. See Howe, 'The Refuge of Art: Gustave Moreau and the Legacy of Symbolism', in *Mystic Masque: Semblance and Reality in Georges Rouault, 1871–1958*, ed. Stephen Schloesser (Chestnut Hill: McMullen Museum of Art, Boston College, 2008), pp. 45–61.

[56]   Paul Claudel, 'Le Précieux sang', *Autres Poèmes durant la guerre* (1916), in *Oeuvre poétique* (Paris: Gallimard 1962 [1957]), p. 533.

The fantastical

Ernest Hello was not only an author of religious meditations but also of *fantastical* short stories. Two years after *Paroles de Dieu*, Hello published his *Contes extraordinaires* [Extraordinary Tales] (1879), reprinted in 1900, 1926, 1945 and most recently, in 2006.[57] This genre was strongly influenced by the stories of Edgar Allan Poe, which had been translated into French thanks to the devotion of Charles Baudelaire.[58] Gareth Healey has recently noted with respect to Poe: 'Poetry with a macabre theme interested Messiaen'.[59] I might suggest a slightly different approach: it was not so much the 'macabre' that interested Messiaen as the *fantastique*.

The *fantastique* [fantastical] originated as a genre specifically opposed to the novel.[60] The novel was seen as a supremely realistic and positivist genre. The *fantastique*, on the other hand, was anti-realist and became associated with short stories. The *fantastique* juxtaposed realistic elements with anti-realistic ones – dreams and nightmares, drug-induced hallucinations, and 'supernatural' elements (ghosts, fairies, vampires, demons, spells). In ghost stories, the reader knew the causes of things and the narrative's conclusion was neatly closed. The *fantastique*, by contrast, left causality inconclusive and the reader's judgment insolubly uncertain. Did the protagonist *really* surrender to the devil or was he merely dreaming?[61] Because of this ambiguity, the reader needed to propose alternative possible solutions: favourites included mysticism, madness, nightmares and hallucinogenic drugs. Hence the evolution of an associated popular term: the *hallucinant*.[62]

Messiaen himself made explicit the link between the fantastical and Shakespeare, saying that he loved the Bard mostly because of the 'magic, the

---

[57]   Ernest Hello, *Contes extraordinaires* (Paris: Sandre, 2006).

[58]   Edgar Allan Poe, *Histoires extraordinaires*, trans. Charles Baudelaire (Paris: M. Lévy, 1856); Poe, *Nouvelles histoires extraordinaires*, trans. Baudelaire (Paris: M. Lévy frères, 1857); Baudelaire, *Notes nouvelles sur Edgar Poe* (Paris: M. Lévy frères, 1857); Poe, *Histoires grotesques et sérieuses*, trans. Baudelaire (Paris: Michel Lévy frères, 1865). See also Schloesser, 'From Spiritual Naturalism to Psychical Naturalism', p. 83.

[59]   Healey, 'Messiaen – Bibliophile', p. 162.

[60]   Schloesser, JAC, pp. 36–37.

[61]   For an example in Georges Bernanos's *Sous le soleil de Satan* (1926), see Schloesser, JAC, pp. 248–249.

[62]   '*Hallucinant* can be traced back through Gautier, Hugo, and Balzac: its primary association was with opium, hallucinations, and sense-misperception; its secondary usage was like that of 'dream', 'idealism', 'fantasy', and 'imagination' – i.e. terms opposed to 'realism'. Alfred Jarry used *hallucination* in opposition to *perception* as denoting the difference between anti-representation and representation. Schloesser, JAC, p. 344, n. 99.

sorcerers, the goblins, the phantoms and the apparitions of every sort'.[63] As a boy, Messiaen enjoyed both scaring people as well as being frightened, pleading with his blind grandfather: 'Grandad, scare us!' At the age of ten, Messiaen said to his mother: 'Mummy, you're a poet just like Shakespeare. Like him, you have suns, planets, ants, frightening skeletons. I prefer things which are frightening.'[64]

As Paul Festa has recently shown in his film *Apparition of the Eternal Church* (2006), Messiaen's music is capable of evoking responses of dread and fear (along with images of gothic ghouls and serial killers) even in those who have no idea what they are listening to.[65] This element of fear or dread is a constituent part of awe or what medieval scholar Caroline Bynum calls the 'wonder response'.[66] It is the confrontation of the self with something Other that cannot be consumed, appropriated or domesticated. We fear what we cannot tame. The transcendent is terrible and terrifying. 'To speak of eternity, the unknowable', says Messiaen, 'these are words evoking terror. All the traits of God evoke terror …'.[67]

The Surrealist

Messiaen's invocation of the Surrealists Pierre Reverdy and Paul Éluard whisks us quickly from the *fin-de-siècle* into the vortex of the Jazz Age. And yet there remains continuity: insofar as Surrealism sought to shock via unexpected and seemingly irrational juxtapositions, it was a twentieth-century echo of fantastical non-resolution.

In 1924, Breton published his first *Surrealist Manifesto*. Breton acknowledged his debt to Pierre Reverdy for the conceptualization by quoting him: 'The image […] cannot be born from a comparison but from a juxtaposition of two more or less distant realities. / The more the relationship between the two juxtaposed realities is distant and true, the stronger the image will be – the greater its emotional power

---

[63]   Claude Samuel and Olivier Messiaen, *Permanences d'Olivier Messiaen: dialogues et commentaires* (Arles: Actes sud, 1999), p. 32. Messiaen's father Pierre was a translator of Shakespeare.

[64]   Hill and Simeone, *Messiaen*, pp. 12, 10–11.

[65]   Messiaen would undoubtedly have been pleased to know that a six-year-old boy listened to a recording of the 'Apparition of the Eternal Church' and said 'I love it'. When Festa asked him why, the boy responded: 'Because it's scary'. Paul Festa, *OH MY GOD. Messiaen in the Ear of the Unbeliever* (San Francisco: Bar Nothing Books, 2008), p. 71; see also pp. 34–36, 42–43, 45, 48–49, 52–53, 55, 64, 72, 78–79, 84–85, 90–91.

[66]   Caroline Walker Bynum, 'Wonder', *American Historical Review* 102, no. 1 (February 1997): 1–26. For Messiaen on awe and fear, see Samuel, *Music and Color*, pp. 164–165.

[67]   Olivier Messiaen in an interview with Patrick Szersnovicz (29 May 1987), 'Olivier Messiaen: La liturgie de l'arc-en-ciel', *Le Monde de la Musique* (July/August 1987): 34. I am grateful to Robert Sholl for providing this reference.

and poetic reality.'[68] That same year, Breton, Reverdy, and Éluard launched the first issue of the periodical *La Révolution surréaliste* [The Surrealist Revolution] (1924–29). Two years later, Éluard published *Capitale de la douleur* [The Capital of Pain] (1926), a post-war publishing phenomenon that First World War veterans carried in their back pockets:

> The bottle we surround with the bandages of our wounds resists no longing. Let's take the hearts, the brains, the muscles of rage, let's take the invisible flowers of the pale girls and children joined together, let's take the hand of memory, let's close the eyes of recollection, a theory of trees delivered by the thieves strikes us and divides us, all the pieces are good. Which will gather them up: terror, suffering, or disgust?[69]

Messiaen's mother died of tuberculosis in 1927 at age 44. The publication of *The Capital of Pain* around the time of the 18-year-old musician's great grief cannot help but have made an impact as he approached adulthood. This is the swirling passion in which the adolescent Messiaen was immersed:

> Unknown, she was the form I preferred,
> The one who freed me from the weight of being a man,
> And I see her and I lose her and I bear
> The pain like a little sunlight in cold water.[70]

Surrealism was a kind of terrestrial transcendence. It foregrounded the fantastical and the uncanny, the capacity of everyday reality to shock us into the awareness that our rational 'waking life' is not in control.[71] The method depended on the retrieval of a fantastical device – the hallucination. As Éluard wrote:

> When there is a total fusion between the real image and the hallucination it has provided no misunderstanding is possible. The similarity between two objects comes as much from the suggestive element contributing to establish it as from the objective relationship existing between them. The poet, the supremely hallucinated man, will establish similitudes to his liking between the most dissimilar objects (literally he leaves his mark on them) ... .[72]

---

[68]   Breton quoting Reverdy's remarks in *Nord–Sud* (March 1918) in his *Surrealist Manifesto* (1924), cited in Schloesser, JAC, p. 111.

[69]   Paul Éluard, 'Silence of the Gospel', in *Capital of Pain*, trans. Mary Ann Caws, Patricia Terry and Nancy Kline (Boston, MA: Black Widow Press, 2006), p. 113.

[70]   Paul Éluard, 'Just and Small' no. 10, in *Capital of Pain*, p. 147.

[71]   Schloesser, JAC, pp. 112–113.

[72]   Paul Éluard, 'Le miroir de Baudelaire', in *Donner à voir* (1939); in Larry W. Peterson, 'Messiaen and Surrealism: A Study of His Poetry', in *Messiaen's Language of Mystical Love*, ed. Siglind Bruhn (New York: Garland Publishing, 1998), pp. 215–24, at 217.

Having arrived once again at 'hallucination', we are now in a better position to appreciate Messiaen's synthesis of these culturally coded meanings. When asked to explain what he meant in his paraphrase of Thomas Aquinas ('God dazzles us by an excess of truth; music transports us to God by an absence of truth'), Messiaen replied:

> For the surrealists, it was a *hallucinatory* domain; for Christians, it is the domain of *faith*. [...] They haven't seen, but they have a secret *intuition* about what they don't see. Now, I think music, even more than literature and painting, is capable of expressing this *dreamlike*, *fairy-tale* aspect of the beyond [*l'au-delà*], this '*surreal*' aspect of the truths of faith.[73]

It was by means of his peculiar musical language, said Messiaen elsewhere, that he achieved 'possibilities for giving expression to everything *super-terrestrial*, everything that's *supernatural*'.[74]

Surrealism in the 1920s and 1930s can be seen as a twentieth-century successor to the Symbolist and fantastical. All of them shared a fundamental opposition to positivism – and in this they were one with Catholic Revivalism. A signal moment in which these currents intersect occurs at the exact mid-point of the *Turangalîla-symphonie* (1946–48), in movements 5 and 6 (out of 10), where the 'Joie du Sang des Étoiles' [Joy of the Blood of the Stars] is followed by the 'Jardin du Sommeil d'amour' [Garden of Love's Sleep], the first full rendition of the 'love theme'. This voluptuous movement, seemingly suspended in time, is then followed by the 'Turangalîla 2' movement – a largely percussive and atonal section whose contrasting chaos provokes a shock. In this association of the erotic and the shocking, Messiaen demonstrates being influenced by the Surrealists for whom '"convulsive beauty", one of Breton's central categories of experience, is [...] a returning of the experience of beauty to its sexual origins: a convulsive experience akin to the convulsions of orgasmic bliss or, indeed, to the involuntary tremors provoked by an experience of the uncanny'.[75]

---

[73]   Samuel, *Music and Color*, p. 223; cf. Olivier Messiaen, *Lecture at Notre-Dame: An address presented at Notre-Dame Cathedral in Paris, December 4, 1977*, trans. Timothy J. Tikker (Paris: Alphonse Leduc, 2001 [1978]), p. 13; emphasis added. The original nineteenth-century connection between hallucinant and hallucinogenic drugs is evoked by Squeaky Blonde's bong smoking in Paul Festa's documentary film *Apparition of the Eternal Church* (2006). See Festa, *OH MY GOD*, pp. 91–94.

[74]   Messiaen, in Rößler, *Contributions*, pp. 48–56, at p. 54; emphasis added.

[75]   Steven Harris, *Surrealist Art and Thought in the 1930s: Art, Politics, and the Psyche* (New York: Cambridge University Press, 2004), p. 11.

The Catholic

Reverdy and Éluard were one pair joined in Messiaen's 1944 list of influences; Ernest Hello and Dom Columba Marmion were another. As Hello's influence has already been discussed, the following remarks will concern only Marmion.

Messiaen was given a copy of the Benedictine monk's *Le Christ dans ses mystères* [The Mysteries of Christ] (1919) around 1931, that is, shortly after he took over the post at La Trinité.[76] Although Tournemire had been given Guéranger's 15-volume set and Messiaen was given just this single work, the function of both Guéranger and Marmion in the lives of the two liturgical organists was identical: each was impressed with the idea that the organist is one who 'comments on' sacred texts in a 'mystical' way. The 'Mysteries of Christ', as Marmion indicates in the title of his first chapter, are 'our Mysteries'.[77] We are back to radical immanence. Appropriately enough, Marmion's work inspired Messiaen's contemplations on the Incarnation, *La Nativité du Seigneur* (1936).[78]

The tradition, writes Marmion, should not be 'buried, like a dead letter, in the depths of the Holy Scriptures'; rather, we ought to 'contemplate' the 'mystery of Christ'. This should not be a 'merely intellectual study' (echo of Guéranger), which is often 'dry and sterile'; rather, we should 'contemplate Him so as to conform our lives [...] so that our thirst may be fully quenched'. (Compare Messiaen's words in *Technique*: 'to give to our century the spring water for which it thirsts'.) Although Marmion declares that 'in their historical, material duration, the mysteries of Christ's terrestrial life are now past', he believes that their virtue remains, and we can have a share in them. The mode is clear: it is by 'symbolism and ritual' that our interiors can 'assimilate the spiritual fruit of each mystery in the greatest possible measure'.[79]

Marmion's text echoes the Symbolists. It is a 'psychological law of our nature – matter and spirit – that we should pass from the visible to the invisible'. The 'outward elements' of the mysteries are like rungs in a ladder: by means of them we can 'contemplate and love [...] supernatural realities'. These 'outward elements' are the exterior 'fringe of Christ's garment'. We ought not to stop there but go beyond into the mysteries that are above all 'interior' (like searching for the symbol that is outwardly clothed). Again, when we 'contemplate' these mysteries, it is not for a historical project – not merely in order 'to evoke the remembrance of events'. Rather, the point is so that 'our souls may participate in each special state' of the mysteries.[80]

In brief: Marmion's project continued Guéranger's. *La Mystique* is the making really present (re-presenting), by means of contemplation and internalization, what

---

[76]   Massin, *Poétique*, pp. 68–69.

[77]   Dom Columba Marmion, OSB, *Christ in His Mysteries*, trans. Mother M. St. Thomas of Tyburn Convent, 9th edn (London: Sands & Co., 1939), pp. 13–18.

[78]   Massin, *Poétique*, p. 72.

[79]   Marmion, *Mysteries*, pp. 8, 16.

[80]   Ibid., pp. 23, 25.

others leave behind as merely historical or theoretical – remaindered remembrances of a dead past. By concluding his list of influences with two prominent figures in Catholic Revivalism, Hello and Marmion, Messiaen returns to the central dialectic: re-presenting the not-present. Immanence and Emanence. Incarnation and Eschatology.

Conclusion: Dialectical realism

Hello and Marmion should be seen as Messiaen relates them, that is as parallel with Reverdy and Éluard. And yet Catholicism and Surrealism were seen as largely incompatible, even bitterly opposed to one another, in the Jazz Age. How can we reconcile Messiaen's simultaneous prehension of such apparent incompatibilities?

We can explain the phenomenal success of post-war Catholic Revivalism (the *renouveau catholique*) by seeing it as one among a number of 'dialectical realisms' that vied for predominance in that post-war era.[81] By 'dialectical realism' I mean a vision of the world that embraces *both* a 'realistic' aspect *as well as* an 'un-realistic' one. Sur-realism: a dialectic of the dream state and the waking state. Socialist realism: a dialectic of what is 'seen' and what is 'hoped for'. Magical realism: a dialectic of reality and magic. Catholicism, too, is a dialectical realism: a dialectic of outward material that sacramentally embodies invisible reality. Messiaen had memorized the classic Catholic catechism definition by age 10: 'A sacrament is an outward sign instituted to give [inward] grace'. Sacramentalism holds together immanence and emanence in dialectical tension.[82]

This is why, in 1944, Messiaen could quote both Reverdy and Hello in the same breath as two icons for the future. Both shared a fundamental antipathy to the positivist rationalism that privileges only what can be seen. We might interpret Messiaen's introductory notes to his *Technique* (1944) as a manifesto for the post-war world. Like its contemporaneous *Trois petites Liturgies*, it is meant to shock, paradoxically locating presence in apparent absence, integral wholeness in shattered shards: 'Everywhere present, winged mirror of days'.[83]

> 'To express with a lasting power our darkness struggling with the Holy Spirit, to raise upon the mountain the doors of our prison of flesh, to give to our century the spring water for which it thirsts, there shall have to be a great artist who will be both a great artisan and a great Christian.' Let us hasten by our prayers the coming of the liberator. And, beforehand, let us offer him two thoughts. First, that of Reverdy: 'May he draw in the whole sky in one breath!' And then that of Hello: 'There is no one great except him to whom God speaks, and in the

---

[81] Schloesser, JAC, pp. 5–8.
[82] Schloesser, 'Unbearable Lightness of Being', pp. 83–85.
[83] Messiaen, '*Trois petites Liturgies de la Présence Divine*', trans. Spencer; cited.

moment in which God speaks to him' [...] One point will attract our attention at the outset: the *charm of impossibilities*. It is a glistening music we seek, giving to the aural sense voluptuously refined pleasures [...] This charm, simultaneously both voluptuous and contemplative ... .[84]

---

[84]   Messiaen, *Technique*, pp. 5, 6. For the accusation that Messiaen's music was too 'sensual' to be 'spiritual', see Boswell-Kurc, 'Olivier Messiaen's Religious War-time Works', pp. 313–383.

PART IV
Theology in Messiaen's Music

Chapter 10

'Une œuvre simple, solennelle …': Messiaen's Commission from André Malraux

Nigel Simeone

Messiaen's *Et exspecto resurrectionem mortuorum* was a commission from the French Ministry of Culture. Its genesis is documented in the composer's correspondence with government officials, and in his working notes and pocket diaries.[1] These reveal much about the composition process, the evolution of Messiaen's thoughts, and the sometimes frustrating exigencies of writing a state commission that remained true to Messiaen's artistic and religious intentions. The present chapter aims to tell the story of the 'commande Malraux' as Messiaen referred to it throughout the time he was planning and composing *Et exspecto*.

Messiaen had first contemplated a memorial work for brass instruments some 20 years before André Malraux commissioned the piece that was to become *Et exspecto*. In his diary for 1944, at the end of the German Occupation of Paris, a brief annotation mentions a plan that was never realized: 'Write a Requiem for brass instruments, to be played under the Arc de Triomphe […] (in six months)'. It would perhaps be far-fetched to find in this annotation the seeds of a work that was not begun for another two decades, but it is fascinating that the composer already had the idea of a commemorative piece (undoubtedly for the victims of war), scored for brass instruments. Possibly Messiaen had been approached to write something for a national commemoration or some other ceremony that was to take place at the Arc de Triomphe. Whatever the circumstances, it provides a foretaste of the conception – and to some extent the instrumentation – of *Et exspecto*.

Messiaen did not receive his first commission from the French government until 1956. This was for a work that would have been entirely uncharacteristic of Messiaen's output: a *Fantaisie* for organ and orchestra. That such a work was never written is hardly surprising, since Messiaen never showed any inclination to mix the sounds of his organ at La Trinité with the kaleidoscopic sonorities of his orchestral writing. The next few years were traumatic for Messiaen and his family.

---

[1] All letters, documents and diary entries cited in this chapter are in the Messiaen Archives, Paris, unless otherwise stated. My warmest thanks are due to Yvonne Loriod-Messiaen for permission to publish them here. All translations from the French are my own.

His wife, Claire, was increasingly incapacitated, and she had been in an institution since 1954. Messiaen could only look on helplessly as she declined. At the same time, he took refuge in nature: during 1957 and 1958, the second group of pieces for the *Catalogue d'oiseaux* was composed, and the first performance of the complete cycle was given at one of the concerts of the Domaine Musical on 15 April 1959. Exactly one week later, Claire died. The legal wranglings over settling her estate were to prove both time-consuming and distressing for Messiaen, but he never stopped composing: 1959 saw him embarking on *Chronochromie*, commissioned by Heinrich Strobel of Südwestfunk (South-West German Radio).

As yet, the state commission from 1956 remained unwritten, and in 1961 Messiaen wrote to the Ministry of Culture, asking whether its terms could be changed. By this time, at least, it had become a piece that was intended for the centenary of Debussy's birth in 1962. Early that year Émile Biasini, Director of Arts and Letters in the Ministry of Culture, and a close assistant of the minister André Malraux, wrote to Messiaen agreeing to the changes the composer requested, and recalling the origin of the commission:

> I have the honour to inform you that the commission for a *Fantaisie* for organ and orchestra that was awarded to you by a ministerial order of 26 July 1956 [...] has been transformed by a ministerial order of 18 December 1961 into the commission of a musical work for three or four soloists accompanied by a medium-sized orchestra. The fee for the new commission is five thousand francs. As this work is being composed in homage to Claude Debussy on the occasion of the centenary of this composer, I will be happy if your score could be completed before the end of 1962.

Here was a radical transformation indeed: a work for organ and orchestra becoming a piece for an entirely different instrumentation, to be written as a centenary tribute from Messiaen to Debussy. Even though there is not the slightest mention of Debussy in either the printed score, or in Messiaen's writing about the resulting work, the finished piece was to become very well-known. More than a year after the letter from Biasini, Messiaen replied on 19 March 1963:

> This work was required to be written as a homage to Claude Debussy (without any question of imitating this composer's style). In truth, inspiration only came to me following a visit to Japan, which explains the subject of the work but does not in the least preclude the homage to Debussy. I have spoken about it with Monsieur Malraux who is in complete agreement. [...] Here now is the title [...] of the work: *Sept Haïkaï (esquisses japonaises)*.

A little later, Messiaen noted in his diary: 'Debussy commission: this will be the *Sept Haïkaï*. In agreement with MM. Malraux, Biasini (at the Ministry) and Siohan, it will be given its first performance at the Domaine Musical by Pierre Boulez, with Yvonne as soloist, 30 October 1963.'

André Malraux, Minister of State for Cultural Affairs from 1959 to 1969, was – according to some of his critics – more prone to dreaming than to efficient administration in his government post. In the world of political affairs, this may have been a fair judgement.[2] But in the world of the arts, and among artists themselves, Malraux enjoyed several close and cordial friendships. He was also fond of travelling the globe as the figurehead for promoting French culture on the international stage.

It is worth considering some of Malraux's activities and achievements in the cultural sphere during the early 1960s, the time he commissioned Messiaen's *Et exspecto*. On 4 August 1962, parliament adopted the so-called 'Loi Malraux', which assured the safeguard of historic districts and provided the official establishment of *maisons de la culture*. The same year, he commissioned Marc Chagall to paint a new ceiling (inaugurated by Malraux in 1964) for the Palais Garnier, home of the Paris Opéra. In 1963, Malraux gave a speech in the presence of US President Kennedy and his wife to celebrate the exhibition of Leonardo da Vinci's *Mona Lisa* at the National Gallery of Art in Washington, DC. That September, at the Louvre, he gave the memorial address for his friend Georges Braque, and then attended the artist's funeral service at Varengeville-sur-mer. The same year, he commissioned André Masson to paint a new ceiling for the Théâtre de l'Odéon, and asked Olivier Messiaen to write a new composition in memory of the dead of two world wars. A dreamer he may sometimes have been, but in his position as De Gaulle's culture minister, he was able to make some of these dreams a reality.

The first explicit reference to a new work for Malraux is a note scribbled by Messiaen on a letter inviting him to a meeting of the Commission Nationale d'étude pour les problèmes de la Musique [State Commission to Study Current Problems in Music], held on 6 May 1963. At the foot of the page, Messiaen has jotted a reminder: 'Speak again about the Mass for Malraux (in memory of the war dead)'. The earliest idea thus seems to have been for a relatively conventional sacred work, perhaps a Requiem Mass.

Six months later, on 30 October, Malraux was present at the world première of the *Sept Haïkaï* at the Théâtre de l'Odéon. *Le Monde* published the following review on 2 November 1963:

> The evening's star attraction was a new work by Messiaen entitled *Sept Haïkaï*, inspired by the composer's impressions gathered during his recent trip to Japan. In his mind, this was intended as a substitute for a chamber music score that had been commissioned by the Direction générale of des Artes et Lettres on the occasion of the Debussy centenary. This substitution was made with the agreement of M. André Malraux. It was thus a genuine commission given

---

2   For an assessment of Malraux's political acumen regarding Algeria, see, for example, Olivier Todd, *André Malraux, une vie* (Paris: Gallimard, 2001), p. 465: 'Concerning Algeria, his [Malraux's] intentions were good, but ill-conceived, detached from the realities of the war, and had the effect of trying to slice through water with a sword'.

directly to a great contemporary composer by the minister, who lent this gesture all the proper formality by being present in person at the first performance, thus demonstrating the serious interest he has shown in the art of living music. [...] This was truly a magnificent evening, the result of relentless hard work (eighteen rehearsals) under the authoritative direction of Pierre Boulez, mastermind of the Domaine Musical, who had the admirable idea of dedicating the concert to the memory of Roger Désormière.

Who was the author of this unusually well-informed review, a critic who was even aware of the change to the terms of the original commission? It was none other than Robert Siohan, Inspector General for Music Education, and a member of André Malraux's cabinet at the Ministry of Culture. Siohan's is a name that will appear several more times in this chapter. Another critic, Maurice Fleuret, writing in *France Observateur* noted wittily that the Domaine Musical seemed to be becoming a semi-official organization, receiving ministerial benediction:

After the generous televised publicity, the microphones of the RTF were present, along with M. Malraux and even M. Bondeville, at the first concert of the Domaine Musical. You might be led to believe that here was henceforth a national institution, at which *La Marseillaise* will soon be sung on a twelve-note row!

Two weeks after this concert, Émile Biasini, Director General of Arts and Letters at the Ministry, sent Messiaen the official commission for 'a musical work in memory of the dead of the two world wars', offering a fee of 5000 francs. Messiaen quickly accepted, and went to see Malraux to discuss the project with him again. According to Messiaen, Malraux asked for 'a work that is simple, solemn, and very loud'. As for the precise scoring, Messiaen noted down several options: 'chorus, organ and orchestra; or chorus and organ; or chorus, brass and organ; or chorus and orchestra; or chorus and brass. It will be performed either at Notre-Dame de Paris, or La Sainte-Chapelle, or at Chartres Cathedral.'

At this stage, the plan was clearly for a choral work, though Messiaen says nothing about a possible choice of text. Was he, perhaps, still thinking of a Mass, or a Requiem Mass, as he had been when the commission was first mentioned informally? A note in his diary in December 1963 suggests as much, outlining plans for a work to be performed by a large chorus and brass instruments, apparently inspired by Machaut's *Messe de Notre Dame*, which was often performed at the time by choir with brass accompaniment. Moreover – Messiaen noted – it needed to be a work for the dead, maybe a setting of the *De Profundis*: 'Commande Malraux: write a work for chorus (300 singers) and brass (50 players). See the Machaut Mass – but a work for the *dead* (a *De Profundis?*), which will be played in 1964 at Notre-Dame, La Sainte-Chapelle, Chartres Cathedral, etc. Six performances.'

The start of 1964 brought some good news about the commission. Biasini wrote to Messiaen on 16 January:

> I am pleased to inform you that, given the importance of this commission, the
> Minister of State, having taken advice from competent authorities, has decided
> to raise the fee to nine thousand francs in place of the five thousand francs
> initially proposed.

During March 1964, Messiaen developed the idea of composing a choral work.
According to the plans noted in his diary, he had added 'a large orchestra, with
a lot of brass and percussion', and he also envisaged a piece that would be 'very
long'. There is, however, still no mention of the possible texts Messiaen might
have been considering.

After a few weeks of reflection, Messiaen evolved a very different new scheme.
The idea of a chorus was now abandoned, but here, at last, we find the subject that
would serve as the basis for what was now to be a purely instrumental work. He
wrote to Robert Siohan on 25 April 1964. As already noted, Siohan was Malraux's
Inspector General of Music Education, but also the same Robert Siohan who had
conducted the first performance of Messiaen's *L'Ascension* at the Concerts 30
years earlier, on 9 February 1935. Messiaen wrote as follows:

> Following our conversation about the recent commission by Monsieur le
> Ministre André Malraux, for a musical work about the glorious dead of the two
> world wars, I would like to clarify certain points:
> 1. The commission will be delivered at the end of 1964.
> 2. It will be a work for an orchestra of brass instruments concerning the
> Resurrection of the Dead.

This shows that Messiaen was starting to fix his plans for both the instrumentation
and the subject of his new work. Incidentally, the postscript of this letter includes
a most unexpected personal note to Siohan:

> I am literally a martyr to the tax inspector who – considering that I have two
> sources of income, from my salary as a professor at the Conservatoire and the
> performing rights on my musical works – treats me as if I am a film star, in
> the highest tax bracket. Would it be possible for the Cabinet of the Minister to
> request on my behalf that I could be put in a lower tax band? (In effect, half of
> my earnings go in tax). Over the last five years I have lost of great deal of my
> time having to deal with questions of inheritance, and repeated enquiries about
> allocating funds to family members, even though I have paid everything asked
> for in connection with the subject. Would it also be possible to help me on this
> point?

In Messiaen's diary for June 1964, his thoughts on the project have started to
crystallize, and the duration has been reduced – instead of talking about a work
that was to be 'very long', he seems to be contemplating a piece of much more
modest dimensions:

> The Malraux commission: a work on the Resurrection of the dead – *Et exspecto resurrectionem mortuorum* – for a very large orchestra of brass instruments. See plainchant, Boul[ez] chords, birds of Africa and Amazonia. Needs to be delivered by 15 November 1964 with the material copied. Duration: 10 minutes. The work will be played in public on the occasion of the Commemoration of the anniversaries of 1914 and 1944. Payment for the commission: 900,000 Afs. Contact Robert Siohan or M. Biasini of the Direction générale des Arts et Lettres.

On a small piece of paper, jotted down at about the same time, Messiaen noted some more developed ideas about the instrumentation – he was now contemplating a vast array of brass and other wind instruments:

> Malraux commission […] a work with a duration of 10 minutes (or 15 minutes). […] I am authorized to compose a work on the Resurrection of the Dead. Brass only: bugles, horns, trumpets, trombones and woodwind (100 musicians).

At the end of the academic year at the Conservatoire, Messiaen went, as usual, to his little house at Petichet in the Dauphiné, where he was able to compose in peace and quiet. On 27 June 1964, he noted in his diary that he needed to: 'Prepare everything for the Malraux commission'. He got down to work without delay, beginning composition of *Et exspecto* on 7 July, and completing the majority of the piece during these summer months in the countryside. The summer was not spent entirely on the new commission: Messiaen made weekly visits to the Grenoble Conservatoire with Yvonne Loriod to work on the complete cycle of Mozart piano concertos that she was preparing to play in Paris that autumn. For these private rehearsals, Messiaen himself played the orchestral reduction on a second piano.

For relaxation, and to make the most of the mountain air, Messiaen and Loriod also took a number of day-trips on Sundays. On 2 August, the couple went to the village of La Grave and its great glacier of La Meije (about 35 miles east of Petichet), and a week later, on 9 August, the Messiaens went for a long walk on Mount Tabor, close to Petichet. Messiaen had been having a lot of trouble with his knee, but this was cured thanks to the acupuncture used by his doctor, who had the splendidly apt surname for Messiaen of Dr Regard. According to Loriod, her husband was back on form as a great walker as a consequence, but the summer of 1964 was mostly spent on hard and intensive work on his new composition.

Malraux's staff made repeated requests – three times during September alone – for a date by which the new commission would be finished and delivered. There was even an idea at the Ministry that the work might be performed one month later, in October 1964. Biasini wrote to Messiaen that Malraux 'has the intention of having your work heard on the occasion of the commemoration of Charles Péguy at Chartres, this coming October. I would thus be very happy if it would be possible for you to send me your work with the least possible delay.' This wholly impracticable suggestion was for a performance just a few weeks hence, and Biasini's letter was swiftly followed by two others. Messiaen was understandably worried: his work was not yet finished, and the mention of a performance in October, for a celebration of Charles Péguy (who had died 50 years earlier, in 1914) struck the composer as alarming, as well as completely impossible.

According to the terms of the commission, the Ministry had requested that the work should be ready by 15 November, and Messiaen had indicated that it would be finished by the end of the year. In something of a panic, he noted in his diary at the end of September:

> Write a personal letter to André Malraux: explain the history of the commission – the five pieces – that I will not have finished before 25 December – that I have looked at the subject from a Catholic perspective – speak of the Resurrection of the Dead – say how much I regret (as a believer) that the Charles Péguy commemoration in October is impossible – but that the fifth movement cannot be cut – assure him that it will be finished by Christmas.

Messiaen duly wrote to Malraux on 6 October, after returning to Paris from Petichet. It is quite a long letter, somewhat exasperated, but also thoroughly practical: he explains something of the story of the commission, and speaks for the first time of the form of the work (noting that a composition that had originally been planned as a single movement had evolved into a five-movement piece), of the orchestration (already completed for the first three movements) and of what he has tried to express in the work itself:

> I have received three letters in succession: 1. from Monsieur Biasini; 2. from Monsieur Siohan and 3. from Mademoiselle Moreau, asking me to deliver your commission for an orchestral work in honour of the dead of the two world wars at the start of October – this on account of the ceremony commemorating Charles Péguy in Chartres Cathedral.
>
> I am sorry, because it would have been a great joy for me to have taken part in this ceremony. But unfortunately I promised you this commission for the end of this year, 1964, which in my view indicates around Christmas time. I thus continue to promise that I will have it finished for Christmas.
>
> Here is the history of the commission. Having the good fortune to be a Catholic, and a profound believer, I have looked at the subject very broadly and have thus written five pieces on the *Resurrection of the Dead*. These pieces require a large orchestra of woodwind (full) and of brass (very full, ranging from the piccolo trumpet in D to the bass saxhorn). In addition, metallic percussion (bells, gongs and tam-tams). In all: 40 players.
>
> I spent this summer in the High Alps so as to work in peace, and I orchestrated for ten hours a day over three months. The music is entirely finished. Movements 1, 2 and 3 are orchestrated, as is half of the fourth. So it remains to orchestrate the other half of the fourth and all of the fifth movement. It is impossible to perform a work such as this in fragments, and in any case, even when I have

finished, it will be necessary to allow another three weeks for copying the orchestral material.

I therefore expect to be able to show you the finished score around 25 December, and for the parts to be copied by the end of January.

Of course, I could have finished sooner, if I had considered this work an ordinary commission. But it seemed to me that the nobility of the subject necessitated this powerful and majestic orchestration, suitable for a cathedral, and also the open air, and if I have composed five pieces instead of one, it is because the quotations from Holy Scripture on which the work is based required it, as well as the overall balance of the piece.

As soon as it is finished, I will send you a letter. Permit me, dear Monsieur le Ministre, to express my deepest gratitude for the beauty of the work which you have requested from me. […] Olivier Messiaen.

Malraux replied on 12 October, a soothing letter, written in a spirit of encouragement – clearly he had no wish to give Messiaen any more cause for concern:

Mon cher Maître, I am delighted by all that, and above all by the joyous confusion that emerges from your letter, and which so often accompanies great works. It follows from this that you must take whatever time you need: my colleagues wrote to you on account of the commemorations, but Chartres Cathedral will welcome you for another ceremony – one that will not, of course, cancel that which is already planned for La Sainte-Chapelle. In all confidence, and a little impatience (but not for the 'delivery') […] André Malraux.

Yvonne Loriod has recalled the days after Christmas at the rue Marcadet, at the end of December 1964 and the start of January 1965: 'The year finished in the benevolent calm of his studio, with regular work each day, devoted to the composition of the work commissioned from André Malraux'.[3] *Et exspecto* was finished in the first few days of January 1965. After his customary review of the manuscript, Messiaen began immediately to make arrangements for preparing the orchestral material. On 29 January, he took his score – already photocopied and microfilmed as was his habit – to his pupil Raymond Cremers who was going to copy the orchestral parts. The 'Note pour la copie des parties d'orchestre' that Messiaen wrote to Cremers shows something of the obsessive care the composer took over such matters: to copy each instrument separately, and to take particular care over transpositions as the score was written at sounding pitches – just to be sure, Messiaen appended a little lesson in transposing instruments. He commented also on how he wanted the parts for gongs and tam-tams written, how to write complex bars and on the distrubition of the three ranks of cencerros: 'There are three players – *three separate parts!!!*'.

3   Yvonne Loriod, personal communication with the author.

Two days after his meeting with Cremers, Messiaen noted in his diary that he still needed to show his new work to Malraux. A visit was duly arranged, but before it even took place, Messiaen was being badgered once again by Biasini. In a letter dated 8 February, Malraux's zealous assistant wrote:

> You have informed me that the musical work [...] which was commissioned from you by the State in 1963 would be ready at the end of December 1964. [...] Having received no news from you about this work, I have the honour of requesting that you inform me of the date on which it will be possible for you to deliver the work to me.

Three days later, on 11 February, Messiaen visited Malraux at the Ministère des Affaires Culturelles, at 3 rue de Valois, and took with him a photocopy of the score. Remarkably, he left this score with Malraux for a few days – it was altogether exceptional for Messiaen to lend a hitherto unperformed work in this way. Two days later, Malraux's secretary returned the precious score to Messiaen's apartment in the rue Marcadet.

With the work completed, there was now a question of finding a conductor, and of fixing the dates of the first performances. According to Messiaen's diary, André Malraux had the rather grandiose idea of inaugurating a new national and religious day of commemoration for the dead of the two world wars:

> André Malraux wants a national and religious event for the dead of the two wars – like the antique ceremonies of Mesopotamians, Assyrians, Egyptians, Greeks etc. It would take place every year on 9 May. I am the first composer to be chosen. I will be paid in April. After the performances on 8 and 9 May, I can hand over my score and give it to Leduc. No hire fee on the orchestral material for these two performances.

In February, Messiaen wrote a note in his diary about the rights for the work and the organizers of the concerts. Here, too, he considered the important question of the choice of conductor:

> The work belongs to Malraux for the two first performances in France. It belongs to me after that. Siohan (Ministry, credits) and Werner (payments, orchestra, conductor), will assist me in preparing the first two concerts:
> 1. At La Sainte-Chapelle in Paris – official performance.
> 2. At Notre-Dame de Chartres – second official performance with General de Gaulle. The work will be given on its own, played twice, each time with a sermon on the Resurrection?
> 3. Orchestra of the Domaine Musical and Boulez? Or the Orchestre National (Maderna? Or Baudo? Or Cluytens?). Cremers will have the material finished around 20 March.

One of the most important consequences of this commission was that Messiaen became an Establishment figure, an 'official' composer, very much in the public eye. On 30 March there was even a lunch at the Elysée Palace, recalled by Yvonne Loriod with great charm, though also, it must be admitted, a certain starry-eyed view of General de Gaulle's intellectual interests:

> Simplicity is always best, said the General. A lunch during which the conversation between De Gaulle and Malraux amazed Messiaen through the culture of these two beings. The questions posed by the General to Messiaen were also full of warmth, of curiosity and of profound theological understanding.[4]

Malraux's plans for a national commemoration seem to have been abandoned, and the date of the first performance of *Et exspecto* was fixed for 7 May 1965, at La Sainte-Chapelle, conducted by Serge Baudo. All the rehearsals were noted in Messiaen's diary:

> 3 May: Sainte-Chapelle with Baudo, Siohan and Werner to look at the placement of the music-stands and lighting. At 6 p.m. Woodwind rehearsal.
> 4 May: Morning: Brass. At 5 p.m. Percussion.
> 5 May : 6 p.m. Tutti.
> 6 May: General rehearsal. Malraux will be there.

Messiaen's reaction to the performance is noted in his diary on 7 May:

> The first private performance of *Et exspecto resurrectionem mortuorum*, conductor: Serge Baudo, with musicians of the Domaine [Musical], the [Orchestre] national, the Garde Républicaine, the 6 Percussions de Strasbourg. [...] 150 guests. A marvellous performance with the reflections of the sun in the blue and the red of the stained-glass windows – and with all that resonance!! It was recorded by the radio.

Messiaen himself prepared the text of the programme for this performance, and even the wording of the printed invitation cards that were sent out to 150 guests. But who were these guests? According to a letter from Messiaen to Alain Trapenard at the Ministry of Culture, the first 40 invitations were for the musicians in the orchestra 'who wouldn't otherwise be able to get in', then the personal guests of André Malraux, of Serge Baudo, and, above all, of Messiaen himself, who requested that 54 invitations be sent to his home address, for himself, his family, his publishers, and a few pupils and friends. It is possible to reconstruct the guest-list thanks to notes kept by Yvonne Loriod. As well as officers of the Ministry (Malraux, Biasini, Siohan and others), there are also old friends including those who were among Messiaen's class-mates at the Conservatoire – Gaston Litaize,

---

4   Yvonne Loriod, personal communication with the author.

Jean Langlais, Daniel-Lesur and Elsa Barraine – and also those who are or were pupils in Messiaen's own class – such as Maurice Le Roux, Jean-Pierre Guézec, Iannis Xenakis and Jacques Charpentier – along with representatives of his publisher Leduc and his recording company Erato. Table 10.1 gives as complete a list as possible of those present, based on Loriod's notes.

Table 10.1   Guests at the performance of *Et exspecto resurrectionem mortuorum* in La Sainte-Chapelle, 7 May 1965

Ministry of Culture	Friends, family, etc.	Pupils
André Malraux (2)	Elsa Barraine	Solange Ancona
Alain Trapenard	Mme Baudo et amies	Jacques Charpentier
Albert Beuret	[Yves?] Bonnefoy	Raymond Cremers (2)
Émile Biasini	André Boucourechliev (2)	Michel Decoust (2)
M. Lombard (architect)	Jacques Chailley	Françoise Gervais
Gaëtan Picon	Gabriel Dussurget	Jean-Pierre Guézec
Robert Siohan (2)	Mlle Gaussens	Jean-Paul Holstein
Maurice Werner (2)	Monique Haas et	Paul Méfano (2)
M. Lombard (architect)	Marcel Mihalovici	Maurice Le Roux
	Daniel-Lesur	Françoise Rieunier (2)
Organists	M. et Mme Loriod	Camille Roy (2)
Jean Bonfils	Pierette Mari (2)	Pia Sebastiani
Ferdinand Klinda	Pascal et Josette Messiaen	Akira Tamba
Jean Langlais (3)	Michel Philippot (2)	Iannis Xenakis
Christiane de Lisle	Olivier Revault d'Allones (2)	
Gaston Litaize (2)	Jean Roire	**Publishers**
Guy Morançon	Claude Rostand	Michel Garçin (Erato)
	Jean Roy	Mme Alphonse Leduc
Clergy	Claude Samuel (2)	Gilbert Leduc (2)
Chanoine Hollande	Nelly Sivade	
(Trinité)	Pierre Souvtchinsky (2)	
Chanoine Paléstinien	Suzanne Tézenas	

A few weeks later, on 20 June, *Et exspecto* was performed in the presence of De Gaulle himself, at Chartres Cathedral, given by the same performers as in La Sainte-Chapelle, and again conducted by Serge Baudo. A general rehearsal was held in the Cathedral the day before, on 19 June, closely supervised by Messiaen. These preparations were filmed for television – a broadcast was produced by Luc Ferrari and directed by Gérard Patris, with rehearsals of each movement interspersed with commentaries by Messiaen himself, as well as unscripted exchanges between Messiaen, Baudo and the musicians.[5]

---

[5]   This 45-minute programme, made by ORTF, was broadcast as part of the series *Les Grandes répétitions* on 11 November 1965.

Messiaen drew a plan of the instrumental layout he wanted in the Choir of Chartres cathedral, and this turned out to be his ideal disposition for performances elsewhere: in the printed score the orchestral layout is identical to his Chartres plan – all that is missing is the mention of a Cathedral (see Plate 10.1).

After the Chartres performance on 20 June, some reviews of the work appeared. On 24 June Claude Rostand wrote in *Figaro littéraire*:

> The work is a monumental invocation, without voices, but for instruments alone. Since it resembles no conventional liturgical or musical form, I don't know what terms to use to describe it. As is his custom, Messiaen uses some elements from the rhythms and timbres borrowed from the East (India, Japan, Bali) but very little birdsong. The whole work is carried by the intense lyricism which is his nature, and is expressed using a sonorous palette that has astonishing richness and power.

The same day, 24 June, *Le Monde* published a review by the critic Jacques Longchampt. This may be the earliest public mention of the possibility of performing *Et exspecto* in the open air, and certainly of the specific Alpine location Messiaen had in mind: according to Lonchampt, 'Messiaen wished that it could be heard in front of the massif of La Meije, in the Alps'.

For Messiaen himself, the Chartres performance was a very moving occasion. 'Everyone in their places at 9.15', he noted in his diary. 'De Gaulle arrived and High Mass began. It was the Feast of Corpus Christi. At the end of Mass, at 10.30 precisely, the low A flat sounded from the contra-bassoon and the saxhorn, reinforced by the third tam-tam, and all of a sudden the immense Nave was filled with a noble and overpowering presence.'

The first concert performance of *Et exspecto* took place at the Théâtre de l'Odéon on 12 January 1966. It was at a concert of the Domaine Musical, conducted by Pierre Boulez. According to Messiaen's own note to himself on his copy of the score, the concert was a 'succès formidable!!!' (with three exclamation marks).

The following day, the same performers, with Boulez, recorded the work in the church of Notre-Dame de Liban, the Maronite church in the rue d'Ulm, in the Fifth Arrondissement – it was a favourite venue for Erato sessions. Photographs of Messiaen and Boulez taken during the recording show them smiling, resembling a pair of conspiratorial twins. The finished result is arguably the finest recording the work has ever received.

Before the score was engraved for publication, Messiaen carefully reviewed and revised his manuscript score. He fixed the metronome markings, and changed some tempo indications. For example, at the start of the fifth movement 'Un peu lent' in Messiaen's manuscript score was changed to 'Très lent', with a metronome mark added of $\flat$ = 66. Messiaen made further revisions that took into account the early performances (and the Erato recording) at which he had been present, such as modifications to the tam-tam and gong parts in the third movement, greatly extending the pauses during which their notes die away.

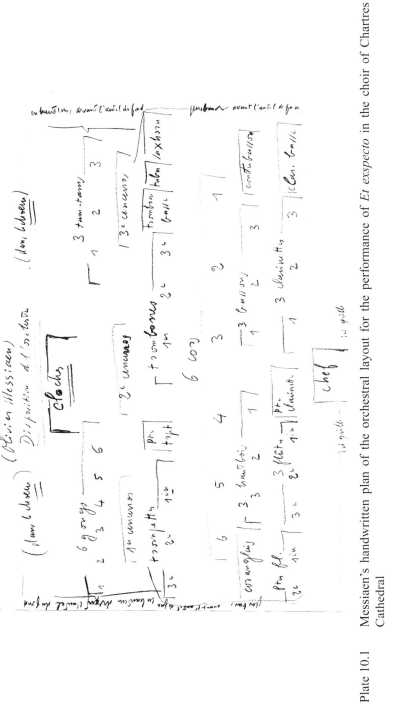

Plate 10.1   Messiaen's handwritten plan of the orchestral layout for the performance of *Et exspecto* in the choir of Chartres Cathedral

The publisher Alphonse Leduc issued the score in February 1967. In this edition, the definitive state of the piece, it can be seen that between the first performances and publication, Messiaen changed his expressive intentions for the work. According to the terms of the original commission, and Messiaen's own commentary for the performance at La Sainte-Chapelle in 1965, *Et exspecto* was dedicated 'to the memory of the dead of the two world wars'. In striking contrast to this, the 'Note de l'Auteur' for the published score makes no mention of any commemorative intention for the work. Certainly, Messiaen states that it was commissioned by André Malraux, but he says nothing on the subject of the war dead. Instead, he preferred to think of the Resurrection, and his note speaks not of those fallen in battle, but of something grander, less connected to a specific memorial occasion – and thus the score became, for Messiaen, an elemental outburst of hope in New Life, destined to be performed in: 'vast spaces: churches, cathedrals, even in the open air and on mountain tops'.

Let us return to May 1965. Messiaen was deeply touched by Malraux's commission. It provided an opportunity to compose a work unlike any other in his output, and for performances in two sacred spaces that each moved him profoundly. In the letter written by Messiaen to André Malraux on 25 May he spoke of his genuine gratitude to the Minister for this significant commission – one that gave him the chance to hear his music performed in the context of the stained glass and the architectural splendour of both La Sainte-Chapelle and Chartres Cathedral:

> Dear André Malraux, having been away in Yugoslavia for seven days for concerts of my orchestral works, I only found your letter on my return. You will forgive me for replying so belatedly. Your letter touched me deeply. You are right to talk about fairy tales, and the Good Fairy is you, for having allowed me to realize a dream that is forty years old: to hear my music among the colours I love – the blues, reds and violets, and the medieval stained glass windows. Thank you for this marvellous gesture![6]

---

[6]   Draft in Yvonne Loriod's hand, Messiaen Archives.

Chapter 11

Olivier Messiaen and the Avant-Garde Poetics of the *Messe de la Pentecôte*

Robert Sholl

Setting the stage

In a small article entitled 'Musique Réligeuse', on the first page of *La Page musicale* (5 February 1937), Messiaen published his challenge to the musical world and what amounted to a compositional call to arms. In this vignette, he contrasts three aesthetic categories of religious music: the conventional, the mystical, and the living. 'La conventionnelle' he associates with exterior effect, but he states, with reference to the heightened religious sentiment of Wagner's *Parsifal* that: 'the expansive chords, like reinforced concrete [*ciment armé*], which adhere to the obligatory formula of such works, will remain the symbol for those who have eyes but do not see'.[1] In other words, for Messiaen, this kind of music is calculated to promote an emotional illusion of grandeur without any sincere Christian identity. Messiaen goes on to distinguish what he calls 'La Mystique' in art, but he cautions the reader against:

> 'sugariness' [*sucreries*], the false ecstasies of a vague religious sensibility! There are few true mystical musicians. Those whose works are most long lasting are those who attach themselves to: **La vivante:** Living by their subject, living by their language. The word 'life' reoccurs constantly in the Gospels; our sacraments, our catholic liturgy, which is above all an organism of spiritual life, and all Christians reach [*tendent*] towards eternal life. The language of a believing musician will search then to express life. This life – inexhaustible and always new to those who search for it – calls for means of expression that are powerfully original and varied. To us [this means] audacious harmonies, shimmering rhythms, sumptuous modes, (and) the timbres of the rainbow! To us [it also signifies] tonal enrichment, explosive [*fusées*] counterpoints, chord clusters, [and] melodies that burn with love! This is behind the door [*derrière la porte*], Bach and the faith of his Chorals, Frescobaldi and the humility of his *elevazioni*, Franck and the expressive nobility of his *Beatitudes*, (and) nearer to us, Tournemire and the luminous arabesques of his *L'Orgue Mystique*. Young composers, if you have this faith, march forward [*de l'avant*], and give

---

[1]   Note the reference to Ezekiel 12:2.

us enlivening and effective religious works to which we can ascribe what the
scripture says of the stars: 'They shine joyously for him who created them!'[2]

One would have thought that such a call to create a new spiritual art would have
been music to the ears of the composer Charles Tournemire (1870–1937), who, in
his unpublished *Mémoires* continually rails against secular tendencies in music,
criticizing almost all of his contemporaries: 'But, why do the French organists
(principally), not understand the idea that organ music from which God is absent, is
a body without a soul!'.[3] Following this indictment, Tournemire refers specifically
to Messiaen's article in *La Page musicale*:

> The young O. Messiaen, (magnificent name), is an accomplished poser. He exploits
> the most holy ideas, without [a sense of] modesty … 'He plays the apostolate' …
> For the rest, this young Messiaen is an anti-musician (the beginnings had been
> good – but, he is in constant regression). He takes pleasure in a sustained ugliness
> [*laideur soutenue*] … and several cretins follow him …. Again Messiaen…In a
> rag [*Dans un canard*] … he has published a little article entitled 'Ciment armé,
> derrière la porte'. In this little article, he dares to assimilate the art of Wagner (in
> his *Parsifal*) with reinforced concrete [*ciment armé*], and more: he consigns the
> path to the company of the rising generations, but he demands then to be covered
> with flowers, so that we might be impressed and not forget them, and at last, he
> places himself at the head of this modern movement, as the only one who is truly
> great, true, sublime … Little fool!! [*Petit sot!!*][4]

This avalanche of invective post-dates and runs contrary to the laudatory tone of
the published correspondence between these composers.[5] Although Tournemire's
reaction to Messiaen's article in his *Mémoires* represents a gross misrepresentation
of Messiaen's thought, nonetheless, it reveals a sense and a recognition of shared

---

[2]   Olivier Messiaen, 'Musique Réligieuse', *La Page musicale* (5 February 1937): 1.
The scriptural reference at the end of the article is from Baruch 3:34 '[…] They shone with
gladness for him who made them' ('The Apocrypha', *Bible*, New Revised Standard Version
(NRSV)). This article is the first in a discourse of articles in *Le Page musicale*. Messiaen's
article was responded to by Eugène Berteaux on 19 February 1937 in an article entitled
'"Ciment Armé" … "derrière la porte"!', and then Messiaen responded on 26 February:
'"Derrière ou devant la porte? …" (Lettre ouverte à M. Eugène Berteaux)'. Berteaux then
responded on 5 March 1937 with 'Devant ou derrière la porte?…'; this seems to have blown
the correspondence out.
[3]   Charles Tournemire, *Mémoires (1886–1939)*, p. 157 (Tournemire's underlining).
[4]   Ibid., (again, Tournemire's underlining). Tournemire had confused the title of the
first response by Berteaux with the original article by Messiaen.
[5]   Joël-Marie Fauquet, ed. 'Correspondance inédite: Lettres d'Olivier Messiaen à
Charles Tournemire', *L'Orgue: Cahiers et Mémoires*, no. 41 (1989–I): 80–85.

values and beliefs.[6] Indeed, in his article for *La Page musicale*, Messiaen had perhaps inadvertently taken his cue from Tournemire, who, writing in the *Revue Grégorienne* seven years earlier, had addressed the issue of what was (for him) an appropriate musical language for the reinvigoration of contemporary art:

> If the Protestant Chorale of inestimable plastic value had inspired musicians of the stature of Scheidt and Bach, could not Gregorian chant, altogether richer, perhaps give birth to a new art, supported by polyphony and polytonality? To penetrate this musical temple of the angelic lines, necessitates prolonged religious and mystical preparation [*mystique prolongée*]. The light at first discrete, brightens faintly; but the addiction to the chant *par excellence* of the church is an adorable thing. Imperceptibly, the soul is illuminated. A profound emotion is felt when an antiphon or an alleluia is heard. *Voilà* the door is open to the sonic edifice where the incense rises up […] . The eternal entices to God (*Lui*) a legion of Christian artists, so that they may purify contemporary art and carry this forth in knowledge and faith![7]

Tournemire's call for a 'legion of Christian artists' could not be closer to Messiaen's own plea for, and amplification of, this concern in his own article. Both men are concerned with the creation of an intrinsically sacred music, beyond the door of the normative and worldly [*derrière la porte*].[8] Yet Tournemire's caustic response to Messiaen's article points to a discomfort with the modernist spirit of Messiaen's musical language, and the ways it usurps the boundaries of what Tournemire might have regarded as an appropriate modern musical language for religious expression.[9] What was uncomfortable for Tournemire in Messiaen's language in 1937 was almost certainly the burgeoning marriage of Catholic evangelism, secular images of love, and the neo-classical use of the organ (in fact an extension and refinement of the symphonic aesthetic of Tournemire). All these

---

[6]   In an entry of Tournemire's *Mémoires* of 18 September 1933 (p. 87), Tournemire writes: 'The young Olivier Messiaen, musician of the future, (this young man has become a terrible "*arriviste*"!!) […] It is, however. remarkable that this young artist is only 24 years old! It is true that he is a believer!'

[7]   Charles Tournemire, 'Des possibilités harmoniques et polytonales unies à la ligne grégorienne', *Revue Grégorienne*, Année 15, no. 15 (September/October 1930), p. 174.

[8]   This is a perennial issue in the discussion of music and the liturgy behind which is an almost aphasic fear, and the unspoken question: in what voice should we address and praise God?

[9]   There may also have been a certain amount of personal ire in Tournemire's comments. In 1937, Messiaen was a rising star in the French musical firmament, while Tournemire was composing monumental sacred works such as his *L'Apocalypse de Saint-Jean* (1932–36), effectively for his own drawer.

were signs, however, of Messiaen's blossoming originality.[10] Most of Messiaen's music of the 1930s and 1940s contains that peculiar flammable, immiscible and radical concoction of language and ideology (understood in Messiaen's case as religion) that has always been at the theoretical centre of avant-garde art. Perhaps Messiaen is rarely thought of in this way, but in the 1930s and 1940s the avant-garde gun was loaded in works such as *Les Corps glorieux*, *Chants de Terre et de Ciel*, *Vingt regards sur l'Enfant-Jésus*, *Harawi* and the Tristan Trilogy (especially the *Cinq Rechants*), pieces that abundantly fulfil his ideal of living works that call for 'means of expression that are powerfully original and varied', and that contain 'audacious harmonies, shimmering rhythms, sumptuous modes, (and) the timbres of the rainbow!'[11]

Rather than being identified with the avant-garde (the domain of secular renunciation), Messiaen's works of 1948–53 are more often portrayed critically as 'experimental', because they extend and refine elements of his previous musical language in unconventional and perhaps unforeseen ways. Evidently, the fusion of surrealism and Christianity in works such as the Tristan Trilogy, already entails avant-garde tendencies in which ideals of sacred and erotic human love are projected through an increasingly technical, abstract, radical and even irascible language.[12] The *Messe de la Pentecôte* (1950–51), a work inspired by Messiaen's own organ improvisations and designed for liturgical use, looks back over its shoulder at these developments, but also searches for the seeds of new means of expression beyond the consequential telos of 'progress'.

In fact, Messiaen's citation of the *Messe de la Pentecôte* in his *Technique de mon langage musical*, his first major attempt to describe his music and his aesthetic language, reveals the ways in which the 'progress' of his own musical language had outstripped his own rhetoric.[13] But the *Technique* was more than merely a

---

[10]   Tournemire's own extraordinary harmonic and monumental achievements of the late 1930s, the *Symphonie-Choral* (1935) for organ for instance, while basking in the afterglow of nineteenth-century symphonicism, represent at least a tentative movement towards a religious musical language that had sublimated, or does not need to rely exclusively on explicitly Christian musical material such as plainchant. In a slightly different sense, this progression is felt clearly in Messiaen's music of the 1930s where symbolism and rhetoric become more powerful signifiers of the music's expressive intent.

[11]   Messiaen, 'Musique Réligieuse', p. 1.

[12]   For more on this see Robert Sholl: 'Love, Mad Love, and the *'point sublime'*: The Surrealist poetics of Messiaen's *Harawi*', in *Messiaen Studies*, ed. Robert Sholl (Cambridge: Cambridge University Press, 2007), pp. 34–62.

[13]   Messiaen himself acknowledges this when he cites the opening of the 'Communion' of the *Messe de la Pentecôte* (as yet unlabelled in 1944) as example E in Ch. VII 'Rhythmic Notations' of *Technique de mon langage musical*. Prefacing these examples (A to G), he writes: 'In appendix to the present chapter and to all those on rhythm, here are some supplementary examples *which do not at all obey the laws of my rhythmic system.'* (my emphasis) *Technique de mon langage musical*, Vol. 1 (Paris, Leduc, 2001 [1944]), pp. 30–31.

documentation of progress or achievements thus far. It was a manifesto (another avant-garde trait), and, like the *Messe de la Pentecôte*, it was a continuation of his earlier thought about a problem fundamental to his art: how could he configure the meaning of his musical language as intrinsically religious or spiritual, and in reconfiguring this relationship, could his music become more potent and spiritually effective? Indeed, by placing shock at the heart of his aesthetics could he bring secular humanity to an encounter with God?

This question was further complicated for Messiaen in the late 1940s. How could he do this *and* respond to the divergent interests of his students, in particular Pierre Boulez? Or to put the problem in another way that perhaps sets Messiaen's originality in relief to a greater extent, Messiaen's music of this period points to one of the fundamental aesthetic issues of twentieth-century music (one that faced Schoenberg, Stravinsky and Boulez): how can music revive and renew itself in the face of the death of the organizing and teleological procedures of tonality?

Beneath the various quests for a solution to this problem we can sense an almost theological thirst for what the sources of music itself are, and an unconscious interrogation of why we respond intuitively to aspects of cohesion and unity. Perhaps this is why Messiaen himself resisted any association of his music with any particular musical label or fashion, but simply stated on a number of occasions that he believed in natural resonance (the overtone series), and in the colour that he perceived (as a result of his synaesthesia) in his own music and that of other composers.[14] Indeed, even in his early article in *La Page musicale*, Messiaen implies that his music attempts to reach beyond partisan lines to a music that sublimates its origins in the creation of revelatory art.

A somewhat dialectical reading of the *Technique* might suppose some truth in Tournemire's suspicions of Messiaen's 'arriviste' tendencies.[15] At the same time as Messiaen is attempting to describe and reconstruct some of the sources of his music, effectively patching together the pieces of the stained-glass window obliterated by the ideal of dazzlement [*éblouissement*] in his music, he is also de-historicizing his music somewhat through his own representation of its originality.[16] This perception of his music as breaking with the past resonates not only with avant-garde precepts, but also with Messiaen's later explanation of his language, based on natural resonance and colour rather than on a sense of historical musical development.

While Messiaen may have whole-heartedly believed that these phenomena underpin his language, his explanation has always seemed to me to be rather glib, resting as it does on scientific fact and a proto-romantic ideal of subjective intuition or revelation. Messiaen does not get out of the historical net quite so easily. He was, like others, caught up as a major participant in an inexorable tendency of

---

[14]   See for instance this discussion in Messiaen's *Conférence de Notre-Dame* (Paris: Leduc, 1978).

[15]   See the entry in Tournemire's *Mémoires* for 18 September 1933, p. 87 (cited above).

[16]   For more on the idea of *éblouissement*, see Sander van Maas's 'Forms of love: Messiaen's aesthetics of *éblouissement*', *Messiaen Studies*, pp. 78–100.

twentieth-century music. The early twentieth century had seen a revalorization of the basic elements of music – melody, harmony, rhythm, counterpoint, and timbre (colour), texture and tonality – such that the old hierarchical supremacy of melody, harmony and counterpoint had been challenged if not usurped. The music of Boulez, Cage and Messiaen would carry this revalorization further by elevating features such as timbre, duration, attack and register to equal or greater importance.

Had Tournemire lived another 11 years and heard Messiaen's *Messe de la Pentecôte*, he would almost certainly have penned another poisonous diatribe against Messiaen. But the *Messe de la Pentecôte* is more than a reinvention of the 'organ mass' as envisaged by Tournemire in his *L'Orgue Mystique* (1926–33). It is a crucible in which Messiaen begins to work out the ramifications of his latest musical researches, as much as a continuation and re-evaluation of his own religious modernist aesthetic, and of how these might be recreated on his own beloved organ at La Trinité.

The avant-garde and the *Messe de la Pentecôte*

In what follows, it will be clear that I am not concerned with the influence of Messiaen on his students (that is another topic altogether), but with the way in which Messiaen absorbs and transforms the aesthetic tendencies of the avant-garde. In some senses the avant-garde, as the literary critic Matei Calinescu has elaborated, have been a constant representation of a politicized vanguard of innovation since the Enlightenment.[17] Usually a small group of individuals with seemingly disparate interests but underlying aesthetic concerns, the avant-garde provide a kind of stumbling block to diachronic history, tripping it up only to be absorbed, possibly normalized or even rejected (but rarely ignored), to some degree upon recovery of equilibrium. For artists that can be classified as avant-garde, radicalism and experimentation are *de rigeur*, but, ironically, alongside this positivist side of the stylistic coin, avant-garde works of art can also use and abuse cliché and even mannerism.[18]

The revolutionary objectives of the avant-garde usually mingle political and artistic momentum. The avant-garde embraces a desire to break free of convention (what is understood to be the atrophied status quo), and to do so in a way that creates

---

[17]   For more on this see Matei Calinescu's *Five Faces of Modernity* (Durham, NC: Duke University Press, 1987).

[18]   My understanding of this has been nourished by a variety of reading but principally Peter Bürger's *The Theory of the Avant-Garde* trans. Michael Shaw (Minneapolis: University of Minnesota Press, 1984 [1974]), and Renato Poggioli's *The Theory of the Avant-Garde* (Cambridge MA: The Belknap Press of Harvard University Press, 1968). For a recent discussion of Bürger see Richard Murphy's 'Theories of the avant-garde', in his *Theorizing the Avant-Garde* (Cambridge: Cambridge University Press, 1998), pp. 1–48.

a clear political and aesthetic demarcation. Often this may be achieved in acerbic and even acrimonious terms that attack the institutionalization and commercial aspects of art promoted by that great imaginary invention of the political left: the bourgeoisie (usually persons unnamed who are to be blamed for oppressing someone else, also unknown, in a manner also, equally, unknown).

For the avant-gardist, such a disassociation from the normative must be achieved at the fundamental level of language in a departure from historical or narrative currents, often through disruptive and violent language. From such a stance, a conflict arises between the negation and confirmation of meaning, context, and the cultural presences in art, an engagement that leads to an all-important semantic reconfiguration. This 'progression' is tangible in the work of the Dadaists, Duchamp, certain strands of Surrealism (Artaud in particular), in Abstract Art (Kandinsky, Mondrian, Rothko, Pollock, Newman) and in the music of avant-garde composers such as Stockhausen, Boulez, Xenakis and Ligeti.

So how does Messiaen fit into this picture? In some senses he doesn't fit into any picture, but it is the nature of his musical originality, its hieratic and iconoclastic qualities, together with the search for a reinvention of language and expression through research and disruption, that put him back squarely in the avant-garde play-pen. Rather than employing an anti-establishment rhetoric, it might be construed that Messiaen takes a powerful concoction of modernist music and places a Catholic theological label on the outside. But, despite giving this impression in his own description of the *Messe de la Pentecôte* in *Traité IV*, Messiaen seems to bring modernism and Catholicism into a kind of Surrealist dialectic of images that renders a new musical substance, strong in its lyricism and potency.[19]

As a work conceived both in and for the liturgy (as a result of weekly improvisations), the *Messe de la Pentecôte* could be understood as an insidious rounding on the bourgeois quality of pre-Vatican II Catholicism, as much as an interiorization of such affirmative beliefs, despite the technical and aesthetic language of negation heard in the music. The radicalism of the language could equally also be understood as an attempt to move beyond social signification (an idea consonant with avant-garde ideals) towards a new level of linguistic communication with the divine (the transcendentalist argument). By instituting this new language into the context of the liturgy, recreating a relationship between art and life (as he implies in his article in *La Page musicale*), was Messiaen trying to re-orient the secular trajectory of the avant-garde (inherent in this language) towards God?[20] Would this not in itself be a truly avant-garde thing to do? There is no doubt that the shock of avant-garde, its utopian and purist aspirations,

---

[19]   For more on this see Robert Sholl, 'Love, Made Love and the '*pointe sublime*': the Surrealist poetics of Messiaen's *Harawi*', in *Messiaen Studies*, pp. 34–62.

[20]   Messiaen, 'Musique Réligieuse', p. 1. Messiaen writes: 'The language of a believing musician will search then to express life. This life – inexhaustible and always new to those who search for it – calls for means of expression that are powerfully original and varied.'

sedimented in the language of the *Messe de la Pentecôte*, was to bring to the surface the profoundly theological overtones (expressed albeit in a secular vein) of avant-garde rhetoric. But if the asymptotic approach to reification or death underlying avant-garde thought is then masked as Christian eschatology, how can we distinguish between (to paraphrase Ecclesiastes) the sting of death, and the euphoria of religious anaesthetic?

What Messiaen's manifesto in *La Page musicale* points to is a desire for a music that breaks with any normative aesthetic correlation of music and meaning, and therefore penetrates beyond the aesthetics of musical gratification. When asked by Claude Samuel, during the recordings sessions for his *Turangalîla-symphonie* in 1961, what advice he would give to an enthusiast who was coming to hear one of his works that would be difficult at first hearing, Messiaen said that the public must come with no 'a priorisms', and with a sort of 'aural virginity' [*virginité d'oreille*]. Samuel then asks:

> 'He must hear a shock?'
> Messiaen (emphatically): 'Yes! A Shock!'[21]

Certainly the *Messe de la Pentecôte* must have provided a shock for parishioners of a conservative disposition at La Trinité, but more broadly this music might act as a critique of the church's apparent lack of engagement with modernity, even as it threatens the audience/congregation's most cherished ideals: the desire to belong to a community that honours tradition, past and present worshippers, and the idea of a benevolent and omnipotent God. The radical quality of the *Messe de la Pentecôte* is clarified further when compared with the organ music of Messiaen's friends, the composers Maurice Duruflé and Jean Langlais. Their music effectively seeks, and serves to perpetuate and gently extend the liturgical traditions of the church, and the symphonic organ thinking of Tournemire in particular, into the concert hall. In other words, their works have an underlying purpose of fulfilling (even perhaps unwittingly) a religious and social function.

In contradistinction the *Messe de la Pentecôte* is in no way subservient to such ideals. Religion for Messiaen is not mere consolation, or a refuge, but, as his short article in *La Page musicale* implies, it is a call to action. Perhaps this is what is so refreshing about the *Messe de la Pentecôte*: action is seemingly not governed by the kind of systematization of the *Mode de Valeurs et d'Inténsites*, or Boulez's *Structures 1a*. In many ways, it is because Messiaen is able to incorporate and subsume systematic musical thinking and religious imagination that the piece is able to impart a new kind of semantic communication, a language befitting the beauty, mystery, and *theologia gloriae* of Pentecost.

For instance in Messiaen's description of the first piece of the *Messe*, the 'Entrée (Les langues de feu)' [The tongues of fire], in his *Traité IV*, he implies

---

[21]   *Entretien avec Olivier Messiaen*, 11–13 October 1961, included with a recording of his *Turangalîla-symphonie* (Vega 30 BVG 1363).

that the work entails a world of an unknown or rarefied language (with its private meanings and overtones of Debussy and Bartók), seemingly free from any conscious necessity to communicate specific meaning. What is surprising perhaps is that there is reluctance in Messiaen's commentary to connect the theological origins of his music and his expressive intentions with the technical aspects of the piece in his commentary on the work. Yet, it is this impasse between spiritual concerns and technical prowess, enshrined in a limited number of musical typologies, that foreground the hermetic and autonomous qualities of the work. Such avant-garde qualities also subsume, perhaps unusually for Messiaen, a reluctance to indulge in prescriptive narrative, while allowing space for the listener's own imagination to engage with the musical imagery of the piece.

In *Traité IV*, Messiaen imparts that, in the 'Entrée', it was images of the tongues of fire that inspired him, and that these were embodied in the innovative combinations of timbres employed.[22] In a certain sense the radicalism of the registrations serves as both a critique and extension of nineteenth-century 'symphonic' organ writing.[23] But perhaps the most radical and cohesive aspect of the piece lies in Messiaen's grid structure of the 'Entrée', which demonstrates 'total control' of archaic Greek rhythms, used as formants independent of timbre (see Figure 11.1)[24]

Despite this background organization, at the surface level of the 'Entrée' Messiaen creates a study of the ways in which subtle gradations of rhythm (difficult to achieve or appreciate in performance) create rhythmic crescendos and diminuendos across, and sometimes despite, the timbral changes.

---

[22] Messiaen wrote: 'I was only attracted [*attaché*] to the symbol of the tongues of fire [*langues de feu*]. According to Saint Gregory, they signify the charity that inflamed the Apostles, and the word that burnt and enlightened their audience like 'a fire of love'. But these tongues of fire were all a real fact, surreal: I wanted to represent the flames in the form of tongues, the astonishment of this strange phenomenon, the presence of the bizarre, the strange, the marvellous, the miraculous, and the mixed admiration which accompanied it.' *Traité IV*, p. 84.

[23] Messiaen uses a bourdon 16 and a three-rank mixture (*cymbale*) on the Swell. This is contrasted with a quintaton 16 and tierce $1^{3/5}$ on the Positive, a diapason (*montre*) and quinte $2^{2/3}$ on the Great, and a 4ft reed stop (*clairon*) on the pedal. The 'mutation' stops (mixture and tierce) used on the positive and swell, which sound harmonics of the note played but not the actual fundamental pitch itself, are used (unusually) without any 8ft or 4ft timbres, while the pedal seemingly fills this registral gap with a reed stop at 4ft pitch. The only 8ft employed by Messiaen, significantly a diapason by itself (not the gentler foundational sounds of a flute and bourdon together that might have been employed more traditionally) together with a quinte, is only used on one note (G) throughout the *Entrée*. In the choice of registrations, there are certain aspects of complicity between the sonorities. The quinte, on the great organ, is present in the positive quintaton 16. The quinte (great) and the tierce on the positive are likewise present as harmonics in the three-rank mixture on the swell.

[24] See also *Traité I*, pp. 236–243 for more on this.

Figure 11.1   Messiaen's table of rhythms for the 'Entrée', *Traité IV*, p. 88

Through Messiaen's swirling rhythmic eddies, the first two staves of the score can be understood almost as a study in the use of the number 3 (see Example 11.1). The flexibility of Messiaen's rhythmic language acts like an extension of plainchant's flexibility (also discussed in *Traité IV*), while his modernist reconfiguration of this sense of freedom (without the actual presence of this archaic musical material) also complements his use of Greek rhythms.[25]

Example 11.1   Olivier Messiaen: 'Entrée (Les langues de feu)', opening

---

[25]   Of course, Messiaen disrupts this sense of 3s in various places, for instance in the last two crotchet beats of 2/1/3, or 2/2/2/beat 1. Articulation and agogic accentuation also takes a role in creating groups of 3. For instance, in the group of '7 in the time of 8' in the pedal at the last two crotchet beats of 2/2/2, the first three notes (C, G, A♭) while notationally conjoined to the following D♭ are separated from this note by a small *luftpause*: Messiaen asks the player to use his right foot for the A♭ and the D♭, which is then followed by a B♮ as part of another group of 3. Likewise at 2/3/2, the groups of three repeated notes are interrupted by the addition of a semiquaver rest, thereby accentuating the final D♭ of the bar and giving it an accent (marked by Messiaen) almost like an accented anacrusis. As it is tied over the bar though, this D♭ both belongs to a 'renegade' group of 4 in bar 2 of that system, and it also creates an additional value to the minim and crotchet that form a group of '3 in the time of 2' in the pedal of the final bar of that system, a foundation for the 'minting' [*le monnayage*] of the wonderful and unusual chords above on the swell.

To a certain extent, Messiaen's kind of grid-like rhythmic organization of Greek rhythms in the *Traité* in Figure 11.1 seems to run contrary to his avowed distrust of 'scientific progress', but, on the other hand, the musical subtlety of Messiaen's employment and interconnection of rhythm and timbre, together with an understanding of articulation (the player and the organ's action itself), creates a new level of intensity and reification of musical materials that has its own distinct expressive power.

These relationships are extended through the use of interversions and their connection with mode and timbre in the 'Offertoire (Les choses visible et invisibles)' [Offertory: Things visible and invisible], where a strong sense of ritual is enshrined in the return and extension of material in the first parts of the piece (pp. 3–11), finishing with an oppressively long and 'torturous' passage of modes and interversions (8/4/3–11/1/2).[26] Perhaps most remarkable for the listener, however, is the connection between the timbre of the organ and what Messiaen describes as 'the law of the rapport between attack and duration' from the second system of p. 11.[27] He writes:

> The pedal transforms the droplet of water [*la goutte d'eau*] (in the right hand) into the sound of a bell, adding to it an echo, a sustained quality, a halo, a lengthening – it gives it a physical power, creating an aura from the halo, and from its attack a reverberating sound.[28]

The way the combination of flute 4, piccolo 1 and the tierce $1^{1/3}$ creates a percussive sound, like a glockenspiel, on the organ at La Trinité, is indeed remarkable.[29] Through registral colour, Messiaen inscribes a relationship between timbre, duration and attack in the music. In moments such as this, we can hear something of Cage's *Sonatas and Interludes* for prepared piano (1946–48), where the play of timbres, registers and resonances creates its own sense of rhythmic vitality that somewhat marginalizes the importance of harmony in this music.[30]

---

[26]   Messiaen, *Traité IV*. On p. 96, Messiaen describes an earlier manifestation of this music as 'a struggle against darkness and the power of darkness, the effect is somewhat muddy, quite torturous'.

[27]   Messiaen describes this law in *Traité II*, p. 101.

[28]   *Traité IV*, p. 100.

[29]   *Traité IV*, p. 99. Messiaen writes: 'I hold very much with the registration of this passage. This combination of timbres, which I found – so that the attacks and the organ writing that accompany them are almost obligatory: it is (a little) "my thing", it is typical of the Messiaen organ style.'

[30]   For more on Messiaen and Cage see Paul McNulty, 'Messiaen's journey towards asceticism', *Messiaen Studies*, pp. 63–77. On p 71, McNulty states that: 'Messiaen invited Cage to play his *Sonatas and Interludes* at the Salle Gounod of the Conservatoire on 7 June (1949) with another (private) performance scheduled for 17 June at Suzanne Tézenas's salon.'

The idea of a 'mélodie de résonances' and a 'mélodie de timbres' is continued in the 'Consécration (Le don de Sagesse)' [Consecration: The gift of wisdom]. The contrast of afferent harmonies surrounding the pedal clairon 4, and the sense of development by registral and melodic disruption in the plainchant material creates a striking juxtaposition. The contrast of elasticity (by kind and degree) of the musical materials, together with their contiguity, engenders a sense of both ritual and play within the work while implying, but ultimately deferring from any referential meaning implied by the text behind the plainchant.

The fixed-explosive sense of the 'Entrée' is revisited in the marvellous central avian improvisation of the fourth piece: 'Communion (Les oiseaux et les sources)' [Communion: Birds and springs]. In this music, Messiaen mixes four different types of music – *les gouttes d'eau* (with reminiscences again of the monody on page 4 of the 'Offertoire') in the left hand on the 'swell' organ, a Blackbird (in the right hand on the 'positif' organ), a Cuckoo (on the 'great' organ, with its almost-fixed pitches [C, C♯ and D♯/E♭ acciaccaturas]), and a solo Blackbird (again in the right hand on the 'positif') – all with different timbres, attacks, articulations, rhythmic and dynamic profiles.[31] The birdsong realizes the capital already invested in the disruption of plainchant in the 'Consécration', while also using the acciaccaturas and ornamental notes used in the variation/reprise of the monody in the 'Offertoire' from 6/4–7/4. In the 'Communion', the possibilities inherent in the systematization of musical elements enable Messiaen to direct and shape birdsong (the voice of God in nature), and to invest greater meaning and lyrical intensity into his music through the technical acquisitions of the avant-garde. In the central avian section of the 'Communion', and in the wonderful centrepiece Lark song of the 'Sortie (le vent de l'esprit)' [Sortie: The wind of the Spirit], Messiaen re-orients the negative political rhetoric of avant-garde art into a private language for the search for God.

Indeed, writing of this passage in the 'Sortie', which uses register and degrees of chromatic durations to create a crescendo of density and intensity, Messiaen states that: 'it is a perpetual ascension towards an always renewed ceiling [...] the bird flies higher and higher: becoming totally invisible ...'.[32] It is this kind of utopian, eschatological aspiration that marks the *Messe de la Pentecôte* as a work of the avant-garde. Even the sense of logical musical destruction, the implosion (system 3 of Example 11.2), and then explosion (systems 4–7 of Example 11.2) at the end of the 'Sortie', embodies, in an eschatological vein, the avant-garde ideal of revitalisation through necessary destruction:[33]

---

[31]   This is the first heterophonic birdsong passage in Messiaen's organ music, and prefigures the 'Pièces en trio' of the *Livre d'Orgue*.

[32]   Messiaen, *Traité IV*, p. 119.

[33]   The ending of the work, again a reworking of the monody from the *Offertoire* (motive B), is in a 'rhapsodic style recalling the improvisations of Tournemire, but more disjointed, tempestuous, frenzied.' *Traité IV*, p. 124. This kind of virtuosity is new to Messiaen's writing and undoubtedly precipitated the 'Les yeux dans les roues' (*Livre*

Example 11.2   Olivier Messiaen: 'Sortie (le vent de l'esprit)', end

This passage exposes the essential sense of incompleteness, the fragmentary, enigmatic and even deliberately unsatisfying qualities of the *Messe de la Pentecôte*. These elements are intrinsic to the rhetoric of reinvigoration in the work, and serve perhaps to deflect attention and even transform the facade of the reified musical language into an austere theological phenomenon.

Messiaen's desire to wrench new expressive means from a musical dead end is a tribute to his compositional originality. Beneath the flotsam of the language are underlying traditional formal elements such as the reconfiguration of motives (mainly A and B in Examples 11.3(i) to 11.3(vi)).[34]

Such underlying coherence contributes to the powerful austerity of the *Messe de la Pentecôte* because the idea of motivic forms breaking from each other and reforming is stronger than any sense of similarity. Together with the concentration on the revalorization of musical elements, this kind of fractured unity is essential to the lyricism and the theological poetry of the work. If Pentecost was the day in which the promise of the outpouring of the spirit is realized, the mystery and confusion of this wondrous event is well complemented by the way in which different levels of disjuncture are underpinned by almost invisible levels of cohesion.[35] The violence and inscrutability of the language has its own type of normative quality commensurate with an avant-garde revalorization of what can be expressed as sacred in music. Messiaen's music, therefore, represents an attempt to dilate the invisible power of the Holy Spirit into the world rather than translate it in any conventional way for consumption.

The symbiosis of seemingly opposing forces is an essential tool in Messiaen's attempt to re-orient the search for the absolute, in Western music, towards God. Such disruptive convergence and divergence foreground the sense in which the avant-garde expression in the work is searching for certainties outside its own sphere of control. Whether Messiaen's religious rhetoric enhances the essentially modernist and ambiguous elements of his art, or religion commodifies his art in a

---

d'Orgue), also written for the Sunday of Pentecost. One can only imagine what Tournemire would have written about these works.

[34] In these examples I assume enharmonic and intervallic equivalence (i.e. a diminished fifth is the same as an augmented fourth), and also inversional equivalence in Example 11.3(vi) (i.e. the rising fifth in A[1] can also be a fourth). It should also be borne in mind that the first appearance of motive B in Example 11.3(ii) has only three distinct pitch-classes, but is presented as a four-note motive. If this appearance is considered as a prime form of the motive, then, when the intervallic configuration of this is changed (for instance in the final bar of the 'Offertoire'), such a transformation reveals the way in which fragmentary nature of these motives are, despite this quality, being employed by Messiaen to impart an intimation of coherence. I have not described all of the different configurations of B in the examples used (these are relatively obvious to the eye), and Example 11.3 is in no way a definitive list of motives or their transformations, but this is not the *raison d'être* of the example.

[35] See for instance *Catechism of the Catholic Church*, 2nd edn (Rome: Libreria Editrice Vaticana, 1997), p. 326 article 1287.

Example 11.3   Olivier Messiaen: Transformation of three musical ideas in *Messe de la Pentecôte*

(i) 'Entrée (Les langues de feu)' opening

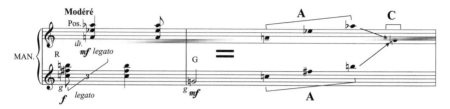

(ii) 'Offertoire (Les choses visibles et invisibles)' 4/4/1–2 and final bar

(iii) 'Offertoire (Le don de Sagesse)' opening

(iv) 'Consécration (Le don de Sagesse)' 16/2

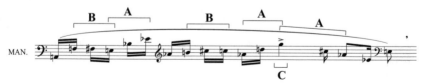

(v) 'Communion (Les oiseaux et les sources)' 18/1/1 and 18/5/2/beats 3–4

(vi) 'Sortie (le vent de l'esprit)' opening, 22/4/3 and 27/1/4

way that undermines the kind of objectivity that was so highly prized by Messiaen's avant-garde musical protégés as intrinsic to modern art, is a tension essential to the poetics of the *Messe de la Pentecôte*. As a work in which an uncompromising and deliberate sense of musical non-resolution complements the perpetual search for the divine, the *Messe de la Pentecôte* continues to provide a challenge and even a provocation to reimagine the way in which the sacred can be evoked through art.

The tyranny of beauty

It is perhaps taken for granted by those who study Messiaen's music that it is beautiful. But what does this really mean when we assert this, and in what sense is this so? Modernity has rather deprioritized this aesthetic aspect of art, both in the theory and practice of art, perhaps because of an assumed understanding of beauty, its historical place, and its relevance and value.[36] The traditional (idealist) understanding of beauty as a form of autonomy free from 'concept and significant content', as German philosopher Hans-Georg Gadamer describes it, or other notions of semblance and resemblance, are all somewhat insufficient for the discussion of Messiaen's music.[37] The idea of avant-garde music being associated with the beautiful might seem oxymoronic, but this antagonism is essential to the complex make-up of the *Messe de la Pentecôte*.

If beauty in a person or thing can be described as the revelation of the intangible through the tangible, always escaping, incomprehensible, untouchable, and if indeed we cannot quantify it, then, in theological terms, it has an essentially apophatic quality (it is beyond description or encapsulation because of its own nature). Rather than understanding this as an eschatological metaphor, receding into the mists of the transcendent, the very intangibility of beauty allows beauty to have a contiguity (if not a synergy) with the implications of the avant-garde's re-engagement with, and reinterpretation of real life. In contradistinction to the notions of disinterested Platonic or Kantian beauty (which might sit fairly comfortably with the narratives of autonomy in modernist art), the ideal of beauty

---

[36]   One of Messiaen's favourite theologians Hans Urs Von Balthasar noted that: 'Beauty is the word that shall be our first. Beauty is the last thing which the thinking intellect dares to approach, since only it dances as an uncontained splendour around the double constellation of the true and the good and their inseparable relation to one another. Beauty is the disinterested one, without which the ancient world refused to understand itself, a word which both imperceptibly and yet unmistakably has bid farewell to our new world, leaving it to its avarice and sadness.' *The Glory of the Lord: A Theological Aesthetics*, Vol. 1, *Seeing the Form*, eds Joseph Fessio and John Kenneth Riches, trans. Erasmo Leiva-Merikakis (Edinburgh: T&T Clark, 1982), p. 18.

[37]   Hans-Georg Gadamer, 'The relevance of the beautiful', in *The Relevance of the Beautiful and Other Essays*, trans. Nicholas Walker, ed. and intr. Robert Bernasconi (Cambridge: Cambridge University Press, 1986), pp. 3–53.

within Messiaen's art is calculated to entice our engagement with his music as a precursor to transformation. It is an essential element of the music he describes, in his early article 'Musique Réligeuse', as *La vivante*.[38] For Messiaen, the terrifying, the shocking aspects of the 'Sortie', the abstract and dirge-like qualities of parts of the 'Entrée', the 'Offertoire' and the 'Consécration', the sense of alienation, desolation, and even the rather anodyne quality of some of the music in these first three movements, together with the depth of semantic reconfiguration inherent in the music, are all powerful signposts by which the listener is asked to examine physical, emotional and spiritual immanence, and thereby engage with the possibility of a renewal of selfhood and an awareness of the divine.

Such a grandiose ambition seems to arise from a negation of beauty as traditionally understood. But this is not just the distrust of appearances intrinsic to aesthetics, the promise of objectivity, and the notion that this objectivity will, if not encapsulate, then offer some accountability of the value of the work concerned and its historical placement or even validity as part of a canon of works, nor is it necessarily the idea that despite appearances, the inner substance of an artwork *à la* Maritain may remain Catholic despite external appearances.[39] It is, however, a conspicuous attempt to inspire and embrace a state of subjective alienation as a springboard for freedom.

Would this then not then be a kind of *éblouissement*? Perhaps, but *éblouissement* also implies a positive saturation of knowledge as intuition, in Christian parlance a knowledge of God as unmediated truth. If confusion is a higher form of knowledge (because of the choices that are available), then in this sense, the listener might also have a choice about what freedom implies that is not merely conditioned on the religious and transcendent trajectory of *éblouissement* as Messiaen conceives it. The saturation of language and images inherent in Messiaen's musical discourse, as a kind of first order of appearances, might offer a beautiful distraction from the pull towards the beauty inherent in the petrifaction of apperception implied by *éblouissement*. Both perspectives seem to defer the necessity for any deeper or more refined critical or ontological perspective. Even if the finality of judgement is perpetually suspended through the desubjectification inherent in *éblouissement*, the possibility of re-enchantment, through the awe and terror of the intimation revelation, which Rainer Maria Rilke's angels signify in his *Duino Elegies* (1923), opens up a space in which the beauty of grace may break through art to reach humanity.[40] Such a sense of beauty would remain unpossessed, unresolved and

---

38   Messiaen, 'Musique Réligieuse', p. 1.

39   For more on this see Stephen Schloesser's *Jazz Age Catholicism: Mystic Modernism in Postwar Paris, 1919–1933* (Toronto: University of Toronto Press, 2005).

40   For more on this idea see Robert Sholl, 'The Shock of the Positive: Olivier Messiaen, St Francis, and Redemption through Modernity', in *Resonant Witness*, ed. Jeremy Begbie and Steve Guthrie (Grand Rapids: Eerdmans, 2008). In the first *Duino Elegy*, Rilke observes: 'For beauty is nothing but the beginning of terror, which we still are just able to endure, and we are so awed because it serenely disdains to annihilate us. Every angel is

even largely undisclosed. In short, it would entail something of the eschatological drama inherent in Messiaen's work: the sense of looking forward to a moment of fulfilment and union that never seems to arrive.

This kind of divine intervention would not be a comfortable experience, but it would, as one might expect from any sort of revelation, be sympathetic to the anti-normative. Part of the beauty of such music would be in its idiosyncrasies, and in its resistance to the rationalization of text-based meaning. In this sense, there is an inherent tension in the *Messe de la Pentecôte* (and indeed in the *Livre d'orgue*) between the rhetoric of desire and disclosure, and a break from any functionality and specificity in their faithfulness to an ideal. The gratification of knowledge as connected to representation and the possible pleasure inherent in recognition is intimated but denied.

This is where Messiaen treads a fine line. There was always a danger of course that his music might rapidly degenerate into the kind of kitsch that art critic Clement Greenberg deplored as relying: 'essentially on representation, narration, and drama' (as Alexander Nehamas summarises it).[41] These qualities might be ascribed to Messiaen's 'Première communion de la Vierge' from the *Vingt regards sur l'Enfant-Jésus*, for instance, with its kinaesthetic representation of the beating heart of Jesus, like the iconography (or idolatry) inherent in some Catholic images of the sacred heart of Jesus.

Clement Greenberg explains that: 'The avant-garde poet or artist tries in effect to imitate God by treating something valid solely on its own terms, in the way nature itself is valid.'[42] Nehamas interprets Greenberg in the following way: 'The avant-garde renounces representation and, in the end unable to imitate God, it turns to the imitation of 'the disciplines and process of art and literature itself'.[43] He goes on to flesh this out a little:

> what that means is that great art has always been concerned with its own medium and devoted to 'formal' problems and that its best audience has always appreciated it for that reason. Modernism just made explicit what had been up to then unknowing and unselfconscious. It shows that content that is easy to understand, telling a story [...] lies outside the proper domain of art, the investigation of what painting or poetry, *as* painting or poetry, can legitimately accomplish.[44]

terrifying.' *The Selected Poetry of Rainer Maria Rilke* (1875–1926), ed. and trans. Stephen Mitchell (London: Picador, 1987), p. 151.

[41]   Alexander Nehamas, *Only a Promise of Happiness: The Place of Beauty in a World of Art* (Princeton: Princeton University Press, 2007), p. 31.

[42]   Clement Greenberg, 'Avant-Garde and Kitsch', in *Art and Culture* (Boston: Beacon Press, 1961 [1939]), quoted in Nehamas, *Only a Promise of Happiness*, p. 31.

[43]   Nehamas, *Only a Promise of Happiness*, p. 31.

[44]   Ibid., p. 32.

The 'formal' problems faced by Messiaen: the absence of tonality, the impetus to re-valorize the elements of music, the inculcation of his student's musical acquisitions etc., were nothing compared to the problem of making a self-validating artwork that of and in itself was not imitative or representational of God. We are therefore returned to the non-normative as a means of the transcendental. Messiaen was not merely intent on making an image of the divine. We are allowed to gaze fixated on the idol, held in a trance by its effect, its aura, but the beauty of *éblouissement* resides not just in this kind of worship, it also lies in the promise that the idol will one day be shattered, that the fixation with the anti-normative will move beyond embodiment (as a lingua-franca), and will come to fulfil its own prophesy.[45]

The *Messe de la Pentecôte* intimates that even beauty that may seem repulsive, repressive and aggressive, textureless, flat and even physically painful may be a signpost on the map of the positive. If modernism inculcates reification and the cult of death as beautiful without the hope of redemption (even assuming this as a glorified hubris), Messiaen's task as a 'great artisan and a great Christian' was surely to reinvent this paradigm.[46] Rather than equating the beautiful with any notion of resolution, the telos of death becomes an eschatological portent of hope. On the other side of this two-edged sword, to contemplate that the beautiful might be an illusion created by ideology or by the appearance of idolatry is also to go to the heart of Messiaen's aesthetics, for it is the ideas of resemblance, desire for alternative being and for ontological change that are fundamental to his art: desire for death becomes the beginning rather than the end. Non-resolution, the non-normative language of the *Messe de la Pentecôte* can then be understood as part of the wallpaper of God's waiting room as much as an indication of the unknowable *derrière la porte*, as Messiaen himself puts it.[47]

What this seems to imply is a kind of masochistic compulsion towards reification where the image of the self is compulsively de-subjectivized, or, more positively, reconfigured. In his *Aesthetic Theory*, Adorno writes that:

> The aporia of art, pulled between regression to literal magic or surrender of the mimetic impulse to thinglike rationality, dictates its law of motion; the aporia cannot be eliminated. The depth of the process, which every artwork is, is excavated by the irreconcilability of those elements; it must be imported into the idea of art as an image of reconciliation.[48]

Put in more eschatological terms, Messiaen's employment of birdsong for example must transcend its own status as imitation of nature, must transcend the urge to be understood, to be formalized, rationalized by notation, by technique and by

---

[45]   See Van Maas in *Messiaen Studies*, pp. 90–94 in particular.

[46]   Messiaen, *Technique*, p. 7.

[47]   Messiaen, 'Musique Réligieuse', p. 1.

[48]   T. W. Adorno, *Aesthetic Theory*, eds Gretel Adorno and Rolf Tiedemann, trans. Robert Hullot-Kentor (London: Athlone, 1997), p. 54.

the desire for audibility, but neither should the birds become mythical iconostatic, kitsch creatures, frozen in art as a seemingly purposeful form of taxidermy. Aesthetics, and to a lesser degree theology, are left to attempt a diremption of these irreconcilable perspectives through analysis and exegesis, with an awareness of the danger that any tendency towards synthesis might become part of the eschatological wish-making machine of Messiaen's aesthetics. This is why the aesthetic immanence of Messiaen's work can too easily be overstepped by the totalizing ambitions of theology: it can become a crutch for what is perceived as lacking or incomprehensible in the music.

The tyranny of beauty is that immanence is caught in its own reflection: the fact that the language needs ideology to overcome reification had become so ingrained in Messiaen's art that the avant-garde elements do not so much efface it as deepen the interdependence. The imperative of, and necessity for, meaning demands this, even as the musical language shakes this tree. Messiaen's art therefore seems to long for a diremptive process that shatters the mirror and takes the music out of this semantic Catch 22. Adorno comes close to providing a reasoned escape route when he states that:

> As figures of the existing, unable to summon into existence the nonexisting, artworks draw their authority from the reflection they compel on how they could be the overwhelming image of the nonexisting if it did not exist in itself.[49]

Rubbing shoulders with this is David Bentley Hart's observation, perhaps inspired by Hans Urs Von Balthasar, that:

> For Christian thought there lies between idolatry and the ethical abolition of *all* images the icon, which redeems and liberates the visible, and of which the exemplar is the incarnate word: an infinite that shows itself in finite form without ceasing to be infinite – indeed, revealing its infinity most perfectly thereby.[50]

---

[49]   Ibid., p. 83.

[50]   David Bentley Hart, *The Beauty of the Infinite: The Aesthetics of Christian Truth* (Grand Rapids: Eerdmans, 2003), p. 15. On p. 60 of *Redeeming Beauty: Soundings in Sacral Aesthetics* (Aldershot: Ashgate, 2007), Aidan Nichols quotes Hans Urs Von Balthasar's *The Glory of the Lord*, Vol VI: *Theology: The Old Covenant*, eds Joseph Fessio and John Kenneth Riches, trans Erasmo Leiva-Merikakis (Edinburgh: Ignatius Press, 1991), p. 91: 'The beautiful does not live in splendour alone; it also needs figure and image, even if what figure does is attest to him who set it up, even if image is beautiful only as the imaging forth of that splendour which is beyond all images [...] . [I]f in the end all worldly aesthetics needs a theological foundation, we can say in anticipation that only biblical theology provides a final, non-tragic justification for worldly beauty, since it is only here that the image, which finite worldly reality is of necessity, can be taken up and secured in the eternal image, which is the archetypal image even as it is the image that transcends all images.'

In this sense, the violence inherent in the musical language, for instance at the end of the *Messe de la Pentecôte* (in Example 11.2 above) while an audible (and visible) manifestation of the ineffable, is also an embodiment of the (invisible) sublime, and a wager on what the sublime could come to signify. It is because we are unable to locate the source of (divine) irradiation through art, that the beauty of this moment (and the promise of its unveiling) remains more potent. The final explosion of the work, and indeed the final chord, comes to signify a form of the sublime, as Bentley Hart, paraphrasing Kant's *Critique of Judgement*, describes it:

> an immensity, grandeur, or force that exceeds representation – because it requires apprehension (*Auffassung*) an 'infinite' activity that surpasses the power of comprehension (*Zusammenfassung*), which is itself dependent upon the inward synthesis of the sense of time and hence finite (§26) – reason must return from the realm of the sensible. But in so doing it discovers in itself a supersensible power that is infinitely free of and infinitely greater than the realm of representation. Precisely when the inner sense of time, exposed to comprehension's defeat, suffers violence at the hands of imagination's contrapurposive power of apprehension, reason discovers through its negative pleasure a deeper purpose within that violence: the entire vocation of the mind (§27).[51]

Taken in terms of the devastating implosion and explosion of sound at the end of the *Messe de la Pentecôte* (Example 11.2 above), evidenced by the performance of Olivier Latry at Notre-Dame de Paris, the immanence of the known (representation, comprehension and our apperception of time) is pierced by the need for apprehension, and most particularly by our desire for knowledge of the unknowable.[52] The inner or private sense of time, what Henri Bergson terms *la durée*, is also a casualty in this diremptive telos.[53] Its intimate quality, and, in Christian terms, its *locus* as a portal for revelation to irradiate human consciousness, is transformed through the kinaesthetic shock of disintegration essential to the utopian poetics of this music. While there is no sense of synthesis, no sense of overcoming, the imagination is left to infer the end of this work diremptively as Christian: the final chord seemingly telescopes the past onto the immediacy of the future while also embracing the eschatological hope essential to Christianity.

Messiaen thus embraces the notion in modernity of the secular sublime as a zygotic twin of Christianity. The depth structure of this sublime requires the imagination of the listener to perceive the kind of 'sustained ugliness' that Tournemire accuses Messiaen of in his *Mémoires*, as a means of usurping categories of the intentional and of the known, and of moving towards a dialogue in which the

---

[51]   David Bentley Hart, *The Beauty of the Infinite*, pp. 45–46.

[52]   Messiaen, *Complete Organ Works*, recorded by Olivier Latry (Universal, DG 471).

[53]   Messiaen discusses the ramifications of Bergson's theory of *la durée* in *Traité I*, pp. 31–36.

listener is taken into and becomes a participant in Messiaen's proclamation.[54] In this way, Messiaen's music acts like the lens through which our eyes may become accustomed to the radiant and enigmatic beauty of the divine, but the desire to gaze stems from a cipher of grace at the basis of human anthropology: a beautiful splinter in the throat of modernity.

---

[54]   Tournemire, *Mémoires*, p. 157.

Chapter 12

Messiaen as Explorer in
Livre du Saint Sacrement

Luke Berryman

There has never been a philosopher who did not finally look down on the philosophy he invented in his youth with disdain, or at least suspicion.

– Friedrich Nietzsche[1]

Neither summation nor improvisation

A clear understanding of the transition between Olivier Messiaen's opera, *St François d'Assise* (1983), and his final organ composition, *Livre du Saint Sacrement* (1986), is required to begin to define his late style. Messiaen employs the various compositional techniques that he had constructed over his career in palpably new ways in the *Livre*, but its theological programmes remain similar to those on which many of his earlier works are based. Critical comparison with the preceding organ cycles, and many other compositions, will bear witness to this. By revisiting aspects of Messiaen's biography from the mid-1980s, while also exploring previously unpublished information about the *Livre*'s commission, I hope to show that self-doubt began plaguing the composer during the completion of *St François*. I will argue that it was this self-doubt that spurred Messiaen to treat his old styles in new ways in the *Livre*. By the dawn of this organ piece, he seems to have begun questioning the ability of his longest-established techniques to express extra-musical material.

Messiaen composed four enormous works between 1965 and 1983; the oratorio *La Transfiguration de Notre-Seigneur Jésus-Christ* (1965–69), the organ cycle *Méditations sur le mystère de la Sainte Trinité* (1969), the orchestral piece *Des Canyons aux étoiles...* (1971–74), and *St François* (begun in 1975 and first

[1]   Friedrich Nietzsche, *Human, All Too Human*, trans. Marion Faber and Stephen Lehmann (St Ives: Clays Ltd, 1994), p. 155. This essay began life as an undergraduate dissertation, and was later presented at the conference 'Messiaen the Theologian' at Boston University (October 2007). I am indebted to Jennifer Bate and to Gale Kramer; Ms Bate kindly provided me with reviews of her UK premiere of the *Livre*, and Dr Kramer generously granted me access to the correspondence between Ray Ferguson and Olivier Messiaen. I am also grateful to those who offered suggestions and comments, particularly Julian Johnson, Andrew Shenton and Evan Cortens. This essay is dedicated, with affection and respect, to the memory of Dr Sam Mindel.

performed in 1983). In contrast to the smaller scale works from the 1950s that precede them, these four are often dismissed as overly long, unimaginative and even gratuitously self-indulgent. Brian Dennis declared in 1970 that *La Transfiguration* is 'long and repetitive, sanctimonious and over-sentimental'.[2] David Lumsdaine asserted in 1973 that the *Méditations*, in the context of Messiaen's major creations, 'could not be described as "important"'.[3] Malcolm Miller said in 1989 that the sonority of *Des Canyons* has a 'gaudy character [... that] seems (to put it mildly) to overreach the bounds of palatable subtlety'.[4] Even as recently as 2007, Robin Holloway found space in a book review to lambaste *St François*, complaining of the 'unsurpassed level of decibels and repetition: that little tag representing *la joie* which induces a spasm of embarrassed but unambiguous *hatred* well before its 1001st time of asking: that death scene for the saint of humility, frugality, self-effacement in a furnace of C major! Trite and banal beyond belief'.[5] Conversely, some scholars receive these works positively by attempting to explain them as a succession of intentional epitaphs. The opening of Arnold Whittall's comparison of Messiaen's late works with Elliot Carter's in *Musical Composition in the 20th Century* is one such example. 'Whereas Carter's music since the mid-1970s has embodied a substantial new stage in his development', Whittall claims, 'Messiaen's might be thought to comprise a series of epilogues – alternatively grand and unassuming – to the achievements of earlier years'.[6] However useful one deems either of these paradigms for analysing the four works from 1969–83, I believe that both are equally inappropriate approaches to the *Livre*, Messiaen's longest organ cycle (and the first composition completed after *St François*). To slavishly catalogue it, and the pieces that followed, alongside the four titanic works of 1969–83 is to misunderstand it; but almost all scholarly reception has done just that. This is evidenced in many discussions of the *Livre* since its 1986 premiere, which can be roughly divided into the two patterns of reception outlined above. It is usually described either as a series of disconnected written-out improvisations, or as an arbitrary epitaph to the organ oeuvre. Both approaches can lead to the conclusion that the *Livre* is an inconsequential work in Messiaen's repertoire. Paul Griffiths offered a prime example of the written-out improvisation model after hearing the *Livre*'s UK debut. His assessment was that 'although it lasts for close on two

---

[2]   Brian Dennis,'Messiaen's "La Transfiguration"', *Tempo*, no. 94 (1970): 30.

[3]   David Lumsdaine, 'Messiaen: *Catalogue d'oiseaux*. Robert Sherlaw Johnson (piano). *Neuf Méditations sur le mystère de la Sainte Trinité*. Olivier Messiaen (organ)', *Tempo*, no. 105 (1973): 38.

[4]   Malcolm Miller, 'Messiaen: *Des Canyons aux étoiles; Couleurs de la cité celeste; Oiseaux exotiques* Paul Crossley (pno), London Sinfonietta *c*. Esa-Pekka Salonen', *Tempo*, no. 169 (1989): 54.

[5]   Robin Holloway, '*Messiaen* by Peter Hill and Nigel Simeone', *Tempo*, no. 239 (2007): 75.

[6]   Arnold Whittall, *Musical Composition in the 20th Century* (Oxford: Oxford University Press, 1999), p. 262.

hours, the work is not a consummation of Messiaen's organ composing but rather a garland of mementoes'.[7] Griffiths has also said in the *Grove Dictionary* that the *Livre* merely 'gathers together ideas developed at La Trinité over many years and so does not represent a new large adventure'.[8] On the other hand, many writers believe that the *Livre* is intimately intertwined with the expansive aesthetics of *La Transfiguration, Les Méditations, Des Canyons* and *St François*. Such opinions abound in reviews of the work's UK premiere, where words such as 'summation' and 'synthesis' appear repeatedly. Malcolm Hayes heard 'a wonderful suffused serenity, as if the process which began nearly 60 years ago with Messiaen's early organ piece *Le banquet céleste* has now come full circle'.[9] Bayan Northcott claimed that 'stylistically, several of these pieces could have been written in the 1930s'.[10] Robert Henderson described the *Livre*'s unfolding as 'leisurely', saying that 'the initial impression created by these 18 substantial, predominantly devotional pieces, is one of summation, of drawing together almost every aspect of his half century of creative activity and experience in a massive, and comprehensive act of synthesis'.[11] In a similar vein to these critics, Christopher Dingle has stated that 'the *Livre*, like *Saint François*, seems to be one "last, big work" – a "summation" to the organ works'.[12] He has also suggested that it has a 'fundamental analogy with the opera; *Livre du Saint Sacrement* is another grand summa. This enormous organ cycle is as much a grand synthesis as *Saint François d'Assise*'.[13]

A close examination of the music, and the circumstances in which it was being composed, reveals that the *Livre* is not best described, as Griffiths has suggested, as a garland of mementoes. Neither does it appear to be a summation as Dingle, Hayes, Henderson and others have posited. In *Livre du Saint Sacrement*, Messiaen in fact seems to have subjected many of his familiar techniques to new treatment,

---

[7]   Paul Griffiths, 'The Arts: Jennifer Bate, Westminster Cathedral', *The Times* (9 October 1986).

[8]   Paul Griffiths, 'Messiaen, Olivier', in *Grove Music Online*, ed. L. Macy, <http://www.grovemusic.com> (accessed 27 January 2007).

[9]   Malcolm Hayes, 'End of the banquet', *The Sunday Telegraph* (12 October 1986).

[10]   Bayan Northcott, 'Messiaen: New celestial colours on a grand scale', *The Independent* (9 October 1986).

[11]   R[obert] L H[enderson], 'Messiaen première', *The Daily Telegraph* (10 October 1986).

[12]   Christopher Dingle, 'Charm and Simplicity: Messiaen's Final Works', *Tempo*, no. 192 (1995): 2.

[13]   Christopher Dingle, *Messiaen's Final Works* (Aldershot: Ashgate, 2009), taken from the pre-publication draft of the Chapter 4, 'Messiaen's Final (Organ) Work: *Livre du Saint Sacrement*'. I am extremely grateful to Dr Dingle for kindly providing me with a copy of this chapter before it went to press.

rather than merely rehashing them in what Dingle has called a 'monumental consolidation'.[14]

The *Livre's* Commission

The reality of the *Livre*'s composition differs substantially from Messiaen's own, apparently spurious, account of it. Attempting to discover the true nature of its conception consequently gives the first indication that the work was an unusually problematic one for its composer. His description of it as an organic outgrowth of his oeuvre, prompted by some divine muse, is worth quoting at length:

> My post as a church organist obliges me to improvise. My wife records these improvisations and I then listen to them with a very critical ear. One Maundy Thursday evening, when the Church commemorates the first Eucharist, I had three minutes to fill, and it was then that I had a flash of inspiration. I played a piece which, at first sight, seems to have no substance whatsoever: a very simple bacchiac rhythm (short – long – short) and a banal chord of a sixth – but I suddenly realised, on re-hearing myself, that this music was like no other. I think that I was inspired by the moment, touched by this service, which was a very beautiful one. I rewrote the piece, calling it *L'Institution de l'Eucharistie*, and began to write the *Livre du Saint Sacrement*, eighteen pieces for organ lasting two and half hours in total. It was more than a year after *St François*.[15]

Peter Hill and Nigel Simeone's examinations of Messiaen's sketches, which show that the improvisation that became 'L'Institution de l'Eucharistie' was performed on Holy Thursday 1981, two years before *St François* was even finished, conflict with this account.[16] Even before 1981, it appears that Messiaen was contemplating a new organ work. One evening in March 1980, he dined with the clergy of La Trinité. During the meal Messiaen was requested to write a booklet about the organ, and to give a recital to mark his upcoming half-centenary of service in December 1981. Presumably engulfed in work on *St François*, he suggested 1984 or 1985 for the performance. Despite this postponement, it appears that he was still giving thought to the concert. Hill and Simeone discovered in his diaries the

---

[14]   Christopher Dingle, '"La statue reste sur son piédestal": Messiaen's *La Transfiguration* and Vatican II', *Tempo*, no. 212 (2000): 11.

[15]   Jean-Christophe Marti, 'It's a secret of love – an interview with Olivier Messiaen' liner notes for *Saint François d'Assise*, cond. Kent Nagano (Deutsche Grammophon, DG 445 176–2, 1998), p. 29.

[16]   Peter Hill and Nigel Simeone, *Messiaen* (New Haven, CT/London: Yale University Press, 2005), p. 343.

telling comment: 'I shall be able to give the first performance of a new work by me for the organ'.[17]

This information can for the first time be placed alongside the previously unexplored correspondence, obtained by this author, between Messiaen and the American Guild of Organists (AGO), who commissioned the *Livre*. Ray Ferguson's letter, sent on 2 March 1982, was designed to whet Messiaen's appetite: 'we want our Convention to make a significant contribution to the repertoire, and only you are able to do this'.[18] Messiaen responded on 1 August 1982, to accept the commission and declare his favoured genre. 'I will definitely be writing you a work for solo organ', he confirmed, 'a suite of about half-an-hour.'[19] Hill and Simeone note that at this time, in his diaries, Messiaen was already thinking about 'organ studies for which he devised titles: "Études on complementary colours, on grace notes, and on light and dark". The same entry in the diary mentioned "a series of pieces on the Blessed sacrament" and a piece about the miraculous parting of the Red Sea'.[20] This all suggests that Messiaen's claim, that the *Livre* was only begun on 19 April 1984, was disingenuous. He had evidently had it in mind for nearly two years by this date. Why he attempted to cover his compositional tracks in this way would be the topic of a different discussion. Of primary importance here is that the *Livre* was clearly a long and carefully considered project, and not a hastily compiled garland of mementoes. In fact, it appears that Messiaen was intent on creating something completely original in this work, even once *St François* was completed, by which time he was approaching 80 years of age.

Struggling with *St François*, struggling after *St François*

Having uncovered the true time frame in which the *Livre* was written, Messiaen's disparaging and often-quoted comments about the future of his career, made around the time of *St François*'s premiere, can be reassessed. It seems likely that it was not just the strains of finishing the opera but also the difficulties that he encountered in writing the *Livre* that caused his bleak mood at the time. When it eventually reached the stage, Messiaen's monumental operatic project had absorbed the best part of a decade's work. He had even hinted, to more than one person, that *St François* would be the composition with which he ended his career. Yvonne Loriod recalled:

> After the work was finished he became very depressed. He was unable to eat or walk or indeed do anything. But a year later he wrote the *Livre du Saint*

---

[17]   Ibid., p. 331.

[18]   Unpublished private correspondence between Ray Ferguson, writing on behalf of the AGO, and Olivier Messiaen. Translated by Robert Jutton.

[19]   Ibid.

[20]   Hill and Simeone, *Messiaen*, p. 343.

Sacrement and then, after that, he wrote a series of four short works, beginning
with the *Petites esquisses*, as a kind of relaxation. He was very doubtful about
the *esquisses* and said, 'I'm tired, I can no longer write, the pieces are not
very good'.[21]

Kent Nagano also remembered Messiaen being increasingly despondent as work
on the opera drew to a close. '[He] told me that his life's work was finished – "I've
lived to write Saint Francois and I feel that I'm not going to write any more"
– and he said this in such a way that I felt he was referring to the end of his
life [… Messiaen said] "I'm serious. I feel something is happening".'[22] Both of
these testimonies indicate Messiaen's belief that *St François* would be the final
composition he successfully completed. On top of the purely musical challenges,
Messiaen was at the same time becoming unwell. Hill and Simeone recorded that, at
the time, 'there were traces of blood in his urine, and he believed he had cancer'.[23]

Perhaps Messiaen at first felt that the AGO's 1982 commission would be an
opportunity to build upon his achievements in *St François*. He certainly hinted
as much in his exchanges with Ray Ferguson. Messiaen was inundated with
commissions when Ferguson first made contact (he had recently turned away Daniel
Barenboim and Mstislav Rostropovich, among others), and so it is unsurprising
that Ferguson was less concerned with the type of composition, and more with
simply securing one.[24] His invitation to Messiaen was consequently open:

Concerning the genre and duration of the work, in order to give you as much
freedom as possible, here are some suggestions of a few types of composition
that you could choose from:
1. A work for organ with exotic percussion or for organ with brass quartet,
lasting 10–12 minutes.
2. A work for organ with large orchestra, or with chamber orchestra, lasting
around 20 minutes.
3. A suite for solo organ, lasting 10–20 minutes, or even a piece for solo organ
lasting 8–10 minutes.[25]

That Messiaen simply ignored Ferguson's suggested time limits seems to reveal
an intention, from the start, to once again compose on a large scale. In June 1984,
Messiaen said to Ferguson that 'I have pondered our project deeply', that the

---

[21]   Peter Hill, 'Interview with Yvonne Loriod', in *The Messiaen Companion*, ed. Peter
Hill (London: Faber, 1995), p. 301. Loriod's faulty chronology can here be overlooked.

[22]   Hill and Simeone, *Messiaen*, p. 340.

[23]   Ibid.

[24]   Hill and Simeone recorded that proposed commissions from Daniel Barenboim (for
the Orchestre de Paris), Marcel Couraud (for the Chorale Marcel Couraud) and Mstislav
Rostropovich (a work for cello and orchestra) all came to nothing. See ibid., pp. 332–333.

[25]   Unpublished correspondence.

new work was 'enormous' and 'will make up a whole concert'.[26] These remarks support the proposal that Messiaen wanted the *Livre* to be some sort of organic step forward from the immediately preceding pieces, even once work on the project was underway.

If he found making it so difficult, this would go some way to explaining the well-documented difficulties that he experienced in the mid-1980s. Admittedly the workload of the opera must have been staggering, but Messiaen had been composing on similar scales long before it. What was it about *St François*, and why was it at this moment in his career, that he should suddenly be struck by despondency? The sheer size of the opera's ensemble is perhaps a distraction in the search for the answer to this question, and it is easy to become fixated upon the novelties in the orchestration (the unusual percussion instruments, such as shell chimes, the Basque drum, the reco-reco, and so on), or the audacious requirement of three ondes Martenots. But ensemble and orchestration are only two (and, perhaps, simply the most immediately obvious) dimensions that he enlarged in the works from 1969–83. Messiaen's actual goal with this series of expansions was most likely to make his theological programmes ever more dramatic, effective and convincing. It is unsatisfactory, for me at least, to conclude that he simply went on increasing his forces for novelty's sake.

Consider briefly Act 3, scene 7 of *St François*, where Messiaen utilizes a basic pattern recognizable from many of his earlier works – namely, the following of a highly dissonant section with an area of harmonic stasis. The programmatic function of such moments always appears to be the dissolution of awe and fear in God's presence into some other emotion: ecstatic joy in some instances, tranquil serenity in others. Here, Messiaen is working on the largest conceivable scale, in terms of ensemble size, scoring and duration. He challenges the listeners with an extended passage built from extremely high vocal lines set to nonsense syllables, note clusters in all parts, and barbaric *ffff* rhythms devoid of melody. The violence of this section is masterfully resolved, however, by the beauty of the ensuing passage in which God calls directly to St Francis. As with the dissonant period, the construction of the resolution section that follows is recognizable from the earlier works. The volume of God's voice suddenly changes to *ppp*, and Messiaen shifts the music to a comfortable vocal register. He even instructs 'breathe individually' in the score, to ensure an unbroken, meditative chord of E major.

It is reasonable to suggest that Messiaen could not have expanded this musical gesture any further, which is essentially how he was able to progress smoothly from one work to the next in the years 1969–83. The large operatic forces *St François*, used over a lengthy duration, enabled him to give familiar techniques their most comprehensive elaborations yet. Perhaps Messiaen felt that the completion of *St François* would end his career because, within it, he surmounted this expressive peak. What to do next must have posed a significant challenge. He was evidently not content to simply recapitulate various methods of old in his next composition

---

[26]   Ibid.

(as Dingle implied in calling the *Livre* 'one last, big work'). Had that been the case, there would have been nothing preventing him from simply regurgitating exactly the music of the 1930s. Writing for an ensemble larger than that of *St François* would have been inconceivable, and a solo instrumental piece that was longer than the opera would have been equally infeasible – and so expansion no longer guaranteed progression, as it had done during the previous 14 years. Perhaps Messiaen even wondered during the half-decade in which the *Livre* was written if it would ever reach a satisfactory conclusion.

An absence of revelation

The musical differences between the *Livre* and its immediate predecessors reinforce the idea of the organ cycle as a transitory work. Messiaen's effort to evoke God's presence on earth, in various forms, is one of the theological tropes that the *Livre* shares in common with earlier pieces. This sort of programme, when encountered in the organ repertoire, is found most frequently in final toccata movements. Messiaen composed culminating, celebratory passages to suggest the emotion prompted by the experience of God's presence. There are several areas in the *Livre*'s programme that could reasonably have been expected to provoke such a response from Messiaen. That they move in noticeably new directions suggests that he had indeed begun to doubt the powers of his older techniques.

Three movements that share, in one form or another, the idea of God's presence on earth are 'Dieu parmi nous', from Messiaen's first cycle *La Nativité du Seigneur* (1935), 'Le vent de l'esprit', the last movement of *Messe de la Pentecôte* (1949–50), and the 18th and final movement of the *Livre*, 'Offrande et Alleluia final'. In 'Dieu parmi nous', the topic is spelled out unambiguously by its title: 'God among us'. The theme of 'Le vent' is the descent of the Holy Spirit to the Apostles at the end of the Pentecostal Mass. Messiaen described the 'Offrande et Alleluia final' as a musical manifestation of the shared joy of all the saints before the presence of God. Although he made many changes to his musical language in the 15 years between 'Dieu parmi nous' and 'Le vent', they still share similarities beyond their superficial theological connections. For example, both open with dissonant sections that are later counterbalanced by a joyful, celebratory passage. This leaves little doubt about Messiaen's understanding of the programme; namely, that the initial fearful awe before God's presence eventually dissolves into overwhelming joy. The opening of 'Dieu parmi nous' consists of a descending chordal pattern in the manuals. This phrase concludes *fff* on a D♭ major 7 chord, which is offset by the *ffff* C♮ in the pedal. The case in 'Le vent' is somewhat different, as Messiaen's musical language had become increasingly complex in the years after 'Dieu parmi nous'. The same basic structure still applies though. The opening of 'Le vent' ends with a rapidly constructed *fff* chord consisting of nine different notes (see Example 12.1).

Example 12.1   Olivier Messiaen: 'Sortie (le vent de l'esprit)', end

It is not until the E-major toccata of 'Dieu parmi nous' that the terror of the opening phrase is overcome. That Messiaen felt this toccata to be a turning point in the piece is a claim verified by the composer himself. In the *Technique of My Musical Language* (1944), he records that the 'toccata in E major is the piece itself, all the large development which precedes having been only the preparation of it'.[27] On the surface, 'Le vent' might seem entirely different and even incomparable with 'Dieu parmi nous', by virtue of the changes in Messiaen's musical language. Even with no clear tonal centre, though, Messiaen writes a joyous central section, marked 'Vif (Choeur des alouettes [Chorus of larks])'. By using birdsong in this way, Messiaen creates a celebratory passage without recourse to a build-up and release of harmonic tension (so crucial in 'Dieu parmi nous'). He also exhibits a greater level of sensitivity to colour, using subtle changes to indicate the movement from the opening awe to the concluding joy. The final *ffff* chord, for example, is a wider-spread version of the opening nine-note chord, which lends it a different, brighter sound.[28] Regardless of how successful the listener finds these passages in their attempt to evoke joy in God's presence (and this endeavour certainly never had a shortage of negative critical response), it is likely that this is the function that Messiaen intended them to serve.

'Offrande', on the other hand, stands apart from these earlier toccatas. The familiar extra-musical themes remain, but the realization of them is quite different. He once wrote lengthy, culminating passages but, by the advent of 'Offrande', Messiaen apparently preferred to express God's presence in greatly compacted terms. The curious decision to abandon the formulae that had so characterized

---

[27]   Olivier Messiaen, *The Technique of My Musical Language*, trans. John Satterfield, 2 vols (Paris: Durand, 1944), Vol. 1, p. 42.

[28]   This recurring nine-note chord may also have numerological significance. For a full discussion of Messiaen's preoccupation with numerology in his so-called 'serial' works, see Richard Toop, 'Messiaen/Goeyvaerts, Fano/Stockhausen, Boulez', *Perspectives of New Music* 13 (1974), pp. 141–169.

previous toccatas can often leave 'Offrande' sounding fragmentary, even anti-climatic, on first hearing. A closer examination of the innovative music may elucidate the reasons behind these changes, and might also determine if this new writing is as effective as Messiaen's older material.

A treatment of the theological programme that is new, both in terms of musical language and compositional structure, is evident from the start of 'Offrande'. A bare, unaccompanied plainchant built of angular intervals begins this toccata. This seems at first an unexpected, and perhaps even inappropriate, method for representing the programme. It is disconnected from and apparently unrelated to the material follows. Given the movement's title and position in the cycle, the assumption that Messiaen would aim in 'Offrande' to evoke joy in God's presence, as with 'Dieu parmi nous' and 'Le vent', is a reasonable one. In 'Offrande' though, every path that he takes towards a section equivalent to the E-major toccata in 'Dieu parmi nous', or the 'Chorus of larks' in 'Le vent', is discarded before it reaches fruition.

More surprising features emerge as the movement progresses. The 'Offrande' has, in its opening pages, a passage similar to one in 'Dieu parmi nous' that Messiaen described as a 'Magnificat, [an] alleluiatic praise in bird style'.[29] In 'Dieu parmi nous' this alleluiatic praise moved gradually towards the E-major toccata. In 'Offrande' however, the equivalent section becomes locked in a rondo with the opening theme (in the pattern ABABA). Eventually Messiaen appears to simply abandon this scheme. He restarts with a new idea that also terminates prematurely; a page of chords, fixed in a repetitive pattern. Where the opening ideas in 'Dieu parmi nous' all led towards the culminating toccata, in 'Offrande' Messiaen interrupts the preliminary material with an unexpected, *fff* declamation in the 'langage communicable', to spell out the programmatic message in the least ambiguous terms possible: 'La joie' [joy] (see Example 12.2).[30] This moment suggests a struggle on Messiaen's part, taking place during the course of composition, to construct a musical passage that satisfactorily matched his understanding of the programme. This was certainly not an issue apparent in 'Dieu parmi nous' or 'Le vent'.

After the octaves of 'La joie', Messiaen begins breaking down the motifs used in the unusually repetitive rondo into their smallest constituent parts. This lends the music a feeling of almost frantic uncertainty. The process certainly bears little resemblance to either 'Dieu parmi nous' or 'Le vent', whose unerring, joyful conclusions were practically forgone once they reached the sections

---

[29]   Messiaen, *Technique*, Vol. 1, p. 42.

[30]   That is, Messiaen's musical alphabet devised for *Méditations sur le mystère de la Sainte Trinité* (1969). By assigning each letter of the alphabet a fixed pitch, duration and register, Messiaen created a system that enabled him to spell out words in their entirety in the course of a composition. For a full treatment of the 'langage', see Andrew Shenton, *Olivier Messiaen's System of Signs: Notes Towards Understanding His Music* (Aldershot: Ashgate, 2008).

designed to counterbalance their bold openings. In 'Offrande', in fact, it is not until the concluding bars that Messiaen reaches a musical passage that seems in any way evocative of the declared extra-musical theme. Within these bars is one of Messiaen's simplest depictions of God's presence: seven majestic pillars of sound that resolve onto a lone C♮ (see Example 12.3). If, as Messiaen himself said, the whole message of 'Dieu parmi nous' is reducible to the E-major toccata, then 'Offrande' is arguably reducible to these seven chords and their moment of resolution – the movement's entire message is compacted into just four bars of music.

The process of resolution is an unusual one. Messiaen attempts to create cadential movement between an 11-note chord of contracted resonance (repeated seven times) and the only degree of the scale it is missing, C♮. Chords of contracted

Example 12.2   Olivier Messiaen: 'Offrande', 'La joie' in 'langage communicable'

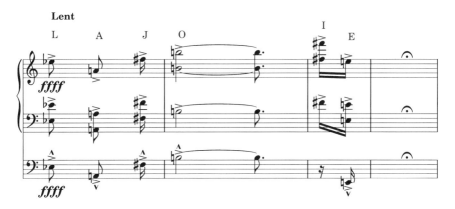

Example 12.3   Olivier Messiaen: 'Offrande', end

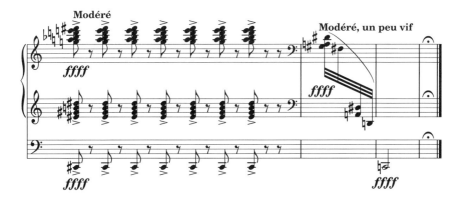

resonance are certainly hallmarks of Messiaen's style, but this shift from an 11-note chord to the one note it was missing, in order to create a sense of completion, seems to derive from serial ideas of note-row completion. It is also possible that he designed this descent to sound like resolution in a tonal sense. This is seen in the careful spacing of the repeated chord of contracted resonance. The intervals are compacted only in the higher register of the manuals, resulting in a sound that is very close to C♯ major. Although 11 notes are sounding simultaneously, the semitone descent to the low C♮ is plainly audible. This note is an exposed, and therefore a rather irregular, ending for Messiaen. When the conclusions of the immediately preceding works are considered (compare it to a moment such as the emphatic C-major completion of *St François*, for instance), this becomes especially apparent.

The role of the plainchant that opens 'Offrande' can now be reassessed in light of the rest of the movement. Unlike 'Dieu parmi nous' or 'Le vent', the relationship between the music and the programme is not immediately obvious. I would venture to suggest that the clear relationship between music and programme in 'Dieu parmi nous', something largely absent from 'Offrande', could be a reason for its sustained popularity among Messiaen's organ works. The opening plainchant may seem logical given its liturgical context; but to begin a grand, symphonic finale with an angular, solo melody disjointed from the rest of the work borders on the nonsensical, especially given the clear contradiction it makes with Messiaen's apparent toccata formulae established in his earlier works. I would posit that the plainchant is possibly more a humble recognition of the lack of a culminating, celebratory section anywhere in the movement, than it is a theological or liturgical symbol.

A similar absence of a culminating section to coincide with the theological programme is found in the 13th movement of the *Livre*, 'Les deux murailles d'eau'. In this movement, Messiaen makes a parallel between Moses's parting of the waters and the breaking of the host in the Eucharist. This again deals with God's presence on earth; in both the host, and in the miracle of divine intervention in the Old Testament. The build-up of musical tension, as in 'Dieu parmi nous', is protracted, and yet a moment never arrives that clearly represents the arresting parallel between the breaking of the host and the parting of the waters. Messiaen's constant reversion to the opening musical panel, which is made up of two sections (a lively toccata and unaccompanied birdsong), again suggests that the composer could find no satisfactory way to realize his own extra-musical agenda. The lengthy, central section of the 'Deux murailles' (which appears after two repetitions of the opening panel) is marked 'the crashing waves'. It appears to be leading towards a climactic passage, presumably to represent the moment when the waves part and the host breaks. Crash though the waves might, at its peak the passage simply leads to yet another statement of the opening panel. The point of culmination that the listener has been led to expect in fact never arrives.

The 'Deux murailles' concludes with a section that mirrors the short introduction. Where it had previously led the way to an alleluiatic Magnificat, the opening scale is now followed by a passage of directionless chords (similar to those mentioned in 'Offrande'). Their extremely dissonant harmonies, *tenuto* markings (which elongate the dissonances) and sheer volume seem indicative, in this context, of frustration on the part of the composer. The final chord, an 11-note chord of contracted resonance from which only E♮ is absent, is a *ffff* superimposition of 'complimentary colours [...] acid green on reddish-brown, yellow on violet'.[31] Even among the reviews of the British premiere cited above (which, it will be recalled, were mostly stereotypical grand summation appraisals), the conclusion of this movement stood out for Robert Maycock. 'The sound of that moment of superimposed colours', he wrote, 'is a shock of astonishing violence, nearer a cluster than a chord'.[32]

There is, for me, a marked difference in Messiaen's approach to the theological programmes of his earlier organ works when they recur in *Livre du Saint Sacrement*. Where the early compositions provide passages of musical culmination that clearly align with the programme, in the *Livre* there appear to be no sections of the sort. The irregularities in the *Livre* suggest to me that Messiaen's own compositional techniques must have indeed felt for him like exhausted expressive tools after *St François*. There is in fact little evidence in either 'Deux murailles' or 'Offrande' to support Paul Griffiths's claim, made in 1995, that a 'supreme and serene confidence [...] had always shone from this composer's scores'.[33] Messiaen's musical language had once served him as a comprehensive lexicon, giving voice to the splendour of his religious beliefs. By the *Livre* he was evidently no longer content to speak with it in the same ways.

Darker darkness and brighter brightness

Evidence that Messiaen hoped to depict theological imagery in the *Livre* still more convincingly than in his earlier works is found, I believe, in the portrayal of the Crucifixion and Resurrection in the ninth and tenth movements of the *Livre*: 'Les ténèbres' and 'La résurrection du Christ'. These two movements constitute Messiaen's largest and most comprehensive consideration of the Resurrection in his organ repertoire, something that becomes obvious when they are examined alongside earlier works for the instrument that deal with the same theme. 'Les Ténèbres' addresses the Crucifixion of Christ, a topic with which Messiaen had first engaged on the organ some 50 years previously in 'Jésus accepte la souffrance' from *La Nativité*. 'Les ténèbres' paints a picture thoroughly different from the purely victorious and apparently bloodless death of Christ depicted in 'la

---

[31]   Messiaen, Introduction to the score of *Livre*, p. [iii].

[32]   Robert Maycock, 'Ovation for Olivier: Westminster Cathedral Unveils Messiaen's Latest Organ Work', *Classical Music* (1986): 29.

[33]   Paul Griffiths, '*Éclairs sur l'au-delà* – the Last Works', in *Messiaen Companion*, p. 511.

souffrance'. Messiaen instead concentrates on the darkness cast over Golgotha on Good Friday, with a succession of chords of contracted resonance. This passage forms a long opening section that precedes an area of dissonant chords and their subsequent resolutions. These exposed clashes suggest agony, rather than glory, on the cross. It is one of the few (and certainly the darkest) portrayals of the Crucifixion in his entire oeuvre. The terrible 12-note concluding chord, a chord of superior contracted resonance, marked *p* and scored in the bass register, is about as far removed from the triumphant ending of a work as 'la souffrance' as is conceivable. Messiaen felt the need to have two separate movements for the Crucifixion and the Resurrection and so, like a passion, 'Les ténèbres' ends with no implication of the Christ's reawakening.

The succeeding movement, 'La résurrection du Christ', continues in the same dark vein. It would be reasonable to expect, especially given the rest of Messiaen's organ output, that a programme such as this would be an occasion for a joyful toccata. From the start, this extraordinary *très lent* movement hardly seems like the celebration that may have been anticipated. If his purpose was not to celebrate the Resurrection, then what was Messiaen aiming to achieve in this movement? Given the continuous stream of very slow, intensely dissonant *fff* chords that make the whole piece a long a protracted struggle to the final F♯-major conclusion, it is possible that Messiaen wanted to musically envision the physical process of Christ's dead body returning to life. The long series of slow chords distorts the sense of passing time, perhaps a way of suggesting three days' duration. A pedal on C♯ (i.e. the dominant of the final key), which Messiaen puts in place as the movement moves towards its conclusion, is held for nine bars with the series of dissonant chords above continuing to struggle onwards. This pedal creates an almost unbearable sense of harmonic tension, and it makes the final F♯-major chord all the more dramatic when it arrives. Perhaps the theological function of this final resolution is to depict the exact moment that Christ awoke.

Given their musical gore, I would argue that Messiaen is more successful in realizing his programme in 'Les ténèbres' and 'La résurrection du Christ' than in his earlier attempts. These movements do not evoke a Christ who wins resurrection easily, as is arguably the case in 'la souffrance', where the Crucifixion and Resurrection are both compacted into one movement. These movements from the *Livre* demonstrate that my notion of the work as a problematic one for Messiaen does not necessarily imply that it is a failure, as might be suspected from the lack of 'revelatory' passages discussed earlier. What I am actually suggesting is that the *Livre* was a large-scale experiment, in which Messiaen searched for new and better ways of musically realizing his theological programmes. The process of experimentation may, in some movements of the *Livre*, have produced music that is less coherent in comparison with previous works. In other areas, though, it undoubtedly resulted in music that is among the most convincing and successful in his entire oeuvre.

A supra-real communion

Another movement of the *Livre* where Messiaen arguably achieves a greater level of success than in earlier works is 'La joie de la grâce'. This is the 15th and (in terms of the programme) pivotal movement of the *Livre*, in which he approaches communion – an event that Gillian Weir correctly describes as 'the mystery at the heart of the church'.[34] In the title and subtitle, Messiaen explains that 'La joie' is intended to evoke the joy felt at the moment of communion. The programme deals entirely with the realm of thought and inner ecstasy, and Messiaen meets this demand with a movement consisting entirely of birdsong. The so-called *style oiseau* is a tool among Messiaen's compositional techniques that he had used to illustrate theological ideas (especially particularly abstract ones such as this) since the 1950s. Twenty years prior to the advent of the *Livre*, Messiaen declared birdsong to be his refuge:

> In dark hours, when my uselessness is brutally revealed to me and all the musical languages of the world seem to be merely an effort of patient research, without there being anything behind the notes to justify so much work – I go into the forest, into fields, into mountains, by the sea, among the birds […] it is there that music dwells for me; free, anonymous music, improvised for pleasure.[35]

Even if Messiaen believed birdsong to be superior to 'all the musical languages of the world', actual birdsongs should not be confused with his transcriptions of them, which incontestably constitute a unique facet of his own musical language.

The music of this movement is, in terms of Messiaen's compositional techniques, distilled in order to obtain the highest possible theological significance. In 'La Joie', he separates the birdsongs from both nature and narrative, setting them instead on a thoroughly ethereal plane. There are no imagined nature-scenes, as in the *Catalogue d'oiseaux* (1956–58); neither is there any external narrative, as in *St François*. Messiaen appears to avoid the inclusion of anything other than the birds, so as not to diminish the purity of this 'free, anonymous music, improvised for pleasure'. In 'La joie', Messiaen no longer felt it necessary to set the birds against any sort of background for the benefit of the listener. For the first time he prescribed nothing, instead allowing the birds to sing alone. He thereby reached a new, higher vista of supra-reality in this movement. In taking birdsong to this level, 'La joie' represents a step beyond the entirely free, *hors tempo*, birdsong of *St François*. As with the aforementioned 'revelatory' passages, I would suggest that whether or not the listener accepts this music as a satisfactory representation of the joy felt at the moment of communion is largely irrelevant. What is more important is that Messiaen found a way, within the terminology of his own musical

---

[34]   Gillian Weir, 'Organ Music II', in *Messiaen Companion*, p. 379.

[35]   Bernard Gavoty, 'Who Are You, Olivier Messiaen?', *Tempo*, no. 58 (Summer 1961): 35.

language, to craft a movement that for him adequately represented the theological profundity of the mystery of communion. It therefore seems fair to conclude that Messiaen's decision to abandon both nature scenes and narratives in this movement was a highly effective and successful one.

Christopher Dingle's suggestion that the *Livre* belongs to the same world as *St François* might have at first appeared valid. It is true that, on the surface, 'there are passages of pure, quasi-tonal modality, such as the contemplations either side of actually receiving the Eucharist'.[36] It is also true that simplistic comparisons between 'Deux murailles' or 'Offrande et Alleluia final' can be made with Messiaen's earlier pieces in the same vein, as both 'contain dazzling toccatas over growling pedal lines recalling the post-Dupré fireworks of "Dieu parmi nous" or "Transports de joie"'.[37] But I hope to have demonstrated that in a deeper sense a new voice – which could justifiably be called a late style voice – clearly started to sound during the composition of this experimental piece.

Towards Messiaen's late style

Messiaen's late works have often been greeted as ones of synthesis, as if their principal function was to represent a job completed. This framework has suited critics, for the compositional techniques of their object of study have never been cast into doubt. The late pieces, *Livre du Saint Sacrement* included among them, have in fact been seen as containing the heady achievement of stylistic perfection – as graceful conclusions to a lifetime of creativity. This belief in Messiaen's discovery of a wisdom that surpasses mere maturity in his dying movements smacks of 19th-century idealism. The widespread acceptance of this belief is owed in no small part to the composer himself, and to the willingness of many Messiaen scholars to allow his (often spurious) versions of events to go unquestioned. His erroneous description of the *Livre*'s birth is just one example of a statement that casts doubt over Messiaen's reliability as a source of factually solid information.

The abandonment of the often encountered misconception that Messiaen's late period consists exclusively of epitaphs or repetitive regurgitations (depending on the taste of the scholar concerned) is long overdue. Edward Said has already observed that there are two broad categories of late works: those that 'crown a lifetime of aesthetic endeavour' and those that are characterized by 'intransigence, difficulty, and unresolved contradiction'.[38] Where monumental compositions such as *La Transfiguration*, *Les Méditations*, *Des Canyons*, and especially *St François* could each conceivably serve as a suitably grand crown for Messiaen's output, I would suggest that the *Livre* falls into Said's second category of intransigence. Messiaen had acknowledged as early as 1961 the great difficulty of composing

---

[36]   Dingle, *Messiaen's Final Works*, Chapter 4.
[37]   Ibid.
[38]   Edward Said, *On Late Style* (London: Bloomsbury, 2006), p. 7.

music that adequately matched his theological programmes, saying that he wished through his work to 'rejoin the eternal durations and the resonances of the above and beyond, to apprehend that inaudible which is above actual music [...] *naturally, I shall never achieve this*'.[39] He may have thought it impossible, but it does seem that Messiaen nevertheless selected a certain route to attempt to move towards this goal. Once he discovered himself to be at the end of this route, he chose not to give up, but to move in a new direction and begin fresh experiments – the only way to uphold a sense of progress towards an ultimately unobtainable end.

Dingle paints a portrait of Messiaen in the 1980s, based on the compositions from that decade, as 'an old man who has fulfilled his task and ambitions and is at peace with the world'.[40] He also advises that, when listening to these works, we ought to 'simply sit back and be charmed'.[41] But this fairytale image of peaceful serenity clashes with Said's very definition of lateness as 'surviving beyond what is acceptable and normal; in addition, lateness includes the idea that one cannot really go beyond lateness at all, cannot transcend or lift oneself out of lateness, but can only deepen the lateness. There is no transcendence or unity'.[42] I hope to have demonstrated that, based on the musical nature of *Livre du Saint Sacrement*, Messiaen did not (as Dingle suggests) transcend his own late style to arrive at some other, ethereal plane. He was instead engaged in a highly critical assessment of the compositional techniques that he had crafted over the course of his entire career. Given Messiaen's apparently unrelenting scrutiny of his own musical language after *St François*, it is clear to me that there is a line by T. S. Eliot that will perhaps serve as the best starting-point for further study of the composer's late works: 'Old men ought to be explorers'.[43]

---

[39]   Gavoty, 'Who Are You, Olivier Messiaen?', p. 36. My italics.

[40]   Dingle, 'Charm and Simplicity', p. 7.

[41]   Ibid.

[42]   Said, *Late Style*, p. 13.

[43]   T. S. Eliot, *Four Quartets* (London: Faber & Faber, 1944): 'East Coker', line 202.

Chapter 13
Buddhist Temple, Shinto Shrine and the Invisible God of *Sept Haïkaï* [1]

Cheong Wai Ling

Sept Haïkaï: esquisses Japonaises pour piano solo et petit orchestre, published in 1966, was the first work to appear after Messiaen and Loriod's long delayed marriage of 1961.[2] Composed in 1962 immediately after their first visit to Japan, *Sept Haïkaï* is understandably rich in Japanese imagery, which Messiaen recorded first hand. More specifically, the imagery is not just conveyed through music; verbal texts arguably play an even more important mediating role. Indeed, Messiaen's commentaries on *Sept Haïkaï* grew in length and substance over the years. The preface to the score is typically succinct. Messiaen then elaborated on the programme of *Sept Haïkaï* when he was interviewed by Claude Samuel in the 1960s and 1980s,[3] but by far the most detailed account did not appear until the posthumous publication of his *Traité V/ii* in 2000. Despite their varying degree of thoroughness, there is little discrepancy in these sources, with one important exception. Simply put, Messiaen confined the programme of the 'Introduction' and 'Coda', the framing pieces of *Sept Haïkaï*, to a footnote in the score, and did not mention them again until *Traité V/ii*.

Apart from these two pieces, the titles are programmatic in nature, and, with the exception of 'Gagaku',[4] draw on places visited on their tour. These include Nara, the ancient capital of Japan, Lake Yamanaka and Karuizawa, where

---

[1]   Research for this study was supported by the Research Grants Council (CUHK441107).

[2]   Messiaen gives a slightly different subtitle on the next page of the score – *Sept Haïkaï: esquisses Japonaises, pour piano solo, xylophone et marimba soli, 2 clarinettes, 1 trompette, et petit orchestre* [Seven haiku: Japanese sketches for solo piano, xylophone and marimba soli, 2 clarinets, trumpet and small orchestra]. 'Haïkaï' is the transliteration of 'haiku', a genre of Japanese poems known for their extreme brevity. Each poem comprises only three lines of, respectively, five, seven and five syllables.

[3]   (Published 1967/1986) The earlier book of conversations with Samuel contains considerably less information: Claude Samuel, *Entretiens avec Olivier Messiaen* (Paris: Belfond, 1967), trans. Felix Aprahamian as *Conversations with Olivier Messiaen* (London: Stainer & Bell, 1976).

[4]   Imperial court music of Japan.

Messiaen notated birdsongs, and finally Miyajima, which, according to Messiaen, is 'perhaps the most beautiful place in Japan'.[5] The movements are titled:

I   'Introduction'
II   'Le Parc de Nara et les lanterns de Pierre' [The Nara park and the stone lanterns]
III 'Yamanaka-cadenza'
IV   'Gagaku'
V   'Miyajima et le torii dans la mer' [Miyajima and the torii in the sea]
VI   'Les oiseaux de Karuizawa' [The birds of Karuizawa]
VII 'Coda'

The suppression of the programme in the titles of the framing pieces is intriguing, especially as the preface already tells of his use of Hindu rhythms and the technique of retrograde, both of which suggest strong links to the underlying programme. In order to address the question as to what could have led Messiaen to suppress the programme until much later, let us first of all examine the seven pieces of *Sept Haïkaï* from the perspective of music–programme interaction, taking into consideration his last words on the programme.

The elaborate use of Hindu and retrograde rhythms in the 'Introduction' and 'Coda' fits well his reference to the *Ni-o* or custodian kings (see Plate 13.1), a retrograde pair of wooden sculptures that guards the entrance gate to a Buddhist temple. The duration series (xylophone and marimba) and the retrograde canon (woodwinds and piano) that traverse the 'Introduction' recur in the 'Coda' in reversed order. The Indian origin of Buddhism and, more specifically, that of the *Ni-o* might have prompted Messiaen to give vent to a preponderant and exclusive use of Hindu rhythms in these two pieces.

'Gagaku', the centrepiece of the set, is closely modelled on Japanese imperial court music, into which Messiaen has skilfully woven his turning chords [TC; *accords tournants*], and selected symmetrical permutations [*permutations symétriques*] into the musical fabric. 'Yamanaka-cadenza' and 'Les oiseaux des Karuizawa', on the other hand, celebrate Japanese birdsongs recorded during the trip. Given some basic knowledge of *gagaku* and Japanese birdsongs, especially the distinctive singing of the uguisu (Japanese bush warbler), the general audience should have no difficulty identifying their indebtedness to Japan. The music and the programme match well in these three movements, with just one minor incongruity – the 'problematic' addition of a Greek strophe [*strophe crétique*] to the prevailing ensemble of Japanese birdsongs at rehearsal number 9 of 'Les oiseaux des Karuizawa'.

In stark contrast to the Yamanaka and Karuizawa pieces, however, French rather than Japanese birds sing in movement II 'Nara' and movement V 'Miyajima'. Here we find the music–programme relationship at its most precarious. Despite

5   *Sept Haïkaï* (Paris: Leduc, 1966), Preface; *Traité V/ii*, p. 506.

Source: Photographs reproduced by kind permission of Todaiji [東大寺] and Bijyutsuin [美術院]

Plate 13.1   Buddhist temple gate guardians *Ni-o* [仁王] at Todaiji [東大寺], Nara [奈良]

Messiaen's detailed commentaries, the deployment of a French nightingale in 'Le Parc de Nara', and a larger number of fabricated French birdsongs in 'Miyajima' remains perplexing. Messiaen was somewhat apologetic about the French nightingale, the only birdsong heard in the 'Nara' movement, reassuring his reader that 'uguisu', the king among all the Japanese birds,[6] will soon take over at 'Karuizawa':

> This bird [...] is the French nightingale. There is no nightingale in Japan! What the Japanese poets call nightingale is the 'uguisu', *cettia diphone cantans*, a Japanese bush warbler that will become the hero in the sixth piece. For the time

---

[6]   *Traité V/ii*, p. 515 (translations are mine unless indicated otherwise).

being, we will make do with the French nightingale, denuded, travestied, but recognizable.[7]

Nevertheless, he did not offer any explanation for the even more active roles played by fabricated French birdsongs in 'Miyajima et le torii dans la mer' (see Plate 13.2). Apart from French birdsongs, both the 'Nara' and 'Miyajima' pieces are also rich in Greek rhythms, yet another non-Japanese element. But perhaps the most unexpected moment is marked by the forceful intrusion of a chorale into 'Miyajima et le torii dans la mer', which slows things down, and in effect drives everything aside, Japanese or otherwise.

There is certainly no simple answer to Messiaen's emphatic use of non-Japanese elements in *Sept Haïkaï*, since he did not touch on this issue, even in his detailed discussion of the music documented in *Traité V/ii*.[8] As argued below, the torii of the Miyajima Shinto shrine seems to provide an important clue to Messiaen's use of a chorale, and also the many birdsongs featured in the same piece.[9] In order to tackle the multiple meanings of the torii explored in *Sept Haïkaï*, however, a good grasp of the chief technical issues of the work will be indispensable. A more detailed discussion of *Sept Haïkaï* thus follows, with Messiaen's use of eight violins constituting the main thread of the inquiry.

The eight violins of *Sept Haïkaï*

Eight violins are the only string instruments used in *Sept Haïkaï*. All except the two pieces devoted to Japanese birdsongs ('Yamanaka-cadenza' and 'Les Oiseaux de Karuizawa') include them. Unlike the 'Epôde' of *Chronochromie* (1959–60), birdsongs are not scored for the strings in *Sept Haïkaï*. Indeed, Messiaen may have barred the violins from playing the birdsongs in the wake of the scandalous premieres of the 'Epôde', in which the audience strongly resisted a diet of close to five minutes of exclusively strings and birdsongs.

Messiaen's preface to *Sept Haïkaï* is on the whole 'extra-musical' in character. When commenting on the first and last pieces of the set, however, he shows greater interest in the technical side of the music:

> The Hindu rhythms dedicated to the three Shakti are played by the cencerros, bells, trumpet, trombone and metallic percussion instruments. The piano and the woodwinds play a retrograde rhythmic canon. The xylophone and marimba play a *métabole* from the Hindu *tâla simhavikrama* (power of lion) to the *miçra-*

---

[7]   *Traité V/ii*, p. 473.

[8]   Messiaen's analysis of *Sept Haïkaï* is arguably the most detailed among all analyses of complete works in the *Traité*.

[9]   I refer to the Itsukushima shrine located on the island of Miyajima as the Miyajima Shinto shrine.

Source: Photographs retrieved May 22, 2008, from Flickr: <http://www.flickr.com/photos/
jameseverett /372471686/> (top); and japan-guide.com: <http://www.japan-guide.
com/e/e3450.html> (bottom)

Plate 13.2   Different perspectives of the torii at Itsukushima Shrine [厳島神社],
Miyajima [宮島]

varna (mingling of colours). With the violins we hear only the first strophe of a melodic phrase (the second strophe being reserved for the seventh piece).[10]

Example 13.1 shows a reduction of bars 1–3 of the first movement of *Sept Haïkaï*. Messiaen marks in the score his use of the Hindu rhythm *miçra varna* (xylophone and marimba) and the rhythms of three *Shakti* (trumpet, trombone and percussion),[11] Not marked in the score but conveyed in his analysis (*Traité V/ii*) are the use of Hindu rhythms in the piano and the retrograde of the same in the woodwinds. In movements I and VII, Hindu rhythms saturate all the instruments except the violins, which play in unison a lyrical line.[12] Curiously, Messiaen tells us not to focus on it, even though it stands out as the most melodious strand of the multi-layered music. Instead, he urges us to listen to the xylophone, marimba, piano and woodwinds, although he also emphasizes that everything counts:

> This piece is finely worked and grimacing, like the two guardian kings that frame the entrance to Buddhist temples. There is no principal melodic part. The violins are of little importance – they express little more than a set sentiment – and constitute but one song among other things. We will hear above all the xylophone, marimba, piano and woodwinds: but we should also pay attention to the rest; *everything counts*.[13]

The eight violins are also used in the second, fourth and fifth movements of *Sept Haïkaï*. Nevertheless, instead of playing in unison, as in the framing pieces, each violin takes up one voice of a chain of octachords that traverses and colours the music. The setting in the eight violins of this succession of octachords or, more specifically, the turning chords, first occurs in Strophes I and II of *Chronochromie*. Following *Sept Haïkaï*, it does not surface again until the fourth movement of *Éclairs sur l'au-delà...*. Henceforth, I shall refer to the octachordal chains as TC chains to facilitate discussion.

In both *Chronochromie* and *Éclairs* a TC chain is superimposed on two other chains of complex chords to form a highly symbolic three-tiered structure (see Table 13.1).[14] The sole use of the TC chain in *Sept Haïkaï* is unique to Messiaen's entire output, and it probably owes much to his decision to appropriate the sustained *sho* chords of *gagaku*, Japan's traditional imperial court music, which is still performed today.

---

[10]   This passage, extracted from the preface to *Sept Haïkaï*, is about the first piece; the passage about the last piece is the same except for its ending.

[11]   *Sarasvatîkanthâbharana, Pârvatîlocana* and *Lakshmîça*. See *Traité V/ii*, pp. 450–452.

[12]   Movement VII is a continuation of *Sept Haïkaï* I.

[13]   This footnote appears twice in the score, on pp. 1 and 124.

[14]   The chords of transposed inversion on the same bass note, and the first chords of contracted resonance.

Example 13.1   Olivier Messiaen: *Sept Haïkaï* I, bars 1–3 (reduction)

Table 13.1   The superimposition of three tiers of chords in *Chronochromie* and *Éclairs*

Turning chords	Eight violins
Chords of transposed inversion on the same bass note	Seven violins
First chords of contracted resonance	Three violas and four cellos

The turning chords, together with the chords of transposed inversion on the same bass note (CTI; *accord à renversements transposés sur la même note de basse*), the first and second chords of contracted resonance (*1er et 2e accord à résonance contractée*), and the chords of total chromaticism (*accord du total chromatique*), are central to Messiaen's repertory of colour-chords. These are special harmonies of his own invention that are valued as much for their audible as for their visual effects. Messiaen codifies their structures in the seventh and last volume of *Traité,* published in 2002, and provides us with detailed descriptions of their colour effects.

All these five categories of complex chords are transposable 12 times, and are, in this sense, diametrically opposed to the modes of limited transposition, Messiaen's other major source of sound-colour materials. He lists in *Traité VII* all 12 transpositions of each category of chords, and numbers them for identification purposes.[15] In the following discussion I shall follow his numbering system; my abbreviation of the turning chords thus reads from TC1 to TC12. Each transposition of the turning chords comprises a group of three octachords; I shall also follow Messiaen's nomenclature and refer to them as respectively A, B and C.

The TC chains of *Sept Haïkaï*

The following discussion of the TC chains of *Sept Haïkaï* II, IV and V will start with the 'Gagaku', since their roles are the most well defined therein. I shall then examine the rather similar TC chain of *Sept Haïkaï* II before venturing into the many changes that set the TC chain of *Sept Haïkaï* V apart from its precedents.

Example 13.2 shows a reduction of bars 1–4 of 'Gagaku'. Two melodies stand out, one of which is played in unison by the trumpet, two oboes and cor anglais, and the other doubled inexactly (i.e. with variable intervals) by the piccolo and soprano clarinet. This setting is derived from traditional *gagaku*, in which the Japanese wind instruments, *hichiriki* [double-reed bamboo pipe] and *ryuteki* [transverse bamboo flute], play heterophonic tunes. In addition, the eight violins play a chain of slow-moving turning chords. The setting of the violins is calculated to mimic the sound effects of the *sho* [Japanese mouth organ], which plays similar roles in *gagaku*. Considerable resemblance is achieved by instructing the violins to play the octachords without vibrato and on the bridge of the instrument ('sul ponticello'):

> Rather oddly, the *sho* is replaced by eight violins. They play sustained chords of divergent lengths. They play non vibrato, sul ponticello, always *forte*, without any fluctuation of nuance, with a tart sound, acidic, as if scraping the strings. The playing – inexpressive, forced, brassy, vinegary, unpleasant – makes the chords sound unusual and unheard-of.[16]

Messiaen notes that the *sho* chords of *gagaku* lie above rather than below the melody, just as the heaven is above the earth, an effect he replicates in his own

---

[15]   The 12 transpositions of different chords are numbered accordingly to different criteria. See Cheong Wai Ling, 'Messiaen's Chord Tables: Ordering the Disordered', *Tempo* 57, no. 226 (2003): 2–10.

[16]   *Traité V/ii*, p. 500. The seventh and eighth violins play *ff* rather than *f*.

Example 13.2   Olivier Messiaen: *Sept Haïkaï* IV, bars 1–4 (reduction)

music.[17] Meanwhile, a number of metallic percussion instruments (cencerros, crotales and bells) play isolated notes according to Messiaen's symmetrical permutation scheme, to create a pointillistic backdrop.[18] There is no question that 'Gagaku' is the most intensely Japanese in style among the seven pieces of *Sept Haïkaï*, and this seems to befit its appearance as the centrepiece of the work.

The TC chains of 'Le Parc de Nara' and 'Gagaku' are strikingly similar, though of course there is no suggestion of Messiaen's hearing *gagaku* in the Nara park. In both cases the eight violins share the same non-vibrato mode of playing, and,

---

[17]   'They [the chords] do not support the melodic line, as is generally the case in a European accompanied melody. They lie above the melody, just as the heaven is above the earth, say the Japanese.' *Traité V/ii*, p. 494.

[18]   The non-pitched percussion plays yet another strand of rhythm.

perhaps more importantly, the same repertory of octachords. Messiaen describes these chords in two places in his *Traité*:

> 1: The chords are special. I invented them especially for *Sept Haïkaï*, and they are
> used only twice: in the second piece 'Le Parc de Nara et les lanternes de pierre',
> and above all in the fourth piece entitled 'Gagaku'. The chords are pre-composed,
> as are those played by the *sho* (mouth organ) in the Japanese *gagaku* [19]
> 2: One remembers that these are the turning chords to which I applied the
> principle of the chords of transposed inversion on the same bass note. I chose
> the three chords of the turning chords (eighth transposition): A, B, C – and I gave
> each chord a certain number of inversions … .[20]

Like the *sho* chords of *gagaku*, the octachords are pre-composed. Having picked the three octachords of TC8, Messiaen processed them by the technique of transposed inversion to arrive at 16 more octachords.[21] Before committing himself to an habitual listing of each and every single chord, he remarked that the colours of the chords are meant to reproduce the marvellous effect of sunlight on the Japanese cedar tree called 'cryptomerias'.[22]

If the colourful TC chain of *Sept Haïkaï* II may be likened to the play of light on the foliage in the Nara park, it also constitutes a nuanced contrast to the piano part, which, according to Messiaen, adopts a dodecaphonic idiom in order to suggest the greyness of the stone lanterns there. This contrast is central to Messiaen's conception of the piece. Apart from the polarity between colours and greyness, the geometric disposition of the stone lanterns as opposed to the irregular shading of light and foliage also constitutes a second polarized pair that Messiaen sought to express in musical terms:

> Extinguished, in the middle of a summer's afternoon, under the sunlight that
> plays amongst the crytomerias, they (the stone lanterns) have a geometrical
> beauty that contrasts oddly with the poetry of the grass and foliage, of the lights
> and shadows. In order to render this contrast, I superimposed two rhythmic
> styles and two harmonic styles, and the marimba solo plays a stylized birdsong
> that unifies them all.[23]

---

[19]   *Traité* V/ii, p. 463.

[20]   Ibid., p. 500.

[21]   See ibid., p. 463.

[22]   'One may consult the table attached herewith in order to understand the analysis of the chords played by the eight violins throughout the second piece of *Sept Haïkaï*. The colours of these chords reproduce the marvellous work of sunlight on the cryptomerias.' Ibid., p. 463.

[23]   Ibid., p. 462.

As Messiaen notes, he has unified the music through use of birdsong. Just as the rhythmic rigour of the octachords, controlled by a sophisticated symmetrical permutation scheme, is reflective of the geometric beauty of the stone lanterns, the free play of light on the foliage is symbolized by the clarinets' indulgence in irrational values.[24]

Half-way through *Sept Haïkaï*, the violins' playing of the TC chain, having traversed and coloured 'Le Parc de Nara' and 'Gagaku', heads on for its final appearance in 'Miyajima et le torii dans la mer'. It is at this point that important differences are introduced to the TC chain for the first time. Indeed, it is questionable whether the TC chain continues to simulate the *sho* chords in *Sept Haïkaï* V, given the number of changes that have been brought into place. Before we address the differences and attempt any explanation, we need to understand Messiaen's compositional features in the work and specifically the 'chorale', which is the principal theme of *Sept Haïkaï* V. Here's how Messiaen describes it in his *Traité*:

> Five elements inform this layering of colours. (1) Top register: the piccolo and the flute play a stylized birdsong that is half invented. (2) High register: rhythmicized sonorities played by the piano, triangle, crotales and cencerros. (3) Medium high register: brilliant melodies, forte, a miniature concerto for two voices played by the xylophone and marimba. (4) Middle register: the turning chords played by the eight violins and the bells. (5) Medium low register: the principal theme, a chorale for woodwind and brass underlined by cymbals, gongs and tam-tams.[25]

'Miyajima et le torii dans la mer' is in many ways the densest piece of the set (see Example 13.3). Not only does it use more French birdsongs and Greek rhythms when compared to 'Le Parc de Nara', the only other piece that pits French birdsongs against Greek rhythms, but the *sho*-like octachordal chain is also set against a layer of percussive tetrachords in pursuit of his cherished notion of 12-tone complementation.[26] Such complexity, though, is shrewdly counterbalanced by extreme brevity; of all the seven pieces of *Sept Haïkaï*, this is the shortest (see Table 13.2).

Central to the multi-layered setting of *Sept Haïkaï* V is the chorale theme. Messiaen accords it great prominence by assigning the soprano clarinet, trumpet, trombone and bass clarinet to play it at three successive octaves.[27] Moreover, each

---

[24]   Ibid., p. 473.

[25]   Ibid., p. 507.

[26]   This approach is subsequently epitomized in Messiaen's chord of total chromaticism [*accord du total chromatique*], 'the most beautiful and richest of all chords', which likewise divides up the 12 tones into pairs of complementary octachords and tetrachords. See *Traité VII*, pp. 106–107 and 181–190.

[27]   The octave doublings are not shown in Example 13.3. The bass clarinet is incidentally left out from Messiaen's discussion in *Traité V/ii*, p. 511.

Example 13.3   Olivier Messiaen: *Sept Haïkaï* V, bars 1–8 (reduction)

note of the chorale is coloured by a block chord played by the woodwinds, which fills out the registral space opened up by the octave doublings. The prominence given to the chorale is unassailable; only the French birdsongs, full of life and rather unrestrained in their pace and volume, may pose any threat to it. In his *Traité*, Messiaen takes great care to list all the chords of transposed inversion used to harmonize the chorale, noting the changes made to individual chords, and also the colour effects of selected CTI.[28] All in all the theme of chorale stands out in 'Miyajima', and marks the most extensive use of the CTI in *Sept Haïkaï*.[29]

---

[28]   Ibid., pp. 513–514.

[29]   The chords of transposed inversion are also used to harmonize the song of the uguisu in *Sept Haïkaï* VI.

Example 13.3 *concluded*

The TC chain of 'Miyajima et le torii dans la mer'

The *sho*-like octachordal chain has previously appeared in *Sept Haïkaï* II and IV, but significant changes are brought to it only when the chorale theme arrives in movement V. In order to speculate on the correlation between the two events, I shall turn now to examine the changes that set this particular TC chain apart from the other two TC chains.

First and foremost, the TC chain of *Sept Haïkaï* V exhibits stringent use of only three octachords. Messiaen no longer uses TC8 and its 16 derivatives as he does in movements II and IV. Instead, the three octachords of TC6 are used in their original settings; even the spacing is scrupulously observed. Whether this reversion to the default format was conceived as a gesture of resolution can only

Table 13.2   An overview of *Sept Haïkaï* V

Stylized French birdsongs	Piccolo + flute (inexact doubling)	Blackcap [*fauvette à tête noire*]
Principal theme (harmonized by CTI)[b]	Wind + brass + CGCT[a]	Theme of chorale
TC[c] octachordal chain (hot colours)	8 violins + bells	Greek rhythmic series Chord series
Stylized French birdsongs	Xylophone	Garden warbler [*fauvette des jardins*]; Melodious warbler [*hypolaïs polyglotte*]; Nightingale [*rossignol*]
	Marimba	Melodious warbler; Nightingale
Complementary tetrachordal chain (cold colours)	Piano + triangle + crotales + cencerros	Greek and other rhythms Chord series

[a] CGCT abbreviates two Turkish cymbals, two gongs, one Chinese cymbal and two tam-tams.

[b] CTI = chords of transposed inversion.

[c] TC = turning chords.

be left to speculation, but Messiaen's description of the colour effects of TC6 in *Traité VII* ('recall a stained glass window of which characters clothed in red stand out from a blue background') strongly suggests that it is best suited to the programme at hand.[30]

Since a lot more octachords are used previously in the TC chains of 'Le Parc de Nara' and 'Gagaku', they are presumably more colourful than the TC chain of 'Miyajima'. Messiaen's self-imposed limitation to the three octachords of the TC6 may arguably be understood as a measure taken to control the spill of colours, perhaps in order to let the chorale, harmonized by a myriad of colourful CTI, shine in the foreground.

Nevertheless, this notion of suppressed colours is contradicted by the fact that the TC chain of *Sept Haïkaï* V alone calls forth the complementary tetrachords of the three octachords. Perhaps even more strikingly, the colour effects of the TC chain, and also two of the three complementary tetrachords, are marked here for

---

[30]   *Traité VII*, p. 169. The three octachords of TC6 also reappear in *Couleurs* at arguably the most important moment of the work (rehearsal number 73), though the spacing of 6A and 6B and also the colour markings differ.

the first and only time in the score.[31] Such colour markings are not added anywhere else in the score of *Sept Haïkaï*, and it is not at all clear why. What is clear is that Messiaen furnished the 'Miyajima et le torii dans la mer' with a wealth of colours, and he tried hard to ensure that they would not be missed.

Messiaen referred to this particular TC chain and the complementary tetrachordal chain as ensembles of hot and cold colours:

> High register: the piano plays rhythmicized sonorities. They are, in fact, three chords. [...] These three chords – their notes, their high register, and the percussion instruments that double them – constitute an ensemble of cold colours that contrasts with the hot colours of the turning chords played by the eight violins. The latter adopts the three chords of the turning chords no. 6 (see table). The overall colour effect is predominantly red, orange, purple-crimson, all of which contain red, the hot colour par excellence.[32]

The hot colours are in part the result of the vibrato playing of the violins, but there is evidence that the choice of chords matters as well, with the overall colour effects of the TC6 rich in the hue of red.[33] Meanwhile, the cold colours are attributed to the complementary piano chords, and the high-register tinklings of the metallic percussion: the triangle, crotales and cencerros.

Sept Haïkaï V marks the first time that the eight violins play the TC chain with vibrato. Moreover, by discarding the previous 'sul tasto' and 'sul ponticello' markings, which may be understood as either too high or too low in position, the normal playing position is regained. In movement V, the violins thus revert to the playing modes that characterize movement I, and subsequently movement VII (see Table 13.3). A sign of reversion is again in evidence, thereby offering a clue to the question as to what could have deterred Messiaen from making significant changes to the TC chain until the arrival of the chorale.

In retrospect, I believe that important changes made to the TC chain in *Sept Haïkaï* V concern colours: the use of the octachords of TC6 for their hot reddish effects, and the addition of a complementary chord chain that furnishes the piece with cold colours. Furthermore, the turning chords recover their default formats, and the violins resume playing with vibrato in the normative position. That the TC chain is overtly altered in *Sept Haïkaï* V may therefore be related more directly to the chorale, the grandeur of which owes much to the colours of the CTI. It is seemingly in response to the colourful chorale that the TC chain breaks loose from its former tie to the *sho*-like timbre and freely explores a new colour scheme, a fine selection of both hot and cold colours.

---

[31]   The colour markings are confined to pp. 58 and 64 of *Sept Haïkaï* V, respectively, the opening and its reprise in the piece.

[32]   *Traité V/ii*, p. 507.

[33]   Ibid., p. 508.

Table 13.3   The shifting roles of the eight violins in *Sept Haïkaï* I, II, IV, V and VII

I	8 violins vibrato	Monodic	Dynamics vary	
II	8 violins + crotales[a] non-vibrato; sul tasto	Octachordal chain[b] TC8 and derivatives	*pp*	Interversion 5
IV	8 violins non vibrato; sul ponticello	Octachordal chain[c] TC8 and derivatives	*f* (upper hexad); *ff* (lower dyad)	Even-numbered multiples of demisemiquavers
V	8 violins + bells[d] vibrato	Octachordal chain[c] TC6 (default format)	*mf*	Greek rhythms
VII	8 violins vibrato	Monodic	Dynamics vary	

[a] The crotales do not double any one of the eight violin parts.

[b] Disrupted only once.

[c] Undisrupted.

[d] The bells double consistently the top violin part.

Throughout *Sept Haïkaï* the TC chains are dominated by other strands of music so they assume a quiet though somewhat unyielding presence. The TC chain of 'Miyajima et le torii dans la mer' is no exception, being overshadowed by other layers of music, the lively birdsongs and the majestic chorale. If we read metaphorically into this setting, which purportedly depicts aspects of Japanese culture, we may detect a covert attempt to import from the West images that are alien to the topic at hand. If they are truly aliens in the mind of the composer, however, they must have been conceived as the most welcomed of the kind. For 'Miyajimaet le torii dans la mer' is unmistakably jubilant in tone. A wealth of materials are included in the scene alongside the French birds and the chorale: Messiaen also brought in a myriad of Greek rhythms, and the unprecedented use of a tetrachordal chain to complement the TC chain.

It is precisely these two chains (teatrachordal and TC) that enable Messiaen to play with the correlation between colours and 12-tone complementation. He had previously depicted the stone lanterns of 'Le Parc de Nara' with recourse to dodecaphony that is, according to Messiaen, sadly greyish in effect.[34] Nevertheless, when faced with the colourful chorale in 'Miyajima et le torii dans la mer', he changed his approach and called forth the hot- and cold-coloured chains to exhaust the 12-tone space. The same 12 tones are thus reassembled through the mediation of brightly coloured chords.

---

[34]   *Traité V/ii*, pp. 462–463.

Multiple meanings of the torii

The recurrent use of the TC chains in *Sept Haïkaï* movements II, IV and V may serve primarily a cyclic function, as a tactic to add coherence to what might otherwise seem to be a disparate set of pieces, but the violins, which mimic the sound effect of the *sho* in 'Gagaku', also acquire in due course distinct Japanese resonances, which unavoidably influence the way we hear them in 'Le Parc de Nara' and 'Miyajima'. They help evoke, if only discreetly, the imagery and colours of Japan.

While the TC chain of *Sept Haïkaï* V is endowed with Japanese flavour, there is also evidence that it resonates with Christian and not just Shinto symbolism. With their heightened emphasis on colours, and the circular repetition of three chords, the TC and the complementary chains tie in well with the Christian imagery of a rainbow, a symbol that often occurs in Messiaen's writing on sound-colour phenomena.[35] For example, a throne encircled by a rainbow appears in *Revelation* 4:3, the first biblical inscription to *Couleurs de la cité céleste*: 'And he that sat [on the throne] was to look upon like a jasper and a sardine stone; and there was a rainbow round about the throne, in sight like unto an emerald'.[36] A rainbow also crowns the mighty angel who announces the end of time in *Revelation* 10:1, and this is of course part of the well-known biblical inscription for *Quatuor pour la fin du Temps*:[37]

> And I saw another mighty angel come down from heaven, clothed with a cloud, and a rainbow was upon his head, and his face was as it were the sun, and his feet as pillars of fire; and he had in his hand a little book open, and he set his right foot upon the sea, and his left foot on the earth […] . And the angel which I saw stand upon the sea and upon the earth lifted up his hand to heaven, and sware by him that liveth for ever and ever, who created heaven, and the things that therein are, and the earth, and the things that therein are, and the sea, and the things which are therein, that there should be time no longer.[38]

The chorale theme, which reigns victoriously in *Sept Haïkaï* V, seems to be even more symbolically potent than the chord chains. Given its broad, overriding arch-like strides, it may suggest the torii of the Miyajima Shinto shrine, which stands in the sea rather than on land. It may also suggest the angel above, who adopts a torii-like gesture in that one foot is set on the land, and the other upon the sea. It could well be the resemblance between the two that attracted Messiaen to the torii in the first place, and the torii in turn conjured up for him the invisible temple.

---

[35]   Messiaen, *Technique de mon langage musical*, Vol. 1 (Paris: Leduc, 1944), p. 46.

[36]   *Revelation* 4:3 (King James version).

[37]   Messiaen's colourful chord chains may also be related to J. S. Bach's *St. Matthew Passion*, in which strings conjure up the imagery of halos in recitatives delivered by Jesus.

[38]   *Revelation* 10:1–2 and 5–6 (King James version).

The Japanese word torii [鳥居] literally means 'the birds' abode'. Although the etymology of the word remains debatable, one legend has it that the torii was first built as a bird perch, upon which cocks gathered to crow. The building of a bird perch was but one of many tricks thought up by the elders to tempt Amaterasu, the sun goddess, to come out from her hiding place, in order that light might return to the land. This legend, documented in *Kojiki* [Records of Ancient Matters], the oldest extant Japanese book, would surely have delighted Messiaen, though there is no documentary evidence that he was aware of it.[39] Nevertheless, the piccolo, flute, xylophone and marimba's lively playing of birdsongs is, for whatever reasons, very much in the foreground of the music. Indeed, with the sole exception of the chorale, all the other layers of 'Miyajima et le torii dans la mer' stand the danger of being drowned out by the birdsongs.

There are indications that this enormous bird perch, or torii, is central to the design of *Sept Haïkaï*. Printed in vermilion on the front page of the score is an image of a torii that stands in the sea.[40] In this drawing the artist also included three stone lanterns, but there is no other sign of the Shinto shrine. The conventional understanding of the torii is a gate or portico that leads to the Shinto shrine and that marks our entrance to the sacred precinct. Messiaen must have seen a good number of torii in Japan, but the torii of the Miyajima Shinto shrine is different because it stands in the sea and not on land. This is an important difference as it helps Messiaen to envisage an invisible temple.

Messiaen goes against convention, and proposes that we view through the torii not the shrine, but rather the sea and sky, the vast expanse, which is for him the 'second temple', the 'true temple'.[41] It is precisely this change of perspective, with the torii as the reference point, that leads him to argue for the 'true temple'. Messiaen's programme, though not the title of 'Miyajima et le torii dans la mer', alludes to an invisible temple. It provides an important clue to the provocative use of a chorale, which unavoidably evokes Christian resonances, given Messiaen's religious stance.

Messiaen's claim that the torii opens out to a stretch of sea and sky is indeed an attractive idea; nevertheless, he left out, deliberately or otherwise, an important point from his discussion. In reality, we do not see through the torii such a vast expanse, but rather the Hiroshima prefecture (see Plate 13.2), the capital of which is the Japanese city most closely associated with the painful memories of the Second World War. Accompanied by a Belgian Jesuit priest, Father Ernest Goossens, the Messiaens visited the Hiroshima city, laid flowers to the Cenotaph for the A-bomb Victims in the Peace Memorial Park, and were moved to tears by a playing of

[39]   Donald L. Philippi, trans., *Kojiki* (Tokyo: University of Tokyo Press, 1968), pp. 81–85.
[40]   A photo of the same torii was reproduced on the front page of the *Conférence de Kyoto: November 12, 1985* (Paris: Leduc, 1988).
[41]   *Traité V/ii*, p. 506.

Fauré's *In paradisum* (from his *Requiem*) in a church nearby before departing for Miyajima in a ferry that afternoon.[42]

Still, Messiaen's idea of a 'true temple' may not be evangelical in intent, because all earthbound temples cannot possibly be true temples, be they Christian, Buddhist or Shinto. Nevertheless, there is evidence that Christianity was a concern at the time he composed *Sept Haïkaï*. His claim to have tried to add 'a Christian dimension' to the 'Gagaku', the centrepiece of *Sept Haïkaï*, has some relevance here,[43] though one wonders if he did not fail to realize it until the following piece, 'Miyajima et le torii dans la mer', through the prominent use of a chorale.

Epilogue

'Miyajima et le torii dans la mer' is the shortest piece in *Sept Haïkaï*, and also the only one marked with colour effects in the score. It is also the only movement to have fully utilized the chords of transposed inversion, acting as a resource of colours for the chorale. The turning chords, which have already been used in 'Gagaku' to simulate the playing of *sho*, also recur here, pitted against their complementary tetrachords to fill out the chromatic space.

Among the seven pieces of *Sept Haïkaï*, 'Miyajima et le torii dans la mer' undoubtedly excels in colours, being inspired by the exceptional beauty of the locale. As noted in Messiaen's programme, there are the green of the pine trees, the red of the maple leaves, the torii and the Shinto shrine, and also the blue of the sea and sky. All these dazzling colours are, according to Messiaen, as much a part of the scenic settings, as of things invisible. In the *Traité* he remarks that 'the torii should lead us towards the second temple, if we know how to listen to the language of the colours of the beyond … '.[44] This is a perplexing remark. It is not at all clear what drew Messiaen to relate the second temple to the hearing of colours, though colours for the ear fit perfectly well with his synaesthesia. Significantly, the vague suggestion of an invisible temple in *Sept Haïkaï* is directly followed by a more extended exploration of a celestial 'hidden' city in his next work, *Couleurs de la cité céleste* (1963). In it, Messiaen draws on a wider range of sound-colour materials to paint the heavenly Jerusalem of the Apocalypse. *Couleurs* also marks his first overt reuse of Christian references in an orchestral work since *Trois petites Liturgies de la Présence Divine* (1943–34).

The expression of his Catholic faith had been less prominent in the works of the so-called Tristan Trilogy (1945–48) up to *Chronochromie* (1959–60), during which time the only clearly stated Christian works are the solo organ works *Messe de la Pentecôte* (1950), *Livre d'orgue* (1951) and *Verset pour la fête de la dédicace*

---

[42]   See Peter Hill and Nigel Simeone, *Messiaen* (New Haven, CT/London: Yale University Press, 2005), pp. 250–251.

[43]   Claude Samuel, *Olivier Messiaen: Musique et couleur* (Paris, 1986), p. 149.

[44]   *Traité V/ii*, p. 506.

(1960). After *Couleurs*, Messiaen's works that lack any explicit reference to his faith diminish markedly in number. Quite apart from the two temple gates of *Sept Haïkaï*, one Buddhist and the other Shinto, we may thus read *Sept Haïkaï* as constituting yet another gateway for Messiaen, through which he turned irrevocably to the expression of the invisible.

Messiaen could have been captivated by the torii of the Miyajima Shinto shrine before he decided that the Buddhist temple gate (with its custodian kings) might forge a pair of gateways. This parallel, which involves the first, fifth and seventh pieces, however, stands in danger of upsetting the other more obvious symmetry of *Sept Haïkaï* (see Figure 13.1).

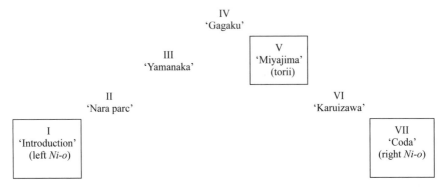

Figure 13.1   Surface symmetry in the programmes of *Sept Haïkaï*

Even a glance at the titles of the seven pieces of *Sept Haïkaï* shows that symmetry is in play. With 'Gagaku' in the middle, the 'Introduction' and the 'Coda', the Nara park and the Miyajima shrine, the scenic Yamanaka and Karuizawa, all strike us as natural pairs.

Regretfully, the beauty of this symmetrical setting cannot accommodate the parallel between the Shinto and the Buddhist temple gates, and the custodian kings stationed there. It could have been this consideration that drove Messiaen to confine the *Ni-o* to a footnote in a rather inconspicuous spot in the score. That all the other footnotes are about performance instructions renders this disclosure of an extra-musical detail all the more intriguing. In any case, this act does help conceal a factor that could have upset the surface symmetry of the design.

If Messiaen was simply interested in the depiction of a Buddhist icon, he could have chosen other things, for instance, the monolithic Buddha statue of the Todaiji, one of the key Buddhist monuments in the Nara park. If he had in mind a parallel to the torii of the Shinto shrine, however, his choice of the Buddhist entrance gate became inevitable. And the parallel goes further. Just as Messiaen's argument that the torii leads not only to the Shinto shrine, but also to the invisible, depends on diametrically different perspectives, he also approached the Buddhist temple gate from directions that are exact opposites of one another. As mentioned above, it is not until *Traité V/ii* that Messiaen fully disclosed the custodian kings alluded to in the first and last pieces of *Sept Haïkaï*. On this occasion, he even goes so far as to specify that the 'Introduction' and 'Coda' symbolize respectively the left and right custodian kings:

> The first and the seventh pieces play the role of the two *Ni-o*, the two statues of guardian kings that guard the left- and right-hand side of the entrance to Buddhist temples. The intricate angry demeanour and the static threat of these two menacing statues is reproduced in the finely wrought grimace of the Introduction and Coda. The Introduction symbolizes the left guardian king, and the Coda symbolizes the right guardian king.[45]

Messiaen's mapping of the left and right custodian kings to the 'Introduction' and 'Coda' may strike us as a rather odd and risky idea; none of the other pieces carries a programme that can be pinned down to just one specific object. In my view, however, the programme may suggest not just the *Ni-o* kings, but, more importantly, a hearing of the two pieces as constituting an entrance gate into Japan, Messiaen's Japan. Therein, we come face to face with his rendition of the quintessentially Japanese sound of *gagaku*, and the adorable uguisu. In the midst of all these Japanese elements, however, we hear also the enthusiastic singing of fabricated French birds, Messiaen's advocate for Greek rhythms, and even the provocative use of a chorale. When we eventually leave *Sept Haïkaï*, we symbolically go through the same Buddhist gate, albeit from the opposite direction, and things can never be the same again.

---

[45]   *Traité V/ii*, p. 567.

Glossary of People

Adorno, Theodor Ludwig Wiesengrund (1903–69). German-born international sociologist, philosopher, musicologist, and composer. He was a member of the Frankfurt School and he was also the Music Director of the Radio Project from 1937 to 1941, in the United States.

Aristotle (384 BC–322 BC). Greek philosopher, a student of Plato and teacher of Alexander the Great. He wrote on many subjects, including physics, metaphysics, poetry, theatre, music, logic, rhetoric, politics, government, ethics, biology and zoology.

Auric, Georges (1899–1983). French composer. Studied at the Paris Conservatoire. A member of *Les Six*, Auric wrote scores for films including Cocteau's *Beauty and the Beast* (1946) and *Moulin Rouge* (1952).

Averroes, Ibn Rushd [known as Averroes] (1126–98). Andalusian polymath; a master of early Islamic philosophy, Islamic theology, logic, psychology, Arabic music theory, and the sciences of medicine, astronomy, geography, mathematics and physics.

Avicenna, Ibn Sina [known as Avicenna] (c. 980–1037). Persian polymath and the foremost physician and philosopher of his time. He was also an astronomer, chemist, geologist, logician, paleontologist, mathematician, physicist, poet, psychologist, scientist, soldier, statesman and teacher.

Balthasar, Hans Urs von (1905–88). Swiss theologian and priest. Best known for his 16-volume systematics (Trilogy), which is divided into three parts.

Bate, Jennifer (1944–). British concert organist. Daughter of H. A. Bate, organist of St James's Church, Muswell Hill in London from 1924–78. An authority on the music of Messiaen, with whom she studied. First performer to record his complete organ works.

Baudelaire, Charles Pierre (1821–67). French poet, critic and translator; a controversial figure in his lifetime, his name has become a byword for literary and artistic decadence. At the same time his works have been acknowledged as classics of French literature.

Beauduin, Dom Lambert (1873–1960). Belgian monk who founded the monastery now known as Chevetogne Abbey in 1925. He had previously been a monk of the Benedictine Mont César Abbey in Leuven, and was deeply involved with the liturgical movement in Belgium.

Bergson, Henri-Louis (1859–1941). French philosopher influential in the first half of the twentieth century. Notable for his work on 'duration', 'intuition' and 'laughter'. Bergson's doctoral dissertation *Time and Free Will: An Essay on the Immediate Data of Consciousness* 1910 [*Essai sur les données immédiates de la conscience 1889*] was widely influential.

Bernanos, Georges (1888–1948). French author with Roman Catholic and monarchist leanings, he was a violent adversary to bourgeois thought and to what he identified as defeatism leading to the conquest of France in 1940. He lived in exile for many years, returning after liberation upon an invitation by De Gaulle.

Bernard of Clairvaux (1090–1153). French abbot and the primary builder of the reforming Cistercian monastic order.

Bloy, Léon (1846–1917). French novelist, essayist, pamphleteer and poet.

Boulez, Pierre (1925–). French composer and conductor. Studied with Messiaen at the Paris Conservatoire. Famous works include *Le marteau sans maître* (1953–57) and *Pli selon pli* (1957, rev. at intervals until 1989).

Bouyer, Louis (1913–2004). French author. Wrote principally on the history of Christianity. Converted from Lutheran ministry to Catholicism in 1939. Exerted significant scholarly influence over the Second Vatican Council.

Bruhn, Siglind (1951–). German musicologist and pianist. Best known for her works on Hindemith and Messiaen.

Cage, John (1912–92). American composer and a pioneer of chance music, electronic music and non-standard use of musical instruments, Cage was one of the leading figures of the post-war avant-garde and, in the opinion of many, the most influential American composer of the twentieth century.

Chapuis, Michel (1930–). French organist and teacher. Studied at the Paris Conservatoire under Marcel Dupré. Served as an organist in Notre-Dame Cathedral in Paris from 1955–64.

Chateaubriand, François-René de (1768–1848). French writer and politician. Often considered to be one of the founders of Romantic French literature.

Chenu, Marie-Dominique [OP] (1895–1990). A liberal Roman Catholic theologian and a founder of the reformist journal *Concilium*. He was invited to be an expert speaker at the Second Vatican Council.

Claudel, Paul (1868–1955). French poet and dramatist. Most famous for his verse dramas, the bulk of which have Catholic themes.

Cochereau, Pierre (1924–84). French organist, improviser, composer and teacher. Studied with André Fleury and Paul Delafosse. Director of Le Mans Conservatory, 1949–56. Appointed titular organist of Notre-Dame Cathedral in Paris in 1956, a post he held until his death.

Cocteau, Jean Maurice Eugène Clément (1889–1963). French poet, novelist, dramatist, designer, boxing manager, playwright and filmmaker in the Surrealist style.

Comte, Auguste (1798–1857). A French thinker and one of the founders of sociology and positivism. He is responsible for the coining and introduction of the term 'altruism'.

Courbet, Gustave (1819–77). French painter who led the realist movement in French painting. Notorious for his erotic works, he believed that painters should portray the world around them.

Danielou, Jean Cardinal [SJ] (1905–74). Theologian, historian and a member of the Académie Française. Served as an expert to the Second Vatican Council, and in 1969 was made a cardinal by Pope Paul VI.

Dante Alighieri (*c.*1265–1321). Florentine poet. His central work, *The Divine Comedy*, is often considered the greatest literary work composed in the Italian language and a masterpiece of world literature.

Debussy, Achille-Claude (1862–1918). French composer and one of the most prominent figures working within the field of Impressionist music.

Delbos, Claire (1906–59). French violinist and composer. First wife of Messiaen. Mother of their only child, Pascal Messiaen, born in 1937.

Duchamp, Marcel (1887–1968). French artist whose work is most often associated with the Dadaist and Surrealist movements. Duchamp's output influenced the development of post-First World War Western art.

Dukas, Paul (1865–1935). French composer and teacher at the Paris Conservatoire. Messiaen was among his pupils.

Dupré, Marcel (1886–1971). French organist, pianist and composer. In 1926, he was appointed professor of organ performance and improvisation at the Paris Conservatoire, a position he held until 1954. In 1954, Dupré succeeded Claude Delvincourt as director of the Paris Conservatoire, where he remained until 1956.

Duruflé, Maurice (1902–86). French composer, organist and teacher. Became titular organist of St Etienne-du-Mont in Paris in 1929, a position that he held until his death. Professor of Harmony at the Paris Conservatoire, 1943–70.

Eliot, T. S. (1888–1965). Poet, dramatist and literary critic. He received the Nobel Prize in Literature in 1948.

Éluard, Paul (1895–1952). French poet. One of the founders of Surrealism, a movement that he abandoned after the Spanish Civil War.

Emmanuel, Maurice (1862–1938). French composer and teacher at the Paris Conservatoire.

Francis of Assisi (Giovanni Francesco Bernardone) (1181/82–1226). A friar and the founder of the Order of Friars Minor, more commonly known as the Franciscans.

Freud, Sigmund (1856–1939). Austrian psychiatrist who founded the psychoanalytic school of psychology.

Fumet, Stanislas (1896–1983). Essay writer, poet, editor, and art critic. Fumet played a paramount role in the art and evolution of ideas in France. He was one of the outstanding figures of social Catholicism.

Gadamer, Hans-Georg (1900–2002). German philosopher. Best known for his 1960 work, *Truth and Method*.

Garrigou-Lagrange, Reginald Marie [OP] (1877–1964). Catholic theologian and prominent Thomist in the twentieth century. He wrote against Modernism and is best known for his spiritual theology. He taught at the Angelicum in Rome from 1909–1960 and wrote 28 books and hundreds of articles.

Gavoty, Bernard (1908–81). Organist and music critic.

Gilson, Etienne (1884–1978). French Thomist, philosopher and historian of philosophy. In 1946 he attained the distinction of being elected an 'Immortal' (member) of the French Academy.

Guardini, Romano (1885–1968). Catholic priest, author, and academic. He was one of the most important figures in Catholic intellectual life in twentieth-century Germany.

Gueranger, [Dom] Prosper Louis Pascal (1805–75). Benedictine priest, abbot of Solesmes Abbey (which he founded in the disused priory of Solesmes) and founder of the French Benedictine Congregation (now the Solesmes Congregation). He is credited with reviving the Benedictine Order in France, and revitalizing the Tridentine Mass.

Guitton, Jean (1901–99). French Catholic philosopher and theologian. He became a member of the *Académie française* in 1961 and was invited as an observer to the Second Vatican Council, the first lay person to be granted this honour.

Hart, David Bentley. Eastern Orthodox theologian, philosopher, writer, and cultural commentator.

Haydn, (Franz) Joseph (1732–1809). Austrian composer. One of the most prominent composers of the classical period, and called by some the 'Father of the Symphony' and 'Father of the String Quartet' because of his leading role in the development of these genres.

Hegel, Georg Wilhelm Friedrich (1770–1831). German philosopher and one of the creators of German idealism. He developed a comprehensive philosophical framework, to account in an integrated and developmental way for the relation of mind and nature, the subject and object of knowledge, and psychology, the state, history, art, religion and philosophy.

Hello, Ernest (1828–85). French critic and devout Roman Catholic. He is principally remembered for his book *Physionomie de Saints* (1875).

Hill, Peter (1948–). English pianist and musicologist. Best known for his biography of Messiaen (2005), co-written with Nigel Simeone, and his recording of Messiaen's complete piano works.

Joan of Arc (*c*. 1412–31). National heroine of France and a Catholic saint. A peasant girl born in eastern France, she led the French army to several important victories during the Hundred Years War, claiming divine guidance, and was indirectly responsible for the coronation of Charles VII.

Kant, Immanuel (1724–1804). German philosopher regarded as one of the most influential thinkers of modern Europe and of the late Enlightenment. His most important work is the *Critique of Pure Reason*, a critical investigation of reason itself that includes an attack on traditional metaphysics and epistemology.

Langlais, Jean (1907–91). French composer of modern classical music, organist, and improviser. Langlais became blind as a result of glaucoma when he was only two years old. He studied at the Paris Conservatoire, obtaining prizes in organ, which he studied with Marcel Dupré, composition, which he studied with Paul Dukas, and improvisation, which he studied with André Marchal. He was titular organist at the Basilica of Sainte Clotilde in Paris, 1945–87.

Latry, Olivier (1962–). French organist, improviser and teacher. Titular Organist of the Cathedral of Notre-Dame in Paris, and professor at the Paris Conservatoire. He has recorded the complete organ works of Messiaen.

Lefebvre, Archbishop Marcel-François (1905–91). French Roman Catholic archbishop. He took the lead in opposing the changes within the Church associated with the Second Vatican Council and, in 1970, Lefebvre founded the Society of St Pius X (SSPX), which is still the world's largest Traditionalist Catholic priestly society.

Loriod, Yvonne (1924–). French pianist, particularly noted for her performances of Messiaen's works. Studied at the Paris Conservatoire. Married Messiaen in 1961 after the death of his first wife, Claire Delbos.

Lourié, Arthur-Vincent (1892–1966). Russian composer. Lourié played an important role in the earliest stages of the organization of Soviet music after the 1917 Revolution but later went into exile. Born into a prosperous Jewish family, he converted to Catholicism while still in Russia. In 1922, he settled in Paris, where he became friends with the philosopher Jacques Maritain and was introduced to Stravinsky.

Lubac, Henri-Marie Cardinal de, [SJ] (1896–1991). French Jesuit priest who became a Cardinal of the Roman Catholic Church, and is considered to be one of the most influential theologians of the twentieth century. His writings and doctrinal research played a key role in the shaping of the Second Vatican Council.

Lustiger, Aaron Jean-Marie [Cardinal] (1926–2007). French prelate of the Roman Catholic Church. He was Archbishop of Paris from 1981 until his resignation in 2005. He was made a Cardinal in 1983.

Mâche, François-Bernard (1935–). French composer of contemporary music; former student of Émile Passani and Olivier Messiaen. He has composed electroacoustic, orchestral, chamber, choral, vocal and piano works. He has been a member of the Académie des Beaux-Arts since 2002 and occupies the chair of the late Iannis Xenakis.

Mahler, Gustav (1860–1911). Austrian composer and conductor. He was best known during his own lifetime as one of the leading orchestral and operatic conductors of the day. He has since come to be acknowledged as among the most important late-Romantic composers.

Maimonides, Moses [also known as Rabbi Moses ben Maimon] (1135–1204). Rabbi, physician and philosopher in Spain, Morocco and Egypt during the Middle Ages. He was the pre-eminent medieval Jewish philosopher whose ideas also influenced the non-Jewish world.

Mallarmé, Stéphane (1842–98). French poet and critic. Major figure in the Symbolist movement, known for hosting meetings in his home of the group that became known as *les Mardistes*.

Maritain, Jacques (1882–1973). French Catholic philosopher raised as a Protestant; converted to Catholicism in 1906. He is responsible for reviving the work of St Thomas Aquinas, and was a prominent voice in the Second Vatican Council.

Marmion, Dom Columba (1858–1923). French theologian and writer. His book *Le Christ en ses mystères* (1919) was a particular favourite of Messiaen.

Massenet, Jules (Émile Frédéric) (1842–1912). French composer best known for his operas. His compositions were very popular in the late nineteenth and early twentieth centuries.

Mauriac, François (1885–1970). French author and member of the *Académie française* (1933); laureate of the Nobel Prize in Literature (1952).

Miller, Alton Glenn (1904–44). American jazz musician, arranger, composer and band leader in the swing era.

Nietzsche, Friedrich Wilhelm (1844–1900). German philosopher and classical philologist. He wrote critical texts on religion, morality, contemporary culture, philosophy and science. Nietzsche's influence remains substantial within and beyond philosophy, notably in existentialism and postmodernism.

Novalis (1772–1801). Pseudonym of Georg Philipp Friedrich Freiherr von Hardenberg. Early German Romantic author and philosopher.

Péguy, Charles (1873–1914). French poet, essayist, and editor. His two main inspirations were socialism and nationalism, but by around 1908 he had become a devout but non-practising Roman Catholic and Catholicism had a major influence on his works.

Poulenc, Francois (1899–1963). French composer and member of *Les Six*. Studied with Ricardo Viñes, 1914–17.

Pseudo-Dionysius the Areopagite (flourished *c.* 500). The anonymous theologian and philosopher of the late 5th to early 6th century whose *Corpus Areopagiticum* (before 532) was pseudonymously ascribed to Dionysius the Areopagite, the Athenian convert of St Paul mentioned in *Acts* 17:34. His surviving works include *Divine Names, Mystical Theology*, *Celestial Hierarchy*, *Ecclesiastical Hierarchy* and various epistles.

Rahner, Karl [SJ] (1904–84). German theologian and one of the most influential Roman Catholic theologians of the twentieth century. Prior to the Second Vatican Council, Rahner, along with Yves Congar, Henri de Lubac and Marie-Dominique Chenu, formed a new school of thought called the 'Nouvelle Théologie'.

Renan, Ernest (1823–92). French philosopher and writer, deeply attached to his native province of Brittany. He is best known for his influential historical works on early Christianity and his political theories.

Reverdy, Pierre (1889–1960). French poet associated with the Surrealist and Cubist movements. Worked alongside Pablo Picasso and Henri Matisse.

Rilke, Rainer Maria (1875–1926). German Roman Catholic poet. Fled from Munich to Switzerland after the First World War, where he stayed until his death.

Roland-Manuel, Alexis (1891–1966). French composer and critic. Studied composition with Vincent D'Indy. Appointed Professor of Aesthetics at the Paris Conservatoire in 1947.

Rößler, Almut (1932–). German concert and church organist. Studied at the Musikakademie in Detmold. Premiered works by Messiaen and recorded his complete organ works.

Rousseau, Jean Jacques (1712–78). Philosopher, writer and composer of the eighteenth-century Enlightenment, whose political philosophy influenced the French Revolution and the development of modern political and educational thought.

Said, Edward (1935–2003). Palestinian-American scholar of literary theory and cultural criticism. Appointed Professor of English and Comparative Literature at Columbia University in 1963.

Saint Bonaventure of Bagnoregio (1221–74). Eighth Minister General of the Order of Friars Minor, commonly called the Franciscans. He was a medieval scholastic theologian and philosopher, a contemporary of St Thomas Aquinas, and a Cardinal Bishop of Albano.

Saint Thomas Aquinas, [OP] (*c.* 1225–74). A priest of the Roman Catholic Church in the Dominican Order, and an immensely influential philosopher and theologian in the tradition of scholasticism. He was the foremost classical proponent of natural theology, and his influence on Western thought is considerable, and much of modern philosophy was conceived as a reaction against, or as an agreement with, his ideas, particularly in the areas of ethics, natural law and political theory.

Satie, Erik (1866–1925). French composer and pianist. Studied at the Paris Conservatoire, which he left before graduating. Noted for the abstract nature of many of his compositions.

Sauvage, Cécile (1883–1927). French poetess, and mother of Messiaen.

Scheler, Max (1874–1928). German philosopher known for his work in phenomenology, ethics and philosophical anthropology.

Schiele, Egon (1890–1918). Austrian painter and protégé of Gustav Klimt, Schiele was a major figurative painter of the early twentieth century.

Schiller, Johann Christoph Friedrich von (1759–1805). German poet, philosopher, historian and dramatist.

Schleiermacher, Friedrich (1768–1834). German Protestant theologian and philosopher. His works inspired Karl Barth's twentieth-century Neo-Orthodoxy movement.

Schoenberg, Arnold (1874–1951). Austrian and later American composer, associated with the expressionist movement in German poetry and art, and leader of the Second Viennese School. He was also a painter, music theorist, and an influential teacher of composition.

Schweitzer, Albert (1875–1965). German musicologist, organist, physician and theologian. Best known for his study of Johann Sebastian Bach, *Le Musicien-Poète* (1905).

Spitta, Phillip (1841–94). German musicologist famous for his exhaustive biography of Johann Sebastian Bach (1873–80).

Thibon, Gustave (1903–2001). French philosopher, Catholic, monarchist and autodidact. In 2000, he was awarded the Grand Prix of philosophy of the *Académie française*.

Thomas à Kempis (*c*.1380–1471). Late medieval Catholic monk and author of *The Imitation of Christ*, one of the best known Christian books on devotion.

Tournemire, Charles (1870–1939). Organist at the Basilique Ste-Clotilde, Paris, between 1898 and 1939. Taught at the Paris Conservatoire. Studied with César Franck.

Viñes, Ricardo (1875–1943). Spanish pianist. Studied at the Paris Conservatoire. Worked with Debussy and Ravel, and gave a number of Ravel premiers, including *Miroirs* (1906) and *Gaspard de la Nuit* (1909).

Voltaire, François-Marie Arouet (1694–1778). French Enlightenment writer, essayist and philosopher known for his wit, philosophical sport and defence of civil liberties, including freedom of religion and free trade.

Wagner, (Wilhelm) Richard (1813–83). German composer, conductor, theatre director and essayist, primarily known for his operas. Wagner pioneered advances in musical language, such as extreme chromaticism and quickly shifting tonal centres, which greatly influenced the development of European classical music.

Waugh, Arthur Evelyn St John (1903–66). British writer, best known for darkly humorous and satirical novels as well as for serious works that frequently manifest his Catholic background.

Xenakis, Iannis (1922–2001). Greek composer. Studied architecture and engineering in Athens and, later, composition with Messiaen (after unsuccessful lessons with Arthur Honegger and Darius Milhaud).

Select Bibliography

Musical Scores

This section includes biographical information for those significant works cited in the text. Full details of Messiaen's oeuvre can be found at <www.oliviermessiaen.net>.

Messiaen, Olivier, *Apparition de l'église éternelle* (Paris: Lemoine, 1936).
—— *Catalogue d'oiseaux* (Paris: Leduc, 1964).
—— *Chants de terre et de ciel* (Paris: Durand, 1939).
—— *Chronochromie* (Paris: Leduc, 1962).
—— *Cinq Rechants* (Paris: Salabert, 1949).
—— *Couleurs de la Cité céleste* (Paris: Leduc, 1966).
—— *Des Canyons aux étoiles...* (Paris: Leduc, 1978).
—— *Diptyque* (Paris: Durand, 1930).
—— *Éclairs sur l'au-delà...* (Paris: Leduc, 1998).
—— *Et exspecto resurrectionem mortuorum* (Paris: Leduc, 1966).
—— *Harawi* (Paris: Leduc, 1949).
—— *Hymne au Saint-Sacrement* (Williamstown, MA: Broude Brothers, 1974).
—— *L'Ascension* [orchestra] (Paris: Leduc, 1948).
—— *L'Ascension* [organ] (Paris: Leduc, 1934).
—— *La Nativité du Seigneur* (Paris: Leduc, 1936).
—— *La Transfiguration de Notre-Seigneur Jésus-Christ* (Paris: Leduc, 1972).
—— *Le Banquet céleste* (Paris: Leduc, 1960).
—— *Les Corps glorieux* (Paris: Leduc, 1942).
—— *Les Offrandes oubliées* (Paris: Durand, 1931).
—— *Livre d'orgue* (Paris: Leduc, 1953).
—— *Livre du Saint Sacrement* (Paris: Leduc, 1989).
—— *Méditations sur le mystère de la Sainte Trinité* (Paris: Leduc, 1973).
—— *Messe de la Pentecôte* (Paris: Leduc, 1951).
—— *Offrande au Saint Sacrement* (Paris: Leduc, 2001).
—— *Oiseaux exotiques* (Vienna: Universal Edition, 1959).
—— *Poèmes pour Mi* (Paris: Durand, 1936).
—— *Préludes* (Paris: Durand, 1930).
—— *Quatre études de rythme* (Paris: Durand, 2000).
—— *Quatuor pour la fin du Temps* (Paris: Durand, 1942).
—— *Réveil des oiseaux* (Paris: Durand, 1955).
—— *Saint François d'Assise* (Paris: Leduc, 1988).
—— *Sept Haïkaï* (Paris: Leduc, 1966).

—— *Timbres-Durées* (Unpublished, 1952).

—— *Trois petites Liturgies de la Présence Divine* (Paris: Durand, 1952).

—— *Turangalîla-symphonie* (Rev. 1990, Paris: Durand, 1992).

—— *Vingt regards sur l'Enfant-Jésus* (Paris: Durand, 1947).

—— *Visions de l'Amen* (Paris: Durand, 1950).

Books, Articles and Reviews

Adorno, Theodor W., *Beethoven: The Philosophy of Music*, ed. Rolf Tiedemann, trans. Edmund Jephcott (Cambridge: Polity Press, 1993).

—— *Aesthetic Theory*, eds Gretel Adorno and Rolf Tiedemann, trans. Robert Hullot-Kentor (London: Athlone, 1997).

—— *Philosophy of New Music*, trans. Robert Hullot–Kentor (Minneapolis: University of Minnesota Press, 2006 [1941/1949]).

Ackroyd, Peter, *T. S. Eliot* (London: Hamish Hamilton, 1984).

Alighieri, Dante, [see Dante].

Alldritt, Keith, *Eliot's Four Quartets: Poetry as Chamber Music* (London: The Woburn Press, 1978).

Andriessen, Louis and Elmer Schönberger, *The Appollonian Clockwork: On Stravinsky*, trans. Jeff Hamburg (Oxford: Oxford University Press, 1989).

Angelier, François, 'Hello, l'explosion de l'unité', in Ernest Hello, *Paroles de Dieu. Réflexions sur quelques textes sacrés* (Grenoble: Million, 1992).

Ansermet, Ernest, 'Introduction à l'œuvre d'Igor Stravinsky', *Revue Pleyel* 2, no. 18 (1925): 15–16.

Aquinas, Thomas, *Summa Theologiae*, 60 vols (New York: Blackfriars–McGraw Hill, 1964–).

Assise, François d', *Écrits*, Sources chrétiennes (Paris: Éditions du Cerf, 1981).

Auden, W[ystan] H[ugh], 'Psychology and Art To-day', in *The Arts To-day*, ed. Geoffrey Gregson (London: John Lane, 1935).

Austin, Guy, *Contemporary French Cinema: An Introduction* (Manchester: Manchester University Press; New York: St. Martin's Press, 1996).

Balmer, Yves, *Catalogue des concerts du fonds Loriod-Messiaen de la Bibliothèque nationale de France* (Paris: Yves Balmer, 2008).

—— '*Je suis né croyant* … Aux sources du catholicisme de Messiaen', in *Musique, art et religion dans l'entre-deux guerres*, eds Sylvain Caron and Michel Duchesneau (Lyon: Symétrie, 2009), pp. 365–389.

Balthasar, Hans Urs von, *The Glory of the Lord: A Theological Aesthetics*, Vol. I: *Seeing the Form*, eds Joseph Fessio and John Kenneth Riches, trans. Erasmo Leiva-Merikakis (Edinburgh: T&T Clark, 1982).

—— *The Glory of the Lord: A Theological Aesthetics*, Vol VI: *Theology: The Old Covenant*, eds Joseph Fessio and John Kenneth Riches, trans. Erasmo Leiva-Merikakis (Edinburgh: Ignatius Press, 1983–91).

—— *The Theology of Henri de Lubac: An Overview*, trans Joseph Fessio and Michael M. Waldstein (San Francisco: Ignatius Press, 1991 [1976]).

Balthasar, Hans Urs von, *Razing the Bastions: On the Church in This Age*, trans. Brian McNeil (San Francisco: Ignatius Press, 1993 [1952]).

Barndollar, David, 'Movements in Time: *Four Quartets* and the Late String Quartets of Beethoven', in *T. S. Eliot's Orchestra: Critical Essays on Poetry and Music*, ed. John Xiros Cooper (New York: Garland, 2000), pp. 179–194.

Barthe, Claude, preface to Ernest Hello, *L'Homme: la vie, la science, l'art* (Paris: Editions de Paris, 2003), pp. 9–20.

Baudelaire, Charles, *Notes nouvelles sur Edgar Poe* (Paris: M. Lévy frères, 1857).

Beevor, Antony, and Artemis Cooper, *Paris After the Liberation, 1944–1949*, rev. edn (New York: Penguin Books, 2004).

Bergonzi, Bernard, ed., *T. S. Eliot Four Quartets: A Selection of Critical Essays* (London: Macmillan, 1969).

Bloom, Harold, *The Anxiety of Influence: A Theory of Poetry*, 2nd edn (New York: Oxford University Press, 1997).

Bloy, Léon, *Ici on assassine les grands hommes: par Léon Bloy: avec un portrait et un autographe d'Ernest Hello* (Paris: Mercure de France, 1895).

Boswell-Kurc, Lilise, 'Olivier Messiaen's Religious War-time Works and their Controversial Reception in France (1941–46)' (PhD diss., New York University, 2001).

Boulez, Pierre, 'Vision et révolution', in *Regards sur autrui: Points de repère, tome II* (Paris: Bourgois, 2005), pp. 436–443.

Bouyer, Louis, *Dom Lambert Beauduin. Un homme d'Eglise* (Paris: Casterman, 1964).

—— *Le Métier de Théologien. Entretiens avec Georges Daix* (Paris: Editions France Empire, 1979).

Boivin, Jean, *La Classe de Messiaen* (Paris: Christian Bourgeois, 1995).

Bruhn, Siglind, *Messiaen's Contemplations of Covenant and Incarnation: Musical Symbols of Faith in the Two Great Piano Cycles of the 1940s* (Hillsdale, NY: Pendragon Press, 2007).

Bürger, Peter, *The Theory of the Avant-Garde* (Minneapolis: University of Minnesota Press, 2004 [1974]).

Bynum, Caroline Walker, 'Wonder', *American Historical Review* 102, no. 1 (February 1997): 1–26.

Calinescu, Matei, *Five Faces of Modernity* (Durham, NC: Duke University Press, 1987).

Cao, Hélène, 'Olivier Messiaen: de la poésie du réel aux mystères de la foi', *Saint François d'Assise Messiaen, L'Avant Scène Opéra* 223 (2004): 3–9.

Cardolle, Chanoine J., *Aux Jeunes. Et toi, connais-tu le Christ vie de ton âme? D'après l'œuvre de Dom Marmion* (Paris: Desclée De Brouwer, 1949).

Catechism of the Catholic Church, 2nd edn (Rome: Libreria Editrice Vaticana, 1997).

Catholic Encyclopedia: St. Thomas Aquinas, available online at <www.newadvent. org/cathen/14663b.htm> (accessed 7 March 2007).

Chaigne, Louis, *Anthologie de la renaissance catholique* (Paris: Alsatia, 1938).

—— *Itinéraire d'une espérance: Pages de journal* (Paris: Beauchesne, 1970).

Chartier, Roger, *Ecouter les morts avec les yeux* (Paris: Collège de France/Fayard, 2008).

Chateaubriand, Viscount de, *The Genius of Christianity or the Spirit and Beauty of the Christian Religion, Book V, The Existence of God Demonstrated by the Wonders of Nature*, trans. Charles I. White (Baltimore: J. Murphy; Philadelphia: J. B. Lippincott, 1856).

Chaubet, François, *Histoire intellectuelle de l'entre deux guerres* (Paris: Nouveau Monde, 2006).

Chenaux, Philippe, *Entre Maurras et Maritain: une génération intellectuelle catholique (1920–1930)* (Paris: Cerf, 1999).

Chenu, Marie-Dominique, *Introduction á l'étude de S. Thomas d'Aquin* (Paris: Vrin, 1950).

Cheong, Wai-Ling, 'Messiaen's Chord Tables: Ordering the Disordered', *Tempo* 57, no. 226 (2003): 2–10.

Chesterton, G. K., *Saint Thomas Aquinas: 'The Dumb Ox'* (New York: Image Books/Doubleday, 1956).

Claudel, Paul, *Art poétique: connaissance du temps, traité de la co-naissance au monde et de soi-même: développement de l'église* (Paris: Mercure de France, 1907).

—— Preface to Louis Chaigne, *Anthologie de la renaissance catholique* (Paris: Alsatia, 1938), n. p.

Cocteau, Jean, *Œuvres Complètes de Jean Cocteau*, vol. 9 (Paris: Marguerat, 1946).

Collins, Larry, and Dominique Lapierre, *Is Paris Burning?* (New York: Simon and Schuster, 1965).

Cooper, John Xiros, ed., *T. S. Eliot and the Ideology of 'Four Quartets'* (Cambridge: Cambridge University Press, 1995).

—— *T. S. Eliot's Orchestra: Critical Essays on Poetry and Music* (New York: Garland, 2000).

Craft, Robert, *Stravinsky: Chronicle of a Friendship* (Nashville/London: Vanderbilt University Press, 1994).

D'Ambrosio, Marcellino, '*Ressourcement* Theology, *Aggiornamento*, and the Hermeneutics of Tradition', *Communio* 18, no. 4 (1991): 530–555.

Daley, Brian, 'The *Nouvelle Théologie* and the Patristic Revival: Sources, Symbols, and the Science of Theology', *International Journal of Systematic Theology* 7, no. 4 (2005): 362–382.

Daly, Gabriel, *Transcendence and Immanence: A Study in Catholic Modernism and Integralism* (New York: Oxford University Press, 1980).

Daniel, Arnaut, 'L'aura amara', in *Lyrics of the Troubadours and Trouveres: An Anthology and a History,* trans. Frederick Goldin (Garden City, NY: Anchor Books, 1973), pp. 210–216.

Daniel-Lesur, Jean Yves, 'Trois Petites Liturgies de la Présence Divine d'Olivier Messiaen', *Revue Musicale de France* (1 April 1946).

Dansette, Adrien, Histoire religieuse de la France contemporaine: l'Église catholique dans la mêlée politique et sociale (Paris: Flammarion, 1965).

Dante [Alighieri] *Literature in the Vernacular [De vulgari eloquentia]*, trans. Sally Purcell (Manchester: Carcanet New Press, 1981).

Davidson, Audrey Eckdahl, *Messiaen and the Tristan Myth* (Westport, CT: Praeger, 2001).

Davies, Brian, *The Thought of Thomas Aquinas* (Oxford: Clarendon Press, 1993).

Deiss, Lucien, 'Cantate brève à la messe de onze heures', *Communio* 6 (1978): 87–91.

Dieuaide, Jean-Michel, 'La Musique, Parole de Dieu prononcée par des voix humaines', *Voix Nouvelles* 43 (2005).

Dillard, Annie, *Holy the Firm* (New York: HarperCollins Perennial, 2003 [1977]).

Dingle, Christopher Philip, 'Olivier Messiaen: *La Transfiguration de Notre-Seigneur Jésus-Christ*: A Provisional Study', 2 vols (MPhil thesis, University of Sheffield, 1994).

—— 'Charm and Simplicity: Messiaen's Final Works', *Tempo*, no. 192 (1995): 2–7.

—— '"La statue reste sur son piédestal": Messiaen's *La Transfiguration* and Vatican II', *Tempo*, no. 212 (2000): 8–11.

—— *Messiaen's Final Works* (Aldershot: Ashgate, 2009).

D'Ioro, Paulo and Daniel Ferrer, *Bibliothèques d'écrivains* (Paris: CNRS Editions, 2001).

Du Bos, Charles, 'Le Génie de Maurice de Guérin, in Maurice de Guérin, *Le Centaure. La Bacchante: précédés de La génie de Maurice Guérin, par Charles du Bos* (Paris: Falaize, 1950).

Duployé, Pie, *Les Origines du Centre de Pastorale liturgique, 1943–1949* (Mulhouse: Editions Savator, 1968).

Durant, Will, *The Age of Faith: A History of Medieval Civilization – Christian, Islamic, and Judaic – from Constantine to Dante: A.D. 325–1300*, vol. 4: *The Story of Civilization* (New York: MJF Books, 1950).

Durling, Robert M., 'Introduction', in *Petrarch's Lyric Poems: The Rime Sparse and Other Lyrics*, trans. and ed. Robert M. Durling (Cambridge, MA: Harvard University Press, 1976).

Duteurtre, Benoît, *Requiem pour une avant-garde* (Paris: Robert Laffont, 1995).

Eliot, T. S., *T. S. Eliot On Poetry and Poets* (London: Faber and Faber, 1957).

—— *Four Quartets* (London: Faber & Faber, 1944).

Éluard, Paul, *Capital of Pain*, trans Mary Ann Caws, Patricia Terry and Nancy Kline (Boston, MA: Black Widow Press, 2006).

Erigena, Johannes Scotus, *Periphyseon [On the Division of Nature]* (Indianapolis: Bobbs-Merrill, 1976).

Études de Pastorale Liturgique, Vanves 26–28 janvier 1944, Coll. Lex Orandi 1 (Paris, 1944).

Fallon, Robert, 'Composing Subjectivity: Maritain's Poetic Knowledge in Stravinsky and Maritain', in *Jacques Maritain and the Many Ways of Knowing*, ed. Douglas Ollivant (Washington, DC: American Maritain Association, 2002), pp. 284–302.

—— 'Messiaen's Mimesis: The Language and Culture of the Bird Styles' (PhD diss., University of California at Berkeley, 2005).

—— 'The Record of Realism in Messiaen's Bird Style', in *Olivier Messiaen: Music, Art and Literature*, eds Christopher Dingle and Nigel Simeone (Aldershot: Ashgate, 2007), pp. 115–136.

—— 'Two paths to paradise: Reform in Messiaen's *Saint François d'Assise*', in *Messiaen Studies*, ed. Robert Sholl (Cambridge: Cambridge University Press, 2007), pp. 206–231.

—— 'Messiaen's Gothic Spirituality and the *Renouveau Catholique*', trans. Martine Rhéaume, in *Musique, arts et religion dans l'entre-deux-guerres: la construction d'une culture en pays francophone,* eds Sylvain Caron and Michel Duchesneau (Lyon: Symétrie, 2009), pp. 347–364.

Fauquet, Joël-Marie, ed. 'Correspondance inédite: Lettres d'Olivier Messiaen à Charles Tournemire', *L'Orgue: Cahiers et Mémoires*, no. 41 (1989–I): 80–85.

Festa, Paul, *OH MY GOD. Messiaen in the Ear of the Unbeliever* (San Francisco: Bar Nothing Books, 2008).

Florand, J. P., 'Y a-t-il un Cas Messiaen?', *Le Littéraire* (20 April, 1946).

Freeman, Robin, 'Trompette d'un Ange secret: Olivier Messiaen and the Culture of Ecstasy', *Contemporary Music Review* 14, no. 3–4 (1996): 81–125.

Fulcher, Jane, *The Composer as Intellectual: Music and Ideology in France, 1914–1940* (New York: Oxford University Press, 2005).

Fumet, Stanislas, *Ernest Hello, ou le Drame de la Lumière*, rev. edn (Fribourg and Paris: Egloff and the Librairie de L'Université de Fribourg, 1945 [1928]).

—— *Histoire de Dieu dans ma vie* (Paris: Fayard; Mame, 1978; Paris: Editions du Cerf, 2002).

Gadamer, Hans-Georg, 'The relevance of the beautiful', in *The Relevance of the Beautiful and Other Essays*, trans. Nicholas Walker, ed. and intr. Robert Bernasconi (Cambridge: Cambridge University Press, 1986), pp. 3–53.

Gardiner, Helen, *The Composition of 'Four Quartets'* (London: Faber & Faber, 1978).

Gavoty, Bernard, 'Who Are You Olivier Messiaen?', *Tempo*, no. 58 (Summer 1961): 34–35.

Gilson, Etienne, 'Doctrinal History and Its Interpretation', *Speculum: A Journal of Mediaeval Studies* 24, no. 4 (1949): 483–492.

Godin, Emmanuel, 'French Catholic Intellectuals and the Nation in Post-war France', *South Central Review* 17, no. 4 (Winter 2000): 45–60.

Goehr, Alexander, *Finding the Key* (London: Faber & Faber, 1998).

Goléa, Antoine, *Rencontres avec Olivier Messiaen* (Paris: Juilliard, 1961; Paris/ Genève: Slatkine, 1984).

Gordon, Lyndall, *T. S. Eliot: An Imperfect Life* (London: Vintage, 1998).

Griffiths, Paul, *Olivier Messiaen and the Music of Time* (London/Boston: Faber & Faber, 1985).

—— 'The Arts: Jennifer Bate, Westminster Cathedral', *The Times* (9 October 1986).

—— '*Eclairs sur l'au-delà* – the Last Works', in *The Messiaen Companion*, ed. Peter Hill (London: Faber & Faber, 1995), pp. 510–525.

—— 'Messiaen, Olivier', in *Grove Music Online*, ed. L. Macy, <http://www. grovemusic.com> (accessed 27 January 2007).

Guéranger, Dom Prosper, *The Liturgical Year*, trans. Dom Laurence Shepherd, OSB, 15 vols (Westminster, MD: Newman, 1952 [1948–1950]).

—— *Historique, mystique et pratique des temps de l'année liturgique* (Grez-en-Bouère, France: Dominique Martin Morin, 1979).

Guérin, Maurice de, *Maurice de Guérin: journal, lettre et poèmes* (Paris: Lecoffre, 1898).

—— *Le Centaure, La Bacchante* (Paris: Falaize, 1950).

Guguelot, Frédéric, *La conversion des intellectuels au catholicisme en France 1885–1935* (Paris: CNRS Editions, 1998).

H[enderson], R[obert] L., 'Messiaen première', *The Daily Telegraph* (10 October 1986).

Halbreich, Harry, *Olivier Messiaen* (Paris: Fayard/SACEM, 1980).

—— 'Une théologie sonore. Par la connaissance vers l'inconnaissable', in *Olivier Messiaen Homme de Foi* (Paris: Trinité Media Communication, 1995), pp. 21–26.

Harris, Steven, *Surrealist Art and Thought in the 1930s: Art, Politics, and the Psyche* (New York: Cambridge University Press, 2004).

Hart, David Bentley, *The Beauty of the Infinite: The Aesthetics of Christian Truth* (Grand Rapids: Eerdmans, 2003).

Hayes, Malcolm, 'End of the banquet', *The Sunday Telegraph* (12 October 1986).

Healey, Gareth, 'Messiaen – Bibliophile', in *Olivier Messiaen: Music, Art and Literature*, eds Christopher Dingle and Nigel Simeone (Aldershot: Ashgate Publishing, 2007), pp. 159–171.

Hello, Ernest, *Paroles de Dieu: Réflexions sur quelques textes sacrés* (Paris: Perrin et cie, 1923).

—— *Textes choisis et présentés*, ed. Stanislas Fumet (Fribourg: Egloff, Librairie de l'Université, 1945).

—— *Contes extraordinaires* (Paris: Sandre, 2006).

Henahan, Donal, 'Atonal Punch and Judy is Slapstick for Adults', *New York Times* (24 June 1988).

Hill, Camille Crunelle, 'Saint Thomas Aquinas and the Theme of Truth in Messiaen's *Saint François d'Assise*', in *Messiaen's Language of Mystical Love*, ed. Siglind Bruhn (New York: Garland Publishing, 1998), pp. 143–167.

Hill, Peter, 'Interview with Yvonne Loriod', in *The Messiaen Companion*, ed. Peter Hill (London: Faber & Faber, 1995), pp. 283–303.

——, ed., *The Messiaen Companion* (London: Faber & Faber, 1995; Portland, OR: Amadeus Press, 1999).

Hill, Peter and Nigel Simeone, *Messiaen* (New Haven, CT/London: Yale University Press, 2005).

Holland, Bernard, 'Remembering Messiaen with Works of His Own', *The New York Times* (10 November 1992).

Howe, Jeffery, 'The Refuge of Art: Gustave Moreau and the Legacy of Symbolism', in *Mystic Masque: Semblance and Reality in Georges Rouault, 1871–1958*, ed. Stephen Schloesser (Chestnut Hill: McMullen Museum of Art, Boston College, 2008), pp. 45–61.

Hudson, Deal Wyatt, and Matthew J. Mancini, *Understanding Maritain: Philosopher and Friend* (Macon, GA: Mercer University Press, 1987).

Ide, Pascal, 'Olivier Messiaen théologien?', in *Portrait(s) d'Olivier Messiaen*, ed. Catherine Massip, with a preface by Jean Favier (Paris: Bibliothèque nationale de France, 1996).

—— 'Olivier Messiaen, un musicien ébloui par l'infinité de Dieu', *Nouvelle Revue théologique* 4 (1999): 436–453.

—— 'Messiaen et la musique sacrée', in *La musica sacra nelle chiese cristiane. Actes du Congrès international d'études, Rome, 25–27 janvier 2001*, eds Académie Nationale Sainte Cécile, Conseil Pontifical de la Culture and Institut Pontifical de Musique Sacrée (Bologna: Alfa Studio, 2002): 187–196.

Jackson, Julian, *France: The Dark Years, 1940–1944* (New York: Oxford University Press, 2001).

Johnson, Robert Sherlaw, *Messiaen* (London: J. M. Dent & Sons, Ltd, 1975; Berkeley and Los Angeles: University of California Press, 1989).

—— 'Rhythmic Technique and Symbolism in the Music of Olivier Messiaen', in *Messiaen's Language of Mystical Love*, ed. Siglind Bruhn (New York: Garland, 1998), pp. 121–139.

Joseph, Charles M., *Stravinsky & Balanchine: A Journey of Invention* (New Haven, CT: Yale University Press, 2002).

Kant, Immanuel, *Kritik der Urteilskraft* (Hamburg: F. Meiner, 1963).

Kars, Jean-Rodolphe, ' L'œuvre d'Olivier Messiaen et l'Année liturgique', *La Maison-Dieu* 3 (1996): 97–98.

Keeley, Anne, 'In the Beginning Was the Word? An Exploration of the Origins of Olivier Messiaen's *Méditations sur le mystère de la Sainte Trinité*', unpublished paper delivered at Messiaen 2008 International Centenary Conference, Birmingham, UK, 23 June 2008.

Kechichian, Patrick, *Les usages de l'éternité: Essai sur Ernest Hello* (Paris: Seuil, 1993).

Kenner, Hugh, *The Invisible Poet* (London: W. H. Allen, 1974).

Kerr, Fergus, *Twentieth-Century Catholic Theologians: From Neoscholasticism to Nuptial Mysticism* (Malden, MA: Blackwell Publishing, 2007).

Keym, Stephan, *Farbe und Zeit: Untersuchungen zur musiktheatralen Struktur und Semantik von Olivier Messiaens Saint François d'Assise* (Hildesheim: Georg Olms, 2002).

Kivy, Peter, 'Another Go at Musical Profundity: Stephen Davies and the Game of Chess', *British Journal of Aesthetics* 43, no. 4 (October 2003): 401–411.

Krieg, Robert A., *Romano Guardini: A Precursor of Vatican II* (Notre Dame, IN: University of Notre Dame Press, 1997).

Labourdette, Marie-Michel, 'La théologie et ses sources', *Revue Thomiste* 46, no. 2 (1946): 353–371.

Laignel-Lavastine, Maxime, ed., *Les Rythmes et la vie* (Paris: Plon, 1947).

Lauerwald, Hannelore, 'Er musizierte mit Olivier Messiaen als Kriegsgefangener', *Das Orchester* 47, no. 1 (1999): 21–23.

Leersnyder, Brigitte de, ed., *Charles Tournemire (1870–1939)*, Cahiers et Mémoires de l'Orgue 41 (Paris: Les Amis de l'Orgue, 1989).

Leo XIII, [Pope], 'Aeterni Patris', in *The Papal Encyclicals*, comp. Claudia Carlen Ihm, vol. 2, *The Papal Encyclicals: 1878–1903* (Raleigh, NC: The Pierian Press, 1990).

Livingston, James C., *Modern Christian Thought*, vol. 1 (Upper Saddle River, NJ: Prentice Hall, 1988).

Livingston, James C., Francis Schüssler Fiorenza, Sarah Coakley, and James H. Evans, Jr., eds, *Modern Christian Thought*, vol. 2 (Upper Saddle River, NJ: Prentice Hall, 2000).

Lourié, Arthur, 'La Sonate pour piano de Strawinsky', *La revue musicale* 6, no. 10 (1925): 100–104.

—— 'A propos de l'Apollon d'Igor Stravinsky', *Musique: Revue Mensuelle* 1, no. 3 (1927): 117–119.

—— 'Œdipus-Rex', *La revue musicale* 8, no. 8 (1927): 240–253.

—— 'Neogothic and Neoclassic', *Modern Music* 5, no. 3 (1928): 3–10.

—— 'An Inquiry Into Melody', *Modern Music* 7, no. 1 (1929–30): 3–11.

Luchese, Diane, *Olivier Messiaen's Slow Music: Glimpses of Eternity in Time* (PhD diss., Northwestern University, 1998).

Lumsdaine, David, 'Messiaen: *Catalogue d'Oiseaux*. Robert Sherlaw Johnson (piano). *Neuf Méditations sur le Mystère de la Sainte Trinité*. Olivier Messiaen (organ)', *Tempo*, no. 105 (1973): 38.

Lustiger, Jean-Marie, 'Musicien de l'Invisible', in *Olivier Messiaen Homme de Foi* (Paris: Trinité Media Communication, 1995), pp. 7–8.

Lyotard, Jean-François, *Allocution à l'occasion de la Remise du Prix Paul VI à Olivier Messiaen, 28 mars 1989*. Unpublished document available at the Archbishopric of Paris, 22, rue Barbet-de-Joüy, F–75007, Paris.

—— *L'enthousiasme: La critique kantienne de l'histoire* (Paris: Galilée, 1986).

—— *Choosing God, Chosen by God: Conversations with Jean-Louis Missika and Dominique Wolton* (San Francisco: Ignatius Press, 1991).

—— 'Adresse au Symposium des Amis de l'Orgue', *Communio* 4 (2000).

—— *Libidinal Economy* [epigraph] (London/New York: Continuum, 2004).

Maas, Sander van, *Doorbraak en Idolatrie: Olivier Messiaen en het geloof in muziek* (Delft: Eburon Uitgeverij, 2003).

—— 'Forms of love: Messiaen's aesthetics of *éblouissement*', in *Messiaen Studies*, ed. Robert Sholl, (Cambridge: Cambridge University Press, 2007), pp. 78–100.

——*The Reinvention of Religious Music: Olivier Messiaen's Breakthrough Towards the Beyond* (New York: Fordham University Press, 2009),

—— 'Denegations and Affimations: Messiaen and Psychoanalysis', in *Génération Messiaen*, ed. Brigitte Van Wymeersch (forthcoming).

Maggiolini, Alessandro, 'Magisterial Teaching on Experience in the Twentieth Century: From the Modernist Crisis to the Second Vatican Council', *Communio* 23, no. 2 (1996): 225–243.

Mahrt, William Peter, 'Dante's Musical Progress Through the Commedia', in *The Echo of Music: Essays in Honor of Marie Louise Göllner*, ed. Blair Sullivan (Warren, MI: Harmonie Park Press, 2004), pp. 63–73.

Mâle, Emile, *The Gothic Image: Religious Art of the Thirteenth Century*, trans. Dora Nussey (New York: Harper, 1958; New York: Harper & Row, 1972).

Mari, Pierrette, *Olivier Messiaen* (Paris: Seghers, 1965).

Maritain, Jacques, *La philosophie bergsonienne: études-critiques* (Paris: Rivière & cie, 1930).

—— *Approches sans entraves* (Paris: Fayard, 1973).

—— *Art and Scholasticism*, trans. Joseph W. Evans (Notre Dame, IN: University of Notre Dame Press, 1974 [1962]).

—— *Le Docteur Angelique*, in Jacques and Raïssa Maritain, *Œuvres complètes*, vol. 4, *Œuvres de Jacques Maritain, 1929–1932* (Fribourg: Editions Universitaires; Paris: Editions Saint-Paul, 1983 [1930]), pp. 10–191.

——'Sur la musique d'Arthur Lourié', *La revue musicale* 17, no. 165 (April 1936): 266–271.

Maritain, Raïssa, 'A Handful of Musicians', *The Commonweal* (29 October 1943): 33.

Marmion, Dom Columba, *Christ in His Mysteries*, trans. Mother M. St. Thomas of Tyburn Convent, 9th edn (London: Sands & Co., 1939).

Marti, Jean-Christophe, 'Entretiens avec Olivier Messiaen', in *Saint François d'Assise, L'Avant-Scène Opéra, Saint François d'Assise: Messiaen, Special Bilingual Program Book of the Salzburg Festival*, L'Avant-Scène Opéra, Opéra d'aujourd'hui, no. 4 (Paris: L'Avant-Scène Opéra, 1992): 8–18.

—— 'It's a secret of love – an interview with Olivier Messiaen', liner notes for *Saint François d'Assise*, cond. Kent Nagano (DG 445176–2, 1998), pp. 17–29.

Martimort, Aimé, 'La réforme liturgique incomprise', *La Maison-Dieu* 192 (1992): 86.

Massin, Brigitte, *Olivier Messiaen: une poétique du merveilleux* (Aix-en-Provence: Éditions Alinéa, 1989).

Massip, Catherine, *Portrait(s) d'Olivier Messiaen* (Paris: Bibliothèque Nationale de France, 1996).

Massumi, Brian, *Parables for the Virtual: Movement, Affect, Sensation* (Durham, NC: Duke University Press, 2002).

Matheson, Iain, 'The End of Time: A Biblical Theme in Messiaen's *Quatuor*', in *The Messiaen Companion*, ed. Peter Hill (London: Faber & Faber, 1995), pp. 234–248.

Mauck, Marchita, 'Gothic spirituality', in *The HarperCollins Encyclopedia of Catholicism*, ed. Richard P. McBrien (New York: HarperCollins, 1995), pp. 575–576.

Maugendre, Louis Alphonse, *La Renaissance catholique au début du 20ᵉ siècle: Emile Baumann* (1868–1941) (Paris: Beauchesne, 1968).

Maycock, Robert, 'Ovation for Olivier: Westminster Cathedral Unveils Messiaen's Latest Organ Work', *Classical Music* (1986): 29.

McCool, Gerald A., *The Neo-Thomists* (Milwaukee, WI: Marquette University Press, 1994).

McInerny, Ralph, *Aquinas Against the Averroists: On There Being Only One Intellect*, Purdue University Series in the History of Philosophy, ed. Arion Kelkel, et al. (West Lafayette, IN: Purdue University Press, 1993).

—— ed. and trans., with an introduction and notes, *Thomas Aquinas: Selected Writings* (London: Penguin Books, 1998).

McNulty, Paul, 'Messiaen's journey towards asceticism', in *Messiaen Studies*, ed. Robert Sholl (Cambridge: Cambridge University Press, 2007), pp. 63–77.

Messiaen, Olivier, '*Ariane et Barbe-Bleue* de Paul Dukas', *Revue musicale* 166 (May–June 1936): 79–86.

—— 'Musique Réligieuse', *La Page musicale* (5 February 1937): 1.

—— *Technique de mon langage musical*, 2 vols [vol. 1: Text; vol. 2: Music Examples] (Paris: Leduc, 1944); Vol. 1 trans. John Satterfield as *The Technique of my Musical Language* (Paris: Leduc, 1956).

—— 'Entretien avec M. Jean Langlais', *Bulletin des Amis de l'Orgue du Québec* 8 (1969).

—— *Conférence de Notre-Dame: prononcée le 4 décembre 1977 à Notre-Dame-de-Paris* (Paris: Editions Alphonse Leduc, 1978).

—— *Conférence de Kyoto: November 12, 1985* (Paris: Leduc, 1988), trans. into Japanese by Naoko Tamamura (Paris: Leduc, 1988).

—— 'Le Musicien de la Joie. Entretien avec Olivier Messiaen 60 Années à la Trinité', *Musica et Memoria* 42 (1991).

—— *Lecture at Notre-Dame: An address presented at Notre-Dame Cathedral in Paris, December 4, 1977*, trans. Timothy J. Tikker (Paris: Alphonse Leduc, 2001 [1978]).

—— *Traité de rythme, de couleur, et d'ornithologie*, 7 vols (Paris: Leduc, 1994–2002).

Messiaen, Pierre, 'Péguy poète national et chrétien', *La revue des Amis de Saint-François* 29 (1941): 19–24.

Miller, Malcolm, 'Messiaen: *Des canyons aux étoiles; Couleurs de la cité celeste; Oiseaux exotique*s Paul Crossley (pno), London Sinfonietta *c*. Esa-Pekka Salonen', *Tempo*, no. 169 (1989): 54.

Miller, Anthony, 'Music in a Vernacular Catholic Liturgy', *Journal of the Royal Musical Association, 91st Sess., 1964–1965* (Oxford, 1964–1965): 21–32.

Moevs, Christian, *The Metaphysics of Dante's Comedy* (Oxford: Oxford University Press, 2005).

Monnet, Henri, ' Thomas et les Imposteurs', *Revue Pleyel* 3, no. 29 (1926): 13–14.

Montagne, Joachim Havard de la, 'Olivier Messiaen (1908–1992)', *Musica et Memoria* 46 (1992) : 25–26.

—— *Mes longs Chemins de Musicien* (Paris: Editions L'Harmattan, 2001).

Moody, David A., 'Four Quartets: Music, word, meaning and value', in *The Cambridge Companion to T. S. Eliot*, ed. A. David Moody (Cambridge: Cambridge University Press, 1994), pp. 142–157.

Moorman, John, 'The Friars and the Universities', in *A History of The Franciscan Order: From its Origins to the Year 1517* (Oxford: Clarendon Press, 1968).

Murray, Paul, *T. S. Eliot and Mysticism: The Secret History of 'Four Quartets'* (London: Macmillan, 1991).

Nehamas, Alexander, *Only a Promise of Happiness: The Place of Beauty in a World of Art* (Princeton: Princeton University Press, 2007).

Nichols, Aidan, 'Thomism and the Nouvelle Théologie', *The Thomist* 64, no. 1 (2000): 1–19.

—— *Say It Is Pentecost: A Guide Through Balthasar's Logic* (Edinburgh: T&T Clark Press, 2001).

—— *Redeeming Beauty: Soundings in Sacral Aesthetics* (Aldershot: Ashgate, 2007).

Nichols, Roger, 'And a little child shall lead them', *The Musical Times* 137, no. 1841 (July, 1996): 17.

Nietzsche, Friedrich, *Human, All Too Human,* trans Marion Faber and Stephen Lehmann (St Ives: Clays Ltd, 1994).

Northcott, Bayan, 'Messiaen: New celestial colours on a grand scale', *The Independent* (9 October 1986).

Nyssa, Gregory of, *Contemplation sur la vie de Moïse*, trans. Jean Daniélou (Paris: Cerf, 1942).

Oury, Guy-Marie, *Dom Guéranger: Moine au coeur de l'église, 1805–1875* (Solesmes: Éditions de Solesmes, 2001).

Pasnau, Robert, and Christopher Shields, *The Philosophy of Aquinas*, The Westview Histories of Philosophy Series, ed. Alan D. Code et al. (Boulder, CO: Westview Press, 2004).

Pasqua, Hervé, *Bas-fonds et profondeur: Critique de l'idôlatrie et métaphysique de l'espérance: Essai sur la philosophie de Gustave Thibon* (Paris: Klincksieck, 1985).

Pereira, José, 'Thomism and the Magisterium: From *Aeterni Patris* to *Veritatis splendor*', *Logos: A Journal of Catholic Thought and Culture* 5, no. 3 (2002): 149–155.

Perrin, Luc, *Paris à l'heure de Vatican II* (Paris: Editions de l'Atelier/Editions Ouvrières, 1997).

Peterson, Larry W., 'Messiaen and Surrealism: A Study of His Poetry', in *Messiaen's Language of Mystical Love*, ed. Siglind Bruhn (New York: Garland Publishing, 1998), pp. 215–224.

Philippi, Donald L., trans., *Kojiki* (Tokyo: University of Tokyo Press, 1968).

Pitwood, Michael, *Dante and the French Romantics* (Geneva: Droz, 1985).

Placher, William C., *The Domestication of Transcendence. How Modern Thinking about God Went Wrong* (Louisville: Westminster John Knox Press, 1996).

Poe, Edgar Allan, *Histoires extraordinaires*, trans. Charles Baudelaire (Paris: Michel Lévy, 1856).

—— *Nouvelles histoires extraordinaires*, trans. Charles Baudelaire (Paris: Michel Lévy frères, 1857).

—— *Histoires grotesques et sérieuses*, trans. Charles Baudelaire (Paris: Michel Lévy frères, 1865).

Poggioli, Renato, *The Theory of the Avant-Garde* (Cambridge, MA: The Belknap Press of Harvard University Press, 1968).

Pople, Anthony, *Quatuor pour la fin du Temps* (Cambridge: Cambridge University Press, 1998).

Poulenc, Francis, 'My Ideal Library', in *Francis Poulenc: Music, Art, and Literature*, eds Sidney Buckland and Myriam Chimènes (Aldershot: Ashgate, 1999), pp. 140–144.

Rahner, Karl, *Foundations of the Christian Faith* (New York: Crossroad, 1978).

Reynolds, Barbara, 'Note on the Structure of the *Vita nuova*', in Dante, *La vita nuova*, trans. Barbara Reynolds (London: Penguin Books, 1969), pp. xiii–xxix.

Ricoeur, Paul, *The Symbolism of Evil* (New York and Evanston: Harper-Row, 1967).

Rilke, Rainer Maria, *The Selected Poetry of Rainer Maria Rilke* (1875–1926), ed. and trans. Stephen Mitchell (London: Picador, 1987).

Rischin, Rebecca, *For the End of Time: The Story of the Messiaen Quartet* (Ithaca, NY: Cornell University Press, 2003).

Roland-Manuel, 'Concerto pour le Piano, de Stravinsky', *Revue Pleyel* 1, no. 10 (July 1924): 27–28.

—— 'Reflexions sur la pureté', *Revue Pleyel* 3, no. 31 (1926): 15–17.

Rößler, Almut, *Beiträge zur geistigen Welt Olivier Messiaens* (Duisburg: Gilles und Francke, 1984); trans Barbara Dagg, Nancy Poland, and Timothy Tikker as *Contributions to the Spiritual World of Olivier Messiaen: With Original Texts by the Composer* (Duisburg: Gilles und Francke, 1986).

Rousso, Henry, *The Vichy Syndrome: History and Memory in France since 1944* (Cambridge, MA: Harvard University Press, 1991).

Said, Edward, *On Late Style* (London: Bloomsbury, 2006).

Samuel, Claude, *Entretiens avec Olivier Messiaen* (Paris: Belfond, 1967), trans. Felix Aprahamian as *Conversations with Olivier Messiaen* (London: Stainer & Bell, 1976).

—— *Musique et couleur: nouveaux entretiens* (Paris: Belfond, 1986).

—— *Olivier Messiaen: Music and Color: Conversations with Claude Samuel*, trans. E. Thomas Glasow (Portland, OR: Amadeus Press, 1994).

—— 'Olivier Messiaen analyse ses œuvres d'orgue', in *Olivier Messiaen Homme de Foi* (Paris: Trinité Media Communication, 1995), pp. 31–67.

Samuel, Claude and Olivier Messiaen, *Permanences d'Olivier Messiaen: dialogues et commentaries* (Arles: Actes Sud, 1999).

Sauvage, Cécile, *'L'Ame en bourgeon'* [The Budding Soul], trans. Philip Weller, in *Olivier Messiaen: Music, Art and Literature*, eds Christopher Dingle and Nigel Simeone (Aldershot: Ashgate, 2008), pp. 191–251.

Schellhorn, Matthew, '*Les Noces* and *Trois Petites Liturgies:* An Assessment of Stravinsky's Influence on Messiaen' in *Olivier Messiaen: Music, Art and Literature*, eds Christopher Dingle and Nigel Simeone (Aldershot: Ashgate, 2007), pp. 39–61.

Schiller, Friedrich, *On the Naïve and Sentimental in Literature* (Manchester: Carcanet New Press, 1981).

Schleiermacher, Friedrich, 'On the Essence of Religion', in *On Religion: Speeches to its Cultured Despisers* (Cambridge, 1996).

Schloesser, Stephen, 'From Spiritual Naturalism to Psychical Naturalism: Catholic Decadence, Lutheran Munch, and Madone Mystérique', in *Edvard Munch: Psyche, Symbol, Expression*, ed. Jeffery Howe (Chestnut Hill: McMullen Museum of Art, Boston College, 2001), pp. 75–110.

—— *Jazz Age Catholicism: Mystic Modernism in Postwar Paris, 1919–1933* (Toronto: University of Toronto Press, 2005).

—— '"Not behind but within": *Sacramentum et Res*', *Renascence* 58, no. 1 (Fall 2005): 17–39.

—— 'The Unbearable Lightness of Being: Re-sourcing Catholic Intellectual Traditions', *CrossCurrents* 58, no. 1 (Spring 2008): 65–94.

—— '*Vivo ergo cogito*: Modernism as Temporalization and its Discontents: A Propaedeutic to This Collection', in *The Reception of Pragmatism in France and the Rise of Catholic Modernism, 1890–1914*, ed. David G. Schultenover (Washington, DC: Catholic University of America Press, 2009).

Schloezer, Boris de, 'A Mes Critiques', *Revue Pleyel* 3, no. 30 (1926): 13–15.

Schultenover, David, ed., *Vatican II: Did Anything Happen?* (New York: Continuum, 2007).

Serry, Hervé, 'Déclin social et revendication identitaire: la "renaissance littéraire catholique" de la première moitié du XXe siècle', *Sociétés Contemporaines* 44 (2002): 91–109.

—— *Naissance de l'intellectuel catholique* (Paris: La découverte, 2004).

—— 'Le double jugement de l'art est-il possible? Les impasses d'une critique catholique dans trois polémiques littéraires et religieuses de l'entre-deux-guerres', *La Société d'études soréliennes: Mil neuf cent* 26, no. 1 (2008): 73–90.

Sexton, Anne, 'The Barfly Ought to Sing', in *Ariel Ascending: Writings about Sylvia Plath*, ed. Paul Alexander (New York: Harper & Row Publishers, 1985).

Shenton, Andrew 'Observations on time in Olivier Messiaen's *Traité*', in *Olivier Messiaen: Music, Art and Literature*, eds Christopher Dingle and Nigel Simeone (Aldershot: Ashgate, 2007), pp. 173–189.

—— *Olivier Messiaen's System of Signs: Notes Towards Understanding His Music* (Aldershot: Ashgate, 2008).

Sholl, Robert, *Olivier Messiaen and the culture of modernity* (London: British thesis service, 2003).

—— 'Love, Mad Love, and the "*point sublime*": The Surrealist poetics of Messiaen's *Harawi*', in *Messiaen Studies*, ed. Robert Sholl (Cambridge: Cambridge University Press, 2007), pp. 34–62.

—— 'The Shock of the Positive: Olivier Messiaen, St Francis, and Redemption through Modernity', in *Resonant Witness*, eds Jeremy Begbie and Steve Guthrie (Grand Rapids: Eerdmans, 2008).

Spender, Stephen, *Eliot* (Glasgow: Collins, 1975).

Smith, Grover, *T. S. Eliot's Poetry and Plays* (Chicago: Chicago University Press, 1956).

Strauss, David Friedrich, *Vie de Jésus ou examen critique de son histoire par le docteur David Frédéric Strauss*, trans. Émile Littré (Paris: Ladrange, 1839).

Stravinsky, Igor, 'Some Ideas about my Octuor', *The Arts* (January 1924): 4.

Taruskin, Richard, *Stravinsky and the Russian Traditions: A Biography of the Works through 'Mavra'* (Berkeley: University of California Press, 1996).

—— 'Sacred Entertainments', *Cambridge Opera Journal* 15, no. 2 (2003): 109–126.

The Jerusalem Bible: Reader's Edition with Abridged Introductions and Notes (New York: Doubleday, 2000).

Tierney, Mark, *Dom Columba Marmion: Une biographie* (Paris: Buchet/Chastel, 2000).

Todd, Olivier, *André Malraux, une vie* (Paris: Gallimard, 2001).

Tölle, Julian Christoph, *Olivier Messiaen, Eclairs sur l'au-delà ...: die christlich-eschatologische Dimension des Opus ultimum* (New York: Peter Lang, 1999).

Toop, Richard, 'Messiaen/Goeyvaerts, Fano/Stockhausen, Boulez', *Perspectives of New Music* 13 (1974): 141–169.

Tournemire, Charles, 'Des possibilités harmoniques et polytonales unies à la ligne grégorienne', *Revue Grégorienne*, Année 15, no. 15 (September/October 1930): 172–174.

Trinité, La (Bulletin published by the church of Sainte Trinité, Paris), cited editions from 1950–71.

Valéry, Paul, *The Art of Poetry*, trans. Denise Folliot, with an Introduction by T. S. Eliot (New York: Pantheon Books, 1958).

Vandermeersch, Patrick, 'The Failure of Second Naiveté: Some Landmarks in the French Psychology of Religion', in *Aspects in Context: Studies in the History of Psychology of Religion*, ed. J. A. Belzen (Amsterdam – Atlanta: Rodopi, 2000), pp. 235–280

Viller, M., et al., eds, *Dictionnaire de spiritualité: Ascétique et mystique, doctrine et histoire* (Paris: Beauchsne, 1964).

Walsh, Stephen, *Stravinsky: A Creative Spring, Russia and France, 1882–1934* (New York: Alfred A. Knopf, 1999).

—— *Stravinsky: The Second Exile, France and America, 1934–1971* (New York: Alfred A. Knopf, 2006).

Waugh, Evelyn, *Brideshead Revisited: The Sacred and Profane Memories of Captain Charles Ryder* (Boston: Little, Brown, 1945).

Weir, Gillian, 'Organ Music II', in *The Messiaen Companion*, ed. Peter Hill (London: Faber & Faber, 1995), pp. 352–391.

Whittall, Arnold, *Musical Composition in the 20th Century* (Oxford: Oxford University Press, 1999).

Williams, Charles, *The Last Great Frenchman. A Life of General de Gaulle* (New York: John Wiley & Sons, 1993).

Williams, Rowan, *Grace and Necessity* (London: Continuum, 2005).

Index

Adorno, T.W. 37, 52, 219, 220
Aeterni Patris 3, 94, 95, 99, 103, 125
Aquinas, Thomas 3, 4, 6–8, 21, 57, 83–5,
    90, 95–6, 101–23, 128, 132, 138,
    141, 154, 179, 268
    Summa Theologiae 7, 57, 101–3, 106–
      11, 114–15, 118, 121, 123, 154
    Thomism, Thomist 3, 4, 6–7, 21, 37,
      39, 64, 83–99, 102–5, 109–11, 114,
      119, 122–3
Aristotle 86, 103–7
Art et scholastique [also *scolastique*] 85–6,
    89, 109
Assisi, Francis of 8, 41–59, 121–2, 128–9,
    136, 141, 217, 229
Audi, Pierre 43, 45
Avant garde 2, 5, 10, 33–7, 39, 109,
    199–222
Averroës 103–5, 107

Bach, J.S. 26, 29, 141, 199, 201, 257
Balthasar, Hans Urs von 3, 7, 8, 59, 71, 84,
    95, 97–8, 216, 220
Baudelaire, Charles 172, 176, 178
Baudo, Serge 193–5
Bergson, Henri 21, 172, 221
Bibliothèque nationale de France 5, 15
Birtwistle, Harrison 50, 53
Boulez, Pierre 10, 16, 26, 34, 37, 186, 188,
    193, 196, 203–6, 231
Breton, André 177–9
Bruhn, Siglind 8, 38, 122, 140, 146, 170,
    174, 178

Cage, John 26, 36–7, 50, 210
Carter, Elliott 224
Catholicism
    catechism 4, 159, 181, 213
    renaissance catholique 19–21
    ressourcement 3, 4, 39, 84, 94–9

theologia Crucis 46
theologia Gloriae 46, 165, 206
Trinity, (for Messiaen's church *see*
    Trinité, La) 33, 106, 115, 118–21,
    129, 138
Vatican 34, 73
Vatican I 3
Vatican II 4, 6, 8, 63–82, 84, 94, 97–9,
    114, 205, 226
Centre de Pastorale Liturgique (CPL) 65–6
Chartres Cathedral 10, 129, 188, 190–93,
    195–8
Chesterton, G. K. 105
Comte, Auguste 169, 171
Courbet, Gustave 171

Daniel-Lesur 31, 167, 195
Dante Alighieri 1, 8, 103, 127–43
Davies, Brian 103, 106
De Gaulle, Charles 76, 164, 187, 193–6
Debussy, Claude 26, 127, 172, 186–7, 207
deçî–tâlas 110, 115, 119, 155
Delannoy, Robert 31–2
Delbos, Claire 33, 130, 166, 186
Désormière, Roger 188
Dingle, Christopher 8, 11, 15, 113, 114, 128,
    154, 172, 174, 225–6, 230, 238–9
Domaine Musical 186, 188, 193, 196
Dupré, Marcel 25–6, 166–7, 238
Durant, Will 103–4
Duruflé, Maurice 76, 206

éblouissement 203, 217, 219
Eliot, T.S. 8–9, 135, 141, 145–61, 239
Eluard, Paul 9, 70, 166, 177–8, 180–81
Erato 127, 164, 195–6

Fallon, Robert 8, 93, 109–10, 127–43
Fauré, Gabriel 69, 259
Ferguson, Ray 223, 227–8

Fumet, Stanislas 18–19, 21, 174–5

Gadamer, Hans-Georg 216
Gaulle, Charles de, *see* De Gaulle
Gavoty, Bernard 31, 102, 237, 239
Goléa, Antoine 33, 36, 110, 150, 152–3,
    168, 175
Gothic spirituality 8, 127–43
Greenberg, Clement 218
Griffiths, Paul 10, 41, 49, 52–3, 155,
    224–5, 235
Guardini, Romano 7, 84, 97
Guéranger, Dom Prosper 6, 9, 64, 168–70,
    180

Halbreich, Harry 47, 75, 78
Hart, David Bentley 220–21
Hello, Ernest 9, 17–18, 70, 102, 166, 170,
    174–6, 180
Hill, Peter and Nigel Simeone 30, 32–3,
    35, 37, 51–2, 67, 70, 93–4, 98, 130,
    138, 146,
150, 163, 167, 177, 224, 226–8, 259
hylomorphism 108–9

improvisation 10, 31, 69, 78, 202, 205,
    211, 223–4, 226

Johnson, Robert Sherlaw 90, 111, 144, 224

Kant, Immanuel 29, 51, 86, 216, 221
Kars, Père Jean-Rodolphe 69, 123
Keym, Stephan 42, 136

Langlais, Jean 75, 195, 206
Latin Averroists 105–6
Leduc (publisher) 30, 33, 38, 72, 75, 94,
    111, 113, 115, 122, 128, 134, 139,
    158, 166, 179, 193, 195, 198,
    202–3, 242, 257–8
leitmotif 117, 119
Ligeti, György 27, 205
Litaize, Gaston 75, 194–5
Loriod-Messiaen, Yvonne 5, 15, 33, 51,
    57, 154, 163, 165, 185, 190, 192,
    194–5, 198, 227–8, 241
Lourié, Arthur 7, 83–5, 87–94, 99, 130
    De ordinatione angelorum, 90–92

Lubac, Henri de 3, 8, 63, 84, 95–8
Lustiger, Jean-Marie 6, 63–82
Luther, Martin 46, 172

McInerny, Ralph 104–6
Mahler, Gustave 35, 50
Magee, Joseph 58
Malraux, André 37, 185–98
Maritain, Jacques 1, 4, 6–8, 18–19, 21, 24,
    39, 83–99, 130, 217
Maritain, Raïssa 7, 18, 84, 88, 90, 95
Marmion, Dom Columba 9, 20–21, 64, 70,
    166, 180–81
Massin, Brigitte 29–30, 39, 41, 48–9, 54–5,
    64, 90, 101, 109, 174, 180
Messiaen, Olivier
    birdsong 11, 35–6, 41, 49, 51, 72–3,
        94, 110, 115, 118–19, 152, 157,
        196, 211, 219, 231, 234, 237,
        242–4, 250–52, 254, 256, 258
    cas Messiaen, le 5, 31, 163
    colour 41–4, 47, 49, 54, 70–71, 111,
        115, 118–19, 129, 138, 158, 198,
        203–4, 210, 225, 227, 231, 235,
        246–8, 252, 254–7, 259
    communicable language, *see* langage
        communicable (below)
    Eglise de Sainte-Trinité, *see* Trinité, La
    Greek rhythms 207, 209–10, 244, 251,
        256, 261
    Hindu rhythms, (see also *deçî–tâlas*)
        41, 155, 242, 244, 246
    langage communicable 36–7, 115,
        117–21, 139, 232–3
    modes of limited transposition 94, 115,
        248
    plainchant 83, 90, 94, 109, 159, 190,
        202, 209, 211, 232, 234
    rhythm 11, 18, 22–5, 35, 41, 71, 89–90,
        94, 111, 115, 118–19, 135, 146,
        150, 152, 154–7, 196, 199, 202,
        204, 207–11, 226, 229, 242, 244,
        246, 250–51, 254–6
    Technique de mon langage musical
        34–5, 38, 133–4, 138, 166, 202, 257
    *Traité de couleur de rythme et
        d'ornithologie* 5, 15–27, 30, 33,
        35, 127–8, 134, 142, 154–6, 173–5,

205–11, 221, 241–4, 246, 248–252, 254–6, 258–9, 261
Tristan Trilogy 33, 128, 130, 134, 202, 259
Works
  Apparition de l'église éternelle 54, 127, 173
  L'Ascension 30, 38, 97, 128, 138, 189
    'Transports de joie' 238
  Catalogue d'oiseaux 36, 38, 50, 132, 186, 224, 237
  Chants de terre et de ciel 30, 97
  Chronochromie 134, 138, 186, 244, 246–7, 259
  Cinq Rechants 128, 202
  Couleurs de la cité céleste 5, 33, 37, 138, 173, 224, 257, 259
  Des Canyons aux étoiles... 29, 36, 113, 131–2, 136, 223–5, 238
  Diptyque 150
  Eclairs sur l'au-delà... 127, 131–2, 136, 138, 170, 173, 235, 246
  Et exspecto resurrectionem mortuorum 9, 37, 111, 165, 185, 187, 190, 192, 194–8
  Fantaisie (for organ and orchestra) 185–6
  Fauvette des jardins 254
  Harawi 33, 128, 130, 202, 205
  Hymne au Saint-Sacrement 30, 32, 94
  La Nativité du Seigneur, 64, 93–4, 97, 173, 180, 230, 235
    'Dieu parmi nous' 11, 173, 230–34, 238
  La Transfiguration de Notre-Seigneur Jésus-Christ 103, 111, 113, 223
    'Perfecte conscius illius perfectae generationis' 114–15, 118
    'Terriblis est locus iste' 114
    'Tota Trinitas apparuit' 115–17
  Le Banquet céleste 30, 167–8, 225
  Les Corps glorieux 59, 110, 120, 131–2

Les Offrandes oubliées 30, 94, 97, 128
Livre d'orgue 5, 33–5, 211, 218, 259
Livre du Saint Sacrement 1, 10, 223–39
  'La résurrection du Christ' 235–6
  'Les deux murailles d'eau' 234, 238
  'Les ténèbres' 235–6
  'Offrande et Alleluia final' 10–11, 230–35, 238
Méditations sur le mystère de la Sainte Trinité 36, 47, 70, 103, 115, 128, 139, 158, 223–4, 232
Messe de la Pentecôte 1, 10, 29, 31, 34, 199–222, 230, 259
  'Le vent de l'esprit' 11, 211–12, 215, 230–31
Oiseaux exotiques 36, 143, 224
Petites esquisses 228
Quatre études de rythme 34
  Île de Feu 134
  Mode de valeurs et d'intensités 35, 38, 206
Quatuor pour la fin du Temps 1, 8–9, 31–2, 35, 41, 51–2, 118, 128, 130, 138, 143, 145–6, 148, 150–53, 155–6, 158–60, 257
Reveil des oiseaux 35, 163
Saint François d'Assise 1, 5, 7–8, 11, 29, 39, 42–59, 71, 101, 103, 113, 121–3, 136, 138, 143, 174, 225–6, 228
  'L'Ange musicien' 121–2
  'La Mort et la nouvelle Vie' 122–3
Sept Haïkaï 1, 11, 131–2, 186–7, 241–61
Timbres-Durées 35–6
Trois petites Liturgies de la Présence Divine 7, 29, 31, 103, 110–13, 143, 163, 166, 173, 181, 259
  'Psalmodie de l'Ubiquité par amour' 103, 110–12
Turangalîla-symphonie, 33, 41, 51, 57, 128, 130, 134–5, 179, 206

Vingt regards sur l'Enfant-Jésus, 31–2, 202, 218
Visions de l'Amen 18, 175,
Messiaen, Alain 21
Messiaen, Pierre 16–18, 21
Modernism 5, 7, 17, 29–39, 64, 83–4, 86, 98, 102, 108, 171–2, 205, 217–19

Notre-Dame de Paris 72, 188, 221

Paget, Henry 6, 78, 80
palingenesis 110
Pasnau, Robert 107–8
Péguy, Charles 17, 20, 190, 191
Petichet 190, 191
Pope John XXIII 4, 8
Pope John Paul II 98–9, 104
Pope Leo XIII 3, 94, 103–4
Pope Paul VI 4, 76
Pope Pius X 4, 65, 171
Pople, Anthony 145–6
Poulenc, Francis 7, 27, 92–4
Litanies à la vierge noire 92
prime numbers 8, 131–2

renouveau catholique 4, 7, 9, 108–9, 128, 169–70, 173, 181
retrogradatio cruciformis 8, 133, 134, 141
Reverdy, Pierre 9, 19, 70, 166, 177–8, 180–81
Rilke, Rainer Maria 217–18
Rößler, Almut 46–7, 56, 165, 269
Rostand, Claude 31, 195–6
Rouault, Georges 24, 175

sacramentalism 109, 172, 181
Said, Edward 238
St Bernard 8, 128, 141
Sainte-Chapelle, La 10, 188, 192–5, 198
Samuel, Claude 1, 17, 30, 36, 41, 47, 67, 70, 102, 121, 133, 138, 163, 174, 177, 195, 206, 241, 259
Sauvage, Cécile 9, 141, 166, 174
Schloesser, Stephen 9, 17, 30, 37, 64, 66, 69–70, 86, 108–10, 163–82, 217
sestina 133–5, 141
Shakespeare, William 9, 21, 141, 166, 176–7

Shenton, Andrew 1–11, 15, 22, 47, 117, 120–21, 145–61, 223, 232
Sherlaw Johnson, *see* Johnson, Robert Sherlaw
Shields, Christopher 107–8
Siger de Brabant 105
Simeone, Nigel (*see also*: Hill, Peter and Nigel Simeone) 8–10, 15, 30–33, 35, 37, 51–2, 67, 70, 93–4, 98, 128, 130, 138, 146, 150, 154, 163, 167, 172, 174, 177, 185–98, 224, 226–8, 259
Siohan, Robert 186, 188–91, 193–5
Solesmes 6, 19, 45, 64, 69, 168–70
Stockhausen, Karlheinz 10, 27, 205, 231
Stravinsky, Igor 1, 7–8, 27, 50, 84–90, 93, 130, 143, 147, 203
Strobel, Heinrich 186
Summa Theologiae, see Aquinas, Thomas
Surrealism 2, 8–10, 81, 163–82, 202, 205
symbols, symbolism 3, 42, 44–5, 70–71, 81, 96, 119–20, 122, 140, 146, 152, 170, 172–3, 175, 180, 202, 257
symmetry [symmetrical series / form] [symmetrical permutation] 8, 131, 134–6, 242, 249, 251, 260

Taruskin, Richard 5–6, 41, 47–8, 50, 84
Thibon, Gustave 20–24
time 9, 15, 22–3, 35, 39, 49, 52–3, 110–11, 121, 134–5, 138, 145–7, 149, 152–8, 160–61, 163–5, 179, 221, 236, 257
torii 11, 242, 244–5, 251, 253, 255–60
Tournemire, Charles 9, 27, 30–31, 37, 39, 69, 92, 166–8, 170, 172, 180, 199–204, 206, 211, 213, 221–2
transubstantiation 109
Trinité, La (Messiaen's church, for Holy Trinity *see* Catholicism –Trinity) 29–30, 34, 41, 67–9, 73–5, 82, 123, 167, 174, 180, 185, 204, 206, 210, 225–6

Xenakis, Iannis 10, 27, 48–50, 195, 205